BECOMING JANE JACOBS

THE ARTS AND INTELLECTUAL LIFE IN MODERN AMERICA

Casey Nelson Blake, Series Editor

Volumes in the series explore questions at the intersection of the history of expressive culture and the history of ideas in modern America. The series is meant as a bold intervention in two fields of cultural inquiry. It challenges scholars in American studies and cultural studies to move beyond sociological categories of analysis to consider the ideas that have informed and given form to artistic expression—whether architecture and the visual arts or music, dance, theater, and literature. The series also expands the domain of intellectual history by examining how artistic works, and aesthetic experience more generally, participate in the discussion of truth and value, civic purpose and personal meaning that have engaged scholars since the late nineteenth century.

Advisory Board: Steven Conn, Lynn Garafola, Charles McGovern, Angela L. Miller, Penny M. Von Eschen, David M. Scobey, and Richard Cándida Smith

BECOMING
JANE JACOBS

PETER L. LAURENCE

PENN

UNIVERSITY OF PENNSYLVANIA PRESS

PHILADELPHIA

Published by
University of Pennsylvania Press
Philadelphia, Pennsylvania 19104-4112
www.upenn.edu/pennpress

Printed in the United States of America
on acid-free paper

10 9 8 7 6 5 4 3 2 1

Library of Congress Cataloging-in-Publication Data

Laurence, Peter L., author.
    Becoming Jane Jacobs / Peter L. Laurence.
    pages cm. — (The arts and intellectual life in modern America)
    Includes bibliographical references and index.
    ISBN 978-0-8122-4788-6
    1. Jacobs, Jane, 1916–2006. 2. City planners—United
States—Biography. 3. City planners—Canada—Biography.
4. Women city planners—United States—Biography. 5. Women
city planners—Canada—Biography. 6. City planning—United
States—History—20th century. 7. City planning—Canada—
History—20th century. 8. Urban renewal—United States—
History—20th century. 9. Urban renewal—Canada—
History—20th century. 10. Sociology, Urban—Philosophy. I. Title.
II. Series: Arts and intellectual life in modern America.
HT167.L353 2015
711'.4092—dc23
                                                                2015022496

CONTENTS

The Unknown Jane Jacobs

How my ideas developed. . . . Oh my God, who knows how their ideas developed?! The nearest I can pin it down is two things: First of all, I had a pervading uneasiness about the way the rebuilding of the city was going, augmented by some feeling of personal guilt, I suppose, or at least personal involvement. The reason for this was that in all sincerity I had been writing for *Forum* about how great various redevelopment plans were going to be. How delightful. How fine they would work. I believed this. Then I began to see some of these things built. They weren't delightful, they weren't fine, and they were obviously never going to work right. Harrison Plaza and Mill Creek in Philadelphia were great shocks to me. I began to get this very uneasy feeling that what sounded logical in planning theory and what looked splendid on paper was not logical in real life at all, or at least in city real life, and not splendid at all when in use.
—Jane Jacobs, 1959

JANE JACOBS'S *The Death and Life of Great American Cities* is considered one of the most important books written about cities. Since it appeared in 1961, it has been required reading for generations of city planners, architects, urban designers, landscape architects, sociologists, urban economists, geographers, and students from other disciplines who are interested in the physical design and social construction of cities. Combined

FIGURE 1. Jane Jacobs in 1957. Gin Briggs/AP.

with her legendary battles against New York master builder Robert Moses and other urban renewal plans and highway projects in New York and Toronto, Jacobs's books and activism made her a heroic figure, but, like other heroes, one often stereotyped and mythologized.

Despite all that has been written about *The Death and Life of Great American Cities*, Jane Jacobs (who was born Jane Isabel Butzner in Scranton,

Pennsylvania, in 1916, and died in Toronto in 2006), and her activism, the notion that Jacobs was primarily a housewife with unusual abilities to observe and defend the domestic surroundings of her Greenwich Village home has persisted since the 1960s. While in the past this description of her observational capacities was often meant, consciously or unconsciously, to demean the scope of her observations and ideas, as Jacobs's ideas found wider validation, her status as a housewife without a formal education in city planning or urbanism became a symbol of her "genius," but no less problematic. The contemporary view has taken the form of deification, with the phrase "What Would Jacobs Do?" (a play on "What Would Jesus Do?") and descriptions of her as "Saint Jane," an "apostle," and a "goddess," suggesting that her divine wisdom and martial powers appeared spontaneously and fully formed, like Athena from Zeus's forehead. This contemporary view admirably celebrates the rejection of sexism and critiques of her since proven wrong, and affirms the abilities and contributions of average citizens, but neither past nor present views take into account the years of experience, the larger history and context, and the local circumstances and influences that contributed to Jacobs's thinking and her writing of *The Death and Life of Great American Cities.*

Yet critics and commentators are not completely to blame for misunderstanding Jacobs or her work. Jacobs's early writing career and the formative years leading up to *Death and Life* remain largely unknown. As late as 1993, even her friend and colleague William H. Whyte, who played an important part in bringing her book into being, could describe Jacobs as someone who had "never written anything longer than several paragraphs" before the late 1950s. For someone who knew Jacobs so well to make such a mistake was remarkable, but little evidence was then available to refute Whyte's point. Almost nothing was known about the great amount of writing she had done prior to *Death and Life.* And although an anthology of papers from Jacobs's archives and other sources was published in 1997 with her assistance, it added little to our understanding of the twenty-five years of her career between 1935 and 1961. Not only were important early essays on the city and a large body of later writing missing, but Jacobs's first book, which was not *Death and Life,* was completely unknown.[1]

There are a number of reasons why even someone as professionally close to Jacobs as Whyte was unaware of her early writing career. Like others, Whyte would have had no reason to know about her freelance work, starting in the mid-1930s, for various magazines or newspapers; her work for a trade magazine called *The Iron Age* in the early 1940s; or her work, in the mid-1940s and early 1950s, for the publication branches of the Office of War Information (OWI) and the State Department (some of it then classified), including her role as a senior editor of the magazine *Amerika*. As for her work at *Architectural Forum*, where she contributed to most of the seventy-seven issues published between her first assignment in 1952 and her departure to write *Death and Life* in 1958, much of her writing, following the editorial policy at the time, was not bylined.

In *Death and Life*, which preceded her celebrity as an activist, Jacobs offered few clues about her previous work. Although the original hardcover edition included a brief biographical sketch that mentioned her position at *Architectural Forum*, within the book itself Jacobs included few autobiographical references and did not describe the extent of her prior experience with the subject matter. Insofar as an attack on claims of expertise was at the heart of her criticism—and she had little in the way of credentials herself—Jacobs relied on the strength of her ideas and arguments to stand on their own. Moreover, while writing the book, she had been specifically instructed by her boss at *Forum*, editor Douglas Haskell, to be cautious that her views not be taken to reflect the editorial position of *Forum* or its parent company, Time, Incorporated. After she was quoted in the *New York Times*, in 1959, with an across-the-board attack on Robert Moses, the New York City Slum Clearance Committee, real estate developers, and the entire urban renewal "gravy train," Haskell told her that she "really should not have sounded off in the *New York Times* without making a check" because she was identified as "an editor of *Forum* and not as an individual." Although he was a great supporter of her work, and had readily accommodated her long leave from the magazine to write her book, Haskell was obliged to tell her to keep a low profile. "We don't see the urban renewal situation as black and white as you do," he said, speaking for *Forum* and Time Inc. Planning to return to her position at *Forum* when her book was finished, Jacobs didn't seek to jeopardize her job. Not knowing the turn her career would soon take, she therefore wrote *Death and Life* "as an individual," although in doing so she distanced herself from her work as a professional writer about cities prior to the book's publication.[2]

After *Death and Life* was published, Jacobs remained quiet about her writing and work prior to its publication. Not the least of the reasons for this is that she eschewed celebrity, partly because of the attention she received as an activist, partly out of a desire to focus on her work and the pressing issues of the day, and partly out of modesty. Despite becoming a public figure, Jacobs was also painfully shy. Moreover, another reason is that, in her early work, Jacobs held ideas that she later attacked in *Death and Life*. As she wrote to her friend Grady Clay while writing the book in March 1959, she harbored feelings of personal guilt for some of her early writing on urban development. Indeed, as she indicated in her letter to Clay, Jacobs not only wrote favorably about a number of public housing projects in Philadelphia, but also wrote favorably about suburban development and urban redevelopment projects in much of her early writing, in her work for both *Amerika* and *Architectural Forum*. Having once idealized the field of city planning, in large part because of her hopes for cities, she had become angry with the planners and developers who were destroying cities, and she was angry with herself for having once believed in the experts and various theories of urban renewal.[3]

When Jacobs became a well-known writer and activist, celebrity seems to have removed her further from her earlier career. Heroism likely made it difficult to admit the evolutionary development of her thinking, which had included—to use her own description of the process—trial and error and learning on the job. This seems particularly true when reviews of *Death and Life* and coverage of her activism sensationalized her attack on Moses, city planning, and urban renewal. Whether partaking of a widely felt hunger for cultural criticism at the dawn of the anti-establishment 1960s, or simply to generate controversy and buzz, early prerelease excerpts of her book emphasized the critical aspects of Jacobs's writing with explosive headlines such as "Speaking Out, the Voice of Dissent: How City Planners Hurt Cities" and "Violence in the City Streets: How Our 'Housing Experts' Unwittingly Encourage Crime."[4] And not being one to negotiate when compromise would not serve cities or neighborhoods, Jacobs would have seen no sense in undermining her own arguments. At the time, urban redevelopment's damage to cities was more important than her biography.

Nevertheless, a consequence of the break between Jacobs's earlier work as a writer and *Death and Life* was that critics quickly stereotyped her as someone with little prior experience, let alone credentials, in her subject matter, and they dismissed her important contributions, in often gendered terms, as obvious or naïve. Describing Jacobs as a housewife watching the "sidewalk ballet" outside her Village home fit the sexism of the times and added to the improbable David versus Goliath story of her fight with Moses. Articles where the character was an "angry woman" made for better copy than describing Jacobs, for example, as the first person to apply complexity science—which few had heard of or understood in 1961—to cities.[5]

Whatever the reasons, the lack of access to Jacobs's work before *Death and Life* has resulted in commentaries that start with her writing and activism in 1961, when the book was done and when Jacobs had already become a public figure alternately antagonized and lionized. However, for someone who spent most of her life as a writer, and who identified herself as a writer, Jacobs's activism has dominated much, and perhaps a disproportionate amount, of what has been written about her, especially when her activism was, for her, a politically fraught community effort and an unwelcome distraction from writing. As a result of the focus on Jacobs as an activist, the evolutionary nature of her thinking, the influences of her early experiences on *Death and Life* and her subsequent books, and the connections of her formative ideas to the larger world of urban history have remained overlooked and understudied. Indeed, as an influential and galvanizing figure in the histories of urban renewal, city planning, urban design, and public housing, Jacobs is closely bound up with these fields. Had we sooner understood, for example, that Jacobs herself also once believed in urban renewal and the redevelopment projects typical of the early 1950s, we might have realized that our understanding of urban renewal and its related histories of the design and planning of cities are also riddled with mythologies, stereotypes, and self-delusions. Had we understood her direct contributions to establishing the field of urban design, an important discipline might have had a greater number of students.[6]

In telling the story of the "first half" of Jacobs's career and revealing a previously underestimated intellect, *Becoming Jane Jacobs* seeks to offer a new foundation for understanding Jacobs's work—not only *Death and Life*, but also *The Economy of Cities* (1969), *The Question of Separatism: Quebec and the Struggle over Sovereignty* (1980), *Cities and the Wealth of Nations: Principles of Economic Life* (1984), *Systems of Survival: A Dialogue on the Moral Foundations of Commerce and Politics* (1992), *The Nature of Economies* (2000), and *Dark Age Ahead* (2004). By shedding light on experiences that led to Jacobs becoming one of the most important American writers on cities already before *Death and Life*, I seek to dispel the stereotype that Jacobs was an amateur when it came to understanding cities and their redevelopment. In contrast to the dilettante whose "home remedies," as the great writer Lewis Mumford called them in anger, were limited to a woman's view of a local, domestic urban routine, I show that Jacobs, who was anything but a stereotypical 1950s housewife and no more of an amateur than Mumford, was a professional writer who, in the years leading up to the book, spent most of her time not in the Village but in three midtown Manhattan office buildings: the Chilton Publishing Company's office on Park Avenue at 42nd Street, the offices of the State Department's Magazine Branch just below Columbus Circle, and Rockefeller Center, where Time and *Architectural Forum* had their offices. Indeed, as Jacobs was careful to explain in *Death and Life*, she witnessed the now-famous Hudson Street "ballet" on her way to work and on her days off. "The heart-of-the-day ballet I seldom see, because part of the nature of it is that working people who live there, like me, are mostly gone, filling the role of strangers on other sidewalks," she wrote. *Becoming Jane Jacobs* accordingly describes Jacobs's knowledge of and writing about neighborhoods other than Greenwich Village and cities other than New York, and it shows that she was as interested in the sciences of the city as her city's "ballet." Neither accidental nor modest in ambition, a depth of experience was the foundation of Jacobs's desire to offer a wholly new vision of cities, not some shortsighted "remedies."[7]

When the evolution of Jacobs's thinking is considered, the historical context takes on a new significance in understanding and interpreting her work. The New York City of the 1930s, where Jacobs's adult life and writing began, certainly influenced her ideas about cities and their economies. Her early writing shows that she already saw the city in ways different than city planners and reformers of the day, but she also understood their ambitions within the context of the widely shared impulse to be modern, live in a modern city, and improve living conditions for the growing masses of city dwellers. Jacobs lived in a changing New York, and she witnessed the evolution of modern urban redevelopment and public housing in the city early on in their histories. As such, Jacobs's critiques of urban renewal were situated within an awareness—influenced by her architect husband, Bob Jacobs, and by her work for *Architectural Forum*—of the history of modern architecture and city planning theory and practice. In her passionate introduction to *Death and Life*, her attacks on the Garden Cities movement founder Ebenezer Howard and the Modernist architect-planner Le Corbusier were certainly memorable. However, in the dispassionate concluding chapter, she sought to understand Howard's and Le Corbusier's thinking in the context of the "history of modern thought." She admitted that their ideas about cities were the product of their times, particularly the epistemologies of their times. Thus, although some have mistakenly seen Jacobs as an antimodernist, her criticisms of modern architecture, planning, and housing were directed more at Modernism's followers than its pioneers. Although Jacobs's fights with Robert Moses have been similarly sensationalized, she sought to understand even Moses's way of thinking when she wrote that, "it is understandable that men who were young in the 1920s were captivated by the vision of the freeway Radiant City, with the specious promise that it would be appropriate to an automobile age. At least it was then a new idea; to men of the generation of New York's Robert Moses, for example, it was radical and exciting in the days when their minds were growing and their ideas forming." However, she was unforgiving of arrested mental development in the younger generation of planners and designers. Anticipating a theme found in her subsequent books, she wrote, "It is disturbing to think that men who are young today, men who are being trained now for their careers, should accept *on the grounds that they must be 'modern' in their thinking,* conceptions about cities and traffic which are not only unworkable, but also to which nothing new of any significance has been added since their fathers were children." Always an advocate of thoughtful experimentation and productive innovation, Jacobs held contempt for superficial modernity.[8]

In the 1940s and early 1950s, Jacobs's experiences as a writer for both the OWI and the State Department also significantly affected her thinking about epistemologies and "systems of thought." As part of the war effort, she had firsthand experience with what she described in *Systems of Survival* as the "guardian" moral system, only to become a target of an extreme version of the guardian syndrome in McCarthyism. It is impossible to say how Jacobs would have written *Death and Life* differently, or whether she would have written it at all, had she not been forced out of her job at the State Department during the McCarthy era and developed even greater anger toward bureaucratic ignorance than she already held as someone suspicious of government bureaucracies. However, *Death and Life*'s criticisms of top-down thinking and mandates read differently when one knows something about her experiences only a short number of years before.

Like the details and influences of Jacobs's experiences in the 1930s and 1940s, the significance of her work at *Architectural Forum*, which has been absent from previous commentaries, cannot be underestimated. Jacobs may have had no formal education in architecture or city planning, but she learned from working with Haskell, who became known as the "dean of architectural editors" (despite having no such training himself), and others in the "academy" of the magazine. She may have held no educational credentials, but, in her position as associate editor at *Forum*, she had access to research and resources, entrée to architectural and academic circles, and a privileged view of the world of modern architecture and city planning. Having already written about both for *Amerika*, Jacobs started at *Forum* prepared to follow urban renewal efforts related to the U.S. Housing Act of 1949. As *Forum*'s expert on shopping center design, she befriended the architect Victor Gruen, who invented the new building typology, and, because of the shopping center's role in suburbanization and its challenge to the relevance of the historic city center, she also soon segued into writing about urban redevelopment and housing. Although Jacobs eventually wrote about redevelopment projects in Cleveland, Ohio, Fort Worth, Texas, Washington, DC, New York, and other cities, she covered a journalistic beat that included Philadelphia, which brought her into close contact with the architect Louis Kahn and the Philadelphia city planning director Edmund Bacon, whose pioneering ideas in urban design shaped her own. *Death and Life*'s foundation was built through Jacobs's contact with these figures, sharing ideas with Haskell and her other colleagues, editing their work and guest columnists' essays (notable among these were essays by the modern housing and planning advocate Catherine Bauer Wurster), attending and participating in historic academic conferences, and interacting with the larger world of architectural and urban theory, particularly with her counterparts at *The Architectural Review* (London).

If it seems improbable that a canonical book like *The Death and Life of Great American Cities* emerged spontaneously from the typewriter of a housewife who had previously written nothing but a few captions, that is because it is improbable. Indeed, it is impossible to imagine the book without the foundation provided by *Forum* and Jacobs's previous writing and without the support of people (despite what she may have said about some of them later, or them about her) including Mumford, Bauer, and Whyte, the sociologist Nathan Glazer, the city planner Martin Meyerson, the University of Pennsylvania Graduate School of Fine Arts dean G. Holmes Perkins; the New School for Social Research president Hans Simons, and the Random House editor Jason Epstein—all of whom wrote letters endorsing her book project. Even more significant were the Rockefeller Foundation's financial support, which allowed Jacobs some two and a half years for research, travel, and writing, and the foundation's intellectual support, provided most notably by its associate director, Chadbourne Gilpatric, who, with Jacobs's help, created a circle of pioneering figures in urban design that included architects, planners, and landscape architects such as Gordon Stephenson, Kevin Lynch, Ian Nairn, Grady Clay, Christopher Tunnard, I. M. Pei, and Ian McHarg. Finally, it is impossible to imagine *Death and Life* without the difficult and imaginative work of writing the book itself, which evolved, through the struggle of its creation, from a less ambitious series of articles into the determinedly pioneering tome we are familiar with today. For Jacobs as a writer, it was an extraordinarily demanding and transformative process—one perhaps well symbolized by the fact that her hair went from auburn to shock white while writing it. While *Death and Life* is extolled for its good sense and readability, Jacobs believed in the writing adage that "the easier it is to read, the harder it was to write."[9]

Apart from discussing Jacobs's early work and the origins of *Death and Life, Becoming Jane Jacobs* has some other primary goals. It seeks to place *Death and Life* in the context of larger debates about the built environment by showing how Jacobs's work fit within the overarching and widely shared early twentieth-century impulse to suburbanize and to make cities, and housing projects in particular, more like suburbia. I discuss Jacobs's participation in debates and her writing about sprawl, and I show how Jacobs's discussions about land use in *Death and Life* connect to these earlier writings, as well as how her strategic decision to focus on cities did not lessen her concerns for the larger environment.

Given Jacobs's rejection of superficial modernism, another goal is to show the relationship of Jacobs's frequent admonishments to study the "use" of things ("the use of sidewalks," "the uses of neighborhood parks," "the uses of city neighborhoods," etc.) to major debates about the collapse of modern/functionalist architecture and urbanism in the 1950s. Jacobs was deeply interested in innovation, "how things work," and complexity as an understanding of how things work. By Jacobs's own description, *Death and Life* was originally conceived of as a study of "the relation of function to design in large cities," and she returned repeatedly to a functionalist critique of functionalist architecture and urbanism. Supporting my argument with evidence from Jacobs's work as an architectural critic, such as her admiration for Kahn's work, and comparisons of her ideas with other critics of modern architecture, such as the architectural critic J. M. Richards and the architect Percival Goodman, I argue that Jacobs can be better understood as a "neofunctionalist," or a reformer of modernism, and as a participant in the eternal renewal of modern architecture and ideas.

Another goal, which relates to Jacobs's lifelong interest in systems of thought, is to address some questions about her ideological position, particularly with regard to the question of planning. Jacobs and *Death and Life* have long served as screens on which various partisans—conservative, liberal, and libertarian—project their own frequently contradictory ideas and values about cities and societies. Some invoke her to preserve neighborhoods from change and to attack real estate development projects, especially if they are large and modern, while others celebrate her as an advocate of markets free from government regulations. Some see a deep respect for people in her fights against top-down urban planning, while others argue she had too little to say about segregation, racism, and gentrification. When contradictions arise, critics are often disgruntled that Jacobs does not adequately address their special interests, and she is used as a straw man for forces beyond her argument, context, time, and control. Again, here an understanding of Jacobs's early work and *Death and Life*'s historical context is helpful, as is a comparison of Jacobs's anti-ideological, scientifically biased, and allegedly antiplanning approach with the thinking from such influential figures as the economist F. A. Hayek, the philosopher of science Karl Popper, and others.

In all of this, finally, is a new attempt to better understand Jacobs's lifework as a whole. While not a traditional or a complete biography, which would require another volume, by going beyond the first half of her career, and also beyond her battles with Moses, *Becoming Jane Jacobs* seeks to shed light not only on *Death and Life*, but also on key ideas found in the six major books on cities and civilizations that followed. Seen as a whole, from her first essays on city neighborhoods, written in her teens, to *Dark Age Ahead*, in which, in her eighties, she reflected on the course of civilizations, consistent themes can be observed within the evolution of her thinking. For example, although Jacobs's first book, *Constitutional Chaff: Rejected Suggestions of the Constitutional Convention of 1787*, was an edited work that contained little of her voice, Jacobs's philosophical and methodological interests in systems of thought, dialogue, and trial and error are evident. By focusing on ideas rather than battles, and beginning at the beginning and not in the middle of Jacobs's intellectual life, I seek to shift deeper attention to Jacobs's *vita contemplativa*. This is no reflection of a desire to diminish the importance of her community activism, her *vita activa*. On the contrary, in *Becoming Jane Jacobs*, I seek to show how Jacobs's writing and her activism grew together.

That said, Jacobs's "attack on current city planning and rebuilding," the first idea in *Death and Life*, is not the first word in Jacobs's lifework. More representative is *Death and Life*'s second sentence, in which she explained her ambition as being "also, and mostly, an attempt to introduce new principles of city planning and rebuilding." While there may be disagreements about the validity of Jacobs's various ideas or the heart of her ideology, all seem to agree that Jacobs was an observer of cities par excellence. If the etymological root of "theory," which is *observation*, still has relevance, then, despite the David versus Goliath stories and Jacobs's own anti-expert/anti-theory rhetoric, Jacobs was a great theorist, as well as a great activist. Favoring the concrete over the abstract, she was probably a great activist because she was a great theorist, and vice versa. Thus, challenging the activist, amateur, and genius stereotypes, *Becoming Jane Jacobs* shows that it was only through a combination of years of observing and writing about the city, of building a writing career and the experiences of her early years, and of interacting with the architectural press, academy, and profession, and many others, that Jacobs had the ambition and confidence to describe *Death and Life* in 1959 as nothing less than a new "system of thought about the great city." It shows, in other words, that Jacobs could not have written *Death and Life* by simply sitting on her Hudson Street stoop and watching the "sidewalk ballet" go by.

CHAPTER 1

To the City

Under the melodramatic roar of the "El," encircled by hash-houses and Turkish baths, are the shops of hard-boiled, stalwart men, who shyly admit that they are dottles for love, sentiment, and romance. Apprentices, dodging among the hand-carts that are forever rushing to and from the fur and garment districts, dream of the time when they will have their own commission houses. Greeks and Koreans, confessing that they have the hearts of children, build little Japanese gardens. Greenhouse owners declare that they would not sell—at any price— the flowers which grow in their own backyards. A dealer plans how to improve the business that his grandfather started. And orchids in milk-bottles nod at field-flowers in buckets.
—Jane Butzner, "Flowers Come to Town," 1937

IN 1934, at eighteen, Jane Jacobs (then Jane Butzner) left her hometown of Scranton, Pennsylvania, for New York City, the great metropolis a hundred miles to the southeast, to begin her career as a writer. Although she did not start writing her best-known book for another two and a half decades, moving to New York was the beginning of *The Death and Life of Great American Cities*, which she later dedicated "TO NEW YORK CITY." Without Jacobs's experiences there, it is difficult to imagine her writing *Death and Life* and many of the books that followed.[1]

Cities, as Jacobs later described them in *Death and Life*—where she typically resisted figurative language despite her early interest in poetry—were lights in the darkness. Although mindful of the analogical fetishes frequent among theorists of architecture and cities, and believing that a city could be best understood "in its own terms, rather than in terms of some other kinds of organisms or objects," she could not resist an analogy here. Imagine, she told her readers, a large, dark field, where "many fires are burning. They are of many sizes, some great, others small; some far apart, others dotted close together; some are brightening, some are slowly going out. Each fire, large or small, extends its radiance into the surrounding murk, and thus it carves out a space." Cities were light and life, and New York was *the* great fire in the darkness. "Life attracts life," she wrote in *Death and Life*. The aphorism, although she did not relate it in the book to her personal experiences, was rooted in her biography: Jacobs understood the attractive powers of great cities from an early age.[2]

Changing rapidly, New York was also the best of places, and the 1930s were perhaps the best of times, to observe great American city dynamics at work. On its way to becoming the greatest of American cities and one of the greatest of the world's great cities, New York was *The City* for many Americans and immigrants, and Jacobs was one of them. In 1935, Berenice Abbott, who later became Jacobs's friend, described her *Changing New York* photographic exhibition as witnessing "the end of something." It was the end of premodern New York.[3]

Consolidated in 1898 and home to the world's tallest building by 1913, New York City had a population that doubled from approximately three and a half to seven million people between 1900 and 1935. Housing shortages and traffic congestion were already problems; slum clearance housing projects and, by the mid-1920s, highway projects were deemed necessary. Only sixteen years after Henry Ford's Model T automobile came to market, in the 1924 *New York Times* article "New York of the Future: A Titan City," the city's police commissioner called for the building of elevated highways: "Commissioner Enright has announced his conclusion that New York is already at the saturation point. Already the motor car, designed to accelerate movement, has by its very multiplicity defeated itself. Consequently the traffic officer has become the town planner." The same article compared New York to Chicago, where "deep in the heart of the town, tenements are being torn down to make way for spacious new thoroughfares." What of New York? "While Chicago talks of its conception of a 'city beautiful' and

FIGURE 2. Oak and New Chambers streets, Lower East Side, as captured in 1935 as part of Berenice Abbott's *Changing New York* WPA photography project. The area was destroyed in 1959 for an expansion of the adjacent civic center. New York Public Library.

works prodigiously, has New York, the greater city, no far-flung plans?" Was it "timid in the face of imperial ideas, parsimonious at the thought of vast public expenditures?" The answer was no, it was not. New York would not be bested.[4]

By 1935, when Jacobs published her first writing on the city, New York was recovering from the Great Depression and determined to shed the trappings of the nineteenth century. Historically, the city was organized in a tight pedestrian neighborhood pattern of what later became called "Jane Jacobs blocks"—where all daily needs could be satisfied by walking one or two self-sufficient blocks containing a grocery store, barbershop, newsstand, butcher, drugstore, deli, laundry, flower shop, cobbler, stationer, bar, hardware store, bakery, and so on. "So complete is each neighborhood, and so strong the sense of neighborhood, that many a New Yorker spends a lifetime within the confines of an area smaller than a country village," wrote E. B. White in *Here Is New York* in 1949. "Let him walk two blocks from his corner and he is in a strange land and will feel uneasy till he gets back."[5]

Yet, prompted by new building techniques and means of transportation, the time was ripe to think about the "modern" city—for new ideas about city planning and civic art, land use, building and rebuilding, rapid transit and highways, housing and new communities, parks and open space, and skyscrapers. As the authors of the *Regional Plan of New York and Its Environs* observed in 1929, "In spite of the great changes that have come over cities in connection with the development of vehicular transportation and steel construction, and of the imminence of new changes as a result of the development of the airplane, much of what may be called 'medievalism' persists in the modern city." "Skyscrapers are as modern as the motor car. Their influence has been great but has really only begun to be felt," they predicted. Land use needed to be reconsidered to provide skyscrapers with appropriate breathing room. "The skyscraper mountains enclose working places that are little better lighted and ventilated than mines. . . . Why can we not have the skyscraper and still get sufficient daylight for it and other buildings?" they asked. Modern architects like Le Corbusier certainly agreed. But Le Corbusier, who visited New York in 1935, and experienced firsthand the city so frequently referenced as an inspiration and counterexample in his *City of To-Morrow and Its Planning* (1929), was not alone. A city organized to provide its residents with sunlight, fresh air, green spaces, decent housing, and ease of movement seemed only natural and common sense.[6]

Indeed, many of the goals and ambitions of postwar urban renewal were established in the 1930s. The decade epitomized the "creative destruction" of Manhattan and anticipated the urban renewal era of the 1950s and 1960s. Apart from the construction of highways and parkways that sought to reduce congestion and traffic fatalities and make new commuter suburbs accessible, the first public housing project in the United States, First Houses, was dedicated on December 3, 1935, by First Lady Eleanor Roosevelt. Modest but expensive, it was a housing experiment clearly inadequate as a model for growing housing needs. With New York's population growth showing no signs of slowing, the plans on drawing boards were ever more ambitious. Thus, while visionaries and reformers like Le Corbusier and the writer Lewis Mumford imagined more humane "Radiant Cities" and "Garden Cities," the problem of

FIGURE 3. A conception of the modern city with "proper restraint of height and density of building, together with well balanced distribution of ground space, overground space above lower buildings and occasional high towers," and a "sunken road for fast vehicular traffic." Thomas Adams et al., *The Building of the City, Regional Plan of New York and Its Environs,* vol. 2 (Philadelphia: William F. Fell, 1931). Rendering by Maxwell Fry.

FIGURE 4. Le Corbusier in New York, 1935. Getty Images.

quickly supplying a huge number of dwellings, and making them affordable, resulted in designs that privileged quantity over quality. The
"pathology of public housing," which Jacobs would observe in East Harlem two decades later, had its roots during this period.[7]

In the meantime, Jacobs's thesis of city "death and life" was also evolving. From 1935, Jacobs's earliest writing on the city reveals that she understood that cities and their neighborhoods changed over time, declining and
regenerating. "Unslumming and Slumming," the title of *Death and Life*'s
fifteenth chapter, described this urban dynamic from the point of view of
human geography and the self-regeneration of neighborhoods. It was, in
part, a personal story. Describing Greenwich Village, where she made her
home soon after moving to New York, as an "unslummed former slum"
in *Death and Life*, Jacobs recognized herself as having participated in the
spontaneous and historic processes of city decline and regeneration that
were of central importance to the book and to her understanding of cities.[8]

Seeking Her Fortune

Viewed from the dark hills of northeastern Pennsylvania, New York City was a great bright light on the horizon. While Scranton's economic lights had started flickering amid the increasing turbulence of competition in its coal and steel industries before the Great Depression, New York grew into a great city. The sparkle of New York's ebullient Jazz Age had dimmed but was not out: The recently completed Chrysler and Empire State buildings were shiny and new, even if largely vacant, and Rockefeller Center, where Jane Jacobs would later work, was pushing rapidly skyward. With a similar resolve, Jacobs later stated, "I came to New York to seek my fortune, Depression or no."[9]

By moving to a great city when she came of age, from a place with fewer opportunities to one where she could experience the richness of city life, Jacobs participated in not only a universal human tradition, but also one familiar in her family. Her mother, Bess Robinson, a nurse who grew up in a small Pennsylvania town, and her father, John Butzner, a doctor who grew up on a Virginia farm, had met in Philadelphia, where they studied and worked before moving to Scranton. Both found city life superior to rural life, and they shared their experiences with Jane and her three siblings (Elizabeth, James, and John), understanding their children's desires and perhaps need to move from Scranton to pursue their livelihoods. Jane's older sister, Betty, who had studied interior design in Philadelphia, had already settled in New York.[10]

In her youth, Jane had decided to pursue a career as a writer. Around the age of eleven, she became serious about poetry and quickly discovered the satisfaction and praise of publication for pieces first published in a local newspaper and in the Girl Scouts' widely circulated *American Girl* magazine in 1927. Although her interest in creative writing continued into adulthood (she continued to write poetry and tried fiction in the mid-1950s, just before becoming significantly involved in urban renewal controversies), her focus turned to nonfiction in high school.

Following graduation from Scranton's Central High School in early 1933 and a subsequent training course in stenography at Powell Business School, she was "thoroughly sick of attending school and eager to get a job, writing or reporting," as she described that time in her life in a rare autobiography. In August 1933, she found a job with the *Scranton Republican*, and, until the newspaper was sold to the *Scranton Tribune* in June

1934, Jacobs worked as an assistant to the society editor but soon took on the responsibilities of assistant editor, covering events like civic meetings and arts reviews, and laying out the Society page, a task previously left to the composing room foreman but later adopted by other departments of the paper. On her own initiative, she assumed the role of cub reporter, seeking out and developing her own feature stories for the city desk.[11]

Laid off from the newspaper and still too young to move away from home, Jacobs spent six months, between May and November 1934, with an aunt who directed a Presbyterian mission in Higgins, North Carolina, a hamlet that was a pinprick of light barely illuminating the darkness of the Appalachian Mountains. Her experience there, referenced directly and indirectly in her books decades later, made a deep impression. As she later explained in *Cities and the Wealth of Nations*, Higgins (which she called Henry in the book) had been dying for over a century, all but cut off from the economies of cities for about a century and a half. Becoming increasingly isolated, the settlement, she wrote, "proceeded to shed and lose traditional practices and skills after it had lost almost all contact and interchange with the economies of cities," eventually reverting to a subsistence economy. In a notable anecdote, Jacobs recounted how her aunt's parishioners had argued against building a church made of stone, despite being surrounded by Blue Ridge Mountain granite. According to Jacobs, the townspeople had lost both the masonry skills and ambitions of their forbears, who had built stone parish churches, even great cathedrals, from time immemorial. "Having lost the practice of construction with stone, people had lost the memory of it, too, over the generations," she wrote, "and having lost the memory, lost the belief in the possibility—until a mason arrived from the nearest city, Asheville, and got them started on a church of small stones." The anecdote was meant to exemplify how cities, as dense repositories of culture, perpetuated even those practices typically considered innately rural.[12]

Regardless of why Higgins's townfolk may have opposed building a stone church, Jacobs's experiences there were fresh in her mind weeks later, when she arrived at her sister's apartment in Brooklyn in November 1934. The contrast, of course, could not have been greater. While the people of Higgins, surrounded by stone, apparently found the prospect of building a small stone church daunting, in New York one of the largest private building projects in modern times, Rockefeller Center, clearly showed that a great city could withstand even a great economic depression. Although Jane

FIGURE 5. Jane Jacobs's high school graduation photo, January 1933. Jacobs Papers.

would struggle to find any work, and she and Betty would be reduced to eating baby cereal, the cheapest food they could find, by the end of 1934, New York had seen the worst of the Depression and there was a sense of cautious optimism in the air. The Central Park "Hooverville" was gone, and Franklin Delano Roosevelt was promising the American people a "New Deal." New York, offering promise for the nation at large, suggested that robust cities would not succumb to Higgins's fate.

Unable to find a position with a magazine or newspaper, Jacobs looked for part-time work and freelance writing opportunities. She made the most of job hunting, which turned out to be a good way to get to know the city's neighborhoods and business districts. From her first New York home, a six-story walkup on Brooklyn's Orange Street (later destroyed by the Cadman Plaza renewal project), and later from Greenwich Village, where she and Betty moved in October 1935, Jacobs explored Manhattan as she answered want ads, sometimes getting off the subway at random stops for the surprise of discovering the marvels of the city, which inspired her to continue her poetry writing. In this way she discovered the working districts of the city, whose vitality, largely undiminished by the economic situation, afforded her some employment and whose energy and complexity captured her imagination after her time in Appalachia.[13]

Jacobs would spend most of the years from 1935 to 1938, when she started college at Columbia University, in Manhattan's working districts, employed as a secretary at various New York manufacturing businesses. Her writing career would not be delayed, however. In 1935 and 1936, at New York University, she took three journalism courses on newspaper feature writing, editorial writing, and magazine article writing. And her first job was working as an assistant to a writer, soon followed by the development of her own writing projects, a preoccupation that led to her first essays on the city, newspaper columns, her first book, and freelance writing that continued until she landed a job where her responsibilities matched her abilities, about a decade later.[14]

Robert H. Hemphill, Jacobs's first employer and landlord, was an early influence on Jacobs's writing career, encouraging her lifelong interests in economics, public policy, and systems of thought. An advocate for national monetary reform and a straight-talking financial writer for William Randolph Hearst's *New York Journal-American*, Hemphill was a proponent of the establishment of a central bank and removal of the dollar from the gold standard (a move that the Roosevelt administration rejected). He was also the chairman of a committee drafting related legislation to be brought before Congress, for which Hemphill hired Jacobs to assist him. She did library research work for him by cutting clippings of useful material and obtaining copies of bills bearing on economics as they were introduced in Congress. Moreover, Jane and Betty rented rooms in Hemphill's Greenwich Village apartment at 55 Morton Street, which was located just six blocks from the building on Hudson Street that Jacobs would later make her home. To dispel the appearance of impropriety, Jane and Betty described Hemphill as their uncle. Although this was untrue, it is clear that exposure to "Uncle" Hemphill's legislative work inspired Jacobs to compile the "rejected suggestions" of the Constitutional Convention of 1787 in her first book, *Constitutional Chaff*, in which she acknowledged his enthusiasm and wisdom.[15] But with only part-time work for Hemphill, Jacobs continued hunting for more work and exploring the city. As she looked for work in the business and industrial districts between Wall Street and Midtown, she wrote about them.

Jacobs found a few weeks of employment working for a stockbroker named George Rushmore, who was writing a book on the stock market, and other temporary work at a drapery manufacturer, the Westclox clock-making company, and Dennison, an office supplies manufacturer. Between November 1936 and May 1937, she worked as the assistant to the vice president of the Scharf Brothers candy manufacturer located at 10th and 51st streets in Hell's Kitchen, and, from June 1937 to September 1938, as a secretary for the Peter A. Frasse and Company, a maker of bicycle, automobile, and aircraft components, in the industrial Lower West Side. At Peter Frasse, where she worked until starting college in 1938, Jacobs's responsibilities evolved from stenographer, to correspondence writer, to what she described as the newly created position of "trouble shooting secretary," where her role was to "step into any department which seemed to be bogging down and help devise ways for getting the work out faster."[16]

Jacobs's work at Peter Frasse, as with her first job at the *Scranton Republican*, followed a pattern of advancement that would be typical of her career. She quickly gained new responsibilities and independently took on new ones. When these were not demanding or interesting enough to satisfy her, she pursued independent writing projects. With the city and the search for work during the Depression preoccupying her, it was the working districts of the city themselves that she quickly gravitated to, and these became the subjects of her first essays on the city. It was the beginning of a lifelong interest in the geography—historical, physical, social, and economic—of cities.

The Radiant City's Working Districts

When Le Corbusier visited New York in 1935 to promote his ideas and an exhibition of his work, the architect-planner described the neighborhoods between the skyscapers of Wall Street and Midtown where Jacobs worked as the "urban no-man's land made up of miserable low buildings." In Le Corbusier's eyes, these low, congested, "ground-killing" neighborhoods were insalubrious and inefficient, while skyscrapers like Rockefeller Center offered evidence that all could see of the power of modern architecture, rational planning, and the city of the future. Jacobs marveled at the skyscrapers too. As captured in the iconic photographs of Lewis Hine, their construction bespoke the aspirations of the city, the nation, and humanity. As for Rockefeller Center, which was under construction during her first years in New York—and where, although she could hardly have dreamed it as a teen, Jacobs worked as a writer for Time, Incorporated in the 1950s— she came to see the complex as proof that a large and unified group of buildings could be strategically inserted into the city's existing urban fabric without the destruction typical of urban renewal projects. However, Jacobs's and Le Corbusier's visions of the city, which would clash so dramatically in *Death and Life*, were diametrically opposed. Soon after moving to New York, she quickly recognized that the city's unpretentious working districts and their old buildings were as significant as its "financial districts" and its skyscrapers, or more so in the wake of the financial collapse. These districts were the radiant energy of the city's "metaphoric space-defining fires."[17]

Although Jacobs had been to New York as a child, both she and Le Corbusier explored and encountered the city anew in 1935, and both recounted their impressions in November of that year. As reported in the *New York Times*, on November 3, the city excited Le Corbusier greatly; it was a "wilderness of experiment toward a new order," whose contrasts elated and depressed him from moment to moment. From the deck of the ocean liner *Normandie*, the city appeared as a dream city, a vision of enchantment; up close, Le Corbusier was appalled by "the brutality of the great masses—the '*sauvagerie*'—the wild barbarity of the stupendous, disorderly accumulation of towers, tramping the living city under their heavy feet." The precious ground was wasted, as was time better spent in work or leisure than trying to cross it by foot and car. Looking at the Empire State Building, the tallest in the world, from the top of the RCA Tower, he declared the skyscrapers too small, although, in experiencing them for the first time, he could now imagine skyscrapers not just as office buildings but as residences. Cast as "the exact opposite" of his revolutionary 1922 "Contemporary City" plan, New York exceeded his low expectations; it was his first real experience with the modern metropolis. He loved the democracy, the internationalism, and the "event" of New York, Grand Central Terminal, the George Washington Bridge, Louis Armstrong and the city's music; the social and economic inequality, the racism, and the slums he found insufferable. From photographs, he presumed the visual cacophony of the city's hodge-podge of buildings to be a social and aesthetic affront; seeing it in person, he admitted that its energy produced moments of sublime greatness. But caught in a series of traffic jams in the "no-man's land" trying to get from uptown to downtown, he was all the more convinced in his ideas. Experience, the historian Mardges Bacon wrote, "rarely changed his preconceptions; reality rarely changed his myths." It was the opposite with Jacobs.[18]

Two weeks after the *Times* reported Le Corbusier's impressions of New York, Jacobs published the first of a series of four essays on the city in *Vogue*. Anticipating ideas later expanded on in *Death and Life*, the essays bookend the decades between the start of Jacobs's writing career and her first book on cities, while contrasting what was important to her with new ideas about the modern city.

In many ways, Jacobs was as much a functionalist as Le Corbusier and other modern architects—possibly more so, because she was not overly concerned with aesthetics. Indeed, while Jacobs first described her idea for the book that became *Death and Life* as a study of the relation of function to design in larger cities, it was in New York's working districts that she first came to understand how "diverse city uses and users give each other close-grained and lively support," as she later described the phenomenon. And as Le Corbusier charged architects to see again, Jacobs would do the same. She wrote in *Death and Life*, "To see complex systems of functional order as order, and not as chaos, takes understanding," and she learned this early in her New York experience. Looking down from the roof of her apartment in Greenwich Village, she watched the garbage trucks on their rounds and thought "what a complicated, great place this is, and all these pieces of it that make it work." Even garbage collection, no small task in the great city, made her think about how the city functioned at its most basic levels.[19]

In writing about the no-man's land between the skyscrapers of Wall Street and Rockefeller Center, Jacobs sought to reveal to her readers how the everyday, pedestrian city worked and evolved. Although the premise went unstated, her essays on Manhattan's Fur, Leather, Diamond, and Flower districts—published between late 1935 and early 1937, when Jacobs was nineteen and twenty—were written to offer *Vogue*'s uptown readers some insight into the material histories of their prized possessions, the invisible processes and networks that preceded their consumption. In the first, "Where the Fur Flies," published in November 1935, Jacobs described how furs followed a rough-and-tumble journey from trapper to fur farmer, auctioneer to dresser, dealer to manufacturer to retailer. In "Leather Shocking Tales," published in March 1936, she explained that cowhide used for shoes went through a process that left nothing to waste: It first had the soles stamped and cut from it; from the remaining network of scraps, heels were cut; then shoe tips, and finally washers for plumbing and buttons were produced. What is left went off to fertilizer factories. "Diamonds in the Tough," published in October 1936, revealed that most of the sparkling jewelry sold in the "tough" and squalid Diamond District was not new but sold by pawnbrokers after the thirteen months stipulated by law had elapsed from the time it was pawned. Lastly, in "Flowers Come to Town," published in February 1937, Jacobs told the story of how flowers traveled by truck, boat, and plane to get to New York. Most, she explained, came by truck from Long Island, Connecticut, and New Jersey, but those from Florida, California, and Canada came by express train, and those from South America and Holland by ship. Occasionally, a shipment of gardenias was flown in from California by airplane, while other flowers left the city again by ocean liners and airships: "All the large passenger liners are supplied from the New York market, and, on her eastward trips, the Hindenburg, too, carries flowers from Twenty-Eighth Street."[20]

Attentive to the networks of productivity and geography, Jacobs revealed the bouquet on the *Vogue* reader's windowsill as more than a pretty arrangement: It was emblematic of the city's station in international commerce. Though not native to the city, all of these goods—furs, leathers, diamonds, and flowers—were city products, products of the city's networks of process and exchange. Having recently experienced living in a subsistence economy,

Jacobs understood the significance of the city economies, the tremendous physical and social infrastructure that brought raw materials to market. Indeed, she already had some latent understanding about the relationship of city and rural economies. As she wrote years later in *The Economy of Cities*, "When we see a factory out in the country, we do not automatically assume that the kind of work being done in the factory originated and developed in the country." Such observations were, intellectually speaking, not far out of reach of the young Jacobs; her interests in economic geography, explored in courses at Columbia University not long after writing these essays, were already well established within her first few years in New York.[21]

Jacobs was not interested only in the productivity of the city's working districts: Her vignettes of the city also described the complex interactions between people, places, and practices that defined the diverse and lively human ecology of New York and other great cities. The significance of history and context, temporal and spatial juxtaposition, and cultural and economic diversity were clear to the young writer. In her essays, Jacobs showed places that most New Yorkers did not understand, due to changes in space and time, and did not visit because they were located in the working-class districts of the Lower East and West Sides, where the uptown Fifth Avenue shoppers did not tread.

Although the Leather District, for example, was under the escarpment of the Brooklyn Bridge, it had once been located outside of the city, a perfect case study of a rural satellite of city commerce. "When Wall Street really had a wall and was the northern boundary of the city," Jacobs explained, "the Dutch citizens of New York asked the tanners and leather merchants to carry on their business beyond smelling distance. They obligingly moved out to a swamp in the wilderness just south of where the Brooklyn Bridge is now, and there they have remained for more than two hundred years, letting the city grow up about them."[22]

By contrast, it was unclear to her why the Diamond District, "a glittering island in the most squalid section of New York City" located between Hester and Canal streets in the heart of the Lower East Side ghetto, grew up where it did. "No one seems to know why this location was chosen or why the district continues here," she wrote. "Twenty-five years ago, the first of the merchants settled in this incongruous setting for no reason now remembered. It is adjacent to no allied centers; it exists by itself, across the street from the entrance to the Manhattan Bridge, surrounded by the almost legendary Bowery life."[23]

What was already clear to Jacobs was that these districts did not develop in a vacuum isolated from history or social, economic, architectural, and geographical context. She took it for granted that the great city was a global metropolis, populated by people from all over the world. And unlike many other observers of the city at the time, there was no hint of condescension in her discussion of the ethnic, working-class districts, which others saw as the home of the unwashed masses. In "Flowers Come to Town," the most poetic of the four essays, Jacobs drew a parallel between her description of the many varieties of flowers on display and the cultural diversity of immigrant shopkeepers, which implied that the great city's diversity paralleled that of the natural world. Although originally centered around the ferry landing at 34th Street and the East River, a new Flower District grew up around 28th Street and 6th Avenue in the Middle West Side as Greek, Italian, and Asian immigrants set up shop behind the neighborhood's nondescript brownstone fronts. Anticipating the chapter "The Need for Aged Buildings" in *Death and Life*, the young Jacobs seems to have already understood the importance of old buildings to city economies as business and culture incubators. As in a natural ecosystem, the city, and its old buildings, sheltered them in ways that modern skyscrapers, no matter how efficient and modern, could not.

Jacobs's nascent understanding of context, interconnectivity and self-organization, history, and city dynamics was in notable contrast to the revolutionary, antihistorical, and utopian spirit of modernism that was taking hold around her. A child of the Machine Age and the suffrage movement, Jacobs was perhaps too young to experience modernity as a rupture with tradition and the dawn of a new epoch, "one of the great metamorphoses of history," as Le Corbusier's generation saw it. Her impressionable moment was the experience of New York City of the Great Depression, which she celebrated for its ability to continue to work. Despite the Depression, and the city's congestion—or rather because of it—the city continued to tick like clockwork, as in the Fur District, where, from morning until the end of the day, "a steady flow of fur-heaped handcarts and racks runs north, and a stream of both empty and full ones runs south." However, if others saw the need to re-plan and re-create the city in the image of the machine, it was, for her, more than a machine.[24]

As Jacobs later explained with her bonfires metaphor, the city defied being reduced to a single and simple "design device" that could express its structures and functions. Her early essays anticipated her rejection of the promise that new architecture and a new city plan could ameliorate the city's disharmonies and inequities. Just the opposite: Jacobs found the spirit of New York and its hope for the future in these working neighborhoods, where diverse city functions and people lent each other "close-grained and lively support." Le Corbusier hated the congested inefficiencies of New York's streets—"the streets of the new city have nothing in common with those appalling nightmares, the downtown streets of New York," he wrote in 1929—but Jacobs found the essence of the city in its vibrant street life. Le Corbusier saw his imagined Radiant City as the promise and expression of a productive and ennobled society, but Jacobs looked for this in the existing city, in how people and the city worked together and created one another.[25]

Slumming and Unslumming

As Paris transformed Charles-Édouard Jeanneret into Le Corbusier, New York transformed Jane Butzner into Jane Jacobs. Greenwich Village—the working district whose primary products were the written word, the arts, and other forms of cultural experimentation—was described in 1935 as "the center of the American Renaissance or of artiness, of political progress or of long-haired radical men and short-haired radical women." The Village was clearly the right place for a twenty-year-old amateur poet and aspiring writer, who soon experimented with the bohemian eccentricities of dress and behavior. If it was possible to reinvent oneself anywhere, Greenwich Village could hardly have offered the young Jacobs greater possibility or inspiration.[26]

Like the larger city, the Village was also changing as people like Jacobs gravitated to it. In fact, Jacobs was a latecomer to the Village's latest wave of gentrification and revitalization, which the young author of the *Vogue* series would have understood from both history and personal experience. As Caroline Ware wrote in *Greenwich Village, 1920–1930*—published in the same year Jane and her sister moved to Hemphill's apartment on Morton Street—African Americans and immigrants had "retreated before the advance of the Villager," and high rents forced out many artists by the late 1920s. A national newspaper headline of 1927 stated "Greenwich Village Too Costly Now for Artists to Live There: Values Increase So That Only Those Who Can Write Fluently in Check Books Can Afford It." As Jacobs later described it in *Death and Life*, Greenwich Village was an "unslummed former slum." It was an exemplary, and personal, case study of the forces of city life, death, and rebirth—of "unslumming."[27]

Greenwich Village's first wave of gentrification had occurred a hundred years before Jacobs moved there, when, in the 1820s and 1830s, epidemics in the walled city of New York drove those who could afford it to the outskirts of the city, where they displaced freed African slaves and created a pastoral suburb. Anticipating future events, an early city-financed urban redevelopment project, which turned a paupers' cemetery into the Washington Square parade ground, contributed significantly to the area's development. In 1836, New York University erected its first buildings on the east side of the square, and the "American Ward," as Greenwich Village became known, soon became the home of libraries, literary saloons, and art clubs, attracting its first "creative class."[28]

As New York grew northward, pushed by waves of immigration into its suburbs, the Village slowly transformed into a crowded and ethnically diverse industrial slum. Warehouses were converted to factories and its deteriorated housing stock was subdivided into hotels and tenements. As Jacobs later wrote in *Death and Life*, colored people and immigrants from Europe eventually surrounded the American Ward, and "neither physically nor socially was the neighborhood equipped to handle their presence—no more, apparently, than a semisuburb is so equipped today." The white middle-class community fled to settle the Upper East Side and a new suburb in Harlem—"a new quiet residential area of unbelievable dullness"—and left Greenwich Village to deteriorate, only to be revived again by a new wave of writers, playwrights, painters, and those that followed them in the decades before Jacobs arrived.[29]

Jacobs came to see herself as part of these city dynamics, the product of many individual decisions—like her decisions to move from Scranton to New York and then to the Village. As she wrote in a subtle biographical allusion in *Death and Life*, Greenwich Village was an "unslummed former slum" because it had attracted an energetic, ambitious, and affluent population. Whereas "dull neighborhoods are inevitably deserted by their more energetic, ambitious, or affluent citizens, and also by their young people who can get away," high-vitality neighborhoods attracted "vigorous new blood"—like hers.[30]

In *Death and Life*, Jacobs used the term "slum" for shock value, challenging notions of what a slum was (or is) and the people who live in them, as well as the inadequacy and imprecision of the term in city planning theory. She explained that the "unslumming" process required longtime residents, in addition to the admixture of "new blood," to participate in a neighborhood's renovation. The process hinged "on whether a considerable number of the residents and businessmen of a slum find it both desirable and practical to make and carry out their own plans right there." Contrasting with paternalistic, top-down decisions of legislators and city planning theorists to move and transform neighborhoods and their residents, "unslumming" represented self-determination, participation, and the latent power of what was "possibly the greatest regenerative forces inherent in energetic American metropolitan economies."[31]

Although Jacobs did not delve too deeply into city history in *Death and Life*, she knew that parts of the city had improved dramatically, despite exponential population growth, in the years before she moved to Greenwich Village and Le Corbusier visited Manhattan to promote his Radiant City. By 1930, the Lower East Side's population had been halved from its high of 530,000 to 250,000, as residents moved to the boroughs of Brooklyn, Queens, and the Bronx. She also knew this was not true for other parts of the city or for other cities. "Colored citizens," she wrote, "are cruelly overcrowded in their shelter and cruelly overcharged for it. The buildings are going begging because they are being rented or sold only to whites—and whites, who have so much more choice, do not care to live here."[32]

Considered the worst slum district in the world by the early 1800s, Manhattan's Lower East Side had already been the focus for the best intentions of housing and social reformers for over a century. Disadvantaged by its swampy geography at a time when Greenwich Village was a bucolic location for colonial agricultural estates, the area, as Jacobs observed in her early essays on the Diamond and Leather districts, was the home of the people and enterprises—freed slaves, Jews, tanneries, slaughterhouses, and breweries—that were expelled from the old walled city. Eventually it became the city's working district for vice, not to mention gangs and impoverished tenement life. In the first in a long series of New York slum-clearance "firsts," after being granted use of the powers of eminent domain by the state legislature in 1800, in the 1830s the city government razed part of the Five Points core and created a park. Anticipating the redevelopment strategies, the enduring overestimation of the virtues of parks, and the gang battles of 1950s New York, all described by Jacobs in *Death and Life*, the paradoxically named Paradise Park soon became a site for gang warfare. Also anticipating the "white flight" of the mid-twentieth century, the mid-nineteenth century saw the design of the first planned suburbs in the United States, among them the aptly named Irving Park (1843), outside of Chicago, and Llewellyn Park (1853), outside of New York. As Henry James wrote during that time, "New York was both squalid and gilded, to be fled rather than enjoyed."[33]

By the 1880s, the late nineteenth-century pastime known as "slumming"—"the latest fashionable idiosyncrasy in London, i.e., the visiting of the slums of the great city by parties of ladies and gentlemen for sightseeing"—had reached New York. An 1884 New York Times article discussed the "best" districts for sightseeing, noting that there were many good places for the curious sightseer "to see people of whom they had heard, but of whom they were as ignorant as if they were inhabitants of a strange country." But the flip side of slum literature and tourism was reformism. In London, "slumming has brought to the notice of the rich much suffering, and led to many sanitary reforms," the author observed, although this was not yet the case in New York: "So far the mania here has assumed the single form of sight-seeing—the more noble ambition of alleviating the condition of the desperately poor visited has not animated the adventurous parties."[34]

However, the urban reform movement, the foundation for urban renewal concepts and programs that Jacobs would later seek to reform in turn, grew quickly. Paralleling the British experience, the popularity of salacious publications about slum life, such as Darkness and Daylight, or Lights and Shadows of New York Life (1892), was followed, and capitalized on, by reform literature such as police-reporter-turned-photojournalist Jacob Riis's exposé How the Other Half Lives: Studies Among the Tenements of New York (1890). Prompted by Riis and growing public attention, the city government razed the "foul core" of the Lower East Side for a second time in 1888 and, with the assistance of the Small Parks Act of 1887, turned the razed site, once again, into a park, repeating a pattern of redevelopment practices that would continue into the urban renewal era of the 1950s and 1960s. In an 1891 Times article titled "A Plea for More Parks," Riis and reformers from the Union for Concerted Moral Effort, a group of uptown religious leaders, declared their mission "to make war on the slums and cut them to pieces with parks and playgrounds."[35]

Located in the heart of the neighborhood that Jacobs later visited for her "Diamonds in the Tough" essay, Mulberry Bend was a few blocks from the Five Points slum clearance of 1833, but more ambitious; it is considered one of the first slum clearance projects on a modern scale. Not without the difficulties of such an effort, almost ten years passed before Mulberry Bend Park (later Columbus Park) opened in 1897. Anticipating future debates about public-private development that would continue into the present, the park's construction was delayed by the familiar dilemmas of determining compensation for the owners of the condemned properties, evicting tenants, and wrangling over whether adjacent property owners—who would ostensibly profit from proximity to a new pleasure ground—should bear part of the cost of the public investment. It was a project exemplary of the "creative destruction" of Manhattan, with all the contradictions that the historian Max Page implied with that term. Also representing the thinking about parks and sentimentalized nature that Jacobs criticized in *Death and Life*, a reporter wrote that a proper and picturesque people's pleasure ground would be "a welcome bit of green nature that will be more than grateful to a wretched and hopelessly poverty-stricken part of the community, comprising people of various nationalities, with scarcely an American among them."[36]

Despite the hoped-for benefits of this green design, transportation, not public space, ultimately transformed the Lower East Side. In addition to advocating for municipal parks for the poor, in 1891 leaders of the Union for Concerted Moral Effort also lobbied for a municipally owned transit system that would solve the problem of city crowding by making less congested districts, such as Harlem, accessible to the working class. By 1890, Manhattan's elevated railroad system was the longest in the world, but it was slow, overcrowded, expensive, privately owned, and had limited connections to neighboring cities off the island. Although far less radical than contemporary proposals to reform land ownership, the idea of a municipally owned transit system was considered by some to be "socialist," but it eventually came to pass.[37]

By the time Jacobs settled in Greenwich Village, one of the worst slums in the world had uncrowded and unslummed, even as the city's population continued to grow, as half of the Lower East Side's population took advantage of the recently expanded subway system and moved to the outer boroughs of Brooklyn, Queens, and the Bronx. Greater New York's first subway opened in 1904, and the privately owned Interborough Rapid Transit line soon carried six hundred thousand people daily. In the 1920s, with the support of Governor Alfred E. Smith, a native of the Lower East Side, the privately owned Brooklyn-Manhattan Transit system added seven new

crossings of the East River. Finally, in 1932, a few years before Jacobs moved
to the city, the municipally owned Independent Rapid Transit Railroad
added 190 miles of subway. The melodramatic roar of the Els, which were
torn down as the subways were built, soon became a lost part of changing
New York.[38]

Thus, Jacobs moved to New York at a remarkable moment. On the one
hand, the New Deal provided the means for a host of reform-minded
projects and infrastructural improvements. Public works funding allowed Mayor Fiorello La Guardia and Robert Moses, his new parks
commissioner—who was by then the chairman of the Emergency Public
Works Commission, a former New York secretary of state, the former chairman of the Committee on Public Improvements, and a mayoral nominee
in the race won by La Guardia—to implement their pre-Depression lists
of proposed building projects, including parks and parkways, bridges and
swimming pools, hydroelectric dams and airports, and public housing. The
year Jacobs moved to New York also saw the birth of the planning organization that she would battle twenty-five years later. In 1934, assisted by the
Works Progress Administration (WPA), La Guardia formed the Committee
on City Planning, which led to the establishment of the New York City
Planning Commission in 1936. Meanwhile, also in 1934, the new NYC
Housing Authority assumed control of housing construction work initiated
by the WPA, and it quickly conceived of the largest slum clearance housing
project ever undertaken, the predecessor of the types of projects that Jacobs
railed against in *Death and Life.*

On the other hand, Jacobs arrived in New York when, because of the
automobile, city life was becoming a choice for the upper and middle
classes. Following the transit-oriented Sunnyside Gardens housing project
(1924), which was located adjacent to an elevated station in Long Island
City, the architect Clarence Stein and the planner Henry Wright's Radburn,
New Jersey, project (1928) was designed to be the "Suburban Garden City
for the Motor Age." Working with Frederick Ackerman, the chief architect
of the new Housing Authority, Radburn's "superblock" plan was meant to
eliminate "the annoyances of old-time towns" and cities by incorporating
the automobile into daily life. In the 1929 *Regional Plan of New York and
Its Environs*, Radburn was held out as "a significant contribution to the
plan of the Region" as a whole, meriting "every possible financial support
and encouragement from public authorities." Although Modernist architects were later blamed for conceiving the superblock plan and automobile-
oriented design, the car and the problems it created were entrenched when

Jacobs was still a teenager. Although equally captivated by the suburb's verdancy, even Le Corbusier recognized the problems. In 1935, he prophetically stated, "The suburb is the great problem of the U.S.A." While also mesmerized by the automobile (and who wasn't?), unlike aggressive decentrists, Le Corbusier's ideas were based on preserving the countryside from the "vast, sprawling built-up area encircling the city," eliminating long commutes "spent daily in the metros, buses, and Pullmans that cause the destruction of the communal life that is the very marrow of a nation," and keeping people and their homes "in the middle of the city instead of in Connecticut." Nevertheless, those who advocated decentralization recognized similar problems with the self-segregation and planned segregation of the suburbs. As Lewis Mumford wrote in *The Culture of Cities* (1938), "Without doubt the prime obstacle to urban decentralization is that a unit that consists of workers, without the middle class and rich groups that exist in a big city, is unable to support even the elementary civic equipment."[39]

Such were the forces and the "historic changes," as Jacobs called them in *Death and Life*, that would shape the fate, and the life and death, of cities. If they could afford it, those seeking more space and greenery moved to the suburbs, just as others had left the walled city of Manhattan for the suburbs of Greenwich Village centuries before. Jacobs naturally believed in the choice of where to live, but unslumming, she wrote in *Death and Life*, hinged "on whether a considerable number of the residents and businessmen of a slum find it both desirable and practical to make and carry out their own plans right there." Cities may have held an attraction for some, but, as Ebenezer Howard observed in *Garden Cities of To-Morrow* (1902), the country was a magnet for others.[40]

First Houses

When Eleanor Roosevelt dedicated First Houses, the first municipally built, owned, and managed housing project in the United States, a crowd of ten thousand attended, despite the cold weather. Le Corbusier, who had been touring the city's slums and housing projects with the Housing Authority's chairman Langdon Post and *House and Garden* editor Henry Humphrey, was there, as was Moses. It is tempting to think that Jacobs, who lived a short distance away, was there to observe the spectacle and to witness the rise and fall of New York City public housing from start to finish.[41]

The First Houses dedication was an event of national significance. A telegram from President Roosevelt read by Post at the dedication called the project an "answer to the great national need for better American homes and housing conditions." Mrs. Roosevelt added, "I hope the day is dawning when private capital will devote itself to better and cheaper housing, but we know that the government will have to continue to build for the low-income groups. That is a departure for us, but other governments have done it." Governor Herbert H. Lehman similarly described the project as the start of "a new field of public responsibility." Observing that the United States was twenty years behind European countries in eliminating slums and providing affordable housing for its citizens, he added that the Depression had made the shortage of housing an emergency situation:

> The clearance of slums and the provision of new dwellings for low-income families in our state has opened up a new field of public responsibility. Previous to the still existing depression, it was assumed by the majority of people that the housing problem was a personal one, a matter of individual responsibility. [But] students of housing have been well acquainted with the great programs of rehousing which cities of Great Britain and continental Europe have been developing in many years past. Over twenty years ago in cities abroad, local communities undertook to serve the housing needs of those families who found it impossible to provide for themselves homes of modern standards at rents within their means. Under the pressure of emergency people have acquired a new sensitiveness to human values and human needs. We are no longer indifferent to conditions which in the past we have taken for granted.[42]

Located at East 3rd Street and Avenue A on the East Side (an area later known as the East Village), First Houses has been described as one of the best public housing projects ever built, in part for its subtle and contextual design. Nevertheless, at the time, it was generally considered a failed experiment. Mayor La Guardia, a Greenwich Village native, was proud of the housing program, and he boasted of the diversity of backgrounds represented on the housing board, which included Post, the Greenwich Settlement House director Mary K. Simkhovitch, the Catholic Charities administrator Rev. Roberts Moore, and the American Labor Party leader

FIGURE 6. First Houses, Lower East Side, dedicated by First Lady Eleanor Roosevelt on December 3, 1935. NYCHA and LGWA.

Charney Vladek. He exclaimed, "Where can you find a housing board to equal it—an idealist on housing, a social worker, a Catholic priest, and a Socialist!" However, as a housing prototype, he called First Houses "Boondoggling Exhibit A."[43]

Designed by Frederick Ackerman and William Lescaze, First Houses' great shortcoming was providing too few apartments at too great a cost. Initially meant to be a renovation of the existing tenements, where every third tenement building on the site would be demolished in order to provide daylight and fresh air, along the way it was discovered that the 1846 tenements were in too poor a state to be rehabilitated. After three of the eight were renovated, all but a few walls and the foundations of the rest were torn down, and new apartments were built from the salvaged bricks. Reuse of the old bricks allowed the new buildings to blend in with the old, but at the time this underscored the project's lack of modernity, while proving renovation to be a very costly approach.[44]

Criticized as "a million dollar extravagance" because of its cost overruns, the first public housing project thus helped to kill the idea of renovation as a slum improvement tactic decades before Jacobs's criticism of postwar urban renewal. In 1936, the housing consultant and attorney Charles Abrams (later cited in *Death and Life*) was among those who argued that "it will be far cheaper to demolish the old buildings and reconstruct the areas anew." Similarly, Jacobs's future friend and foe Lewis Mumford—who believed that even the city's wealthiest citizens lived in antiquated and inadequate quarters—wrote of First Houses in his column for *The New Yorker*, "The external environment remains exactly what it was before: bleak, filthy, ugly. . . . These new tenements would be expensive at half the price. This is 'slum replacement' with a vengeance—it simply replaces an old slum with a new slum. Congratulations, Mr. Post!" Despite becoming known as the great destroyer of city neighborhoods, Moses was among those who defended the idea of renovation. Still bitter a decade later over Abrams's criticism of his advocacy for rehabilitation, Moses wrote, in 1945, "The perfectionist does not want old buildings made sanitary and fireproof. . . . He says this move perpetuates the slum and gives it a new lease of life when it is about to die a natural death. He favors rehabilitation only if every third house is torn down and the two remaining ones completely rebuilt; and he can show that this process is so expensive that it is hardly worthwhile. Yet it is a fact that in most cities plenty of old tenements and other houses can be made safe, sanitary, and fairly comfortable for a number of years at a reasonable cost."[45]

With overwhelming criticism, Post could only concede that First Houses had cost too much and direct his agency to provide more apartments for less money. He answered his critics by stating that the first public housing project had been a useful experiment that was only the beginning of a "vast housing plan" that would rehouse five hundred thousand families throughout the city over the next ten years. First Houses' enduring contribution had been "to test the Authority's power to condemn land for slum clearance—a test which we won," he added. By upholding the Housing Authority's power to condemn two parcels that an intractable owner had refused to sell, a State Appeals Court established a significant legal precedent for the use of eminent domain upon which future urban redevelopment was predicated.[46]

Post's Housing Authority now had something to prove and the legal means to prove it. However, this would not be easy in a severely depressed economic climate. In the Roaring 1920s, housing projects had been far more ambitious. Whereas First Houses had 123 apartments, midtown Manhattan's Tudor City, built only ten years earlier by the speculative real estate developer Fred French on the site of East River slums, had three thousand apartments and six hundred hotel rooms in twelve elevator buildings surrounding a private interior park. The product of a pre-Depression, developer-driven, and pre-Modernist urbanism of hyper-density, Tudor City represented an architectural approach aptly described as "Manhattanism." But while Tudor City was a ritzy precedent, in the early 1930s Manhattanism was an unattainable development dream in public housing circles. Less than five years before First Houses opened, drawings had been made for a "city of the future" to replace the slums of the Lower East Side's Chrystie-Forsyth neighborhood, razed in 1930. In its place was imagined a skyscraper city flanked by a new multilane automobile parkway and viaduct expressway designed to improve circulation to the Manhattan Bridge. With spotlights illuminating the sky and a multilevel transportation system, the proposal was a visionary combination of Beaux-Arts civic design, nineteenth-century technophilia, and Jazz Age futurism.[47]

Among the last pre-Depression expressions of Manhattanism, and one that made First Houses pale in comparison, was a public-private partnership for a high-rise, high-density development of 1,600 apartments called Knickerbocker Village, located just five blocks from Mulberry Bend and completed in 1934 around the time of Jacobs's visit to the Lower East Side for her first working-district essay. The project—also designed by Frederick Ackerman and developed by Fred French, who had acquired the land by the summer of 1929—would not have been completed due to the stock market crash except for the support of Moses, the chairman of the city's Emergency Public Works Commission. As the *New York Times* observed in 1933, "Any undertaking with which Alfred E. Smith and his 'fidus Achates' [faithful Achates] Robert Moses, are associated has a way of moving swiftly and with decision."[48]

Although the site was a notorious, tuberculosis-ridden "lung block," which had been identified as a slum clearance site as early as 1903, French's original plan was to transform Knickerbocker Village into a "high-class" residential development from which Wall Street executives could walk to work. However, with an $8 million loan from President Hoover's Emergency Relief and Construction Act of 1932, secured with Moses's intervention, the project became the federal government's first major involvement in housing development, and Knickerbocker Village was ultimately rented to middle-class families, among them some fallen Wall Street tycoons. In the new economic context, it was also clear that such projects would do little good for the slum dwellers of the Lower East Side, and using public funds to displace low-income tenants, gentrify neighborhoods, and profit real estate developers gave some pause. Indeed, the housing problems that Jacobs later wrote of had a long history. In an April 1933 exposé in *The Nation*, the local Socialist Party organizer Henry Rosner wrote that, despite all the publicity surrounding the demolition of the notorious "lung block," the neighborhood's original residents would only be worse off for being displaced. Anticipating Jacobs's critiques in *Death and Life*, he wrote that "the displaced tenants will merely move into old-law tenements on the next block which will be a little less dreary, dilapidated, and unhealthy. . . . Two blocks of slums will be destroyed, but several others will be perpetuated."[49]

Progressive critics, including Ackerman and Moses, agreed. Commenting on Rosner's article, Moses replied that the solution to large-scale slum clearance and low-cost housing would be federal subsidies—exactly what would soon come to pass in New Deal and later in Urban Renewal housing legislation. Keenly anticipating the future, in a private letter Moses wrote, "I know the limitations of the Knickerbocker Village and I think I have some idea of what ought to be done on a large scale. It was immensely difficult to get this one project under way in the face of the reluctance of city officials to grant tax exemption and the bitter opposition of real estate and other interests. . . . [T]he solution of the problem lies at Washington, and if proper provision can be made by law for slum clearance and low-cost housing as part of a reorganized Federal Public Works program, we can get somewhere. This probably involves a Federal subsidy." In this way, Knickerbocker Village was the end of Manhattanism and also the beginning of slum clearance and housing development with federal legislation and funds, a turn of events that Moses understood as early as 1933, the year Jane Butzner, his future nemesis, graduated from high school.[50]

From "Manhattanism" to the "Radiant Garden City"

While the Great Depression mortally wounded Manhattanism, suburbanism dealt it a deathblow. Whether sympathetic with Howard's exurban "Garden City" or Le Corbusier's urban "Ville Verte," suburban-minded reformers agreed that the Knickerbocker Village housing model was too much like the slums they replaced: It was too dense and covered too much of the ground to provide the desired amounts of light, air, and open space.

Indeed, irrespective of architectural style, the longing for and sentimentalization of nature had been the undoing of cities, and the driver of sprawl,
since long before Jacobs criticized suburbanism in the conclusion to *Death
and Life*. Even as Le Corbusier and the other European architects referred
to by Eleanor Roosevelt at the First Houses dedication were at work, New
York architects were developing an indigenous "garden apartment" type
that evolved into a new model of "suburbanized urbanism."[51]

First built in the suburbs of Queens in the 1910s, the suburban model
was introduced into the city by the 1920s. In those years, the architect
Arthur C. Holden, a future acquaintance of Jacobs, invented a prototypical
urban redevelopment model that was a cross between high-density Manhattanism and the low-density New York garden apartment, seeking to
combine the advantages of urban density and suburban open space. Contemporary attention to modern European housing only seemed to prove
the local model right. In 1932, the Museum of Modern Art's *Modern Architecture* exhibition of 1932 included a companion exhibition on housing
organized by Clarence Stein, Henry Wright, Lewis Mumford, and Catherine
Bauer—also Jacobs's future collaborators, friends, and antagonists—that
made European models hard to ignore. As Douglas Haskell, the architecture critic for *The Nation* and Jacobs's future boss, wrote in March 1932,
European housing, such as Ernst May's fifteen-thousand-family housing
project in Frankfurt, represented "the best that the twentieth century can
do for the average man."[52]

A few years before Jacobs moved to New York, these varied forces
converged in a number of groundbreaking plans by the Philadelphia and
New York–based architectural firm of Howe & Lescaze. One of the most
celebrated American architectural practices after its completion of the first
modernist skyscraper in the world in 1932, the PSFS Building in Philadelphia, Howe & Lescaze embodied the attempt to synthesize European modernism and American suburbanism. Between 1931 and 1933, even as work
on the urbane PSFS Building continued, the firm submitted a proposal for
the still vacant seven-block Chrystie-Forsyth site. Their massive, visionary
scheme was called River Gardens (aka Rutgerstown) and would redevelop
eighteen city blocks on the Lower East Side, from the Chrystie-Forsyth site
on the west across to the East River and from Houston Street down to the
Manhattan Bridge. Influenced by the architectural principles outlined by
Le Corbusier in *Towards a New Architecture* (1931), the Chrystie project
would house 1,500 families in twenty-four elevator buildings with ribbon

FIGURE 7. River Gardens, a housing project proposed in 1932 for the Lower East Side by Howe & Lescaze. Lescaze Archive, Syracuse University Special Collections, Syracuse, NY.

windows and roof terraces set on fourteen-foot columns; without basements or ground floors and bridging the cross streets, all of the ground space would be free for lawns, recreation, and circulation, allowing children to travel to the public school, planned for the block south of First Street, under cover and with minimal street crossings. Architecturally, the scheme was a forbearer for many public housing projects, including one Jacobs consulted on decades later, in East Harlem, in the late 1950s.[53]

River Gardens was originally conceived in 1932 as a $6 million project with nine-story buildings; however, in a revised plan in 1933, the buildings grew to fifteen stories, with a cost of more than $9 million. Ultimately, River Gardens was proposed to house 7,500 families in dozens of midrise buildings of varying height that would occupy only 45 percent of the ground and leave the rest devoted to green space and recreational uses. Designed by Lescaze with the assistance of Carol Aronovici and Albert Fry, who had worked in Le Corbusier's office from 1928 to 1929 (around the time Le Corbusier wrote *The City of To-Morrow and Its Planning*), River Gardens evoked Le Corbusier's "Contemporary City."[54]

Both projects were locally supported and approved for construction in 1933, although neither commission went to Howe & Lescaze. Although their "international style"—to use the term coined by Henry-Russell Hitchcock and Philip Johnson in *The International Style: Architecture Since 1922* (1932)—was not then embraced by all, style was not the issue. While the Chrystie project was the first in New York that clearly referenced European models—and one of only a few U.S. projects featured in Hitchcock and Johnson's 1932 exhibition—*New York Times* articles and editorials celebrated the projects' basic concepts, which were not unique to Howe & Lescaze's proposals. Architectural style was a matter of taste, but the underlying city planning principles, so rational and self-evident, were praised. In support of River Gardens, the *Times* lauded the superblock approach, stating that the building's limited footprints would create large open spaces for park development and would "secure to city dwellers advantages of sunlight, air circulation, and attractive outlook over garden plots—heretofore not to be had in the congested areas of Manhattan Island." Named for the 1750 farm owned by Herman Rutgers that once occupied the site, Rutgerstown would "bring back into the city some of the country that was in that favorite area in 1750." Suburbanism transcended style.[55]

Chrystie-Forsyth and Rutgerstown failed because of land costs and a dynamic that Jacobs later described as "slum shifting" (or what, a few years after her, the sociologist Ruth Glass termed "gentrification"). In a 1933 *Times* article titled "East Side Housing Not for the Poor," John Sloan, the architect ultimately selected for the Chrystie project, explained that the new housing project had to be considered "slum clearance" and not "slum relief." New apartments could not serve the neighborhood's poor, Sloan said, because "it is simply impossible to supply decent housing for them at anything like the figures they are now paying for hovels on the most expensive Manhattan real estate." People who could not pay more than $5 in rent should be transferred to places where land is cheaper, the architect explained, so they can receive decent housing. Sloan suggested that a relocation could occur in Astoria, Queens, near the water's edge or near the gas tanks (the future site of Stuyvesant Town). Anticipating future developments, he continued, "The development of this section will eventually force the hovels out, and it will become a white-collar residential center for downtown office workers. There is no other way to figure it without a government subsidy to make up the difference between what these people can afford to pay and what it costs for the Chrystie-Forsyth land plus the construction of decent housing on it."[56]

Despite the support of the State Housing Board, Mayor John P. O'Brian (who served between Jimmy Walker and Fiorello La Guardia), the Board of Estimate, and East Side community organizations, Rutgerstown was denied the needed $40 million government loan. Secretary of the Interior Harold Ickes, the director of the Public Works Administration (PWA), stated that Rutgerstown was "socially desirable from the standpoint that it would clear one of the worst portions of New York slums." However, there were no more funds available for private housing projects, particularly for expensive Manhattan real estate. As the *Times* noted in "War on Slums Proceeds Steadily," "When Langdon Post Jr., Tenement House Commissioner, attempted to buy property on the lower East Side, he found that the price asked per foot was much more than the city could afford to pay. . . . This also is the case on the lower West Side, in upper Chelsea, where are some of the worst slums in New York."[57]

Such was the background for the iconic modernist Williamsburg Houses project (1934–37), the most ambitious slum clearance housing project then undertaken in the United States. Located in Brooklyn, where the slums were "among the worst" and land was cheaper, Williamsburg would be the Housing Authority's first independently initiated housing project after it took over First Houses from the WPA, and it would bring together the best team that could be assembled. Lescaze, a new member of the Housing Authority's architectural board, was the lead designer, while Ackerman served as the Housing Authority's new technical director; Henry Wright, Arthur Holden, and Richmond Shreve and Irwin Clavan, architects of the Empire State Building (Clavan would later design Stuyvesant Town), rounded out the design team.

Hybridizing the New York garden apartment with European modernism, Williamsburg turned twelve city blocks into four superblocks of four-floor apartments. Green and open space accounted for almost 70 percent of the site, exceeding the 65 percent demanded by the PWA, which funded the project. Adding further to the project's suburban tranquility, storefront buildings were eliminated and shops were limited to only the highest traffic intersections, reducing interior noise and traffic. Meanwhile, light-colored materials, a lack of distinction between the fronts and the backs of the buildings, and the rotation of the echinate buildings fifteen degrees off the

FIGURE 8. Williamsburg Houses, Brooklyn, designed by Frederick Ackerman and William Lescaze, with possible input from Le Corbusier, 1937. NYCHA and LGWA.

city grid reinforced the project's separation from the neighboring age-darkened and cramped tenement buildings and the rest of the old city.

Not all of the architects on Williamsburg's remarkable design team saw eye to eye. A self-described technocrat, Ackerman was a relatively conservative architect; he had studied in Paris and published an extensive survey of British housing and town planning in 1918, and he objected to the project's machine aesthetic and the rotated site plan. Ultimately, Lescaze's hand prevailed, perhaps with the help of Le Corbusier, who visited the Williamsburg site and was a frequent guest at Lescaze's home and office during his visit to New York. Nevertheless, Williamsburg was the beginning of a new amalgamation of urban design ideals, which, irrespective of the modernistic

architectural language, combined broadly shared functionalist and suburbanizing ideas. As presciently described in the *Times* on October 15, 1936,
the day after its dedication, Williamsburg Houses symbolized "the pioneer
epoch in American efforts at slum clearance and rehousing" and deserved
"a notable place in the history of American housing." While Williamsburg
Houses was not the "towers-in-a-park" scheme envisioned for River Gardens, what Jacobs later called "the Radiant Garden City" had taken root in
Brooklyn by the time she was settled in Greenwich Village.[58]

Creating what Mumford called "the streetless house and the houseless
street," Williamsburg Houses exemplified a "new order," where the automobile was accommodated, while residences, retail stores, and automobile
and pedestrian traffic were all functionally separated. As Mumford wrote
in a review of the project, the "first principle of modern neighborhood
planning is to reduce the number of streets, convert more open space into
gardens and playgrounds, and route traffic around, not through, the
neighborhood."[59]

In what was probably her first encounter with the Radiant Garden City,
Jacobs visited a Brooklyn housing project, probably Williamsburg, around
this time, and she wondered about the design and whether people would
like it. Despite any critiques she may have had at the time, however, there
was an enormous demand for housing. Whereas First Houses had received
15,000 applications for 122 apartments, Williamsburg Houses received
more than 25,000 applications for 1,600 apartments; and as Williamsburg
Houses was the most expensive public housing project undertaken by the
Housing Authority to date, and the most expensive ever built in relative
terms, there was ever-increasing pressure to decrease unit costs; to eliminate stores, amenities, architectural fees, landscaping, and materials; and to
push the buildings higher—especially on pricier Manhattan land. East River
Houses, completed in 1941, around the time Jacobs landed her first writing
job, would be the first high-rise housing project. Located in East Harlem,
where Jacobs would later come to understand the flaws in this urbanistic
system of thought, its superblocks and towers destroyed the city's preexist-
ing block structure and eliminated the familiar and contextual urban qualities of scale, orientation, public space, and multiple function that, just a
few years before, First Houses had retained.[60]

Within the conceptual paradigm where it was believed that as much as
"half the residential area of the city is in an advanced blight or slum,"
and where the most expensive residential street in New York City could be

FIGURE 9. Fort Greene Houses, built in 1941 as a barracks for the Brooklyn Navy Yard, had come to symbolize the problems of public housing by 1959. NYCHA and LGWA.

described as a "super slum" because its apartment buildings violated the minimum standards of quiet, sunlight, and fresh air, suburbanization, suburbanized urbanism, and the "pathologies" of public housing, soon exemplified by Fort Greene Houses, were inevitable.[61]

In 1936, Mumford wrote that "what Manhattan needs to overcome its present blight (caused mainly by an exodus to the outskirts and the suburbs) is a series of 'internal' suburbs." And in fact, even as work proceeded on Williamsburg Houses, the suburbanization of the city had begun.[62]

While at work on Williamsburg, Lescaze, Aronovici, Wright, and Albert Mayer began designing a five-hundred-acre "Garden City within the City" that stretched along most of the East River waterfront of Astoria, Queens, from the Queensboro Bridge to within a few blocks of Moses's new Triborough Bridge. Described as a new approach, Astoria's cul-de-sac suburb would have a density of approximately 150 people (and rooms) per acre, with six-story buildings covering 45 percent of a slum-cleared site. Strategically located between two of the bridges off the island, the "new colony" was an ideally located suburb: It was adjacent to Moses's new Grand Central Parkway (1933–36) and connected by mass transit to many of the city's fourteen slum areas, as designated by the Slum Clearance Committee of New York, for which all of the team members served as consultants. Recognizing that transportation was inextricably linked to city planning, slum clearance, and housing development, Mayer noted that proximity to the city's slums with a 5¢ transit fare was "an important factor because the people who move here from the slums will want to visit and be visited by their friends." And with Moses's new parkways, automobile ownership was clearly part of the city's future. In the *Times* article "New Colony Urged as Slum Solution," Lescaze argued for embracing this future: "The old pattern of a city must be thrown aside because of the absurd congestion of traffic. A small plan of many streets worked all right in its time, when horses and walking on foot were the only means of transportation. Why not do the intelligent thing and provide a decent pathway for the automobile?"[63]

Although the Astoria suburb was not built, it was difficult to argue with the underlying logic. Referencing the recently completed *Regional Plan of New York*, in the introduction to *The City of To-Morrow and Its Planning*, Frederick Etchells stated that the "problem of transit and transportation alone is quite enough to demand the reconstruction of the modern city!" Whether the architecture was modern or traditional, high-rise or low, Jacobs's move to New York in the mid-1930s coincided with broadly shared desires to make the city modern, mobile, and green. While Howard's satellite Garden Cities were imagined as possible because of a growing commuter railway system, Le Corbusier's genius was to understand the revolution of the automobile and to predict an automobilized society. And unlike Howard, Le Corbusier believed in the concentration of the great city and opposed sprawl. As he opined in a 1932 *New York Times* editorial, his "green city" would utilize elevated highways such as those being built in New York and be "the reverse of the garden city, fundamentally opposed to it in principle. Since the garden city is situated in the suburbs and so extends the area of the town, it creates a transport problem; but as the green city will reduce the town area this problem will be done away with entirely."[64]

Such was the urban context in which Jacobs arrived in New York, and to which she would respond in her writings on the city in years to come.

As she later observed in her chapter on unslumming in *Death and Life*, "What is new is that unfit neighborhoods can be deserted more swiftly, and slums can and do spread thinner and farther, than was the case in the days before automobiles and government-guaranteed mortgages for suburban developments, when it was less practical for families with choice to flee neighborhoods that were displaying some of the normal and inevitable conditions that accompany city life." In 1961, however, this phenomenon was not new. This kind of "unslumming" had existed long before she moved to her "unslummed former slum."

CHAPTER 2

The Education of a City Naturalist

> Systems of thought, no matter how objective they may purport to be, have underlying emotional bases and values. The development of modern city planning and housing reform has been emotionally based on a glum reluctance to accept city concentrations of people as desirable, and this negative emotion about city concentrations of people has helped deaden planning intellectually.
> —Jane Jacobs, 1961

JANE JACOBS WROTE her first essays on the city soon after arriving in New York, tracing in them relationships between people, geographies, and city dynamics, even as forces converged to break apart those relationships. Soon thereafter, at twenty-two, she decided to go to college to study geography and economic geography, fields of inquiry that she would pursue for the rest of her life. She would not earn a degree, but her coursework led to her first book, *Constitutional Chaff: Rejected Suggestions of the Constitutional Convention of 1787*, an examination of the intellectual foundations of the creation of the U.S. Constitution, published by Columbia University Press in 1941. Soon thereafter, as a government employee during World War II and the Cold War—primarily as a writer for the Office of War Information (OWI) and the State Department—she would further develop her lifelong interest in "systems of thought," the patterns of thinking that shaped intellectual paradigms and approaches. By understanding such systems, she sought to understand differences in the ways people thought things like cities and civilizations should work, and how, as best she could understand them, they actually did work. Speaking through one of her characters in *Systems of Survival: A Dialogue on the Moral Foundations of Commerce and Politics*, her sixth book, Jacobs wrote, "I like uncovering systems."[1]

In *The Death and Life of Great American Cities*, in which she had a similar goal, Jacobs sought to contrast the way the city worked with the wishful thinking of city planning and urban design theories and practices. Describing the book in 1959, she said, "This book is neither a retelling in new form of things already said, nor an expansion and enlargement of previously worked out basic ground, but it is an attempt to make what amounts to a different system of thought about the great city." In attempting to lay the foundation for a new system of thought about great cities, she would inquire into underlying assumptions, emotional and ideological biases, and specious methods, and, as will be discussed in Chapter 7, she sought to replace flawed "images" of the city with better ones.[2]

Like Francis Bacon, who, in the early seventeenth century, contrasted his scientific method with prevailing superstitions, hasty conclusions, and other misguided habits of thought, Jacobs in *Death and Life* judged that "the pseudoscience of city planning and its companion, the art of city design" were similarly founded on conjecture, unstudied presumptions, and misapplied principles—and "anything but cities themselves." Writing her book in the same years when the historian and philosopher of science Thomas Kuhn wrote *The Structure of Scientific Revolutions* (1962) and coined the term "paradigm shift" to describe the destruction and transformation of orthodox conceptual systems in science, Jacobs also consciously sought a paradigm shift through her similar sensitivity to the influence of contexts and social communities on ways of thinking, away from "orthodox" ideas about cities and their design. However, in becoming a target of McCarthyism as a State Department employee after having worked diligently for the federal government, Jacobs had a short fuse for the groupthink of "normal science," as Kuhn called it, when she came to understand the failings of the theories and practices of urban renewal a few years later.[3]

A Geographer and Political Philosopher

In a brief autobiography that accompanied an early review of *Death and Life*, Jacobs wrote, "When I was twenty-two, and had been five years out of high school, I decided I did want to go to school again and learn a lot of things I had become curious about."[4]

Columbia University's Extension program, later renamed the School of General Studies, was ideal for this purpose, because it offered working and returning students, as well as women, access to regular university courses and faculty in a flexible curriculum. So in September 1938, Jacobs (still Jane Butzner) left her position as a secretary at the Peter A. Frasse and Company steelworks headquarters to enroll at Columbia University.

Allowed to pursue her own interests, Jacobs completed two full-time years of day classes in subjects including geography, geology, chemistry, zoology, biology, philosophy, patent law, constitutional law, and the development of legal institutions—nearly all of them subjects to which she returned in her later work. Ironically, one of the courses that Jacobs liked least was in sociology. Although later labeled as a sociologist, perhaps because the back cover of the familiar paperback version of *Death and Life* indicates that the book should be shelved with titles in sociology, Jacobs recalled being very unimpressed by the one course she took at Columbia in the subject. In fact, had she matriculated, it would likely have been as a geography major. Much more of a geographer than a sociologist, Jacobs took the most courses in economic geography, a study that anticipated her books on cities and economics: *The Economy of Cities* and *Cities and the Wealth of Nations* in particular. Despite leaving the academy without a degree, this field remained the natural intellectual location for much of her work.[5]

In the late 1930s, economic geography was a relatively young discipline but an important part of Columbia University's large Department of Geography. With the kind of multidisciplinary approach that appealed to Jacobs, at Columbia, geography was understood to involve at least two fields of learning: physiography and one other, such as economics, history, botany, or zoology. At higher levels of study, the program was administered by a multidisciplinary committee, including a professor of physiography, a professor of economic geography, and other appropriate disciplinary representatives, instead of being in the hands of any one school or department. This reflected the idea that while geography was considered the "mother of the sciences," it was distinct from the physiography or physical geography studied in departments of geology. As defined by the president of the Association of American Geographers in 1922, geography was "the science of *human ecology*"—a study that emphasized the reciprocities between human activity and the environment in ways that also greatly appealed to her. It was a theme that Jacobs had already explored in her first essays on the city, and it would be a central principle in her lifework.[6]

Among the faculty with whom Jacobs studied was the economic geography professor Herman Otte, who specialized in the economics of the Tennessee Valley Authority (TVA), the multistate regional planning agency created by President Roosevelt in 1933, which Jacobs later discussed at length in *Cities and the Wealth of Nations*. There, decades later, she critiqued Otte's (and others') belief that a region could become significantly productive without the economic and cultural development stimulated by a great city.

Nevertheless, it was likely in one of Otte's economic geography courses that Jacobs first read Henri Pirenne's *Medieval Cities: Their Origins and the Revival of Trade* (1925), one of the single most influential books on her thinking about cities. In her last book, *Dark Age Ahead*, she wrote that Pirenne "laid the foundations for modern understanding of cities" and that *Medieval Cities* was "a basic text for understanding how the world's economic networks operate and how they fail." While confirming her esteem for Pirenne's ideas, the acknowledgment actually significantly underemphasized the influence of his book on her own study of cities, economies, and civilization. Jacobs not only cited Pirenne in most of her books, but also expanded on his themes from *Medieval Cities* within *The Economy of Cities, Cities and the Wealth of Nations*, and *Systems of Survival*. In the first book, Jacobs drew heavily on Pirenne's research on the origins of European cities to explain how cities grew and how they failed. In the second, she was influenced by his history of the development of cities into great cities and into city-states that were nations unto themselves. In the third, Jacobs was particularly influenced by Pirenne's discussion of the tensions between economic and political organization, as well as his analysis of the ways that economic changes in the eleventh century simultaneously gave rise to cities and social change that freed serfs from agricultural servitude, created a powerful and productive middle class (the term is Pirenne's), and prompted unprecedented structures of liberty and democracy (viz. civilization). In *Systems of Survival*, Jacobs expanded on the theme of "traders" versus "guardians," her shorthand for the often competing moral systems of commerce (freedom of economic and cultural exchange) and authority (control of economic and cultural exchange) to which Pirenne alluded.[7]

Pirenne's book was also on Jacobs's mind when she set out to write *Death and Life*. Not only had Pirenne outlined the qualities of a great city;

in *Medieval Cities* he offered an explanation of the "death and life" of cities after the collapse of the Roman Empire (a theme also discussed in *Dark Age Ahead*) and the reemergence of cities following the revival of exchange and urban economies. At a time when cities were threatened from within and without by anti-urban and suburban forces, and the geographic allegiances of the middle class—which, as Pirenne had explained, was historically important to the city's prosperity—his book still resonated in the 1950s. Thus, when, in 1958, she first outlined her book proposal for *Death and Life*, Jacobs noted that Pirenne's work had "much to say on how life is organized in contemporary cities."[8]

Among her other studies at Columbia, Jacobs was particularly interested in the sciences. Rather than being random or unrelated interests, as is often supposed, Jacobs's studies in biology, zoology, and geology all fell within the larger field of geography; the study of natural ecology in these courses complemented and informed the study of human ecology in her geography courses. Indeed, the interest in the sciences that Jacobs cultivated at Columbia, especially in the natural and life sciences, synthesized with her studies in geography to produce seminal theories of city functions and dynamics. The life sciences were her key to developing Pirenne's historically oriented theories of "death and life" into new and timeless principles about city dynamics. From the time of her science courses at Columbia, Jacobs followed scientific developments in such emerging fields as genetics, cybernetics, and complexity science, which enabled her to argue that concepts and research methodologies familiar to the life sciences could be applied to cities. In *Death and Life*, she thus compared the "immense and brilliant progress" made in the life sciences between the 1930s and the 1950s to the stultification of the "pseudoscience" of city planning during the same period with intellectual conviction, not just rhetorical bluster. Discoveries in the life sciences, which revealed the complex workings of biological systems, helped to corroborate her belief that fully functioning cities cannot be spontaneously generated from utopian and artistic desires. Rather, cities had to be considered a part of nature, functioning like other natural and living systems. Together, Jacobs's studies in geography and the sciences would soon lead her to think of herself as a "city naturalist."[9]

Toward the end of her life, Jacobs recalled that she had "a wonderful time with various science courses and other things that I took there [at Columbia]. And I have always been grateful for what I learned in those couple of years." Her appreciation for her studies, and their significance in the development of her lifework, however, was in significant contrast with her feelings about the academy as an institution and with the bitter ways she also recalled her abridged college experience. After two years, Jacobs was effectively expelled, or at least that is how she saw it, because she had taken too many classes for an Extension student, earning sixty-five credits in two years. As she later related, "After I had garnered, statistically, a certain number of credits, I became the property of Barnard College [Columbia's women's college]." Barnard, however, rejected her application on the basis of her high school grades, replacing the good feelings that she had developed for higher education after high school with a lifelong bitterness toward academia. The only consolation was that she would not be obliged to follow Barnard's required curriculum and so, making the bitter best of the situation, considered herself "allowed to continue getting an education." Years later, she would reject numerous honorary degrees in continued protest of what she regarded as higher education's greater concern with selling degrees than educating.[10]

Yet while this part of Jacobs's early encounter with the academy has often been repeated, less well known is the fact that around the time that Barnard College rejected her application, Columbia University Press accepted her first book proposal. Indeed, while Jacobs was taking more classes than she should have as an Extension student, she was also writing a book inspired both by her courses in constitutional law and the development of legal institutions and by the "enthusiasm and wisdom" of her friend, landlord, and former employer, Robert Hemphill. While the exact nature of Hemphill's involvement in *Constitutional Chaff* is unclear, she wrote in 1949 that "the idea of such a study, and the method for working it out was my own conception. It was done during the time I was attending Columbia, but was not a part of my school work. When it was completed, I submitted it to the Columbia University Press, which accepted it for publication."[11]

With similar enthusiasm, the press advertised Jacobs's first book with this statement:

No better, no more instructive way of showing the extent of the compromise (worked out by the Constitutional Convention delegates) has ever been prepared. Here, article by article, paragraph by paragraph, sentence by sentence, and even clause by clause, are

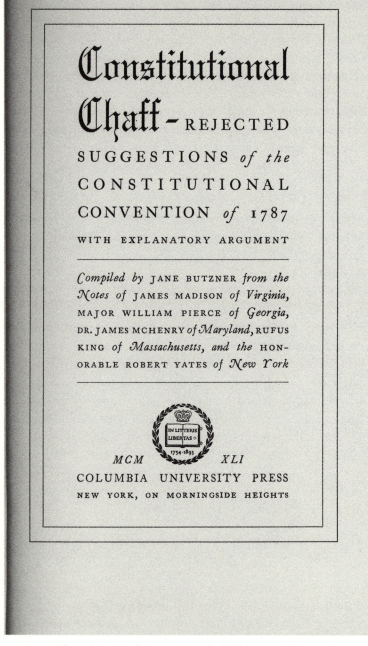

Constitutional

Chaff – REJECTED

SUGGESTIONS *of the*

CONSTITUTIONAL

CONVENTION *of* 1787

WITH EXPLANATORY ARGUMENT

Compiled by JANE BUTZNER *from the Notes of* JAMES MADISON *of Virginia,* MAJOR WILLIAM PIERCE *of Georgia,* DR. JAMES MCHENRY *of Maryland,* RUFUS KING *of Massachusetts, and the* HONORABLE ROBERT YATES *of New York*

MCM XLI

COLUMBIA UNIVERSITY PRESS

NEW YORK, ON MORNINGSIDE HEIGHTS

FIGURE 10. The title page of *Constitutional Chaff* (New York: Columbia University Press, 1941).

the components of our present Constitution and the ideas which
they displaced.[12]

Constitutional scholars agreed. It received favorable reviews from the
eminent constitutional scholar Max Farrand and the Department of State
historian E. Wilder Spaulding, who described the book as an important
contribution for being "so ingenious and so effectively carried out." Likely
unaware that Jane Butzner was also Jane Jacobs, scholars continued to cite
the book decades later.[13]

City Building and Law Making

When Jacobs found that she could not return to Columbia to start her
third year of college, her thoughts turned again to writing about the city.
She was still working on the manuscript for *Constitutional Chaff*, but just
as she had done when she first came to New York looking for a job, she
turned to freelance writing, and, following up on her essays on the city's
working districts, she wrote about how the city worked. In an investigation
comparable to her essays on the historical geography of the city's working
districts, she now examined the city's infrastructural systems in an article
titled "Caution, Men Working," published in *Cue: The Weekly Magazine of
New York Life* in May 1940.

Particularly notable in this short article was Jacobs's suggestion of a
field and a method of study: Jacobs described herself as a "city naturalist."
As she stated in a distinctly geographic metaphor, Jacobs explained that
the city naturalist could understand the city by following and studying the
"rivers," "trails," and "tributaries" of the city's infrastructure. "Despite the
almost hopeless variety," she wrote, "the city naturalist, keeping an eye on
the letters of the covers, can tell whether he is following the course of one
of the great underground rivers, whether he is on the trail of a main stream
of electricity, or gas, or one of the tributaries, whether brine to chill the
produce markets or steam to heat the skyscrapers, is running under his
feet."[14]

Although this explanation was metaphorical, it suggests the continuity
of her interests and the impact of her education; her exposure to the ideas
and methods of human and natural ecology in her geography courses was
evident. Years later, in the introduction to the 1993 Modern Library edition
of *Death and Life*, Jacobs noted that, in the course of writing the book in

the late 1950s, "I realized I was engaged in studying the ecology of cities." However, her 1940 article suggests that her study had in fact started much earlier.[15]

What is more, in the spring of 1940, as Jacobs charted the paths of the city's underground infrastructural networks, the essential life force hidden below the city's surface, she was also writing a radical intellectual archaeology of a fundamental social institution, the U.S. Constitution. Here, Jacobs's studies of urban ecology and systems of thought were both at work, later to be combined in *Death and Life*, *Systems of Survival*, and *The Nature of Economies*, among her other works.

Unfortunately, there is otherwise relatively little of Jacobs's voice in either "Caution" or *Constitutional Chaff*. The edited book was a serious academic exercise but with only a short introduction by her, and the magazine article was light reading for a subway ride. "Read the monograms on manholes and you will know what runs underneath," went the article's hook. Nevertheless, for Jacobs, both studies were close readings of things that people usually took for granted but that were essential to their lives.

At a superficial level, "Caution" explained the emblems a city dweller might observe on manhole covers and other street plaques. The embossed acronyms CT&ES Co, W-U-TEL Co, ECSCOLTD, NYS Co, MR Co, MRC, and NYM&NT, for example, revealed the location of, respectively, Consolidated Telegraph and Electrical Subway Company's electric wires, Western Union's pneumatic tubes, Empire City Subway Company's telephone wires, New York Steam Company's pipes, Manhattan Refrigeration Company's brine lines, Merchants Refrigerating Company's brine lines, and New York Mail and Newspaper Tube Company's tubes that linked the main post office to branch stations. Others included the USTD (the pneumatic tube system of the U.S. Treasury Department), the HPFS (High Pressure Fire Service), DPW (Department of Public Works), and the small covers marked BPM (Borough President of Manhattan), which were found on sidewalk corners and covered the locations of sunken surveying monuments.

More than a simple field guide, however, the article was an early exercise in observing the city. The diversity of manhole and service box covers was evidence of the city's complexity and a reminder of the easily overlooked infrastructure of underground utilities, which kept the "working districts" working. City infrastructure also had a history: Croton Water System emblems recalled the first supply of fresh water from outside the city in 1842 and its collection in a monumental Egyptianate building that was in fact a massive reservoir; later replacing the storage of water with books, the building cum reservoir became the New York Public Library. Like a palimpsest, the city's maze of pipes and cables became more intricate with the passing years, as "new covers with new and varying designs are added to the accumulation of nearly a century." Jacobs implied that the accretions of technology, rather than contributing to the city's artificiality, had actually enhanced the city's naturalness and its durability.

Despite the essay's unlikely subject matter, "Caution" demonstrated that the young Jacobs already regarded the city as a historical topography, a critical bridge in the gap between past and future, and a living artifact of civilization created from and inscribed on the old city and handed forward from one generation to the next. Rapid, large-scale "tabula rasa" urban redevelopment would necessarily destroy the sinews and systems of the urban body.

As unlikely as it may seem at first, Jacobs's *Constitutional Chaff* was a similar investigation. Jacobs was very keenly aware that the Constitution was a living artifact of similar significance, part of the infrastructure of society and civilization, while being an open framework within which the adjustments necessary to accommodate new needs could be fashioned. As she wrote in her introduction, "The authors of the Constitution were compelled to set up *some* organization and endow it with *some* power." But, on September 17, 1787, "the Constitution was signed, and the rest was up to the people."[16]

It is unlikely that the similarities between the city as a framework and the Constitution as a framework were lost on Jacobs. Both the Constitution and the city created the public realm, and urban history revealed the reciprocity between cities and the constitution of social order. As Pirenne observed, the rebirth of Western cities in the Middle Ages created a middle class and new liberties: "Freedom, of old, used to be the monopoly of a privileged class," he wrote. "By means of the cities it again took its place in society as a natural attribute of the citizen." In order to secure the blessings of liberty to ourselves and our posterity, the Constitution did something similar.[17]

Later, in *Systems of Survival*, Jacobs would cite Hannah Arendt, who, in *The Human Condition* (1958), had observed that in antiquity law making and city building both belonged to the highest ranks of political life. "Before men began to act," Arendt wrote, "a definite space had to be secured and a structure built where all subsequent actions could take place, the space being the public realm of the *polis* and its structure [being] the law." The Greek idea that the city, the polis, was embodied in its citizens resonated with Jacobs. Her understanding of the simultaneity of the city and its citizens was evident from her earliest essays. In 1955, as Jacobs's ideas for *Death and Life* began to catalyze as she observed urban redevelopment breaking the link between past and future, she wrote, "Hundreds of thousands of people with hundreds of thousands of plans and purposes built the city and only they will rebuild the city." This idea was closely related to her feeling that once the Constitution was signed, "the rest was up to the people." For both city building and governance, in other words, Jacobs looked to—or idealized—an engaged and self-determined citizenry, a true polis. In *Death and Life*, and in subsequent works including *Cities and the Wealth of Nations* and *Toronto: Considering Self-Government*, Jacobs took up the topic of self-government directly, and in all cases this was closely related to the city. In the second to last chapter of *Death and Life*, "Governing and Planning Districts," Jacobs described the city council chamber of New York's City Hall as a microcosm of the city. "Whole segments of city life, problems of neighborhood upon neighborhood, district upon district, parades of remarkable personalities, all come alive in this room," she wrote. She may have been thinking of Pirenne, and anticipating *Systems of Survival*, as she observed, "The members of the Board listen, interject and sometimes hand down decrees on the spot, like rulers holding court in the manor during medieval days."[18]

Despite the reputation that Jacobs later developed for fighting with City Hall, and her own feelings of aggravation for having to do so, she believed that debate was central to the system of government established with the Constitution. As she learned in writing *Constitutional Chaff*, debate was the means of balancing the powers of control from above and democratic self-government from below. As she wrote in *Systems of Survival*, "Where democracy means more than having the vote, many citizens engage part-time in public affairs."[19] Similarly, in *Death and Life*, while Jacobs described herself as "a fierce and rooted partisan," she could still remark of New York's city council members that "their energy, wits, patience, and human responsiveness are, on the whole, creditable. I see no reason to expect great improvement from finding better." In this, her words echoed the Constitutional Convention delegate Benjamin Franklin, whose intelligence and intellectual curiosity Jacobs long sought to emulate, and whose words the young Jacobs quoted in the introduction to *Constitutional Chaff*.

Commenting on the debates from which the Constitution emerged, Franklin had also remarked that he could "expect no better": "When you assemble a number of men to have the advantage of their joint wisdom, you inevitably assemble with those men, all their prejudices, the passions, their errors of opinion, their local interests, and their selfish views. From such an assembly can a perfect production be expected? It therefore astonishes me, Sir, to find this system approaching so near to perfection as it does. . . . I consent, Sir, to this Constitution because I expect no better, and because I am not sure that it is not the best."[20]

In this light, *Constitutional Chaff*—a study of the *rejected* proposals for the Constitution—was the reconstruction of a process tending toward the good, as well as a reflection of Jacobs's interest in truly understanding others' points of view, which, like her intense desire to understand the basis of ideas and the workings of things like cities, was central to her intellectual approach. Understanding did not substitute skepticism for agreement or acceptance, however. As Jacobs explained, when arguments for the inclusion of certain constitutional provisions were won, what the advocates "thought time would prove has given way to what we think time has proved." Her study was accordingly one in which "the Constitution we have is contrasted with the constitutions we might have had."[21]

Of particular interest to Jacobs, young and old, was the central debate on the fundamental issue of balancing local self-determination with federal governance. James Madison's proposed provisions for regional planning and interstate cooperation, for example, anticipated forever vexing national and urban issues. Seeking a bridge between competing states and a limited federal government, Madison had argued, "Power should be vested in Congress to grant charters of incorporation in cases where the public good may require them and the authority of a single state may be incompetent. The primary object of this is to secure an easy communication between the states, which the intercourse now to be opened, seems to call for." Thinking of large public works that would not otherwise materialize, like canals (or today's high-speed rail) connecting the coast to "western settlements," James Wilson of Pennsylvania concurred. That the new TVA, which Jacobs later criticized, was a rare instance of such a congressional charter of incorporation, created despite the fact that such constitutional provisions had been rejected, would not have been lost on her.[22]

That Jacobs had opinions about federalism and the nature of authority by this time is clear. *Constitutional Chaff* did not include her commentary, but its structure provides some evidence of her thinking. Although the book was organized by chapters corresponding to the articles of the ratified Constitution, followed by the losing or rejected suggestions of the delegates pertaining to each section of the given article, Jacobs also included a few appendices. One of these highlighted a special debate of the Constitutional Convention: the question of the length of the chief executive's term of office. As it happens, when Jacobs wrote this in 1940, Franklin Delano Roosevelt was running for an unprecedented third term. Apparently opposed to FDR's expansion of the federal government through New Deal legislation, she would have been all the more opposed to this precedent. As the authors of the Constitution determined, while a single term of office "tended to destroy the great motive to good behavior, the hope of being rewarded by a re-appointment," too long a period of service for the executive magistrate would tend to centralize power.[23]

In keeping with her lifelong critiques of top-down decision making, Jacobs's dissatisfaction with FDR led to her support for his opponent, Wendell Willkie. In fact, she felt strongly enough about this to volunteer at the Willkie Clubs New York campaign headquarters.[24] For financial perhaps as well as political values, Willkie, who was originally a Democrat and FDR supporter, became a public critic of New Deal programs that competed with private enterprise; as the president of a New York–based business that was the nation's largest electric utility investment company, he was an outspoken critic of the TVA, which Willkie argued would create government-funded competition for private power companies. Although he had never held an elected office, he rose to become the Republican Party nominee for the 1940 election. While it is hard to say whether she embraced what Willkie stood for as much as she opposed Roosevelt's federalism, when it came to supporting the people's power of democratic self-government from below, Jacobs was already "a fierce and rooted partisan."[25]

"Ex-Scranton Girl Helps Home City"

Jacobs's enthusiasm to leave high school and begin her career in New York found new expression when, finished with Columbia and *Constitutional Chaff* in late 1940, she could immerse herself again in the "great world of work outside oneself." Always interested in "how things worked" in her later writing, she would delve into a deep investigation of the "morals and values that underpin viable working life." But in January 1941, she was happy simply to land a permanent job as a secretary to the managing editor of *The Iron Age*, a weekly trade magazine for the metals industry published by the Chilton Company, which, through her persistence, would turn into her first full-time writing job. Hardly a dream job, it nevertheless presented an opportunity to support herself, to develop her writing career, and to learn something about the world of work.[26]

Aligning with her interests in economic geography, *The Iron Age* would offer Jacobs a bird's-eye view of an elemental part of the national and regional economy. And being from Scranton, and having some practical understanding of the metals industry from her work at Peter Frasse, as well as some basic knowledge of geology and chemistry from her courses at Columbia, she already had experience and knowledge to build on. Never one to passively accept a job description, she would work to understand it all and make it all work better.

Following a pattern typical of her early years of employment, Jacobs's efforts and initiative at *The Iron Age* quickly resulted in a promotion from secretary to editorial assistant. With more responsibilities came the broader horizon of observation that she relished. Among her first tasks had been collecting information about the production rates of blast furnaces and other industry data through telephone calls, and this soon expanded to making weekly trips to Philadelphia and traveling around the Northeast to visit metals industry firms and scrap-metal dealers, to gather news and information on market conditions in person. While the subject matter may have been tedious and specialized—at least until World War II made industrial production, especially of metals, of vital national interest—Jacobs began to develop an understanding of a regional economy, which she would draw on in her later books, even as she became increasingly familiar with a New York–Philadelphia–Washington beat that she would cover again as a writer for *Architectural Forum*.

Over the next two years, Jacobs accrued greater responsibility and independence as she was promoted to associate editor. While cutting her teeth on the long technical articles that were *The Iron Age*'s lead stories, she was placed in charge of several small editorial departments, including new products, new literature, and a new metal powders department. By late 1942, she took on such tasks as attending scientific conferences and important industrial meetings throughout New England, the Northeast, the Ohio Valley, and the Midwest, choosing papers to be abstracted in the magazine and developing news items from conference talks. She sought out contributions from scientists and metallurgists directly, worked with them on presenting their ideas, edited their manuscripts, and laid out their articles. When necessary, she visited the magazine's press in Philadelphia to handle last-minute layout and editing problems, and during a vacation period, she managed the magazine's Cleveland office—perhaps her first trip to a city that she would later write about for *Architectural Forum*.

As associate editor, Jacobs also had the autonomy to initiate and write her own features, technical articles, and special projects, and she had the job security—or so she thought—to pursue activities of special interest to her. She continued to travel, visiting mining operations, refiners, fabricators, and other large-scale metals purchasers in order to seek information and ideas for her own articles.

After the bombing of Pearl Harbor on December 7, 1941, *The Iron Age* tapped into the war effort and, although she had been an isolationist before Pearl Harbor, Jacobs found herself on the domestic frontline. *Iron Age* was soon full of reports of wartime production; photographs of women building airplanes and fashioning bayonets; stories of the latest American, German, and Japanese airplanes, ships, and subs; and advertisements by the makers of helmets, shell casings, tanks, and their suppliers. Jacobs traveled often to Washington, where she visited contacts and officials from various government agencies, including the War Production Board (WPB), the Board of Economic Warfare, the War Department, the Navy, the Department of the Interior, and the Department of Labor, to gather news, discover ideas for new articles, and obtain interpretations of facts gleaned elsewhere.

Jacobs's first bylined article for the magazine, "Non-Ferrous Metals" (as J. I. Butzner), was a comprehensive overview of the new industrial metals landscape, and in it she discussed the supplies and uses of copper, aluminum, magnesium, zinc, tin, lead, and silver by the Army, Navy, Signal Corps, Ordnance Department, and private industry, as well as by allies and enemies. "All the common non-ferrous metals have become precious metals, sought after and hunted down, cherished and pampered, aliens to thoughtless use and ordinary ends," she reported. Describing the new economics of tin, for example, she reported, " '*Lost by enemy conquest*' is the brief and inexorable reason for the tin shortage. No more tin from Malaya, Thailand, or the Netherlands East Indies. No consolation that the enemy doesn't have enough either."[27]

In writing this long and detailed report on the metallurgical landscape, Jacobs was particularly interested in innovations to deal with shortages.

Anticipating her lifelong interest in practical as well as conceptual experimentation (she was later rumored in FBI reports to tinker with inventions herself), she missed no opportunity to discuss creative solutions to shortages in all of the nonferrous metals, as well as future peacetime applications. Also characteristic of her expansive interests, a discussion of silver ranged beyond industrial production, and, for *The Iron Age*, into unexpected discussions of anthropology, economics, and politics. "Silver is taking a new role in culture," she observed. "Since man first prized it, it has been primarily a decorative and monetary metal, used in tiny amounts by industry other than the 'arts.' In the last year, however, silver has become truly an industrial metal." Meanwhile, the importance of silver brazing alloys triggered debates over monetary policy and various Senate hearings over whether the Treasury should sell its silver and gold, recalling policy debates introduced to her by Robert Hemphill.[28]

Two years into her job at *The Iron Age*, things started to turn sour. Jacobs's managing editor, T. W. Lippert, was uninterested in the storytelling and editorializing in "Non-Ferrous Metals" and indicated that she should stick to technical writing. In "Silver Alloy Brazing with High-Speed Localized Gas Heating," Jacobs gave him what he wanted, returning to the subject of silver in mind-numbing metallurgical detail, her tone now as cold as a knife's edge. Later describing Lippert as a chauvinist, Jacobs also seemed to be showing him that she could write a technical article as well as anyone. And with the editorial authority to select her own illustrations, she seems to have had the last laugh by accompanying her silver alloy article with photographs of young women in flower-print dresses operating radiant gas superheat burners and brazing marine-lighting fixtures.[29] She didn't stop there, however. Jacobs turned her frustrated energy toward trying to unionize the office's clerical workers, particularly the women; advocating for equal pay; freelance writing; and eventually activism on behalf of her hometown.

Some years later, during the Red Scare of the late 1940s, Lippert told the FBI that Jacobs was "a very brilliant, intelligent young lady," who initially "conducted herself in a very nice, respectable manner and did her work properly." (Other colleagues similarly recalled that she was "the type of person who could talk on any subject. . . . She was a very intelligent person and could do the work of three girls.") However, Lippert soon found her to be contrary and queer (she sometimes smoked a pipe in the office) and described her as "a trouble-maker and an agitator who would cause trouble no matter where she went." Looking back on Jacobs's employment with *Iron Age*, which ended five years before, Lippert offered that she was probably a communist fellow traveler all along. "She followed the Communist Party line all during her period of employment," he stated, also suggesting her support of a second front in the war, when Germany attacked Great Britain and Russia, as evidence of her communist sympathies.[30]

Jacobs's eccentric behavior was not the issue, however. At the time, the USSR was an ally and Jacobs, the author of a book on the U.S. Constitution, was no communist. Nonetheless, with millions of men going to war, and women taking on new roles in the world of work on the homefront, it was a time of great social change—and changes in the domestic workforce gave new impetus for unionization.

As Jacobs described in two of her freelance articles for the *New York Herald Tribune*, written in 1942 and 1943, women were taking on the work of men who had gone overseas and were entering fields that were formerly the exclusive domain of men. In her freelance article "Women Wanted to Fill 2,795 Kinds of Jobs," Jacobs explained that, according to the U.S. Employment Service, five million women entering the workforce in 1943 were taking on many jobs traditionally filled by men. She observed that, before the war, "no women were listed as electricians, welders, draftsmen, or engine-lathe operators" in the Employment Service directories. "Women are working now at all of these classifications," she wrote, "and before the end of the war probably will have tackled the whole list and more." She went on to joke about the manly titles of some service directory jobs—anti-squeak men, blow-off men, hotbed men, sweater men, keep-off men, and odd-shoe men—but her point, in all seriousness, was that "it can hardly be said that any occupation is absolutely unsuitable for women." Within the military, as Jacobs reported in "Waves and Waacs Go Through Assignment Classification Mill," another freelance article, the trend was similar, with women in the Navy and Army auxiliary units "doing virtually every operation that male officers do ashore."[31]

Having established that women worked as well as or better than men in industry, Jacobs concluded that a discussion of equal pay naturally followed. As she later explained to the Loyalty Security Board in 1949, which was suspicious of communist infiltration of U.S. unions during the Red Scare, any arguments that she used to convince others to join a union in the early 1940s were "solely to do with wages, particularly equalization of pay between men and women for similar work, and job security. Neither my motives nor my comments regarding unionization had anything to do with political ideologies." Collective bargaining was simply a tool for advocating basic equality.[32]

Moreover, although Lippert later described these activities as evidence of Jacobs's communist sympathies, he admitted that Jacobs had told him of her intentions at the time and that he had respected the workers' freedom of choice in the matter. The subject was then in no way out of the ordinary. After the labor movements of the 1920s and 1930s, union membership was common in New York workplaces. And Jacobs's union was hardly radical at a time when liberal politics in New York were robust, with socialist and communist groups being a significant presence in the political landscape, even in city government. (Two avowed communists held seats on the New York City Council during the war years.) Jacobs's union, the Book and Magazine Local of the United Office and Professional Workers of America International, was a mainstream choice, moderate in comparison with others.

Thus, when Lippert apparently fired Jacobs (or "let her terminate her services") in November 1943, it was not her politics that were the issue so much as that she had become so absorbed in projects extraneous to the magazine's primary business and was "taking so much time from her work to engage in these activities" that she was no longer focused on her job.[33]

Frustrated by the lack of opportunities to write her own articles and clearly constrained by the technical writing format, Jacobs spent an increasing amount of time on freelance work, becoming a regular freelancer for the *Herald Tribune* starting in February 1942. She eventually contributed over twenty Sunday feature articles, frequently the cover stories of the Science, Education, or Editorial sections. Likely irritating Lippert further, these articles sometimes expanded on her research and work for *Iron Age*— although from her point of view, the freelance versions told the larger and more important human and urban stories denied by *Iron Age*'s technical focus.

One of these, "Trylon's Steel Helps to Build Big New Nickel Plant in Cuba," described the reuse of the steel from the New York World's Fair "Trylon" and other abandoned buildings to construct a new mining operation in Cuba. Jacobs had mentioned the new plant, which would offset a significant portion of the U.S. wartime nickel shortage, in her article "Non-Ferrous Metals." There, however, she was not permitted to discuss the geographic, cultural, and economic transformation of the Cuban peninsula on which the plant and three new towns were being built. Particularly interested in the way that the location of the plant had caused the towns to grow, she wrote, "Until last May [1942], the palm-covered peninsula was inhabited only by one family of Cuban subsistence farmers living in a tiny shack. Now 6,000 construction workers and engineers have built a railroad, pier, roads, and housing, and are working twenty hours a day pushing to completion about fifteen plant buildings." The story likely reminded Jacobs of her time in rural Appalachia, and it was reminiscent of her essays on New York's working districts, while also anticipating her books on city economies.[34]

Apart from freelance writing and encouraging her colleagues to advocate for equal pay, a third activity that grew out of her work and frustrations at *The Iron Age* was organizing a campaign to protest the policies of the WPB and the Commonwealth of Pennsylvania, which Jacobs believed were contributing to the economic decline of her hometown of Scranton. In doing so, Jacobs combined her writing and activism for the first time, bringing together her interests in cities and urban economies in an effort that ultimately resulted in an outcome that would encourage her later work on behalf of cities.

Jacobs's Scranton campaign began in late 1942, about a year into the war effort, and focused on bringing attention to the city as an attractive location for war production. She knew the city, of course, from having lived there, but she also understood the larger industrial landscape from her visits to metals industries in the Northeast and her visits to war production agencies in Washington. Further armed in April 1942 with a report by the Federal Anthracite Coal Commission, which recommended the Scranton region for war plants, she helped to organize a targeted letter-writing campaign with the Scranton Chamber of Commerce, a local foundation, and a local newspaper.

As Jacobs reported in "30,000 Unemployed and 7,000 Empty Houses in Scranton, Neglected City"—an unbylined "News of Industry" section story published in *Iron Age* in March 1943—the city was one of "eighty-two paradoxical industrial areas of unemployment and empty houses" being underutilized at the same time when manpower and housing were in short supply in war production centers. Nevertheless, she reported that it had proved difficult to convince government officials of the city's merits:

Since the first of the year, letters have been written to 400 officials
of the Army, Navy, and WPB, setting forth in detail, in many
instances with charts and figures, what Scranton has in surplus
electric power, labor, sites, transportation, etc. More than 300
answers have been received and have been examined by a member
of *The Iron Age* staff [Jacobs]. They provide a post-graduate course
in the run-around.[35]

Jacobs's meeting with the office of a Pennsylvania senator, Joseph Guf-
fey, who was also the chairman of the Senate's Mines and Mining Committee, proved equally frustrating and quickly turned unpleasant. Talks with
the senator's aide collapsed when Jacobs was told that the Scranton region
had been declining for years and that a few war plants would not help.
When Jacobs countered that this opinion conflicted with the findings of
the Federal Anthracite Coal Commission, the aide asked "whether his ques-
tioner wanted information or an argument."[36]

Jacobs must have known that the senator was right about Scranton,
and in this sense she may indeed have acted the part of a civic-minded
troublemaker. She had, after all, left the city because of the general economic decline that followed the collapse of the coal mining industry, and,
as she reported in "30,000 Unemployed," another twenty thousand people
from Scranton had since left the city for "crowded war boom cities." She
understood the magnetism of great cities, of course. As she wrote in "Waves
and Waacs," an article written within days of the Scranton piece, "Location
is a prime concern with the girls. Most want to be in New York or some
other metropolitan center."[37]

Thus, although it was decades before she wrote on urban and regional
economies in *The Economy of Cities* and *Cities and the Wealth of Nations*,
Jacobs probably knew that, despite any new factories, Scranton's postwar
fate would remain fundamentally unchanged. Indeed, her attempts to cajole
the politicians and WPB to promote industrial relocations in Scranton was,
in the context of her general mistrust of bureaucracy, an unusual engagement with the government in pursuit of federal intervention. It was a mem-
orably frustrating encounter with what she later described in *Systems of
Survival* as the "guardian moral syndrome."

The story about Scranton's "30,000 Unemployed" was nevertheless an
important short-term success for Jacobs and the city. Making the first of

many public speeches for local causes, the twenty-six-year-old was a key-note speaker at a labor protest rally in Scranton's Casino Hall, a downtown theater. In her speech, as with her article, Jacobs called on the government to utilize the resources of the region for the war effort, in fulfillment of recommendations of the president's economic commission. She also followed up on her *Iron Age* piece with a freelance story in the *Herald Tribune* and another, "Daily's Effort Saves City from 'Ghost Town' Fate," in *Editor & Publisher*. "For the first time in U.S. history," Jacobs boasted, "a mining town whose veins of mineral wealth have been worked out is avoiding a ghost town fate." Read by newspaper editors and executives around the country, more than three hundred newspapers picked up the story, leading a number of small companies and the Murray Corporation's factory for Boeing B-29 wings to locate their operations in Scranton.[38]

The success of Jacobs's campaign to save Scranton from a "ghost town fate" was such that a representative of the city's Chamber of Commerce recommended that March 25, 1943—the date of Jacobs's article in *Iron Age*—should "go down in the history of Scranton as IRON AGE Day, for that day marks the turning point in Scranton's history." Had her article carried her byline, and *Iron Age* given credit where it was due, it might have been "Jane Butzner Day." The magazine was pleased to take credit and ran a two-page spread promoting itself. Although it included her name, the *Scranton Tribune* did the same with a one-page ad that highlighted the newspaper's role in publicizing the manufacturing campaign. Later that year, in September 1943, *The Scrantonian* finally recognized Jacobs's efforts directly with the headline "Ex-Scranton Girl Helps Home City: Miss Butzner's Story in *Iron Age* Brought Nationwide Publicity."[39]

Two months later, Jacobs left *Iron Age*. Although her first writing job had been a frustrating one, she would leave with a sense of the power of her writing, as well as a feeling for writing itself as an activist project—something that she would return to in earnest with *Death and Life*.

"Guardians and Traders" at War

In the autumn of 1943, Jacobs left *Iron Age* and joined the war effort as a propaganda writer for the U.S. government. In November, she applied for a position with the News and Features Bureau of the OWI, located in the Argonaut Building, General Motors' former New York headquarters at the corner of 57th Street and Broadway. She was hired as a feature writer

for the Overseas Division, and on November 29 she signed the OWI's Dec-
laration of Secrecy, which charged her to bear true faith and allegiance to
the United States of America, to serve the country honestly and faithfully
against all their enemies whomsoever, and to keep secret any information
about the OWI's purposes and methods of propaganda and psychological
warfare. One of her last freelance articles for the *Herald Tribune*, which was
about the U.S. Army's *Air Force* magazine, may have helped her application;
it received praise from Henry Arnold, the commanding general of the U.S.
Army Air Forces.[40]

For the next two years, Jacobs served with conviction, honed her writing and editing skills, and earned praise and promotion from her supervisors. Less than a year into her work for the OWI, Jacobs handled many of
the bureau's top assignments, including special psychological warfare articles for European outposts. In October 1944, her bureau chief observed
that she had "developed into one of the mainstays of the feature-writing
staff." Two things, he noted, had been responsible for this: Jacobs's "quick
grasp of the propaganda job to be done, and her ability to do a fast, efficient
and well-handled piece of work with any assignment given her."[41]

The nature of Jacobs's propaganda work during the war, at least what
is known about it, was not especially cunning. It was not unlike her freelance work. More public relations than misinformation, much of her work
consisted of telling the story of the United States and its government, people, and way of life. She sometimes worked with overseas intelligence
services to monitor and respond to false information in foreign media,
whether borne of ignorance or counterintelligence, and she may have contributed to reports that overstated U.S. war production, military readiness,
and the like. Jacobs was engaged, in other words, in what she called the
guardian moral syndrome, which applied particularly in wartime. Characteristics of this mentality, moral system, or "syndrome," as she defined
it in *Systems of Survival*—after the Greek word meaning "things that run
together"—included being nationalistic, shunning exchange, exerting
prowess, being obedient and disciplined, respecting hierarchy and tradition,
maintaining territory, and deceiving for the sake of the task.[42]

All of these guardian qualities were exemplified in her work for the
OWI, but this was not the moral system that best suited Jacobs's nature,
and her work for the government during World War II and the Cold War
likely helped her to come to understand this about herself. Although it was
years before she formulated the distinctions between the guardian and the

FIGURE 11. Jane Jacobs, ca. 1945, around the time she left the OWI and joined the State Department's publication branch. Jacobs Papers.

trader moral systems—and explicitly expressed her identification with the trader system—she already prized exchange; valued dissent; was open to initiative, enterprise, inventiveness, and novelty; shunned force; believed in voluntary agreement; and collaborated easily with strangers and aliens. All of these characteristics were part of the trader, or exchange-oriented, moral system described in *Systems of Survival*.[43]

Thus, although the trader moral system was generally inappropriate during wartime, Jacobs was inevitably oriented by its principles in her propaganda work. Whether by temperament, security classification, or previous experience, most of her writing assignments were articles and pamphlets about American history, government, and culture for use by U.S. Information Libraries, especially in nonaligned nations. Drawing on her research for *Constitutional Chaff*, she wrote a pamphlet about the United States for distribution to Indian troops at the request of the British government. It outlined U.S. history and the country's system of government, cultural achievements, productivity, education system, and social status of women and minorities. A series of articles about the history of American labor, which was used in magazines in Switzerland and other countries, drew on her own experience with unionization, as well as her support for the American Labor Party (ALP) in the 1940s. (Jacobs volunteered for ALP's candidate for Congress, Roger Baldwin.) A weekly column on aspects of American culture whose topics were chosen by Jacobs, and other articles in a light but informative vein, including biographies of noted figures in U.S. government, education, business, and culture, were written for placement in foreign newspapers and magazines in Portugal and Spain, Sweden and Iceland, Switzerland, and the Soviet Union—countries for which Jacobs served as a special liaison.[44]

Jacobs already identified with the trader moral system. There is evidence that she consciously regarded her propaganda work as a straightforward act of communication and exchange rather than of deception. Moreover, during the same years that she worked for the OWI, she became interested in interpersonal dynamics and social structures as their own subjects of study.

In March 1944, soon after she began her work at the OWI, Jane met Robert Hyde Jacobs Jr. They married in May with a modest ceremony, officiated by a pastor from a local Presbyterian church, at the Butzner home, and she became Jane Jacobs in name. A honeymoon of bicycling in northern Pennsylvania and upstate New York followed.

FIGURE 12. Jane and Bob Jacobs with their son Jim at 555 Hudson Street, ca. 1950. Jacobs Papers.

A year younger than she, Bob Jacobs had attended Bard College before graduating from Columbia University's School of Architecture with a bachelor's degree in architecture in 1942. After that, he went into Columbia's "In-Training Program in Aircraft" as part of the war effort. In the early 1960s, he taught as an adjunct associate professor of architecture at Columbia and specialized in hospital design. When they met, however, Bob worked for Grumman Aircraft Engineering Corporation on Long Island, where her sister, Betty, also worked as a designer and engineer. Jane and Betty had moved out of Hemphill's Morton Street apartment in October 1935, and Bob joined them at 82 Washington Place until 1947, when Bob and Jane, going against the grain, had saved enough money to buy a three-story "slum building" at 555 Hudson Street. While Betty would later move to the middle-class Stuyvesant Town project, the Jacobses renovated the decrepit storefront building, formerly a convenience store situated between Mr. Halpert's laundry and Mr. Koochagian's tailor shop, on a block of other storefront businesses described in Jacobs's famous Hudson Street ballet. With little money themselves, the Jacobses' renovation project exemplified the unslumming she later wrote about. What Jacobs managed to prove, a reporter later noted, was that her neighborhood may have been low-rent, but it was not a slum.[45]

Bob Jacobs would have a great influence on Jane's thinking. He knew a great deal about modern architecture in theory and practice, as well as New York City, having learned a lot about the city's organization and workings from his father. Robert H. Jacobs Sr., a transportation engineer, was born in upstate New York and had worked as a division engineer for New York City's transportation department during the city's subway design and construction building boom. Jane Jacobs's critiques of modern architecture and transportation planning, in other words, were shaped in part by having a modern architect for a husband and a transportation engineer for a father-in-law.

Of her husband, she wrote in the acknowledgments to *Death and Life*, "by this time I do not know which ideas in this book are mine and which are his." Their partnership would also include activist work. She later described him as the political mastermind behind many of their neighborhood battles.[46]

Apart from bicycling (other bike trips would follow), in 1945 one of the couple's early shared activities was joining the American Sociometric Association. Founded in New York by the psychiatrist-sociologist Jacob L. Moreno, the organization sought to advance the study of the foundations of human society and interpersonal relations. Moreno, whose early theory of "the encounter" influenced Martin Buber's "I and Thou" thesis on the interpersonal nature of human existence, had a particularly metropolitan sensibility. Moreno later wrote that it was "only in New York, the melting pot of the nations, the vast metropolis, with all its ethnic and psychological problems and its freedom from all preconceived notions," that he could fully explore the concepts of sociometric group research. Moreno, who had criticized Freud for destroying the spontaneity of everyday life in the artificial and intimidating setting of his office, believed that it was only "on the street" and in people's natural surroundings that social dynamics could be effectively studied.[47]

This geographic and urban sensibility, as well as Moreno's emphasis on "concreteness" in his study of social systems, likely appealed to Jacobs. "We have to consider every individual in his concreteness and not as a symbol, and every relationship he may bear to each other person or persons in its concreteness and not as a symbol," wrote Moreno. He believed that sociometry could "produce as a counterpart of the physical geography of the world, a psychological geography of human society." At a more practical level, he believed that sociometry could be considered "the cornerstone of a still undeveloped science of democracy." Influenced by John Dewey's writing on democracy, Moreno wrote, "Sociometry can assist the United States, with its population consisting of practically all the races on the globe, in becoming an outstanding and permanent example of a society which has no need of extraneous ideas or of forces which are not inherent in its own structure."[48]

These ideas were especially appealing to many during the war years, especially after the horrific bombings of Japan in August 1945. Across the nation and around the world, people sought new ways to rebuild an international dialogue. In October 1945, the United Nations was formed. Within the American Sociometric Association, members, including the anthropologist Margaret Mead, sought ways of building intercultural tolerance, assisting war veterans, and studying American attitudes toward the Soviet Union in order to prevent future conflict.[49]

Although the extent of Jacobs's engagement with sociometry seems to have been brief, her membership in the society suggests self-consciousness of the intersubjective sensibility that she brought to her writing, including her propaganda work. As she later suggested in discussing her work for the OWI, she served the war effort not with an ambition to be duplicitous, but with the goals of an empathetic writer. She explained that "in writing these, and other, articles [for the OWI], it was necessary for me to have gained an insight into misapprehensions concerning America current abroad; a basic understanding of which common facets of American life are totally unfamiliar abroad; facets of the American scene likely to elicit the greatest interest and admiration; and methods of giving foundation and background knowledge without becoming pedestrian."[50]

This sensibility, which was certainly typical of her thinking and writing, posited a dialogic process between writer and reader, based on an assumption of the other's intelligence and point of view. While Jacobs's dialogue books—*Systems of Survival* and *The Nature of Economies*—made this explicit, her work as a propagandist caused her to become more conscious of her native empathetic orientation. Jacobs certainly sharpened her rhetorical weapons during her years of work for the government, but what was more exceptional about her approach was its apparent similarity to what she did before and after the World War and Cold War—including her writing and thinking about cities. In approaching war propaganda as she would most any writing, through the trader moral system, her propaganda was a bridge-building effort. However, as might be expected, this approach would soon cause her trouble with those who believed that any honest and open-minded communication with the enemy was suspect.[51]

Amerika and Jacobs's "Un-American" Activities

The end of World War II allowed the OWI to be shut down. Anticipating her last paycheck in December 1945, Jacobs searched for new work. She took on freelance writing projects that kept her busy until October 1946, when she returned to government work and a nearly identical job for the State Department at the Argonaut Building.[52]

In her freelance work of the late 1940s, Jacobs cast a wide net and hauled in a mix of unexpected projects. Taking advantage of her experiences at *Iron Age* and a sixty-three-hour training course in physical metallurgy that she completed shortly before leaving the magazine, she edited numerous technical articles for *Powder Metallurgy Bulletin* and a textbook published by Macmillan called *Powder Metallurgy*. She wrote an article on Christmas traditions for *Junior Bazaar* and several articles on New York State government for *The Empire Statesman*. Closer to her special interests in geography and human ecology, she wrote an essay for *Harper's Bazaar* on coastal islands between North Carolina and Maine, in which she "studied the way of life of their people, researched their history, and interpreted the changes in island life which had occurred," following the pattern of her early essays on the city.[53]

Other projects included editing a book on historical anthropology, about which little is known, and writing memoirs for others, including a popular memoir of wartime intelligence work in the South Pacific by the Royal Australian Navy commander Eric Feldt called *The Coast Watchers*, published by Oxford University Press in 1946. For Feldt's book, Jacobs took satisfaction not just in organizing the chaotic bundle of material and maps handed to her, but also in interpreting the author's intentions and translating them for an American audience. "One portion of the task entailed making everything understandable to American readers without loss of the distinctively Australian character of the account," she wrote. "To do this," she continued, "I applied in reverse, so to speak, the special knowledge I had gained at the Office of War Information of the techniques of writing for a foreign readership."[54]

Another notable project that Jacobs pursued in December 1945 was a writing trip to Siberia. Editors at the *New York Herald Tribune, Harper's Magazine*, Oxford University Press, and *Natural History* all expressed great interest in her proposal for a feature article, and with their letters in hand, Jacobs and her husband applied for visas at the Soviet consulates in New York and Washington on three occasions. Their visa applications were ignored. Perhaps aware that she had worked for the OWI, the Soviets may have considered her a potential spy, but more likely they wanted to avoid any sightseeing trips in the vicinity of Stalin's gulag prison camps.

Without visas, the project never materialized, but it would haunt her. Although the Soviet Union was still an ally when she conceived the project, her desire to visit the USSR became cause for suspicion in 1948, when the FBI investigated her for communist sympathies and connections to a suspected espionage ring. Although tensions between the United States and USSR had been growing, only months before her visa applications, Stalin had indicated his willingness to enter the Pacific War. The Soviet Union was, moreover, not only part of Jacobs's OWI assignment, but, as she indicated in response to a second investigation by the FBI and Loyalty Security Board in 1949, there was considerable curiosity in America about Soviet life and Siberia at the time.

Moreover, a trip to Russia would help her write a very salable story, and it was natural that Jacobs, who had been part of the OWI's USSR team, would be interested to see the country. While at the OWI, her group had launched a Russian-language magazine, the outcome of an agreement to exchange information, which was drafted by Roosevelt and Stalin at the Yalta Conference in February 1945, shortly before the war's end. Known as *Little Amerika*, it was the precursor of the larger, full-color magazine *Amerika Illiustrirovannoye*, or *Amerika Illustrated*, which Jacobs focused on while at the State Department's Russian Magazine Section, part of its International Press and Publications Division.[55]

In the months between Jacobs's employment with the OWI and her return as a staff writer for the State Department in October 1946, *Amerika* had been reimagined as a lavishly illustrated magazine modeled on *Life*. As *Time* reported in 1946, "*Little Amerika* left the Russians cold; *Amerika Illustrated* was hot stuff." Full of pictures and stories, many written by Jacobs, of quintessentially American scenes—Arizona deserts, TVA dams, Radio City Music Hall, the bluegrass country, the Senate in session, New York and Philadelphia, Benjamin Franklin, and Manhattan's garment district—the magazine quickly became a popular and coveted object in the USSR. Unlike its exchange counterpart (*Soviet Life*), *Amerika* reportedly generated long lines at Soviet newsstands and black-market prices, which were only increased by distribution problems and a limited initial circulation of ten thousand copies. Although circulation was expanded to fifty thousand, and although *Amerika*'s official price in 1946 was 10 rubles (83 cents) a copy, "in the black market Russians have eagerly paid 1,000 rubles ($83) for a look at the Amerika most of them will never see, except in pictures."[56]

Despite the pictures and greatly increased production budget, *Amerika* published articles very similar to those that Jacobs had first written for the OWI. The public relations mission was much the same: to present a sympathetic and appealing vision of how Americans lived, worked, and played. To this end, in addition to presenting the most favorable aspects of American history and culture in specially written or commissioned articles, *Amerika* reproduced articles from a variety of U.S. publications like *Life, Fortune*, and *Architectural Forum*. The approach was "strictly factual, never boasting, and never political. Never are there any direct criticisms of the worker's paradise." Comparing *Soviet Life* and *Amerika* in 1956, the *Christian Science Monitor* observed, "Both put their countries' best foot forward. Both emphasize the good things of life, the cultural interests of their people, their sports, and home life. Both steer clear of any political arguments or dialectics."[57]

For Jacobs, *Amerika* was thus another opportunity for genuine cultural exchange. Although she indicated in her State Department application that she had viewed her previous propaganda work as no less straightforward than everyday communication during the Cold War, her viewpoint nevertheless became increasingly suspect.

Jacobs worked for *Amerika* for close to six years, one of a staff of some twenty people, including five Russian editors and translators. As a "publications writer," she was required to be knowledgeable about American

FIGURE 13. Cover of *Amerika* no. 43, which focused on urban redevelopment. Columbia University Libraries.

history, institutions, politics, and customs and to have a basic understanding of the history and psychology of the Russian people, in addition to creative literary ability, the ability to work simultaneously with words and pictures, and an understanding of the State Department's objectives. Her day-to-day tasks included a responsibility for proposing, planning, developing, and writing "the more difficult and complex articles and those dealing with delicate and controversial subjects for publication." Because they were producing an illustrated magazine, writers and editors thought carefully about the combination of text and images, and she worked closely with a photographer and illustrators to choose the best images to accompany each article.[58]

Jacobs recognized that the subject matter was "often potentially controversial, as respects our readership (e.g., articles on facets of the American economic system, the press, the U.S. system of government, the American

FIGURE 14. Betty Butzner Manson, Jane's sister, holds an infant and stands with a friend outside a new A&P grocery store near Stuyvesant Town, where Betty lived. The photo was taken in early 1948 and published in *Amerika* no. 23. Around the time of this issue, Jacobs modeled maternity clothes for a feature in the magazine. In the same year, John Jacobs, Bob's cousin, joined the magazine's staff. Columbia University Libraries.

legal structure) and must be treated with discrimination and judgment, to convince rather than to antagonize." During the Cold War, Soviet newspapers tended to emphasize the worst aspects of American life—crime, homelessness, unemployment, and racism—while also spreading rumors that the majority of the U.S. population was poor and threatened by starvation. Stories were also subject to Soviet censorship, and the goal was to avoid that. A great deal of time was invested in the development, writing, translation, and review process for each article. With all of these parameters in mind, Jacobs understood that her magazine's writing required not only "clear, interesting, and literate presentation," but also "a constant consciousness of the appropriate choice of words, specific facts and types of logic necessary to create the precise impression desired upon a Russian readership which is much misinformed by its own press regarding America and lacks background information, both in detail and in the large, which is taken for granted by Americans."[59]

As she gained experience and responsibility, Jacobs participated increasingly in editorial and planning meetings in which articles, sequence, and overall magazine impact were decided. She also supervised article and overall magazine graphics; supervised and edited junior writers' work; evaluated research material; and assigned and edited freelance work. She had greater discretion in initiating contact with and interviewing prominent figures for original magazine articles in all fields, from politics to science to culture, as well as in soliciting reprinted articles from other magazines and books.

The work, in other words, was, for the most part, what she had long wanted, a permanent editorial position with a magazine of some substance and significance. Despite its unique mission, *Amerika* offered Jacobs welcome opportunities to pitch and write almost any story of interest to her and to be in contact with the editors of other magazines in the city from whom she could solicit stories of interest. She excelled at the job, and, not long after a maternity leave in 1948 for her son Jimmy (James Kedzie Jacobs), she was formally promoted to publications editor in November 1949. By that time, she was already fulfilling many of the responsibilities of the chief of the Russian Magazine Section. As she wrote in explanation of her request for promotion in September 1949, "My supervisory and planning responsibilities have consistently grown and now occupy approximately seventy-five percent of my time; the remainder being devoted to developing and writing of complex articles."[60]

FIGURE 15. Jacobs (left) at the State Department, ca. 1949. Jacobs Papers.

Following another maternity leave in 1950 for her son Ned (Edward Decker Jacobs), Jacobs was formally promoted to chief of the Pamphlets and Graphics Unit in October 1951. As an editor-in-chief, she planned future articles; reviewed story ideas; worked closely with the copy and publications editors and the art director; critically analyzed all copy by staff, senior writers, and outside contractors; and interviewed, hired, and supervised freelance writers. She had come a long way since writing her first freelance articles fifteen years earlier.[61]

Having served her country, earned the respect of her colleagues, received excellent reviews from her supervisors, and otherwise dedicated herself to her work for *Amerika*, Jacobs was probably not worried to receive a letter from the FBI in April 1948, indicating that they would be conducting a background check on her. The U.S. Information and Educational Exchange Act of 1948 (the Smith-Mundt Act), required government employees like her to fill out a personnel data form for review. In particular, the law required the State Department to "take all appropriate steps to prevent any agent of a foreign power from participating in educational and cultural exchange programs" regulated by the new law, including *Amerika* and short-wave broadcasts by the Voice of America.[62] (The latter, originally a counterpropaganda project created by the OWI, was transferred to the State Department after the war's end, along with *Amerika*.)

However, the law was part of the growth of America's "second Red Scare," which had previously seen President Truman sign an executive order called the Loyalty Order in March 1947. The order required the establishment of loyalty programs within federal government departments, and the State Department accordingly established its Loyalty Security Board, whose activities would, at first, seem rather pro forma to Jacobs. What began as a pro forma background check in 1948, however, turned into a four-year investigation, the extent of which Jacobs was perhaps unaware; it lasted until *Amerika* was shut down and she resigned from the State Department in 1952.

Indeed, unbeknownst to Jacobs, she had already drawn the attention of security authorities. Her application for a visa to visit Siberia in December 1945 had sent up red flags with SODAC, the FBI's Soviet Diplomatic Activities unit, and was recorded in a 1946 security file. As part of an exchange of information agreement, Secretary (and NKVD/KGB agent) Pavel Fedosimov of the Soviet Consulate General in New York City reported to U.S. authorities that Jacobs and her husband had applied for a visa and had been learning Russian in anticipation of their visit.[63]

The real trigger for the FBI's investigation of Jacobs and her husband, however, was her contact with Alger Hiss, whom the FBI had been investigating as early as 1945. Various FBI informants had claimed that Hiss, a State Department employee since 1936, had been a communist and a Soviet agent. Unaware of this, in 1945, Jacobs had turned to Hiss, one of her supervisors at the State Department, for assistance in applying for her Soviet visa, and he referred her to contacts at the Soviet Embassy. Moreover, in 1948—at just the time that all of Hiss's State Department–Soviet interactions were being investigated—Jacobs listed Alger Hiss as a personal reference on her 1948 investigation data form. And so, in June 1948, J. Edgar Hoover, the FBI director, wrote a memo stating that the pro forma background investigation of Jane Jacobs should become part of the larger "Voice of America" investigation concerning Hiss.[64]

A few months later, in August 1948, Hiss appeared before the House Committee on Un-American Activities, where he was accused of being a former Communist Party member. Following additional accusations and court trials, in January 1950, he was charged with perjury (not espionage) and sentenced to five years in prison. In February 1950, Senator Joseph McCarthy made an infamous speech in which he claimed to have a list of known communists who were working in and shaping policy in the State Department. Jacobs was likely among them. McCarthy was adamant that all State Department employees who had transferred from war agencies like the OWI, especially those associated with "the now-convicted traitor" Hiss, be investigated. As he explained in a speech made to the Senate on February 20, McCarthy believed that there were "thousands of unusual characters in some of those war agencies" and that they required additional screening.[65]

McCarthy was aware that the majority of war agency transfers had been screened prior to their reemployment. For Jacobs, this would have taken place in early 1946, between her employment for the OWI and State Department. Moreover, McCarthy was aware of the activities of the Loyalty Security Board. However, he claimed that while "approximately 4,000 employees [had] been transferred to the Department of State from various war agencies such as the OSS, FEA, OWI, OIAA, and so forth," one thousand of these had not been subjected to a preliminary examination. Recognizing his political motivation, the *Washington Post* coined the term "McCarthyism" in a March 1950 political cartoon.[66]

The FBI's investigation of Jacobs was personally supervised by Hoover on account of the connection to Hiss. Agents questioned her friends and family members; former teachers, neighbors, and landlords; and former and current neighbors, employers, coworkers, and personal references around the country. By October 1948, agents had conducted no fewer than thirteen interviews. The most clearly reliable informants were emphatic that Jacobs was loyal to her country. However, some—including T. W. Lippert (her former supervisor at *The Iron Age*), a disgruntled former coworker, and some old Greenwich Village neighbors—made disparaging remarks about her character and offered suspicions of her politics and communist sympathies. Coming remarkably close to Jacobs's self-described approach

FIGURE 16. Senator Joseph McCarthy (seated) giving a press conference in 1950. McCarthy targeted State Department employees like Jacobs. Getty Images.

to communicating with a foreign readership, one informant told an FBI agent that Jacobs "was always trying to present as closely as possible the picture of the average working man in America as being identical with the average working man in Russia," which the informant felt was untrue and therefore made her "a bad security risk."[67]

Supplied with such information by the FBI, in mid-1949, the State Department's Loyalty Security Board interrogated her for the first time, asking Jacobs to reply to questions concerning her union membership, her voting registration with the communist-infiltrated ALP in the 1940s, her support or affiliation with the Communist Party, subscriptions to communist literature, her proposed trip to Siberia, her association with suspect individuals, and why a former employer had described her as a "troublemaker."[68]

In early 1950, around the time Hiss was convicted of perjury, Jacobs was placed on probationary status at the State Department pending further investigation, despite a recent promotion. A few months later she was required to sign yet another Oath of Office; the document had recently been updated to include a new affidavit regarding subversive activity and affiliation, which required government personnel to affirm that they were not "Communists or Fascists."

In 1952, at the height of McCarthyism, Jacobs was interrogated again by the Loyalty Security Board. This time, perhaps aware for the first time that she was the subject of unusual attention, she replied at length to repeated questions about her union membership and activities, including her membership in a prohibited union of federal employees, the United Public Workers of America; her views on communism and foreign policy; her ALP affiliation; her alleged subscription to the *Daily Worker*; her association with suspect individuals; and her views on the Communist Party, the Soviet system of government, and the aims and policies of the Soviet Union.[69]

When first asked by the Loyalty Security Board about her suspected affiliation with the Communist Party and its front organizations, Jacobs had replied that she thought "too much of the Bill of Rights to become involved with that party," assuming that a short but succinct answer would suffice. When writing at greater length on the subject in 1952, however, she explained that, in contrast to the Soviet system, she believed in decentralized, participatory, and local self-government, with "control from below and support from above"; free and uncensored experimentation, innovation, and self-expression; and humanity and moderation. She wrote:

> I abhor the Soviet system of government, for I fear and despise the
> whole concept of a government which takes as its mission the
> molding of people into a specific "kind of man," i.e. "Soviet Man";
> that practices and extols a conception of the state as "control from
> above and support from below" (I believe in control from below
> and support from above); that controls the work of artists, musi-
> cians, architects and scientists; that controls what people read and
> attempts to control what people think; that turns every agency of
> society, as unions, schools, recreational clubs, and all economic
> and production activities, into instruments for the state's purposes;
> that centralizes into the monolithic state every activity which
> should properly be controlled locally or by individuals; that makes
> free experimentation in any field, from manufacturing to teaching,

impossible; that leaves its people without channels to express their
opinions on, or to direct, the basic questions of national policy;
that deals with opposition by executing, imprisoning, transporting
or otherwise silencing dissidents. I think the Soviet system, in common with all totalitarian government, is a system which, once
instituted, inevitably makes people the helpless victims of those
with an appetite for power. I think that, as a system, it therefore
puts a premium on the cynical and the ruthless, and that its methods automatically tend to elevate to power people with these qualities and to eliminate from positions of power the humane and the
moderate. I believe that it subordinates every other human value
to the purpose of power—power over its own citizens and power
internationally among nations.[70]

She explained further that she believed that the fight against communism would be won by showing that it is possible to overcome poverty,
misery, and decay by democratic means. "We must ourselves believe, and
must show others, that our American tradition of the dignity and liberty of
the individual is not a luxury for easy times but is the basic source of the
strength and security of a successful society," she wrote.[71]

As for her admitted penchant for argumentation and critique, Jacobs
defended herself by deploying her rhetorical skills and turning her ques-
tioners' questions around, arguing that her fondness for "chewing over odd
ideas" was perfectly consistent with American rights and ideals of individualism and free speech. She believed in "the right of Communists, or anyone
else, to speak and publish and promulgate ideas in the United States," just
as much as she believed in her own right to "criticize my government and
my Congress." She stated, moreover, that this was a personal credo that
must be collectively defended for the good of the nation:

I was brought up to believe that there is no virtue in conforming
meekly to the dominant opinion of the moment. I was encouraged
to believe that simple conformity results in stagnation for a society,
and that American progress has been largely owing to the opportunity for experimentation, the leeway given initiative, and to a gusto
and freedom for chewing over odd ideas. I was taught that the
American's right to be a free individual, not at the mercy of the
state, was hard-won and that its price was eternal vigilance, that I

too would have to be vigilant. I was made to feel that it would be a disgrace to me, as an individual, if I should not value or should give up rights that were dearly bought.[72]

In a coup de grâce, she argued, finally, that the greatest threats to American democracy were not from without but within. Identifying two such threats—"the current fear of radical ideas and of people who propound them"—she wrote, "In the case of the first threat, the international threat of Communist systems of government, I have been able to do something practical through my work in the State Department. In the case of the second threat, that of McCarthy—or of the frame of mind of which McCarthy is an apt symbol—there is little practical that I could do other than take a stand in assertion of my own rights."[73]

Although it is hard to imagine that someone at the Loyalty Security Board was not moved by these heartfelt words, in March 1952, the State Department announced that its Publications Branch would be shut down and moved from Manhattan to Washington, DC, a move that Jacobs and her coworkers protested. As reported in the *New York Times*, nearly seventy of the department's seventy-five staff members refused to relocate, and the branch chief, Marion K. Sanders, Jacobs's immediate supervisor, quit in protest of the reorganization plan. The *Times* supported the protest; a June 1952 editorial explained that the United States "has only two means of communicating with the people of the Soviet Union: the Voice of America broadcasts—which are more or less successfully jammed—and *Amerika*." If *Amerika* was abolished, it continued, the Soviet censors would win.[74]

Although it was many years before Jacobs wrote about the trader and guardian moral syndromes in *Systems of Survival*, the symbolism of *Amerika*'s move from New York, city of exchange, to Washington, city of government guardians, was unlikely lost on the younger Jacobs. From the time of her first essays on New York's working districts, she recognized that the city was largely synonymous with exchange; she may also have remembered Pirenne's histories of the growth of the middle class, municipal institutions, and freedom from hierarchal powers as the merchant class claimed power from religious authority. One of Jacobs's coworkers, quoted in another *Times* editorial, observed that moving *Amerika* from New York to Washington "removes publication specialists from the New York area, where our nation's printing, photographic art, and editorial facilities are concentrated." For those who believed that *Amerika*'s mission was to exchange information, its purpose was thus undermined, in various ways, by the move.[75]

Like many of her colleagues, Jacobs refused the move to Washington (which was apparently expected) and, in April 1952, she submitted her resignation as chief of the Pamphlets and Graphics Unit, Magazine Section, Publications Branch, International Press Service, effective May 2. This had the benefit, apparently unknown to her, of ending her investigation by the FBI, and it provided her with the opportunity for a career change in the U.S. capital of the publishing world. Through *Amerika*, which frequently borrowed articles and images from other magazines, she had connections, as well as a résumé that included skills such as managing staff; working on layout, graphics, and production; and having a background as a senior writer and general editor. With experience writing and editing articles on topics including American architecture, U.S. cities, and urban redevelopment for *Amerika* (and a husband who was an architect and an architecture magazine subscriber), she started work with *Architectural Forum* in May.

Although Jacobs was soon employed as an associate editor at a Time, Incorporated, publication, and free of the interrogatories and communist hysteria, her encounters with McCarthyism contributed to her lifelong suspicion of "control from above" and the "dominant opinion of the moment." Even unaware of the extent of the suspicions against her, the idea that someone who was so deeply invested in the traditions of American idealism, who had authored a book on the U.S. Constitution, and who had faithfully served the war effort and government was engaged in "un-American" activities was embittering.

In the decade ahead, she would unleash her frustrations in a counterattack against the Urban Renewal Administration and its cronies in *Death and Life*. When she came to realize the problems, she was only emboldened in taking what, for many years, was a minority position about urban redevelopment. An ideal architectural and urban design critic, she considered dissent to be both a personal and a national tradition. In her 1952 interrogatory, she wrote of a distant Quaker relative, a woman who believed in "women's rights and women's brains" and who had "set up her own little printing press to publish her own works without a masculine nom de plume." She recalled Virginian ancestors who had opposed slavery, secession, and their state's participation in the Civil War, and a grandfather who ran for Congress on the Greenback-Labor platform in 1872. Speaking of third parties like the Greenback party, which supported labor rights and women's suffrage, but also of her years of support for the ALP, she wrote, "I am pleased to see how many of that party's planks, 'outlandish' at the time, have since become respectable law and opinion." Although she parted intellectually with the ALP's platform, she had been attracted to it as a "lively third party rooting for a good many ideas which I too thought were good at the time"—including its positions on state-supported housing. Although her ideas had changed, she continued to register in the ALP, despite knowing that communists were in control of the party, because she resented the idea that she should be afraid to exert her right to do so. "You are surely aware of the fear which government workers feel over how their every action will be interpreted," she wrote to her interrogators. "To live in such fear seemed, and seems, to me a miserable state for a free, self-respecting American to find himself in."

"The fact of being in a minority does not, in itself, trouble me, nor do I see anything un-American about being in a minority position," she stated. "Quite the contrary. The minority views of one day are frequently the majority views of another, and in the possibility of this being so rests all our potentiality for progress." *Death and Life* came out of such courage, and it strengthened her conviction in her own system of thought.[76]

CHAPTER 3

"We Inaugurate Architectural Criticism"

> Would you like to know how a critic feels? As if he were building up a
> world of buildings. The architect uses plans and elevations. The critic
> uses architects. A new architect comes into his hands as into the
> architect's own office comes a sample of a marvelous new material:
> perhaps it is just a new tar that will more cheaply guarantee his roof
> against a leak, perhaps a new truss that will greatly change construction,
> or perhaps a new reflector that will help flood a whole room with
> mysteriously invigorating light. And so for the critic every architect serves
> his turn, according to his own worth whether as nail or ridgepole, to
> enlarge or illuminate the critic's growing City.
> —Douglas Haskell, 1930

WHEN THE CLOSURE of the State Department's New York publications
office ended Jacobs's eight years of work for the government, she was in
need of a new way to help support her family. She was also ready for a new
chapter in her career as a writer.

After *Amerika*, Jacobs followed her interests in geography and the life
sciences and briefly pursued a position with *Natural History* magazine,
whose editors she had approached in 1945, the last time she was out of
work, with the idea of a story on Siberia. But her interests in cities, and
better pay, led her to the offices of *Architectural Forum*, a Time, Incorporated, magazine located in Rockefeller Center. She had become a regular

reader because of Bob Jacobs's subscription and liked it. Moreover, she may already have become acquainted with *Forum*'s staff during her work as an editor at *Amerika Illustrated*: Her work for *Amerika* included articles on American architecture, school design, housing, urban redevelopment, and American cities and neighborhoods that were illustrated by photographs borrowed from magazines including *Progressive Architecture* and *Architectural Forum*.

Whether because of her prior experience and writing on architecture, or prior acquaintance, Douglas Haskell, the editor of *Architectural Forum*, didn't hesitate in offering Jacobs a trial assignment and quickly bringing her into his close-knit circle of associate editors. She may have hesitated when he told her *Forum* needed a new hospitals and schools department editor and handed her the rolls of drawings of the first building she was to review, but with some help from Bob Jacobs, within a few months, Haskell was relying on her advice and opinions. Although he was more than twenty years her senior, Haskell had compatible sensibilities and other things in common that contributed to a close working relationship. He had followed a similar career path; he had dedicated himself to a writing career and had no academic training in architecture. Equally significant, they shared a sense of the enduring importance of cities at a time when suburbanization was a powerful cultural force.

At *Architectural Forum*, Jacobs learned to be an architectural and urban design critic. Although she had risen to the level of senior writer and editor at *Amerika*, writing propaganda for the State Department and a Soviet audience had required a subtle approach in which she treated controversial subjects with restraint and was careful to lure and convince rather than antagonize. By contrast, at the moment when Jacobs arrived at *Forum*, Haskell was at a turning point in his lifelong mission to reinvigorate American architectural criticism. Liberated from some of the constraints that had previously thwarted him, he wanted *Forum* to emulate other emergent forms of cultural criticism and the more aggressive approach of the British *Architectural Review*. He was ready to see his magazine publish the kind of architectural criticism that came dangerously close to the threat of libel lawsuits and he recognized in Jacobs someone who could help him do so.

Ultimately, Jacobs would take architectural criticism in directions unanticipated by Haskell, beyond his expectations and comfort. However, her new vision of cities, and her contributions to the new field of urban design, emerged from her work at *Forum*, where she contributed to most of the issues published over a six-and-a-half-year period, quickly becoming, with Haskell's support, its expert on urban redevelopment and, according to him, its best writer on the subject. These years, which were dominated by debates about the crises and next steps for modern architecture and cities, were the critical backdrop of *The Death and Life of Great American Cities*. Indeed, understanding the contexts, sources, and evolution of Jacobs's ideas makes it difficult to imagine the book coming into being without the knowledge, experience, network, and support that Jacobs gained at *Forum*. From her first article for the magazine, in which she analyzed the functions of a hospital in Peru, to *Death and Life*, which was initially conceived as a study of the relationship between function and design in cities, architectural debates informed her thinking. Building on *Forum*'s editorial agenda for architectural and urban criticism, Jacobs turned critiques about architectural functionalism into a new conception of the functional city.

Architectural Forum's New Editorial Agenda

Jacobs arrived at the *Forum* offices in May 1952 with characteristically good timing. Some months earlier, in January 1952, *Architectural Forum, The Magazine of Building* had split into two magazines: *House & Home*, a new magazine devoted to the "brand new postwar industry" of home building, and *Architectural Forum*, which would focus on schools, hospitals, shopping centers, office buildings, and large-scale urban redevelopment projects. Since acquiring the magazine in 1932, Henry R. Luce, the cofounder of Time, Inc., and *Forum*'s editor-in-chief, had worked to make *Forum* the leading chronicler of the anticipated postwar construction boom, and he hired Haskell in 1949 as the magazine's new architectural editor. By January 1952, when *House & Home* was published under its own cover, Haskell was editorial chairman of two magazines and his personnel was spread thin. He needed more staff. In particular, he needed a new hospitals and schools editor, and so he offered Jacobs a trial assignment to review a new hospital designed by Edward Durell Stone.[1]

Despite needing some coaching on reading architectural drawings from Bob Jacobs, who, conveniently, was a hospital architect, Jacobs was well qualified for the position. She had almost ten years of experience at the associate editor level, in addition to years of freelance work, and she had served for a number of years as an editor of a magazine with a strategic and sensitive editorial agenda. Including her early freelance articles on Manhattan's working districts, she had already written close to a dozen articles on architecture and cities. In writing a lengthy two-part series "New Horizons in Architecture" for *Amerika*, she had described the development of modern American architectural thinking and practice. In two other long articles, she wrote on modern housing and urban redevelopment. In fact, the articles "Planned Reconstruction of Lagging City Districts" and "Slum Clearance," published in *Amerika* in 1949 and 1950, were apparently among the earliest extended treatments on the new U.S. Housing Act of 1949 published in any magazine. If Jacobs had not been paying attention to the redevelopment projects around the city in the 1930s and early 1940s, these articles had caught her up with pre–Housing Act developments even before she started at *Forum*. Perhaps of greater interest to Haskell at the time, however, Jacobs had also written an article about modern schools and had edited an article on modern hospitals for *Amerika*.[2]

"Two-in-One Hospital," an eight-page feature on a state hospital in Lima, Peru, designed by Stone and the U.S. Public Health Service, was published in June 1952. In her first assignment as an architectural critic, Jacobs showed herself to be characteristically observant and analytical and to be sympathetic to the aims of modern architecture, while notably valuing the building's life-enhancing features, its functional qualities, and its innovations over its formal and aesthetic subtleties. She described the Peru hospital as noteworthy for 1) "its simple organization of tremendously complex functions; 2) its open, patio-dotted ground floor, certainly one of the world's pleasantest and easiest to navigate for patients and staff; 3) its careful regard for the customs of those who will use it; 4) its complete and decisive division of some facilities and its equally complete and convenient integration of others; and 5) its thoroughgoing traffic rationale, consistent in detail and in the whole."[3]

In her first critique of a building, Jacobs thus demonstrated an interest in the functionalism of modern architecture in a truly comprehensive sense. The essence of the design problem for this "double hospital" was, as Jacobs summarized it, "how to make the maternity hospital and the general hospital completely distinct and yet completely integrated." In doing so, she appreciated the way that the building's thoughtful design enabled its basic purposes, while at the same time separating the healthy and the ill. Recognizing architecture's subtle but inevitable influence on daily life and experience, she commended the design for providing comprehensibility of

Плановая реконструкция отстающих городских районов

FIGURE 17. The cover image of Jacob's article on slum clearance in *Amerika* no. 45 (1950) shows the construction of Alfred E. Smith Houses, located in New York's Lower East Side, which began in 1950. The caption translates as "Planned reconstruction of lagging city neighborhoods." Columbia University Libraries.

organization and movement, as well as a pleasant experience for staff and visitors. However, going beyond strict functionalism, she also admired the way that the design preserved and facilitated local custom. In Peru, she noted approvingly, "child-birth is regarded as an exciting, wholesome event which has nothing to do with illness." As a subtle critique of the American approach to childbirth, which she knew from personal experience, her review offered the design in Peru as a good model for hospitals, practices, and attitudes at home.[4]

The article became Jacobs's first feature as the magazine's new hospitals and schools editor. Haskell was duly impressed by Jacobs's trial assignment, which recommended her as someone with a progressive, unconventional, and critical mindset. For Haskell, moreover, someone without professional training in architecture—and therefore less likely to be personally invested in an architectural style, school, or the work of a *Meister*—was an asset.

Although Jacobs may have suffered later in her career for not having the right academic degrees, this made Jacobs and Haskell good working partners. Both had started out as freelance writers, and Haskell, as a new permanent staff member at *Architectural Record* in the mid-1940s, had covered the schools department. He had become a respected authority on prefabricated housing in the 1940s, and he would have believed Jacobs capable of developing similar specialties. Both had deep commitments to the social consequences and possibilities of cities and buildings, and they were largely free of doctrinaire beliefs and allegiances in achieving these. Both were pluralists who believed in a diversity of viewpoints, and they were genuine modernists in the sense that they instinctively questioned dogmatic ideas and practices no matter how modern they claimed to be. Just a few months before he hired Jacobs, Haskell had written a memo for the executive staff at *House & Home* titled "Why We Publish Modern," in which he declared that "the trouble with 'traditionalism' is that it cuts off at the source those mental habits which lead to deeper thinking and better solutions." His words could have been hers: Jacobs's deep-seated interest in "how things work" manifested itself as an expectation that *modern* architecture meant something more than aesthetics.[5]

Both Jacobs and Haskell, moreover, had an anti-utopian streak: a desire to solve problems now and with the tools at hand, rather than wait for a wholesale transformation of the context in which better conditions and solutions would prevail. This trait had brought Haskell into conflict with his longtime friend and sometime adversary Lewis Mumford, whose proposals were typically building "from the ground up." The same would later happen with Jacobs. In their individual ways, both Haskell's and Jacobs's views were expressed in an interest in a building's participation in larger contexts: with its users, with the city, and with the "world" that they contributed to building through their writing.

Haskell, finally, was no chauvinist: His coeditor at *The New Student*, a weekly that he directed following his graduation from Oberlin College in 1923, had been a woman, and he considered his spouse, Helen Haskell, his equal. During his years of freelance work, Helen had been the steady breadwinner, and since then, the Haskells took equal responsibility in the ownership and management of Camp Treetops in upstate New York, a nondenominational summer camp that emphasized diversity and progressive education.[6]

With this common ground quickly established, Jacobs was introduced to Haskell's small team of associate editors early in the summer of 1952. As Peter Blake wrote in his memoir, *No Place Like Utopia: Modern Architecture and the Company We Kept*, they were a "small kernel of people who believed in the magazine's 'mission' and in a degree of editorial sophistication and quality." The editors included Walter McQuade, a bright, witty, and rather sardonic writer who had been trained as an architect at Cornell, and Louise Cooper, an economist who supplied the magazine with relevant expertise. Blake, who knew the staff even before Haskell's tenure, rounded out the team. In the 1930s, Blake had worked as a freelance draftsman for the long-time *Forum* art director Paul Grotz, and, before the war, he had worked as a writer for the managing editor George Nelson in 1942. In August 1950, Blake rejoined *Forum* on Haskell's staff as an associate editor, fresh from a stint as the curator of architecture and design at the Museum of Modern Art (MOMA).[7]

With this team in place, on July 23, 1952, Haskell released a six-page staff memo outlining the magazine's new editorial agenda. After years of effort and the distractions of reorganizing the magazine, Haskell had won the support of Henry Luce and Time, Inc.'s executive editors for a new approach to architectural journalism. This new approach would manifest itself in all of the magazine's departments, even within its features on particular building types, then the traditional focus of architectural magazines. In response to new postwar building trends, which Haskell described as a "more advanced stage of the Industrial Revolution," these studies had assumed new importance. In fact, such developments had prompted the reorganization of the magazine and the spin-off of *House & Home*, which focused exclusively on housing and the home-building industry. *Forum*, meanwhile, would take a progressive approach to the other major building types. In Haskell's new editorial agenda, this meant "not just *industrial plants* is our subject, but *why new defense plants must be different*. Not just *hospitals*, but *what makes the 1940 hospital obsolete*. Not just *schools*, but *Forum's proposed school for the 1950s*."[8]

In all aspects of the magazine, a new focus was required. *Forum*, he declared, would "inaugurate architectural criticism." After years of seeking to break down the barriers set up by professional gentlemen's agreements, editorial complacency, and publishers' fears of libel lawsuits, Haskell had Luce's blessing to restore "the lost right" of architectural criticism.

Since the 1930s, Haskell explained, American architectural criticism had been stifled by the threat of libel suits. He wrote, "Ever since about 1929, architectural criticism in the United States has been in effect illegal, partly because of court decisions then rendered and partly because of the cowardice then of editors of certain national magazines who set the precedent of settling cases out of court. Never since has an architectural magazine stepped out of narrow bounds of architectural criticism. It was tacitly assumed that nothing could be done."[9]

But now, Haskell told his staff, Luce and Time, Inc.'s lawyers had agreed to support a more outspoken approach: "My news to you is that *The Magazine of Building* in both editions [*Forum* and *House & Home*] has quietly restored genuine architectural criticism—not the wrist slapping kind, but the kind where you first consult your lawyers about possible action. . . . Our encouragement for doing this came from the first-class lawyers who serve Time Inc. who told us that in case of attack, they would be delighted to defend us for the purpose of restoring to the United States the lost right of architectural criticism."[10]

Finally, as part of the magazine's new direction, *Forum* would intensify its effort to address the "problems of cities." Haskell boasted that *Forum* was already the most up-to-date American architectural journal where urban redevelopment was concerned. "We have traced the impact of redevelopment on Pittsburgh, Chicago, St. Louis, Philadelphia (twice), Norfolk, and now Washington," he reminded his staff, referring to articles published between May 1950 and April 1952. "While we have been doing all these stories," he continued, "the strictly architectural magazines have published not one. They have been fast asleep and snoring."[11]

This agenda, inaugurated just as Jacobs joined Haskell's team, would become the foundation both for her work for the magazine and for *Death and Life.*

Learning from "the Dean"

Jacobs was too smart and independently accomplished to admit to having a mentor (perhaps other than Bob Jacobs), but she was influenced by many people. While *Forum* provided her with an alternative to the academy, a place of collegiality, research, study, feedback, and institutional support, Haskell, later dubbed "the dean of architectural editors" for contributions to American architectural criticism and journalism that spanned from the 1920s to the 1970s, was one of her most important teachers.[12]

Although his career is little known, Haskell was one of the most influential figures in American architectural journalism. As the historian Robert Alan Benson has pointed out, he was among the first critics of modern architecture in America and, after Lewis Mumford, among the most accomplished.[13]

Like Jacobs and Mumford, Haskell began to write as early as high school, thinking he could earn a livelihood while making a positive difference in the world. He was born in the Balkans to a family of missionaries in 1899, and the influence of his uncle Henry J. Haskell, whose career in journalism won him two Pulitzer Prizes, suggested to the teenager an alternative to missionary work. Following six years in a German boarding school at Wilhelmsdorf—the idea of his Swiss-German stepmother—he returned to the family home in Oberlin, Ohio, to attend high school, and he soon became involved in small publishing endeavors. At Oberlin College, which Haskell entered in 1916 (the year Jacobs was born), at seventeen, he continued printing as a small business, providing some needed income.[14]

Although Haskell left college in 1923 without a strong conviction about his future path, his fluent German led to the opportunity to help organize a student exchange tour to Germany, funded by the philanthropic Pratt family of New York, during the summer after graduation. A visit to the four-year-old Weimar Bauhaus, where he met Walter Gropius, fused his interests in art and social reform in a life-changing revelation. His immediate reaction was to return to school to study architecture, but upon reflection, Haskell, then a newlywed, could not see returning to school, and he

FIGURE 18. Douglas Haskell, ca. 1965. Haskell Papers.

instead took an opportunity to coedit a Pratt-endowed, progressive weekly called *The New Student*, in which he promoted the optimistic, Nietzsche-influenced spirit of early Weimar Germany. As Jacobs would do about a decade later, Haskell moved to New York and started his writing career.[15]

The New Student gave Haskell few occasions to write about the new modern architecture, but the April 1925 issue, which used campus architecture as the thematic jumping-off point, was a notable exception. As a survey of recent writing and examples of modern architecture—including the work of Louis Sullivan, Frank Lloyd Wright, Claude Bragdon, Lewis Mumford, and a number of Dutch writers and architects—Haskell's essay "Shells" was among the earliest comprehensive assessments of the modern movement. The most prominent American architectural magazine, *Architectural Record*, did not publish a comparable analysis of European modernism until the following year. For its prescience, Haskell's article received not only praise from Bragdon and Mumford, but also attention from *Time* and Herbert Croley, the founder of *The New Republic* and a former editor of *Architectural Record*.[16]

"Shells," Haskell's first work of architectural criticism, critiqued recent historicist campus architecture with a rhetorical style similar to that later employed by Jacobs. He proposed that university architecture based on period styles was representative of a school's "enslavement to shadows, to predetermined notions, petrifications, parchment, self-adulation, pretense, and the higher bunk." If MIT's architecture, for example, was neoclassical, what then, he asked, "can we believe about their reverence for their science, their technology? What do they know about *doing*? And what of education?" The idea that the new modern architecture, by contrast, could reveal the "imagination, independence, and the virility" of a university's—or a society's—reactions to the "real world" reflected the influence of not only Gropius but also the progressive education theorist John Dewey. Dewey was a contributor to *The New Student* and admired by Haskell and his wife, Helen; one of Dewey's students had founded the Connecticut school where Helen was a teacher. Although Jacobs did not acknowledge any special debt to Dewey herself, she often similarly stressed the significance of "doing," experience, and "how things worked in the real world."[17]

In the following five years, Haskell left *The New Student* to take up freelance writing on architecture and museum exhibits, and he made a series of quick advances in architectural journalism, moving from a position as an editor for *Creative Art* to a temporary position as associate editor at *Architectural Record*. First turned down for a permanent position at *Record* on account of his lack of technical architectural knowledge, he was asked to substitute for the man hired, who had just won a traveling fellowship from the Harvard Graduate School of Design to visit Rome and study the antiquities. Haskell's humbling experience seems to have ensured that neither pedigree nor lack of technical knowledge would become an obstacle for Jacobs's work as an architectural critic.

Soon thereafter, Haskell landed a long-running and prestigious position as the architectural critic of *The Nation*, and, having followed the development of modern architecture since the early 1920s, he was well prepared to write about it at the moment it was legitimized by art historians and museum curators in the early 1930s. Following a five-month trip to Europe, from October 1931 to February 1932, to study firsthand the new modern architecture in Holland, Austria, Switzerland, and Germany, Haskell wrote reviews of the three exhibitions that introduced modern architecture to America. These exhibits—the Architectural League of New York's *Exposition of Architecture and Allied Art*; the *Rejected Architects* show of 1931, organized by Philip Johnson; and the definitive *Modern Architecture: International Exhibition*, organized by Philip Johnson and Henry-Russell Hitchcock for MOMA in 1932—continued to resonate for decades to come.

Because Haskell was open-minded in ways that came easier to someone not trained as an architect, his reviews for *The Nation* typically mixed criticism and approval in reflection of the belief that modern architecture should be an open-ended and nondogmatic engagement with life. After living in Ernst May's Siedlung Römerstadt (1928) in Frankfurt for a number of weeks with his wife, and studying how the project came into being, interviewing some fifty residents, and observing how the buildings had weathered, Haskell sincerely believed that modern architecture could improve the lives of those historically neglected by architects and that it was more than a style. He was therefore quick to criticize young modernists for having already become devotees of what Henry-Russell Hitchcock described in *Modern Architecture: Romanticism and Reintegration* (1929) as the "international style."[18]

In Haskell's view, the "rejected architects" had "not yet begun to fight." Anticipating criticisms that Jacobs and others would make later, he observed that "their imaginations are held captive by Le Corbusier; they are inhibited; and so, although the science and technology to which they profess devotion hold in them a greater diversity of means and a larger range of types than we have ever had before, most of these men clung tenaciously to the flat box type hung on interior posts just as the older men clung to column and to gable." Moreover, Haskell criticized the exhibition's focus on the single-family home (a criticism still relevant): "Although for city purposes our best knowledge discards the freestanding house, their town planning exhibit retained it."[19]

Thus, while suggesting that privileging the detached, single-family house—a housing type associated not only with the suburbs, but also with a privileged clientele—represented a failure to embrace the need for multi-family housing and the possibilities of modern architecture, Haskell described these young modern architects as not being modern enough. Later, in *Death and Life*, Jacobs would similarly chide architects of the late 1950s for clinging "to old intellectual excitements . . . *on the grounds that they must be 'modern' in their thinking.*"[20]

At its heart, their shared argument—although Haskell arrived at his conclusions years before—was that the superficial acceptance of a stylistic architectural language undermined the potential inherent in functionalism, whose virtues transcended style. In "What the Man About Town Will Build," a review of the *Modern Architecture: International Exhibition*, Haskell similarly predicted the popularization of modern architecture and warned of the consequences of its becoming a style. Published soon after his return from Europe in April 1932, Haskell wrote, "A house that is a sort of box or aggregation of boxes—flat top, flat sides with plenty of glass in them, color generally white, and the whole thing preferably raised on stilts—this, loosely described, is what you were given to see at the Museum of Modern Art. . . . And, considering events, we can be quite sure that houses more or less like these are what the man about town will build."[21]

In his 1932 essay "Is It Functional?" Haskell went on to question fake functionalism, and what Jacobs would frequently criticize as "wishful thinking." Illustrating his text and argument with before and after photographs of Peter Behrens's apartment at the Weissenhofsiedlung, Haskell showed that supposedly "functional" modern buildings, which claimed a machinelike reciprocity between form and function, had actually weathered far worse than more traditional buildings. The captions of the photos of Behrens's apartment, which in just five years had deteriorated terribly, read "Too 'functionalist' even to be functional. Stucco trying to imitate the smoothness of the machine looked handsome at first" but "in five years

Nature took revenge. Mechanical looking 'functionalism' was not so functional after all." He wrote that "common rain water was functionally destined within five years to wreak unusual havoc upon the smooth stucco surface. It would leave ugly stains under the windows and run a broad crack down from the roof, doing damage against which the pre-functional house with its wider sheltering projections was better protected, and under which the new one, again just *because* it looked so very smooth and so very fresh when new, would become more hopelessly disreputable and bedraggled when just a little older."[22]

The points of Haskell's essay were at least threefold. First, although "functionalism" should indicate nothing but "exact technique," he argued that exact technique was impossible in architecture. In reality, functionalist architecture was metaphoric, an "architect's fairy tale" caught between an "inevitable collision between the functioning of brutal fact and function." Second, accepting this reality opened functional architecture to a greater range of inspirations. The machine was neither the only nor the best functional metaphor; Frank Lloyd Wright's organicism, or organic functionalism, was one well-known alternative. Haskell concluded, "I do not think that the twentieth century is ready to limit its resources. Is not mankind limited enough from the beginning in that its creation always goes largely by metaphor and simile? Can we stretch a single one of these to shelter our whole life? A 'machine' in which to carry on a conversation; a machine in which to make love. A subtle machine, the last. Other symbols can be found that carry a share of truth: for instance, there is that of the tree."[23] Third, regardless of the metaphor, whether machine or tree, the success of the architectural creation depended on the architect's imagination. "Each architect a poet according to the depth of his imagination. . . . All we can ask is that his fairy-tale come true," he wrote.[24]

Among his published work, the line "Each architect a poet according to the depth of his imagination" perhaps best reflected Haskell's characteristic willingness to look for the best that each architect had to offer. But Haskell's genius as an architectural critic was even more apparent in two unpublished essays from the early 1930s, which articulated part of the editorial agenda that shaped Jacobs's time at *Forum*.

In "Three Architects," Haskell recognized that modern architecture, at its best, was a pluralistic endeavor. As suggested by the title, he identified three different modern architectural attitudes, based on the figures of Wright, Erich Mendelsohn, and Le Corbusier, and argued that each of their

approaches was not only equally modern and valid, but also equally necessary for a full exploration of the possibilities of modern architecture. In
another essay, "On Architectural Criticism," Haskell used the image and
metaphor of a city to illustrate the importance of diversity in the modern
movement. Although it is unlikely that Jacobs ever read these essays, Haskell's notion that the architectural critic played a "city-building" role in "a
world of buildings" made him an empowering and ennobling mentor for
his editorial staff. "Would you like to know how a 'critic' of architecture
feels?," he asked rhetorically, going on to describe how a critic can shape a
world using the work of many architects, just as the architect can use plans
to shape a building. "For the critic every architect serves his turn, according
to his own worth whether as nail or ridgepole, to enlarge or illuminate the
critic's growing City," he wrote.[25]

Haskell's "world of buildings" was not quite a fully formed parable,
but the moral was clear, and Jacobs would have loved the metaphor. As
diverse buildings made up the city, the diversity of architectural ideas made
up the modern movement. And, just as many hands formed the city from
various architectural ideas, no single architect had a monopoly on the truth.
The corollary of this was another belief that Haskell and Jacobs would
share: the impossibility of a city designed by a single mastermind.

Many years later, in a letter to his friend William Wurster, Haskell
returned to the "world" metaphor to explain that his approach to criticism
was different than that of "propagandists and prophets." Among these, he
wrote, "You can count on [Sigfried] Giedion to say that Le Corbusier and
he alone should have had the UN to do; and you could have fairly counted
on Lewis Mumford to say that Le Corbusier is wickedly 'mechanistic' in all
his ways." By comparison, Haskell affirmed, he and *Forum* would try "to
do what the great Victorian critics of literature used to try, which was to
give the artist—each artist—credit for trying to produce a world, his world,
that particular artist's world."[26]

As compared to Jacobs, Haskell may have had a greater willingness to
give each artist credit for creating unique worlds—she did not believe that
cities were canvases for artists. However, they shared, or came to share, a
belief that architecture must be imagined in the "real world." The architect
could not be only a philosopher, theorist, engineer, sociologist, or aesthetician.
Because architecture needed the trials of weather and marketplace and politicians and users, the architectural critic must think beyond the parts and personalities. Concluding his essay on architectural criticism, Haskell thus wrote,

Where philosophy gains by purity and detachment, architecture
gains by impurity and mingling with the marketplace. It is all
action. 'Till the stone and concrete of the foundation rest in the
actual mud, nothing has really happened. The thought is translated
back into physical reality. Everywhere exposed. To merciless
Nature and her weather. To the landshark. To the money shark.
To politician, walking delegate, contractor, assessor, building
inspector, and to the client's use or misuse. What an epic process!
That is why small critics are always trying to divide architecture
into one of its parts. Their appetite fails. Architecture becomes
sociology only, or aesthetics, or construction.[27]

This appetite for the "epic process" in which the real world weathered
and misused architecture and shaped cities was perhaps the strongest desire
shared between Haskell and Jacobs. They ultimately favored life, an epic
process through which the common ground of architecture and cities was
constructed, over buildings.

Criticism and the Crisis of Functionalism

If *Death and Life* can be seen as being part of modern architecture's
phase change into postmodernism, it is significant that by 1952, when Haskell hired Jacobs, both modern architecture and modern urbanism were
already in crisis. As the editor James Maude (J. M.) Richards, Haskell's
counterpart at *The Architectural Review* (London), put it in 1950, "The
present is a moment of crisis, not any longer because we need modern
architecture, but because we have got it."[28]

To be sure, although Haskell was an early critic of modern architecture,
he was certainly not the only one. In a keynote presentation at the annual
meeting of the American Institute of Architects in 1936, the Philadelphia
architect, archaeologist, and art historian Leicester B. Holland could already
describe modern architecture's functionalism as a "cult," presciently adding
that, like other architectural cults, it was invariably valueless and soon to
become the trivial plaything of magazine advertisements. In his paper "The
Function of Functionalism," Holland observed that if the function of functionalism was "just to combat a popular hankering after period decoration,
it is fighting a losing battle against straw men, for it can only substitute one
fashion for another."[29]

Holland's critique echoed through the twentieth century. Playing with the modernist dictum "form follows function," he invented others, including "form is a fiction that flowers out of function." Anticipating later criticism, he condemned as "diabolic" the doctrine that "Commodity and Firmness are alone essential to Well Building, and that Form or Delight is not in itself functional." With a conviction that the Vitruvian architectural triad of firmness, commodity, and delight still had meaning in modern times, he mocked the over-"exposure of construction" in favor of a more modest "expression of construction." Using the analogy of the human body, he offered that it is "one thing for an athlete to slough his restricting garments, and quite another to have a visitor take off his overcoat, and then all his other clothes, and skin, as well."[30]

By 1940, functionalism had become the focus of an early attempt to establish regular architectural criticism in Anglo-American architectural journalism. In a column titled "Criticism" in *The Architectural Review*, J. M. Richards opined that the problem of interpreting functionalism stemmed in large part from the polemical statements of early modern architects themselves. Writing under the pseudonym "James MacQuedy," the young architect and writer explained that the "overstressing of functionalism in the past for propaganda purposes by the prophets of modernism themselves has led to much of the present misunderstanding." It was clear enough to anyone who has studied Le Corbusier's books and his buildings, he explained, that the great architect's provocative and much-quoted remark about a house being a *machine á habiter* was a clever bit of rhetoric and one that had exactly the iconoclastic effect it was meant to have. "It was intended to *épater le bourgeois,* not to state an architectural philosophy," Richards observed.[31]

Richards—the critic for a magazine that would have a great influence on Haskell, *Forum,* and Jacobs—accordingly sought to move beyond functionalist rhetoric and popular misconceptions. The popular belief that "modern architects are 'functionalists,' and rely on efficiency to produce beauty of its own accord," he offered, "has been reiterated quite as often as the error that makes a disclaimer necessary." Richards believed that it was time to leave behind an exclusive concern for "sheer reasonableness and efficiency" in architectural design.[32]

However, alternatives to the strict observance of modernist tenets were difficult to identify and defend. In a notable countercritique, Philip Johnson and Henry-Russell Hitchcock effectively demonstrated how little room there was to avoid the charge of catering to public taste. In 1946, they criticized one of the pioneers of functionalist architecture, J. J. P. Oud, for "slipping back" into a popular architectural language with his design for the Shell Building (1942) in The Hague. "What did Oud find lacking in his earlier approaches?" they asked. "In this instance was he unconsciously slipping back into an easily popular answer or was he seeking something new?"[33]

In reply, Oud turned the table by defending his design for the Shell Building in functional terms. Alluding to his canonical functionalist workers' housing and factory buildings of the 1920s, he stated that he didn't believe in applying the forms of housing and factories to office buildings, town halls, and churches. By contrast, he explained that an ornamental relief, which adorned the Shell Building's entrance and was ridiculed by Johnson and Hitchcock as "embroidery," fulfilled a "spiritual function." Oud also defended the building for being a great success functionally, despite transgressing some of the functionalist tenets of the 1920s. "Do you know that the Shell Building up to now already has been used for five years—sometimes by 600, sometimes by 1,000 employees—and that I never heard one complaint about the practical functioning of the building?" he wrote. "What do you think 'functionalism' could do more in this respect? And why should it be forbidden to give functional doing a spiritual form? Functioning alone as a leading principle—my experience taught me this—results in aesthetic arbitrariness," Oud countered.[34]

After World War II, the critique of functionalism intensified. The war and its conclusion with the atomic bombing of Hiroshima and Nagasaki in August 1945 dispelled many people's faith—including that of Le Corbusier and other spokesmen of the Machine Age associated with the Congrès Internationaux d'Architecture Moderne (CIAM)—in the emancipatory powers of the machine and similar symbols of progress. As Richards and the editors of *The Architectural Review* wrote in a column titled "The Functional Tradition," "The most sinister thing about the atom bomb is not so much that it may go off as that whether it goes off or not, its effects tend to be the same. Western civilization rests on its oars, awaits the issue. Result, a very appreciable slowing down of what used to be called Progress or the March of Events."[35]

By 1947, Richards could state that functionalism, the only real aesthetic faith to which modern architects could lay claim in the interwar years, was now called into question, if not repudiated, by opponents and former supporters alike. The new question was how to address functionalism's shortcomings. Prefiguring some of the ideas that he and his colleagues, and later Jacobs, would develop, Richards offered an article titled "The New Empiricism" as a step toward a less abstract modernism, one that would seek "to humanize theory on its aesthetic side and to get back to the earlier rationalism on the technical side." Appealing to rationalists, he argued that the New Empiricism brought modern social and life sciences into the picture: "Man and his habits, reactions and needs are the focus of interest as never before," he observed. Initially applied to the humanistic modernism of Scandinavia, New Empiricism, as Richards saw it, was part of a widespread tendency, as architects around the world faced the challenge of postwar rebuilding efforts. "That this tendency is not purely a Swedish one is obvious from the concern being expressed in other countries," Richards wrote, "where other empiricists apparently fear that the enormous postwar opportunities of rebuilding may too easily result in the stereotyping of the functionalism of the thirties under the old argument of establishing it as the international vernacular."[36]

Only a few months later, in October 1947, these words echoed around the United States, where Lewis Mumford, a longtime critic of functionalist architecture, quoted Richards's repudiation of it. In an article that became better known than its inspiration, Mumford laid out an American version of Richards's essay on "Sweden's latest style," linking New Empiricism with the "Bay Region style" of the U.S. West Coast. "What was called functionalism," Mumford wrote, "was a one-sided interpretation of function, and it was an interpretation that Louis Sullivan, who popularized the slogan 'Form follows function,' never subscribed to." The so-called Rigorists, like Giedion and Le Corbusier, he argued, had elevated "the mechanical functions of a building above its human functions; they neglected the feelings, the sentiments, and the interests of the person who was to occupy it. Instead of regarding engineering as a foundation for form, they treated it as an end." Mumford, by contrast, advocated "the continued spread, to every part of our country, of that native and human form of modernism which one might call the Bay Region style, a free yet unobtrusive expression of the terrain, the climate, and the way of life on the Coast."[37]

Because of what was at stake for Modernism's champions, Mumford's attack on orthodox modern architecture and the International Style sparked further debate. In response, Hitchcock and MOMA director Alfred Barr organized the 1948 symposium "What Is Happening to Modern

FIGURE 19. Lewis Mumford speaking at the Museum of Modern Art symposium "What Is Happening to Modern Architecture?," 1948. Roy Stevens.

Architecture?" Although this rhetorical question alluded to the New Empiricism that was springing up in Sweden, England, the United States, and elsewhere, the primary purpose of the conference was to defend the International Style and to separate it from the now-disfavored functionalism. Barr was quick to point out in his introductory remarks that, "in spite of every effort on our part, the term [International Style] has often been used interchangeably with the word, 'functionalism.'" It was true, he continued, that "the principle of functionalism helped generate the new architectural forms of the 1920's and thereby contributed to the International Style, but functionalism was and still is a principle of building design which stops short of architecture." To distinguish the International Style as a new phenomenon, "We even considered using the term, 'post-functionalism,' to make absolutely clear that the new style was superseding functionalism," but this was not an adequate description of the movement they sought to identify. Thus, in spite of the deficiencies of the label, "it was obvious that the style had been born and needed a name. . . . Since then, architects and critics alike have questioned the term, often referring to it as the 'so-called' International Style; yet no one since that time has thought of a better term."[38]

After defending the International Style, Barr and Hitchcock counterattacked. Ignoring Mumford's or Richards's underlying regionalist approach, they condescendingly described Bay Region architecture, the American counterpart of the New Empiricism, as the "New Cottage Style." To underscore the supremacy of their architectural idiom, they observed that Bay Region architects such as William Wurster, Bernard Maybeck, and others resorted to the International Style when designing office and institutional buildings. "It is significant," Barr observed, "that when such a master of the Cottage Style as William Wurster is faced with a problem of designing an office building or a great project for the United Nations, he falls back upon a pretty orthodox version of the International Style." Shutting out other modernisms, Hitchcock added that "it has seemed to me almost as if we could now consider International Style to be synonymous with the phrase 'Modern Architecture.'"[39] For a few more years, Hitchcock's 1948 definition of modern architecture as the International Style prevailed. But his seemingly unequivocal faith in the style was near its end.

As Haskell predicted in 1932 in his review of Johnson and Hitchcock's *Modern Architecture* exhibit, by the early 1950s, the International Style had become "what the man about town will build." While many Americans were indeed unwilling to accept the machine á habiter for their domestic lives, Lever House (1952), the first significant postwar office building in the modern idiom, showed that corporate America had fully embraced the International Style. Meanwhile, "Googie architecture"—a term named after a Los Angeles restaurant called Googie's and coined by Haskell to describe the emergence of modern architecture in popular and commercial forms— expressed a "progressive" sentiment in popular culture. However, for many architects, both corporate and popular modernism indicated the degradation of modern architecture's formal and social aspirations into a consumable architectural style. As the International Style's advocates themselves had long been aware, becoming just another style would undermine modern architecture's raison d'être.[40]

Thus, in 1951, a year before Jacobs joined *Architectural Forum*, one of modern architecture's greatest defenders admitted that a historic line of thinking had run its course. In a 1951 essay, "The International Style Twenty Years After," Hitchcock admitted that the International Style had developed into "a form of academicism . . . in prominent architectural schools and in large highly institutionalized offices." While taking pride in his role in defining an important historical movement, he concluded that "we stand now at another change of phase in modern architecture between a 'high' and a 'late' period." Resigned to debasement and decline, Hitchcock wrote, we "must expect many vagaries in reaction against the too literal interpretation of the International Style" and "an academic current which is encouraging the repetition of established formulas without creative modulation."[41]

Having entered the period of Late Modernism, the fundamental question was what would come next—what could possibly come after Modernism, let alone "late modernism"? This was the architectural crisis, soon compounded by an urban crisis, that Jacobs faced as a fledgling architectural critic.

Richards knew that a new revolution was not the answer. He had faith in the liveliest of all the attributes of the human character: "its ability to change profoundly while essentially remaining the same." The answer, he wrote in "The Next Step?," was not to abandon functionalism, but to conceive of a "functionalism of the particular":

There is therefore no call to abandon functionalism in the search for an architectural idiom capable of the full range of expression

FIGURE 20. Lever House, designed by Gordon Bunshaft of Skidmore, Owings & Merrill, was a pioneering work of late modern architecture and "corporate modernism." Getty Images.

FIGURE 21. "Googie Architecture" by Douglas Haskell, *House & Home*, Feb. 1952, 85–86. The term described populist and "uninhibited" modern architecture. In the postwar period, modern architecture was recognized in professional circles as being in intellectual crisis at just the time that it was embraced by the public.

its human purposes require; only to understand functionalism itself, by its very nature, implies the reverse of what it is often allowed to imply: not reducing everything to broad generalizations—quality in architecture belongs to the exact, not the approximate—but relating it ever more closely to the essential particulars of time and place and purpose. That is the level on which humanity and science meet.[42]

Although it is unlikely that Jacobs read this essay at the time—she was still working at the State Department when it came out—it exemplified the ideas and writing that made Haskell, Jacobs, and their colleagues at *Forum* great admirers of *The Architectural Review*. Indeed, not only did Haskell's team read the *Review* and follow its debates, Haskell shaped the new editorial agenda for architectural criticism with the *Review* in mind. In one of his first major editorials following *Forum*'s "inauguration" of architectural criticism, Haskell would echo Richards's sentiment: "Now we cry for human architecture. Modern architecture can no longer live on its promise of simple functionalism."[43]

The influence on Jacobs was ultimately important and direct: The concept of the "functionalism of the particular" was taken up by Gordon Cullen and Ian Nairn, Jacobs's counterparts at the *Review*, with whom she would collaborate in the years before she wrote *Death and Life*. As she recalled decades later, in the foreword to the Modern Library edition of her book, the writers at *The Architectural Review* were especially influential on her thinking about architecture and the city and her effort to expose "the unworkability and joylessness of anticity visions." Her book, which she described in its earliest phase as "a study of the relation of function to design in large cities," would be part of a long effort to reframe the modern functionalist tradition.[44]

"Modern Monsters" Strike Back

Despite the need for architectural criticism, the tradition had withered in both the United States and the United Kingdom in the decades preceding the postwar period. As Richards wrote in a November 1950 editorial, there was then "no regular criticism of current architecture comparable with art criticism, dramatic criticism, or music criticism" because of the threat of libel suits. In a memo to his executive editors a year later, Haskell paraphrased Richards's argument in making a case for a more critical editorial agenda at *Forum*. However, despite the concessions Haskell had won by the time Jacobs had joined his staff, progress was slow. It would take until the late 1950s—just the time that Jacobs was prepared to attack urban renewal practices—for expectations to change, and even then her writing would be considered shocking.[45]

Haskell had decades of experience with the limits of American architectural criticism and had long worked to push the boundaries since the 1930s, when he became an architectural critic for *The Nation* and wrote freelance articles for *Architectural Record* and other magazines. As compared to the professional architecture magazines, however, more rigorous architectural criticism was possible in *The Nation* because the professional magazines had to maintain working relationships with architects and had therefore developed gentlemen's agreements and codes of conduct that maintained a status quo. And even in magazines of general readership, caution was necessary when critiquing a building. In writing his "Sky Line" column for *The New Yorker*, for example, Mumford often omitted architects' names in order to avoid the threat of a libel suit.

In fact, before 1964, when the Supreme Court ruled strongly in favor of the freedoms of speech and press in *New York Times Company v. Sullivan*, publishers were frequently threatened with lawsuits over statements that architects deemed harmful to their reputations. As Talbot Hamlin observed in the 1930 essay "Criticism Might Help Architecture: Let's Try It?," an architect criticized in print looks for "a dollars-and-cents remedy and runs to court with a libel suit." This distressingly prevalent attitude, Hamlin continued, undermined "any definite attempt to evaluate current work, save by means of praise or simple description; adverse criticism can only be hinted in the most general terms."[46]

Recalling the writing of one of America's first architectural critics, Montgomery Schuyler, Hamlin lamented a bygone age of lively criticism: "Gone are those bold days of Montgomery Schuyler's 'Architectural Aberrations' that enlivened the *Architectural Record* of the nineties. . . . [Now] even the better class magazines generally avoid actual criticism; the ogre of a libel suit not unjustly stares at them continually from afar, and even a witty criticism may bring the architect pouncing down with bared claws." In concluding his essay, Talbot expressed the hope that, someday, "some architectural magazine [would] establish a column of sound and careful criticism."[47]

Haskell harbored the same hope for many decades. When he joined *Architectural Record* as a full-time associate editor in 1943, more than a decade after his temporary position at that magazine had begun, architectural criticism remained problematic. What Hamlin had actually failed to mention was that even Schuyler's "Architectural Aberrations" column—which had run from 1891 to 1913, when *Record* was a young and rambunctious magazine—had been published anonymously and that the architects whose buildings were criticized went unnamed. As Peter Blake later wrote, *Record* was "a favorite with advertisers: it made no waves." For that reason, Blake explained, "Doug was not especially happy on its staff—he was an old-fashioned American radical."[48]

So, in 1949, when Henry Luce and Perry Prentice, *Architectural Forum*'s publisher, offered Haskell a job, he took the position in part because he saw his promotion as a chance to reinvent American architectural criticism. At the first opportunity, in November 1951, with subscriptions at record numbers, he hoped that Luce and Prentice would repay his efforts with support for taking *Forum* in a new direction.[49]

Haskell's first attempt at establishing a regular column of architectural criticism at *Forum* was tentatively called the "Monsters column." Reminiscent of Schuyler's "Architectural Aberrations," "Monsters" would chastise the worst architecture and make a case for reinvigorated principles. Soliciting confidential nominations for the award of "most monstrous" postwar architectural projects from a handful of prominent architects, he described his goal as isolating "what might be called illiterate efforts by large enterprises whose public responsibility demands that they not uglify their respective cities." Haskell's associate editors, including Blake, supported the column, as did the architects contacted for "monstrous" nominations.[50]

Prentice had reservations, however. "I am all for the Monsters story," he wrote in a brief memo, "but I think we should get legal advice on it before we publish it." The executive editor, Joe Hazen, concurred. "Doug," he wrote, "please give me a memo on your plans for this department and I'll check the legality." Haskell replied with a draft of the first column. "You might submit the following to the lawyers," he wrote Hazen, "as a probable lead."[51]

What Haskell submitted for the lawyers' perusal was an editorial that would never be published, but it was the first step toward the criticism about urban redevelopment and urban design that Jacobs would develop. Although he focused on a critique of functionalist and utilitarian architecture, Haskell made a case for architecture and for a new architectural criticism that recognized architecture's civic design responsibility and its larger place in the arts. To call attention to this situation, the "Monsters" column would discuss how examples of each of the three most public modern building types—governmental, commercial/industrial, and institutional—had failed to live up to their potential and responsibilities to cities and society.

Haskell's premise was that, in earlier times, "important buildings were all carefully weighed to get the best not only in utility but in architectural art." However, in the mid-twentieth century, he observed, "Our highly placed officials . . . have many of them forgotten the old discussion . . . that whereas building is for utility, architecture is an art."[52]

Haskell's critique was two-pronged. On one hand, he argued that functionalist architecture and architectural utilitarianism, which had been thoroughly embraced by the larger culture, had to be reformed. "The great public buildings, the great commercial buildings, the great industrial buildings, and the great institutional buildings have a job to do beyond satisfying practical requirements. They represent not only the institutions that they house but, in a broader sense, the culture of the United States." On the other hand, he argued that the nation's leading citizens had an obligation to improve the built environment and that a new case had to be made for civic design: "The old literacy about architecture has regrettably gone lost. The idea that it is an obligation on the part of leading citizens to improve the streets, roadsides [sic] of their country not only in point of wealth but as a visual treat seems somehow to fail even to register."[53]

To avoid worrying the lawyers, Haskell carefully directed criticism away from architects and assigned responsibility to an abstract class of "highly placed officials," "leading citizens," and "supposed leaders." Moreover, no criticism would be made of these buildings' "usefulness, of their efficiency, of their adequacy to the program for which they were set up," he conceded. "We are, in other words, not criticizing them as buildings. We are criticizing them as architecture." In doing so, *Forum* would strive to end the confusion that "satisfying the physical functions ended their duty and . . . that a well-functioning building must turn out beautiful simply because it is practical." Finally, he argued that he and his staff would be doing nothing very different that what was done in other cultural arenas. Architectural criticism, he argued in conclusion, echoing Richards, "should be on a par with that of art, music, the theater, and other cultural manifestations."[54]

Despite all of these arguments, libel fears killed the "Monsters" column. Following Prentice's request, Hazen dug up a 1937 legal memo written to Prentice's predecessor, who had established the magazine's cautious editorial policy. As had been explained to the former publisher by counsel in 1937, "fair comment of architectural works is privileged in precisely the same manner and to precisely the same extent as fair comment on other matters of public interest." Published statements of fact, if true, were immune from liability. However, comment or opinion, in order to come within the protection of "fair comment," had to pertain to matters of public interest, not assert alleged matters of fact, and had to be fair. In other words, the architectural critic was fully justified in criticizing architectural failures that could be measured with a ruler but was on shakier ground when stating that a building was "not in keeping with its surroundings"—the truth or falsity of which would be a matter of opinion and "not susceptible of satisfactory proof since there may be (and usually are) honest differences of opinion." And, of course, if the critic's opinion was not fair—if it was spoken with malice, ill will, or was other than "a fair minded man might reasonably hold"—the critic and the magazine's publisher could be found guilty of libel. Just describing a building as not respecting the urban context or as being at odds with civic design principles could therefore land the critic in some trouble.[55]

Moreover, from the publisher's point of view, outspoken criticism was not good for business. The business of running an architectural magazine was a competitive one, and journals vied for rights to publish stories about the best buildings by the best architects, while avoiding wasted pages and praise on projects that might later be seen as lesser works. Haskell and, to a lesser extent, his associate editors accordingly spent much of their time in building relationships with the most publishable architects and in negotiating the layout, number of pages, and cover image privilege with architects whose work they wanted to publish. Haskell knew that *Forum* criticized the work of notable and famous architects, like the young Louis Kahn, Frank Lloyd Wright, or Le Corbusier, at its peril. A wrong word could result in Wright or another exclusive story going to another magazine. Wright, in fact, frequently threatened this. A famous story at *Forum* involved an unexpected visit from Wright, who, while poking around the managing editor George Nelson's office, came upon an unfavorable review of his updated *Autobiography* by newcomer Peter Blake. Enraged by what he read, Wright stormed out of the office, leaving in his wake the expectation that Blake would be fired immediately and that Wright would sever his connections with the magazine, which, in Blake's words, had invested "very large sums of money in buttering up the old egomaniac in the manner to which he had become accustomed." However, Wright was quickly assured of a better review by a senior editor, which was soon delivered by Nelson himself. Despite Wright's thorough hatred of the city, the magazine's relationship with him is likely why he escaped Jacobs's censure in *Death and Life*; since she was planning to return to *Forum* after her book was published, she could not risk antagonizing her magazine's most valuable editorial property.[56]

Lawyerly caution and self-censorship thus prevailed into the early 1950s, the McCarthy years, and beyond. In February 1952, only a few months before Jacobs arrived, Haskell's article on "Googie architecture," published in one of the first issues of *House & Home*, gives a sense of what this meant. Despite his senior position, Haskell's next attempt at criticism took the form of a morality tale reminiscent of Louis Sullivan's turn-of-the-century writings. In a heavy-handed conceit, Haskell spoke through the voice of a fictional professor (Professor Thrugg), who explained to his reader-students that "Googie" architecture, aka "Modern Architecture Uninhibited," revealed the architects' Howard Roark complexes. Like *The Fountainhead*'s hero, they seemed continually compelled to create unprecedented works through the exploitation of abstract form, modern construction methods, and new materials. "The Googie architect," opined the professor, feels "that somehow he has to surpass *everybody* if he can—and that includes Frank Lloyd Wright."[57]

Although it now appears mild and quaint, Haskell later described this essay as not only serious criticism, but also "definitely dangerous since it pointed out specific examples"—even though the three projects in question, all presented anonymously, were a student's design project, the Googie's restaurant in Los Angeles, and an apartment building in Houston.[58]

Further tempering his criticism, Haskell characteristically found a number of genuinely favorable things to say about the works. For example, Googie architecture was said to have "brought modern architecture down from the mountains and set ordinary clients, ordinary people, free." Like Jacobs, he believed that "sometimes fantastically good ideas result from uninhibited experiment." And he opined that "Googie accustoms the people to expect strangeness, and makes them the readier for those strange things yet to come which will truly make good sense."[59]

Nevertheless, the popular phenomenon of Googie architecture and its Formica boomerangs convinced Haskell of the necessity of real and robust architectural criticism. What was needed in a world of populist modern architecture were responsible critics who could separate good ideas from the bad and simply strange. The ordinary people now interested in modern architecture had neither education nor leaders to guide them. Caught between mortgage lenders who inhibited innovation "on one side and Googie geniuses on the other, how can they know their way? There are no responsible critics in the middle!" Through architectural criticism, Haskell offered, "something better than accidental discoveries might come even from Googie." Criticism was needed to guide both the public and the profession.[60]

Forum's New Architectural Critic

Jacobs did not appear as a permanent fixture on the *Forum* masthead until September 1952. However, within two months of her trial assignment, she was freely stating frank and even sardonic opinions of which buildings were worthy of publication in the magazine.

In a July 1952 memo to Haskell typical of their interoffice and personal communication during the decade ahead, Jacobs offered critiques of a new school, a hospital addition, and a housing project for the elderly, recommending the publication of the school project and rejecting the others. Focusing her comments on use or function, broadly conceived, not aesthetics, Jacobs observed that the school design, with internal organization like "little neighborhood units" and general adaptability, presented a model of a "reasonable, flexible way to go about school building under certain circumstances." By contrast, she was dubious about the hospital design, particularly the addition's connection to the old building, the phasing of additional expansion plans, and other decisions that apparently had "no thinking behind them." Jacobs had discussed the project directly with the architect, who left their meeting saying he would get back to her with answers to her various questions. She wrote Haskell wryly that "I encouraged him to do [this] because I secretly thought that even though we would not use this [building in the publication], supposing the reasoning is as faulty as I suspect, these are things he ought to know anyhow." Describing the elderly housing project, Jacobs's empathy came to the fore. She criticized the architect for knowing nothing about the "people it will house, how long they are apt to live there (he never heard anybody bring that up), whether they bring or would like to bring anything with them, etc. They are numbers, one to a bed. It is a barracks." Her remarks anticipated the criticisms she would later make of public housing projects then on architects' drawing boards.[61]

Such editorial work, which included meeting architects and discussing their projects, sometimes visiting buildings in person, discussing with Haskell and other associate editors what to publish, and collaborating on articles, occupied much of Jacobs's time at *Forum*, when she was not working on her own stories. For her first few years, when the magazine continued its practice of publishing staff articles without a byline, she remained focused on hospitals and schools, although soon thereafter a new large-scale building type, the regional shopping mall, became part of her repertoire.

Following Haskell's agenda of a critical approach to building types, the magazine's theme for 1953 was "New Thinking," with monthly features on new thinking regarding hotels, industrial buildings, parking garages, college buildings, and so on. In 1953, most issues therefore included an article by Jacobs on a new school and a new hospital, with special editions including a hospitals issue in May 1953 and a schools issue in October 1953.

By focusing on hospitals, schools, and shopping centers, and covering a geographic territory that included Philadelphia, among the architects whose friendships Jacobs cultivated were the Philadelphia architects Vincent Kling and Louis Kahn, and Victor Gruen, a pioneer in shopping center design. Some of these relationships became quite close and influential, whether or not their names later appeared in *Death and Life*, but initially it was all business. A letter from Haskell to Kling, in which they negotiated putting one of Kling's projects on the cover, gives a good sense of Jacobs's role at the magazine. After pitching Kling with *Forum*'s growing circulation and its number of published prize-winning projects—"There is rarely an important job that hasn't appeared first in the *Forum*," he wrote—Haskell said he would wait for Jacobs's opinion. "As for promising ahead of time that we'll give you the cover, that I can't yet do, not having seen the material," Haskell told Kling. "We really can't dispose of space in the *Forum* on a competitive basis with other magazines—the strength of *Forum* has always lain in the fact that the editors were free to splurge themselves on really good stories. If the opinion of Mrs. Jacobs, our very competent hospital editor, counts for anything, I would say there is a mighty good chance in the case of Hunterdon [Hospital]." Ultimately, Kling's hospital got six pages in Jacobs's December 1953 article "Hospital for the Well," but not the cover; the issue was dedicated to new churches, and so was the cover.[62]

Jacobs's early interactions with Gruen were similar, typically including discussion about when and what would be published. As she wrote Haskell in a March 1953 memo, "This morning I was talking with Victor Gruen, and I suggested that when Southdale [Shopping Center] is finished it would be interesting to do a story on the design of the separate stores within the center. He replied that Northland [Shopping Center], being closer to completion, would be a much better vehicle for this. . . . He also said that if we plan to do Northland he would like a firm promise on it from us as he has the other magazines at his heels." In the end, Jacobs recommended a feature story for when the project was finished, which she visited and wrote up for publication in June 1954.[63]

With others, including Kahn, Jacobs was more aggressive about pursuing rights and agreements to publish certain projects. Although Kahn was still early in his career, she was captivated by his creative mind and work. In May 1955, she summarized a long meeting with him by saying that *Forum* needed to get the rights to publish Kahn's Mill Creek housing project and "Trenton Bath House":

> If any or all of these prospects seems as interesting to you as they did to me, I think a note from DH [Douglas Haskell] expressing our interest and wishes to see them would be good. [Kahn] is being very coy about letting us use his Mill Creek housing in July—in fact at this point is saying leave it out (because it will be along with other people's work!!). I have a plot to try to get him to change his mind, which I hope works, and it would probably help if he got a note expressing interest in these *other* things—especially Trenton which we ought to get our hooks into soon if we want it.[64]

Apart from a behind-the-scenes look at Jacobs's work at the magazine, the memo is remarkable both because of her enthusiasm for Kahn's work and because the Mill Creek housing project was one that later changed Jacobs's mind about such urban redevelopment projects. At the time, however, she expressed no doubts and did not criticize Kahn later (at least directly) because of her lingering admiration. When they were new projects, she described Kahn's Trenton Bath House and Yale Art Gallery as delightful, imaginative, and marvelous creations, and she sought to convince Haskell of their virtues:

> [Kahn] has a structure for an outdoor swimming pool in Trenton on which bids are to come in this week. It seemed to me a marvellous creation. The columns are actually little rooms (he is all for hollow columns, the interiors of which are used), some of them for toilets, some for the mazes by which people enter and leave the dressing areas. . . . The roofs will be awnings, very gaily particolored, stretched over space frames. The space frames make V's on the roof down which the water will pour when it rains, and the water will spout off like fountains. The main areas are a women's dressing room, a men's ditto, and a common space, sort of a lobby,

FIGURE 22. The Mill Creek housing project by Louis Kahn, with Anne Tyng, commissioned in 1950 and seen here in 1956. Kahn Collection, University of Pennsylvania and Pennsylvania Historical and Museum Commission, De Lellis Gallery for John Ebstel.

between. It should be completed by this fall. It seems to me that it will be most delightful, and its structure is certainly imaginative.[65]

And although "marvellous" was not a word Jacobs used often, she found occasion to use it two more times in her summary of the recently completed Yale Art Gallery:

Doug, [Kahn's] idea of how he would do the Yale Art Gallery over is that instead of 27 or some such number of columns, he would have only 9, of a vastly more ingenious form. From there on, his idea takes off on the subject of columns and spaceframes and does not pursue the Art Gallery further. He has marvellous sketches (he showed me slides of them) and marvellous constructions which would make terrific photographs. If he does the article at all the way he ran through this with me, it would not be "How I Would Do the Yale Art Gallery Now" (though that could be the lead-off, and a very good one), but instead on what ideas he has on framing. If the sketches and photos kept popping up in the article with his words, I think it would be terrific. He sure has some mind.[66]

Although Jacobs would later acquire the reputation for being opposed to modern architecture, and is not usually thought of as interested in architectural structures, her praise for Kahn's work was fully consistent with her characteristic interest in invention, experimentation, and function. In *Death and Life*, she praised the Lever House (published in *Architectural Forum*, June 1952), the Pepsi-Cola Building (1960), and the Union Carbide Building (1960)—all designed by Gordon Bunshaft and Skidmore, Owings & Merrill—and Mies van der Rohe's Seagram Building (1958) as "masterpieces of modern design." Although Kahn, like Wright and Buckminster Fuller, escaped her reproach in the book, he could hardly be described as an "orthodox" thinker with "stultifying" ideas—two of her harshest epithets.[67]

In her work for *Forum*, another project review that exemplified her attitude toward modern architecture, as well as her work on buildings other than hospitals, schools, and shopping centers, was her study of the models and plans of Lorimer & Rose Architects' design for City College of New York's new library (now the college's School of Architecture, Urban Design, and Landscape Architecture) in 1954. Impressed by the organization and functional distributions of the plan, she informed Haskell, "It has one of those remarkable simplicities of plan and organization that never turn up, somehow, without a great deal of analysis and thought." An example of this was the vertical organization of primary building functions in terms of the visitors' use of the building. "There is a very good allocation of functions by floors," she observed. "The first floor, with standard texts and the 'study hall' elements, peels off most of the users; the second floor is the main reference section, and takes off most of those remaining; the top floor has special, less used reference sections. . . . In excess space above the ramp endings are the carrels, which are used by fewest people and also, it seems to me, are properly placed psychologically, up in the attic away from it all." On the other hand, Jacobs was disappointed by some of the building's detailing. "While the general fenestration looks swell on the model," she reported, "I wonder how it will look in the finished building. Possibly if the grid that holds it is bold and strong looking enough, it will come off."[68]

However, Jacobs's greatest disappointment concerned the primary circulation and organizing element, a ramp on the entrance side connecting the sidewalk and the building's three floors. To best reveal the functional order of the building, she thought that the ramp should have been made visible through the use of clear glass instead of opaque stone walls, glass block, and corrugated wire-glass. She was sorry to learn that this more dramatic design approach had been rejected as too radical. "I think it is a shame the ramp was not made visible across the front of the building; it would have been very dramatic," she wrote. "It was not, because the city did not want to maintain the glass area, and because there was reluctance to be so 'radical' in design. Visually, the thing is left as a distinct element, with blank limestone facing and narrow glass walls at the ends, but it gives no hint of what it is. A pedestrian solution and a great chance missed."[69]

City College's library, in other words, was a smaller, architectural version of an argument she would later make in *Death and Life*. Design, as she offered there, should pursue "a strategy of illuminating and clarifying life and helping to explain to us its meanings and order."[70] In the case of the library, a transparent ramp not only would have enhanced the urbanity of the local context by contributing "eyes on the street," but also would have dramatically illuminated the building's functional order. A more radical design would have revealed how both the building and the city worked.

In *Death and Life* and beyond, Jacobs remained committed to the concept of functional architecture. Asked in 1962, in a postpublication interview, "How much do you think that fashionable architecture has to do with the disease of cities?," Jacobs responded at length in functional terms. Architects, she replied, had fallen back on novelty in their abandonment of functionalism. "If [architects] had an esthetic based on function, on the way things work, they wouldn't have to fall back on nice effects, novelties, grotesque exaggerations," she explained. Recalling the roots of modern architecture, she continued: "Function, which is supposed to be the basis of modern architecture, has almost unnoticed taken on a very different meaning from that it had in the beginning. Then function was meant the way a building was used. Frank Lloyd Wright revolutionized the home on this basis. . . . Various buildings were really rethought in these terms." But human use had been replaced by self-reference and autonomy: "now function has come to mean not the way the building is used, but the function of the structure itself, the function of the material. So that architecture with a capital A has become more and more interested in itself and less and less interested in the world that uses it."[71]

Jacobs went on to conclude that the "lack of attention to function today is not just a disease of architecture or city planning"—it was a societal problem. Making an analogy between locomotives that revealed their workings and the streamlined style that came later, she observed, "People no longer seem to know how things work. Idealized designs of many kinds ignore what objects do, or conceal what they do and how they do it. It's like locomotives we used to see, with their wheels and the whole business exposed. Then a skirt was put over them, concealing as much as possible. Much of what is called design today is cover-up." Her thought was similar to one she had made in *Death and Life*, where she wrote, "It may be that we have become so feckless as a people that we no longer care how things do work, but only what kind of quick, easy outer impression they give."[72]

Jacobs was thus very much a modernist: A good design revealed how things worked. While supportive of preserving historic buildings, she did not advocate the design approach later known as "contextualism"—the idea that a new building design should be generated by mimicking the stylistic and formal precedents of its neighbors. Quite the contrary, as an advocate of visual diversity and innovation, she rejected the idea that architectural design should create aesthetically disciplined environments. Unlike design contextualists, she believed that the *Gesamtkunstwerk* approach—the attempt to create cities as a total work of art—was a reflection or symptom of a closed, controlled, or arrested society. Such environments, she wrote in *Death and Life*, may "look to us like works of art in their physical totality" and we may regard them with "admiration or a kind of nostalgia." However, she believed that aesthetic discipline was a reflection of social discipline: "the limitations on possibilities and the strictures on individuals in such societies extend much beyond the materials and conceptions used in creating works of art from the grist of everyday life." Architectural style and aesthetics imposed on a city or a city neighborhood could be regarded not only as "cover-ups" of the inner workings or actual functioning of buildings or cities, but also as a form of social control.[73]

CHAPTER 4

Advocating the "City-Planner Approach"

"The city planner gets a problem and he has to start from scratch. The architect usually asks for a program," Rosenfield observes. Working either as a consultant or architect, Rosenfield uses the city-planner approach, does his own studies right down to digging out the facts on family income in the community. His facility with this kind of research comes out of his three years' training as a social scientist. He is suspicious of all rules of thumb and initial assumptions.
—Jane Jacobs, 1952

IN JUNE 1952, the same month in which Jacobs's first article for *Architectural Forum* was published, Douglas Haskell announced his plan to redouble the magazine's efforts on the problems of cities. Haskell explained that, unlike its rivals, only *Forum*'s writers had recognized "the potential in urban redevelopment and the new instruments given private enterprise by the Redevelopment Section of the 1949 Housing Act," which, "for the first time, gave private interests a major chance to operate in large sections in the middle of the city which formerly could not be assembled."[1]

Like most Americans, including Jacobs, Haskell believed that the urban redevelopment powers extended to city housing authorities by Title I of the U.S. Housing Act of 1949 had the potential to improve cities that had remained in a state of deferred maintenance after the war. The nation's housing stock, which was already inadequate and aged before the war, had deteriorated further due to wartime material rationing and domestic construction restrictions. And with millions of military servicemen and -women returning from overseas ready to begin new lives, the country's postwar enemy was a nationwide housing shortage. As the country singer Merle Travis crooned in his 1946 song "No Vacancy," "Now the mighty war over there is won, / Troubles and trials have just begun, / As I face that terrible enemy sign, No Vacancy."[2]

With the Marshall Plan put in place to assist the rebuilding of Europe in 1947, and construction restrictions lifted, the United States mobilized for an equally ambitious and long-awaited postwar rebuilding program at home. As part of the "Fair Deal" launched by President Truman in his 1949 State of the Union address, the new federal initiative would finance slum clearance and urban redevelopment (Title I of the Housing Act of 1949), guarantee mortgages through the Federal Housing Administration (Title II), and provide funds for the construction of one million affordable public housing units by 1955 (Title III). With support from city planners, the home-building industry, and public housing advocates, the bill addressed the interests of diverse constituencies, who sometimes had very different visions for the future of the American city. There were those who believed in building new towns and others who advocated modernizing cities, and, among these, many questioned whether the city could, or *should*, survive in its present form.[3]

Skyrocketing automobile ownership, extensive highway construction, the mass production of suburban housing stimulated by guaranteed home mortgages, the age-old lure of suburban life, and Cold War fears of nuclear attack on urban centers combined to make *decentralization* a buzzword of the early 1950s. Although the idea of planned decentralization dated back at least to Ebenezer Howard's *To-Morrow: A Peaceful Path to Real Reform* (1898), in the postwar period, Clarence Stein and other advocates of Howard's Garden Cities movement believed the time was "ripe for complete change in the form of the urban environment." In *Toward New Towns for America* (1950), Stein predicted that the coming decades would see "a new era of nation-wide decentralization" for reasons of defense and better living. The editor Harold Hauf, Haskell's counterpart at *Architectural Record,* agreed. Hauf believed that the "growing congestion and concentration in urban areas is no more desirable in peace time than in war." But with the added threat of nuclear attack, in a December 1950 editorial "City Planning and Civil Defense," Hauf explained that every slum clearance project should be considered an opportunity to advance the strategic depopulation of cities. "Today urban dispersal appears to be the only fully effective means of minimizing the effects of atomic bombing," he wrote. "If we are alert to the implications, we can identify this means of defense with measures for making our cities better places in which to work and live."[4]

In other words, during the Cold War, and especially during the height of the Red Scare, *Forum*'s support for the modernization of central cities—despite being targets for bombs—was not to be taken for granted. Covering stories on *urban redevelopment*, which became known as *urban renewal* after the U.S. Housing Act of 1954, was an expression of support for the continued existence of the city in both a physical and an existential sense. It was, moreover, a sensibility that was not unrelated to the fact that *Forum* and its staff were based in Manhattan. If one believed in the possibility of nuclear attack, then, deep down, their survival and the city's were one and the same. And there was no better place than a New York–based architectural magazine from which to follow urban redevelopment and renewal projects.

In this light, it should not be surprising that Jacobs sided not only with cities, but also with the urban redevelopment and city planning initiatives that supported them. In fact, although she later came to regret her role in supporting urban renewal, Jacobs was initially an enthusiastic advocate of urban redevelopment and the city-planner approach. In the years before the failure of urban renewal was apparent, this was almost necessarily true for those who supported cities over decentralization. For Jacobs, the same commitment to cities that led her to become *Forum*'s urban redevelopment specialist, and ultimately the author of *The Death and Life of Great American Cities*, initially included hopes for the improvement of cities through redevelopment and renewal.

Saving the City Through "Slum Surgery"

In the years around the passage of the Housing Act of 1949, the belief that American cities were "beyond mild measures" was widely shared and invasive "slum surgery" was widely considered to be the "progressive" approach. *Architectural Forum*'s early articles on urban redevelopment, most often written then by Walter McQuade, Ogden Tanner, and Mary Mix Foley, usually supported heavy-handed and large-scale slum clearance. Their articles, written while Jacobs was still working for *Amerika* and also

FIGURE 23. Titled "Bomb vs. Metropolis," this image, which superimposed the Bikini Atoll Baker bomb test cloud onto the Manhattan skyline, sought to show both the relative scale of an atomic explosion and the fragility of cities in such an attack. Images like these, and fears of Soviet nuclear attack, contributed to arguments for urban decentralization during the Cold War. *Operation Crossroads: The Official Pictorial Record* (New York: Wise & Co., 1946), 215.

writing articles on the subject, give a sense of what was considered acceptable and of how ideas were changing. In 1951, for example, the magazine praised the Pruitt-Igoe housing project, still in its design phase. In 1952, however, some of *Forum*'s writers began to question the large project approach, categorizing it as the "Robert Moses method." In other words, by the time Jacobs joined the magazine, there was a precedent for criticism of what McQuade called the "neighborhood leveling techniques of planners like blockbusting Bob Moses."[5]

For *Architectural Forum*, the story of urban renewal began with "Redevelopment of Norfolk," which documented the "first full-scale try-out" of Title I slum clearance and urban redevelopment in May 1950. First in line for Title I funding in August 1949, beating even New York's Robert Moses to the punch, the head of Norfolk, Virginia's Redevelopment and Housing Authority, who had served as the president of the National Association of Housing Officials, would set a precedent for how Title I funds would be used.[6]

Comprising a third of Norfolk's downtown area, the city's plan was unprecedented in scale, a first in size and kind. Comparing the undertaking to Manhattan's Stuyvesant Town, the previous benchmark for postwar slum clearance and housing projects, *Forum's* (unbylined) writer observed that "Stuyvesant Town is the biggest housing project erected anywhere since the war, but its 75 acres of slum-cleared land is little more than a third of the 207 acres now scheduled for redevelopment in Norfolk." The first phase of the Norfolk redevelopment plan alone, a third of the total acres designated for redevelopment, made it "the biggest [slum-clearance] program ever."[7]

Typical of urban renewal projects to come, the part of Norfolk's downtown planned for reconstruction was also home to the city's African American community. Racism, segregation, and poverty had combined to make this part of the city one of the worst slums in the country, where "inside toilets [were] practically unknown and running water indoors the rare exception" and whole families were frequently crowded into a single room. Although the writer did not go so far as to condemn the underlying social injustices, he did observe that housing for whites in the city had kept pace with population growth related to military production during the war, while "the only new units erected for Negroes since 1940 were two public housing projects for a total of 1,200 families," despite a population increase of 20,000 in the black community.

Anticipating James Baldwin's famous 1963 description of "urban renewal" as "Negro removal," only a fraction of the formerly African American neighborhood would be rebuilt for its residents. Along with a road-widening and -straightening program and the construction of a new belt highway, most of the downtown neighborhood would be rezoned for commercial and industrial uses in the interest of economic development. The twelve thousand displaced "slum-dwellers" who qualified for public housing would be relocated to four new "Negro projects" and one white public housing project to be built beyond the downtown area.[8]

A few months later, an almost identical story was told in Forum's August 1950 issue. In this case, "Chicago Redevelops" described the Lake Meadows area of South Side Chicago as "America's biggest slum." The plan would match perceptions. The redevelopment proposal, the author observed, "is no gentle therapy; it is drastic surgery. But cities like Chicago are beyond mild measures."[9]

Similar to the situation in Norfolk, while Chicago's South Side African American population had almost doubled between 1930 and 1950, segregation crowded people into "blocks of miserable old mansions, inhabited sometimes in shifts." Redevelopment would dislocate 85 to 90 percent of the neighborhood's residents, although few would be able to afford the moderate-income rents of the Lake Meadows housing project. Moreover, only an estimated quarter of the displaced residents would be eligible for public housing elsewhere. The remaining evacuees would be relocated ("slum shifted") by Chicago's Land Clearance Commission into "equivalent dwellings" elsewhere in the designated slum district.

Despite the great need for housing, the new neighborhood would be mostly open land. With suburbanized urbanism thoroughly entrenched as the prevailing planning paradigm, 92 percent of Lake Meadows's ground would be left unbuilt. Designed by a blue-chip architectural firm, the project was defined by two facing "horizontal skyscrapers," each twenty-three stories high, one apartment deep, and one-third of a mile long. With relatively small footprints, the gigantic apartment blocks would leave "vast stretches of open green area." In this way, the project sought to "compete with the suburbs" by creating a new "suburb" just minutes from downtown. The proposal, later critiqued by Jacobs in Death and Life, perfectly encapsulated the principles of "Radiant Garden City" planning.[10]

"Slum Surgery in St. Louis," published in April 1951, described the redevelopment plans for approximately 40 percent of downtown St. Louis in a similar pattern. Years later, in 1972, the demolition of Pruitt-Igoe, the proposed housing project at the center of the city's renewal scheme, would symbolize the failure and death of modern architecture and modernist urbanism.[11]

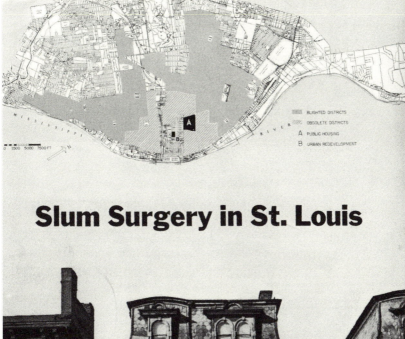

Slum Surgery in St. Louis

FIGURE 24. Published in April 1951, a year before Jacobs arrived at *Architectural Forum*, "Slum Surgery in St. Louis" was an early article on urban redevelopment. It set the stage for Jacobs's writing on the subject in the following years. The article also introduced designs for the infamous Pruitt-Igoe housing project. *AF* (Apr. 1951), 128.

Although many factors—social, financial, and physical—contributed to Pruitt-Igoe's downfall, its failure resulted largely from the expectation, typical of the prevailing paradigm, that an architectural solution could solve a larger urban problem. "Slum Surgery in St. Louis" described a "vertical neighborhood for poor people in a city which up to now has lived 90% in single houses," with no regard for the residents' experiences, let alone desires, of living in single-family houses or in a neighborhood of such houses. By contrast, the project's architectural success was judged by the fact that the Pruitt-Igoe building's skip-stop elevator plan was 16 percent more efficient than the typical cross plan of New York City public housing. On this account, the unbuilt Pruitt-Igoe housing project was described as having "already begun to change the public housing pattern in other cities."[12]

Within only four years of the project's completion, as Pruitt-Igoe began to decline, "Slum Surgery in St. Louis" become a quiet source of embarrassment for *Architectural Forum*. Although she was careful not to name the project or cite the source of the accolades it had received (her own magazine!), in *Death and Life*, Jacobs contributed to the "Pruitt-Igoe myth" by opining that the "expert praise" that the project had initially received was evidence of the bankruptcy of urban redevelopment and design theory. While obviously flawed, some residents found the housing project to be better than the homes they left, at least until larger systemic problems— among them, racism, minimal architectural and maintenance budgets, and a declining city—took their toll.[13]

Despite Jacobs's hindsight, the St. Louis plan was regarded in the early 1950s as a "rescue pattern" to preserve a shrinking city. The author of "Slum Surgery" reported that while "today everybody wants to move out" of the city, the mayor wanted to "preserve" St. Louis, with the hope that the St. Louis plan "might well set a new rescue pattern for other tight-collared U.S. cities who are watching their substance disappear to the comfortable suburbs." In this sense, *Forum*'s editorial position remained urban and opposed to decentralization and suburbanization. The author observed that some "social planners in St. Louis think the population should be allowed to disperse, that even public housing projects should be built outside the city." But then, he asked, "what happens to the city?" The answer seemed to be "progress or death." Quoting a representative civic leader in St. Louis, *Forum* asked its readers to imagine that "the whole city did turn itself inside out and disappear to the suburbs. . . . [O]nce that had happened completely, the implications of the life of the city as a whole, including those suburbs, might be something to worry about. You don't go on walking without a heart." Jacobs would have agreed.[14]

"The Philadelphia Cure"

Although Haskell committed magazine resources to covering redevelopment stories, when Jacobs started at *Architectural Forum* in 1952, there were still not many projects to write about, for better or worse. No Title I projects had been completed, and, in the interest of keeping real estate prices from spiking and to keep critics at bay, redevelopment plans were typically kept quiet, if not secret, until all funding and other agreements were in place.

In New York, for example, the first seven urban redevelopment plans—two projects in Greenwich Village, two in Harlem, and three more located in Williamsburg, Corlears Hook, and on Delancey Street—received little notice. People, reporters included, were slow to grasp the significance of Title I slum clearance or of Moses's appointment as chairman of a new Mayor's Committee on Slum Clearance. (Moses also held the titles of construction coordinator and planning commissioner.) However, as Robert Caro wrote in *The Power Broker*, "on the landscape of New York's history, that appointment stands out like a mountain." With the combination of Title I's powers of eminent domain and Moses's new power, "his control was complete at last."[15]

Typical of Moses's approach and such projects in general, Moses avoided presenting his projects until they were done deals—sites selected and mapped, design proposals drawn, and federal financing assured. Indeed, in 1951, the Slum Clearance Committee's plan to raze twenty-six blocks (fifty-four acres) south of Washington Square had attracted only a passing mention in the *New York Times*, despite the fact that it would remove almost "every familiar landmark" in the process. It was not until March 1952, when a significant but relatively small part of Moses's Greenwich Village redevelopment plan was ready to move forward, that the avant-garde among protesters began to mobilize the community. In response to a subsequent report in the *Times*, Shirley Hayes, the Parks Committee director of the recently established Greenwich Village Community Planning District, formed the Committee to Save Washington Square Park in order to fend off Moses's proposal to extend Fifth Avenue through the park and create a Parisian-style traffic circle around the Washington Square arch. Still virtually unknown were Moses's intentions to connect these new roads to a newly created boulevard, Fifth Avenue South, which would be developed with two superblock housing projects, Washington Square South and the South Village, on the razed twenty-six blocks.[16]

Although opposition gathered against the reconstruction of the park, the widening of existing roads bisecting the square, and the extension of Fifth Avenue, this was not true of the proposed slum-clearance projects for Greenwich Village itself. In August 1952—some years before Jacobs joined the fight for the park—Lewis Mumford voiced his support for the Hayes committee's counteroffensive to stop the reconstruction of Washington Square by eliminating all traffic through the park. However, Mumford advocated a renewal plan even larger than that proposed by Moses. Apparently unaware of the two housing projects already proposed, he wrote that the "area south of the Square, a ramshackle one at best, is ripe for a large-scale housing development." He believed that a plan was needed "for the redevelopment of the whole area south of the park, right down to Canal Street." Consistent with widely held beliefs about functional city zoning, such a plan would include "the ultimate removal of all industrial functions from the area." Without a comprehensive plan of this scale, Mumford argued, "nothing can save Washington Square, much less redeem it."[17]

Indeed, in the early 1950s, a "progressive" approach to city redevelopment meant avoiding a "piecemeal" approach and renovating large sections of the city from the ground up. It meant destroying more slums to build more modern housing, even if this meant displacing more people. In an August 1952 *Forum* article, "What Is Urban Redevelopment?," Mary Mix Foley accordingly editorialized in favor of a plan for Washington, DC, that would displace three-quarters of the existing population, as compared to a more "conservative" plan that would displace only one-half. Privileging redevelopment for the middle and upper incomes by moving poor people out of the city center was seen as part of this progressive approach. Siding with private redevelopment against the public housing–oriented position of the National Capital Park and Planning Commission, Foley presented overtly class-based, and not so subtly race-based, arguments for the "high-class residential areas" and "top-rank investment" for a "well-to-do tenancy" that would allegedly ensure the success of the redevelopment project. This, in Foley's eyes, was "bold use of the redevelopment title of the 1949 Housing Act" and like what was familiar in Norfolk and New York.[18]

The "Robert Moses approach" to slum clearance was not the only kind of urban redevelopment, however. Indeed, the so-called conservative approach that Foley rejected for Washington, DC, had spokesmen well before Jane Jacobs. As part of their contribution to the Southwest Washington redevelopment plan, the architects Louis Justement and Chloethiel Woodard Smith described a diversified community plan that would avoid dull "islands of families with similar income levels, interests, and ages"; keep the "old corner grocery"; and use public and semipublic buildings to provide "welcome breaks in design and scale." They valued the social, economic, and physical diversity of the city in ways like those articulated by Jacobs some years later. Challenging the architects' plan for diversity, Foley expressed the position of those who were drawn to the clarity of standardization and segregation: "To provide this variety within a large redevelopment is to take the hard way in planning. It is particularly difficult in southwest Washington," she opined, "because this area is predominately a Negro slum."[19]

Nevertheless, other city planners besides Smith were willing to take the hard way. In *Forum*'s April 1952 issue, published just before Jacobs started with the magazine, another alternative to the "Robert Moses approach" was described in "The Philadelphia Cure: Clearing Slums with Penicillin, Not Surgery." Viewed as a "conservative" but "startling new way" to rebuild the city, "the Philadelphia cure . . . escapes the violent postwar redevelopment pattern in our largest cities—the neighborhood leveling techniques of planners like blockbusting Bob Moses of N.Y., who smash enormous rundown areas off the map, and then hand the aching sites to single large agencies or insurance companies for slide-rule housing solutions."[20] This critique was very similar, both conceptually and rhetorically, to what Jacobs articulated later. Indeed, she wrote a very positive follow-up article to "The Philadelphia Cure" in 1955 and adopted many of the Philadelphia School's planning ideas as her own.

As developed by the City Planning Commission director Edmund Bacon and the chief coordinating architect-planner Louis Kahn, the Philadelphia cure emphasized six points of the Philadelphia approach—most of which were later explicitly advocated by Jacobs.

FIGURE 25. "The Philadelphia Cure," published in the month Jacobs sought employment at *Architectural Forum*, was another early article on urban redevelopment and a precursor to Jacobs's writing about Philadelphia. *AF* (Apr. 1952), 112.

First, smaller redevelopment areas were defined to avoid "monstrous single-project solutions" that depended on "big insurance company financing," like New York City's Stuyvesant Town.

Second, rebuilding sought to minimize the dislocation of present inhabitants for their own sake and in order to avoid the "political headaches" experienced, for example, in Chicago, with evictions and the threat of them.

Third, community meetings were conducted prior to drawing redevelopment plans in order to foster "democracy and good feeling" and avoid "the friction generated in such cities as New York when a planning boss such as Bob Moses confronts the neighborhood at a 'hearing' with a plan already cooked in total disregard of [local] feelings."

Fourth, the preservation of local institutions such as churches, schools, and clubs was regarded as protection of "the social structure of the area *as a neighborhood* held together by an institutional structure which other cities in their redevelopment and housing projects have unwittingly destroyed." Treating "only the spots of worst infection, Philadelphia expects the cure to spread" naturally.

Fifth, to coordinate development and make "whole city areas harmonious" while avoiding monolithic approaches to urban order, the Philadelphia cure would engage "architects skilled in urban design (as distinguished from spot architecture) to co-operate with the various architects hired by the separate builders of the separate projects."

Finally, sixth, the Philadelphia approach sought to "preserve the historical past of the area," its landmarks and "depth in time." Despite the greater expense, this plan maintained "strong spiritual values in giving a sense of *continuity of life* from generation to generation." According to Bacon, "There is a structure of institutions (in all neighborhoods) which has vitality . . . which ties the people together. Redevelopment, whenever possible, should give these institutions new strength and validity."[21]

In their physical design, Kahn's master plans—developed with the architects Kenneth Day, Louis McAllister, and Anne Tyng; the landscape architect Christopher Tunnard; and Bacon—generally avoided superblocks, instead arranging buildings with reference to existing city blocks. Although they continued to advance the modernist idea of space planning, influences came equally from traditional urbanism, making the scheme a notable interjection of architectural history into a field that had sought for decades to deny it. Influenced by Kahn's 1951 trip to Greece, the proposed organization of "promenades leading to open spaces" was described "as old as the oldest Greek towns." Bacon was also a student of city planning history. In *Design of Cities* (1967), he would trace the history of urban design from Greek and Roman cities to Philadelphia.[22]

Despite perpetuating the sick city metaphor, the Philadelphia cure reversed the widely held "medicine vs. surgery" argument, a motif of urban theory prescribed decades earlier by Le Corbusier in a similarly titled chapter in *The City of To-Morrow and Its Planning*. In addition to accepting a less radical and invasive approach, the physical, social, and procedural aspects of the Philadelphia plan were the beginning of the shift away from modernist urbanism. In the next ten to fifteen years, various aspects of the

Philadelphia plan would develop into disciplines and specialties in their own right: community planning, in-fill development, historic preservation, and urban design. When she later followed up on "The Philadelphia Cure" article, Jacobs quickly recognized the plan's virtues, and she absorbed the innovative aspects of Kahn's and Bacon's city planning ideas into her own urban theory.[23]

Praise for the City-Planner Approach

Jacobs's first article as a full-time staff member was a profile of the architect Isadore Rosenfield. But even while working the hospital and schools desk at *Forum*, she thought about the city. Thus, rather than write a typical hospital-of-the-month story, she decided to write an article about an architect she considered exemplary for approaching his projects like a city planner. Indeed, in contrast with her frequently negative opinion of architects and city planners in *Death and Life*, her September 1952 article is evidence that Jacobs idealized the city planning profession in the early 1950s.[24]

Jacobs met Rosenfield in July 1952 as part of her early hospital research and liked him immediately. Rosenfield was a Harvard-trained architect and the designer and consultant for more than sixty hospitals, as well as the chief architect of the New York Department of Hospitals and of the city's Department of Public Works. He also consulted for other architects, including Kahn, who designed the Radbill Building of the Philadelphia Psychiatric Hospital, which likely led to Jacobs and Kahn's first meeting, in advance of her January 1953 article "New Hospital Type." (In that article, Jacobs praised both the design and functionality of the building. "Kahn has given his building gentleness and joy," she wrote. "[But] there is nothing namby-pamby about the gentleness of Kahn's design, no homogenized simplicity. 'I like my buildings to have knuckles,' he says. The bend in the slab at the knuckly corridor intersection is primarily to express different functions of the short wing on first and third floors and to give variety to [the] second-floor interior vista. The bend also makes best use of slope and garden space for [the] ground-floor dining room.")[25]

As with Kahn, it was less Rosenfield's aesthetic sensibility than his non-dogmatic way of thinking that Jacobs found most compelling. Anticipating themes and rhetoric in *Death and Life*, she described his "inquisitive and

ROSENFIELD AND HIS HOSPITALS

He approaches his jobs like a city planner

FIGURE 26. In "Rosenfield and His Hospitals," Jacobs's first article as a full-time staff member of *Architectural Forum*, she praised the architect's "city-planner approach." *AF* (Sept. 1952), 128.

independent approach to social thinking" as "unorthodox" and "like nothing taught in schools of architecture." Rosenfield, Jacobs related, had moved from the study of social ethics and settlement-house work into the study of architecture in the 1920s, but he had maintained in his work his sensitivity to the human element. She approved of the way Rosenfield made hospital service "dignified" and made patients "feel they are really considered as individuals." This sensitivity extended from physical aspects such as site specificity to an "elastic definition of function" that included "not only the machinery, but the emotional content."[26]

What particularly distinguished Rosenfield's methodology from that of "academic" architects was his city-planner approach. In her idealized view in 1952, this meant not unquestioningly accepting the client's program or secondhand knowledge, but engaging the design problem with empirical and user-oriented research. Setting out her expectations of architects and city planners for years to come, she praised Rosenfield's method (see the epigraph for this chapter).[27] Although her ideas about city planning changed, Jacobs saw and projected the empirical, inductive, and people- and context-oriented methodology that she advocated in *Death and Life* as important habits of thought for studying cities already in one of her first articles as an architectural critic, which also demonstrated her determination to write about cities and urban redevelopment, despite her initial job description.

Jacobs's writing focused on hospitals and schools for the next year, but it was not long before she reviewed larger design projects that provided a bridge to writing about urban redevelopment. Her first break came in late 1952, as *Forum*'s editors prepared for the "New Thinking" theme for the magazine in 1953, in the form of the regional shopping mall, a new building type that had a significant relationship with the city and suburb. By her own account, "New Thinking on Shopping Centers," published in March 1953, was the first in a list of articles that she considered most relevant to her self-described "interest in writing about the nature of cities."[28]

"New Thinking on Shopping Centers" was a twenty-four-page feature meant to rival the special issue on shopping centers published by *Progressive Architecture* a year earlier. It examined four case studies of the new building typology, which had been largely invented by the architect-planner Victor Gruen to replace or compete with traditional downtown shopping districts. Jacobs argued that "the time has come for downtown to begin borrowing" ideas from such successful shopping centers. It was an idea that she may actually have also heard from Kahn, who, in his 1953 article "Toward a New Plan for Midtown Philadelphia," proposed "stimulat[ing] more imaginative development of [the city's] shopping areas, along the lines of the new suburban shopping centers, which already provide a pattern of movement sympathetic to the pedestrian and the motor."[29]

The four case studies in Jacobs's essay were Gruen's Southdale Shopping Center in Minneapolis; Mondawmin in Baltimore, Maryland, developed by James Rouse and a design team including the MIT dean of architecture Pietro Belluschi and the landscape architect Dan Kiley; Parker Square in Wichita Falls, Texas, by Ketchum, Gina & Sharp Architects; and Stonestown in San Francisco, by Welton Becket and Associates. In preparing the article, Jacobs got to know Gruen and Rouse, both of whom she later cited in *Death and Life*.[30]

FIGURE 27. Jacobs visiting the Mondawmin shopping center in Baltimore with the developer James Rouse in October 1952 while conducting research for her March 1953 feature "New Thinking on Shopping Centers." Jacobs Papers.

Indeed, all four shopping centers meant to compete with Main Street, USA. Unlike the more homogeneous retail venues that shopping centers have become, these were all multiuse developments, planned with adjacent middle-class housing projects, medical centers, supermarkets, office buildings, community centers, and upscale restaurants designed to pull in shoppers "who might otherwise go downtown." Although located three miles from the center of Baltimore, Mondawmin was specifically designed to be "a second 'downtown.'" As in Southdale, a broad "buffer" zone— containing offices, a medical center, a large new residential subdivision, and miles of new roads—was designed to control so-called parasitic competition and create an atmosphere conducive to shopping. In addition to being monopolistic, these developments wielded the suburban version of the urban renewal tool known as "excess condemnation," through which the developer or authority profited from the anticipated spike in neighboring real estate values.[31]

Although she came to regret her early writing about urban redevelopment, Jacobs uncritically repeated the real estate boosters' arguments.

Describing Gruen's Southdale development, she reported that the "town-plan conscious" developers had created a "blightproof neighborhood to increase and stabilize the value of the site." To forestall decay, she continued, "the land plan protects residential areas from center traffic; uses office buildings, apartment houses and landscaped strips as transition zones between commercial and residential areas; and protects other residential borders with parks." The Dayton Company, she continued, "will get the benefit of higher land values created by the shopping center." These ideas were aligned with the centralized, functionalist, monopolistic, and suburban approach to urban redevelopment that Jacobs would later attack, not that of the integrated and multifunctioning city she later championed.[32]

Indeed, through at least 1954, Jacobs made the case for the position she would later condemn. She advocated applying the lessons of suburbia to downtown, city planning, superblock redevelopment, and urban renewal. "Since the war, almost nothing had happened downtown. There has been no big store construction," she wrote. "Now the shopping centers are so far ahead, the time has come for downtown to begin borrowing back."[33]

Likely influenced by Gruen here, Jacobs argued that city planning was essential for urban redevelopment. "The first—the most elementary—lesson for downtown is simply the importance of planning," she wrote. "Every unplanned suburban strip losing out to a planned shopping center is a lesson in survival that cannot be ignored." By this she did not mean just avoiding competitive anarchy or visual blight, but the very type of controlled planning—with condemnations and the clearance of all "non-conforming (as residential) buildings and blighted structures"—that she later excoriated. In Chicago, these lessons were being applied by the city's Planning Commission to rehabilitate two shopping districts north and south of the Loop. Jacobs wrote approvingly of the creation of superblocks with "one-way traffic perimeters, elimination of most interior streets, and removal of blighted and irrelevant buildings" to "help save the city's core."[34]

Real estate developers also offered lessons in realistic and community-oriented planning. In order to protect their investments, the best shopping center planners, Jacobs reported, have "become community planners in self defense." A year of planning preceded Southland's zoning approval, and it included the distribution by the developers of more than five thousand "attractive little brochures to everyone in the area, explaining exactly what they proposed to do and why, showed slides of the project, invited and answered questions." At the crucial town meeting, three hundred voters turned up, and only three persons voted against rezoning. City planners, she concluded, could learn something from the real estate developers: "The developers explained their purposes to the citizenry and won zoning changes in a way to give experienced city planners pause. Here is the idealism of town planning actually become reality—not another buried report—because it fits the cold facts of good merchandising. Frightened downtown merchants, please take note."[35]

Jacobs's favorable attitude toward current trends in city planning persisted into 1954, as evident in a review of Gruen's Northland Regional Shopping Center in Detroit. Although she later condemned Clarence Stein's planning ideas as being fundamentally anti-urban, at this time she actually praised Stein and Henry Wright's design for Radburn, New Jersey, a "suburban Garden City for the motor age." Northland, Jacobs wrote, "is a classic in shopping center planning, in the sense that Rockefeller Center is a classic in urban skyscraper-group planning, or Radburn, N.J. in suburban residential planning." It was "a new thing in modern town planning."[36]

Indeed, Northland was truly a "classic" suburban mall—it was a giant suburban building surrounded by a sea of twelve thousand parking spaces and a ring of highways. Blind to its inadequacies, Jacobs saw its best attributes, and probably what Gruen wanted her to see: "a city within a city," a modern version of the traditional city. Gruen's charm on her was clear. Northland, she wrote, "is a rediscovery rather than an invention." Jacobs reported that the most frequent comment by visitors—up to fifty thousand a day—to the shopping mall was "you wouldn't know you were in Detroit." Nevertheless, she saw in Northland the architectural imitations of the city: The ground floor simulated "Main Street." The basement level provided "what side streets are to the downtown area." And the "strong, clear, overall architecture" was designed "to permit downtown variety."[37]

Writing about Northland must have reminded Jacobs of her first essays about the city, as well as her reading of Henri Pirenne's books on the rebirth of cities and commerce in the Middle Ages. Despite the cars and the acres upon acres of parking lots circling the mall, Northland had "old roots." She saw within it an echo of medieval market towns, like old Ludlow in Shropshire, a plan of which illustrated her point. Northland had an "urban-character" that was different than the typical American attitude toward open space, which she described as having the "rural-character" of the minimally defined village common. It was also unlike the typical vehicle-oriented Main Street: Although one could only get to Northland by car, within the mall, "Shopping traffic has come full circle. It is right back where it started—with the pedestrian." Northland was thus "a planning classic because it is the first modern pedestrian commercial center to use an urban 'market town' plan, a compact form physically and psychologically suited to pedestrian shopping."[38]

These were lessons that Jacobs believed could be naturally applied within the city, and in this sense, Jacobs's interpretations may have influenced Gruen in turn. Suggesting an approach to urban redevelopment, she wrote that Northland's "flexible market-town use of open spaces looks like a natural for coping with rehabilitation of blight-spotted decaying shopping districts." Whether she suggested this to Gruen, or vice versa, is uncertain. However, prior to Northland, Gruen was a forceful advocate of decentralization, and his shopping centers were specially designed to compete with downtowns. In *Mall Maker*, the historian Jeffrey Hardwick indicates that Gruen began applying the "market-town" idea to decaying downtown shopping districts around December 1954. But regardless of who influenced whom, Gruen's plan for the redevelopment of Fort Worth, Texas—which sought to stem the flight of commerce out of the city that he had helped to accelerate with the invention of the suburban shopping center, and which Jacobs praised in a 1956 review—would attempt to apply the old "market-town" ideas to the redevelopment of the modern city.[39]

Decentralization Is Centralization

Jacobs later condemned the displacement of local stores by supermarkets and chain stores, and she bemoaned downtowns that were "lackluster imitations of standardized suburban chain-store shopping." She characterized shopping center planning as a form of "monopoly planning" and "repressive zoning" that created not just commercial monopolies but civic ones. "Monopolistic shopping centers and monumental cultural centers cloak, under the public relations hoo-haw, the subtraction of commerce, and of culture too, from the intimate and casual life of cities," she wrote. This type of planning, she explained, "artificially contrives commercial monopolies for city neighborhoods . . . [but] although monopoly insures the financial success planned for it, it fails the city socially." Jacobs's experience as one of the first architectural critics to review shopping centers made her especially sensitive to the deployment of shopping-center planning principles within the city.[40]

In fact, Jacobs's doubts about top-down, monopolizing, segregating, and suburbanizing planning approaches appeared soon after "New Thinking on Shopping Centers," but in another unexpected venue—her favorable review of a modern elementary school in New Orleans.

In the April 1953 article "Good-by Neighborhood Schools?" (a pun on *good-bye*, to *do good by*, and *good buy*), Jacobs took aim at decentralization, arguing that a plan by the City of New Orleans to consolidate city schools into a new suburban school complex for financial reasons was bad for social reasons. Prefiguring her critique of shopping centers in *Death and Life*, she observed that the planners had "hit, *at least economically*, on a plausible solution to the intolerable poverty of the public schools in many of our big rich cities." However, she regarded the city's proposal for busing city children to a centralized, suburban "school village" as a substitution of bureaucratic regimentation and standardization for local participation in neighborhood affairs and influence over the school. Although the suburbs, she argued, were thought to advance physical and social decentralization, the opposite was actually true: "It has become fashionable to call shifting anything to the suburbs 'decentralization.' But the school village idea, suburban or no, is centralization. It makes a homogenous big thing out of diverse little things. It carries the potential (perhaps inevitable?) flaw of centralization: loss of 'amateur' community participation, increase in remote and ingrown bureaucratic control."[41]

The so-called school village in the suburbs, Jacobs believed, was "inherently unfitted to play the easy, intimate role in community life" that the neighborhood school could play in the city, and it would do nothing to meet the needs of a community that lacked in "almost any sort of meeting hall, banquet room, exhibit gallery, library and clubrooms." She regarded the neighborhood school, in other words, not only as embodying community participation and control, but also as functioning as a multipurpose community building that served everyone in the neighborhood, not just students.

On these grounds, Jacobs argued against the suburban superschool and in favor of a new neighborhood school design. Jacobs had many good things to say about the Thomy Lafon Elementary School—a long, corridorless, modernist bar building raised on piloti, built in 1954—whose architects, Curtis & Davis, became known for their regional modernism and received an American Institute of Architects award for the project. However, she was certainly less interested in the design than in the building's social function in the community context. She recognized the validity of the arguments of New Orleans' reformers, who felt that the children bused to the new "school village," mostly African American children from a slum known as "Back-A-Town," would have an opportunity to spend their school day away from "a pretty nasty environment" known for high illiteracy, disease, crime, and delinquency rates. Nevertheless, she offered that one needed to look beyond the superficial appearances of the disenfranchised neighborhood and recognize its underestimated community values. Rehearsing her arguments about the hidden order that could be found under the superficial chaos of cities, she stated:

> the tangible beauty, charm and spaciousness of good schoolhouses are easy to recognize as excellences. The queer, complicated excellences that are able to abide with happenstance ugliness and inefficiency—but not with imposed perfection—are harder to see; and how are they to be valued? What is the worth of a PTA that aggravates a principal as much as it supports him? What is the worth of a paper boat in a sidewalk puddle between home and school? It takes some mighty delicate scales to find the answers, but the answers are vital.[42]

With these remarkable questions, which suggest the return of Jacobs's independent voice after the constraints of *The Iron Age* and government work, Jacobs saw the city's virtues through the veneers of ugliness and inefficiency in the years just before the proliferation of urban renewal projects.

A month later, Jacobs wrote more on the topic of local knowledge and self-determination. Although again not directly concerned with city planning, her May 1953 article "Marshall Shaffer: Teacher-at-Large of Hospital Architecture," which was part of the feature "New Thinking on Hospitals," provided the opportunity to discuss her changing views of the design and planning professions. Whereas her profile of Rosenfield had praised his city-planner approach, her ideas now had much more in common with the critical views that she would articulate in *Death and Life*.

Marshall Shaffer was the director of the Hospital Facilities Division of the U.S. Public Health Service and a former associate of Richard Neutra. In Shaffer, Jacobs found an exemplar of good government and a teacher unencumbered by dogmatism. His philosophy, which Jacobs quoted in *Death and Life*, was summed up in a sign that hung above his desk: "A fool can put on his clothes better than a wise man can do it for him."[43]

Shaffer expressed the wisdom that Jacobs later used to criticize paternalistic city planners. Rather than set up a centralized federal hospital authority, with its own hospital design staff or list of approved firms, Shaffer created a "decentralized" regional network designed to train local architects to build hospitals for their own communities. "When the government prepared to parcel out money for locally owned hospitals [under the Lanham and Hill-Burton Acts of 1941 and 1946]," Jacobs wrote, "he could have argued convincingly that the hinterland was not ready to cope with the design problems." This would have been the "logical" thing to do, she acknowledged. But when it came to hospital design, Shaffer asserted, "These jobs must be done by *any architect* the local community or hospital board chooses. If he [the architect] doesn't know how to design hospitals we will help him learn. . . . You can't legislate good design. Let's have no cut-and-dried answer. Let's keep booby traps out and red tape down. Good design has to come up from the architects, not down from the government."[44]

Shaffer, like Jacobs, rejected paternalism. "He runs a government office," Jacobs underscored, "*that does not duplicate anything that outside individuals or organizations can be taught to do for themselves.*" Redefining the slogan concerning regional "decentralization," she believed that this approach required "imagination, gregariousness, ingenuity, and a passionate belief in decentralization." Embracing the overarching principle that "all architects are created equal," Shaffer set up a regional and state network to assist local architects during six key stages of the design process. In doing so, he regulated only "an absolute minimum, a floor; there never would be a design ceiling or even . . . 'suggested standards' or 'ideals.'" Rather than overdesigning, he found that the most common problem was "design that skimps too much at the expense of reasonable quality." "One of the best things about this job," Shaffer told Jacobs, "has been watching the architects rise to the occasion, and I mean especially the men nobody had ever heard of outside their own town. . . . They've done a magnificent job, better than Washington could possibly have done for them."[45]

Shaffer was clearly cut from the same cloth as Jacobs, and years later, when Jacobs wrote *Death and Life*, she recalled his approach as she thought through the problems of public housing. City, state, and federal housing authorities had set qualitative and quantitative caps on public housing, she observed, but there was no logical reason for the government to dictate so severely the use of public housing subsidies. Government did not, as a rule, take over the running of museums that receive public subsidies, nor did it run subsidized hospitals, she argued, with the late Marshall Shaffer's—and perhaps others'—ideas about decentralizing decision making in mind.

Pittsburgh's Radiant City Experiment

Nineteen fifty-three was a year of firsts for *Forum*'s writing on cities. It was during that year that *Forum* would write about Kitimat, British Columbia, "the first complete new town in North America." It was the year *Forum* reviewed the first completed Title I slum clearance and redevelopment project, Pittsburgh's Gateway Center. And it was the year that Haskell first came to recognize Jacobs's abilities as a writer on cities and redevelopment issues: Within a year of her start at *Forum*, Haskell picked her to write the feature on Kitimat, telling the executive editor Perry Prentice, "It seems to me the only writer we can assign to this is Jane Jacobs. She alone will have the capacity of giving it the human touch while digging into the details."[46]

In the end, Albert Mayer, who designed the town with Clarence Stein, wrote the Kitimat story himself, although Jacobs edited the piece for publication in July 1954. Nevertheless, working on the story offered an opportunity to study Stein's prior housing and town plans—Sunnyside Gardens, Radburn, Chatham Village, Baldwin Hills village, and the Greenbelt towns—all of which she would criticize in *Death and Life* for being fundamentally anti-urban. Although it would be about a year before she had another chance to write a major city feature, editing the Kitimat article exemplified how her day-to-day work at *Forum* provided part of the education necessary to write her great book, even when she wasn't writing the articles.

Meanwhile, writing at *Forum* passed another new threshold of architectural criticism, setting the stage further for Jacobs's future writing. In this case, the author was Haskell, who described his review of Pittsburgh's Gateway Center, "Architecture: Stepchild or Fashioner of Cities?," to his friend William Wurster as "the first piece of architectural criticism that has been so direct and outspoken since around 1928, when two or three magazines retreated in the face of libel suit threats."[47]

FIGURE 28. Gateway Center was one of the first major postwar urban redevelopment projects. In an article, Haskell praised planning concepts attributed to Le Corbusier, and he argued for greater participation of architects in the urban design process. *AF* (Dec. 1953), 112–13.

Located at one of the points of Pittsburgh's Golden Triangle, Gateway Center was a slum clearance redevelopment project first reviewed by Haskell in September 1950, not long after the passage of the Housing Act of 1949, when the project was being prepared for construction. Although *Forum* reviewed only important projects before completion, Gateway Center deserved special attention. It was an early urban redevelopment project, and it was being orchestrated by large, pre–Title I public-private redevelopment interests in New York, including the real estate giant Robert Dowling, the Equitable Insurance Company, and the architectural firm Eggers & Higgins, who were also architects and consultants for a number of Robert Moses's slum-clearance plans. Irwin Clavan, the project architect, had been a job captain for the Empire State Building and a key member of the "Board

of Design" for Williamsburg Houses, Parkchester, and Stuyvesant Town—
projects whose site planning and building forms bore a resemblance to
Gateway's design, as well as Le Corbusier's Radiant City ideas of the late
1920s. However, as Haskell had indicated in "Pittsburgh and the Architect's
Problem," his preconstruction review, "Perhaps no other project drama-
tizes so clearly the problem of the architect at mid-century."[48]

The problems of the architectural profession at midcentury, and of
Gateway Center, were indeed complicated, but in ways unfamiliar since
Jacobs wrote *Death and Life*. When Gateway Center was completed in 1953,
Forum's December 1953 review was headlined "Le Corbusier Made This
Prophetic Sketch in 1922: Now, at Last . . . Office Towers in a Park" and
was accompanied by an image of Le Corbusier's City for Three Million.
The article said, "Some may see in Gateway not much more than three
rather undistinguished buildings. To planners, however, Gateway is surely
something more important: Here, for the first time in US city planning, the
concept of office towers in a park has made good sense in economic terms.
It has made sense to men who may have never heard of Le Corbusier's
'Ville Radieuse.' And having once made sense to these eminently practical
men, the concept can no longer be shrugged off as the dream of some
unrealistic visionary."[49]

Decades after Le Corbusier's original idea, Gateway Center played out
a scenario from the architect's thirty-year-old proposal to rebuild the city
center to ensure its economic and productive success. This, however, was
not seen to be a problem. Haskell described the project, which replaced a
twenty-three-acre derelict industrial district with a park adorned by three
cruciform office towers (similar to Le Corbusier's Cartesian skyscrapers),
as making "good sense." His words were written without cynicism. On the
contrary, as Haskell wrote in 1950, "The basic concept of big city office
buildings widely spaced in a 23-acre park is indeed noble—the first realiza-
tion of Le Corbusier's generation-old dream." Although he had reservations about the buildings' design, which he repeated in his 1953 editorial,
the underlying city planning concept made the completed project a "major
accomplishment."[50]

In contrast with Jacobs's criticisms in *Death and Life*, what Haskell and
others regarded as the problem was that Gateway Center's planning and its
similarities to Le Corbusier's Radiant City were *accidental*. As revealed in
discussions with Robert Dowling, despite an architectural tradition dating
back millennia, site planning, or "plot design," was not regarded as part

of the architect's purview. Plot design, Dowling asserted, "has to do with economics. It is basically an economic question." Only after the financial structure and the rentable space were accounted for were architects brought in, and, "if they have any better ideas, it is too bad, because the basic plan has already been worked out."[51] The idea that the architect was excluded from the planning stage, and only brought in to "clean up" the design, was so dissatisfying to Haskell that he organized a roundtable on the subject "The Need for Better Planning" in order to discuss the problem and the project.

In the discussion, which Jacobs edited for publication, Haskell asserted that an architect *had* contributed to the project's basic design. The credit for this, Haskell argued, had to go to Le Corbusier. "One reason that Mr. Dowling got the plot plan that he has for his Gateway project in Pittsburgh is because of ideas thought out by that great man, Le Corbusier, in France, many years before. He maintained that you should put your cities into parks instead of putting parks into cities," Haskell explained. "If it hadn't been for that architect's idea, Mr. Dowling's plot plan would bear no resemblance to what it now is." To this Dowling replied, "Despite Le Corbusier, with all his greatness, we were not conscious of his influence." Gruen, a roundtable participant, retorted, "Either consciously or subconsciously, that is where it came from."[52]

This discussion, in other words, revealed that, thirty years after their conception, the modernist city planning ideas of the 1920s—what Jacobs later called "orthodox" modernism—still had tremendous momentum, were still considered novel and experimental, while being tested for the first time. Nevertheless, architects were not making the planning decisions: Haskell's complaint, although misguided, was that architects were not the direct agents of the plan. As Jacobs later observed in *Death and Life*, possibly with Gateway Center in mind, "Bankers and government administrative officials who guarantee mortgages do not invent planning theories nor, surprisingly, even economic doctrine about cities. They are enlightened nowadays, and they pick up their ideas from idealists, a generation late."

Moreover, although Le Corbusier and other idealists may have set these ideas spinning, as Jacobs later charged, by the time Gateway Center was built, Le Corbusier had abandoned his machine aesthetic and other principles of the 1920s, thereby contributing significantly to the impending breakup of the Congrès Internationaux d'Architecture Moderne (CIAM), which had already begun to fracture over dissension about CIAM's city planning principles. CIAM's eighth meeting in July 1951, held in England and focused on the theme "The Heart of the City," was a forum for postwar postmortems of prewar ideas and various doubts and attacks on the Functional City ideas of the 1930s.[53]

In 1953, however, the dissolution of CIAM, and the collapse of orthodox modern architecture that it symbolized, was still some years off. Thus, although the tipping point was on the horizon, at the time Gateway Center was completed, Haskell felt no need to criticize the underlying modernist planning concepts that were visible in the Pittsburgh project, and he focused his critique on the architectural design and the architect's absent role in site planning.

In the architectural critique he later boasted of, Haskell decried Gateway's stainless steel–clad buildings as "painted-on" architecture and a "weak modernique, lacking in proportion, texture, and dignity, let alone the mystery or power that would differentiate them from 'up-ended diners.'" This was not a completely new line of criticism for him, or of Irwin Clavan. It echoed two of his earliest pieces of architectural criticism: his 1930 appraisal of the "modernique" Chrysler Building and his 1931 review of the Empire State Building, in which he described Clavan's mooring mast design for the Empire State as among the building's worst parts. The criticism connected the "vulgarization" of modernism in the Art Deco period with that of Late Modernism; it also raised new failures of functionalism. The architect's problem, Haskell stated, would "not be resolved until everyone abandons the hope that naïve functionalism is any guarantee of beauty." Although this aspect of his critique was not well articulated, Haskell and his contemporaries, including Jacobs, recognized that vulgarized modernism was beginning to have an impact on the city through new urban redevelopment, and, in order to solve the crisis of modern architecture, "naïve functionalism" needed to be replaced by a more meaningful modern architecture.[54]

While Haskell did not object to the tower-in-a-park concept, he made a few important arguments. First, he advocated for a greater role for the architect in the site and city planning process. In Gateway Center, he felt that the plan was uninspired and that this was because the architects had been "[left] out until the last minute," until after "the basic pattern had been set." As a consequence, the architecture was "not up to the genuine poetry of its ideas" or its site; the "arrangement of the towers in their park [was] purely mechanical"; and "the landscaping between them [made] no fresh statement about our grand new world." Haskell emphasized that "a great architect *working with the planners from the very start* could have contributed . . . the inspiration to make the whole greater than the parts, the creativeness to make the buildings really sing." Dowling confirmed that it was real estate developers and other economic interests, not architects, who were defining postwar city planning.[55]

Finally, Haskell made a general argument for city building in the remainder of his editorial, which would open the door to Jacobs's later criticism and urban theory. Citing Florentine and Venetian civic spaces, Haskell argued that architecture had a city-building function and that Gateway Center had missed an opportunity to create a "civic center" that would be "the crown and focus of urban life." As such, his argument was part of the widely felt stirrings of the revived field of "civic design."

In this sense, when Haskell told Wurster that his 1953 editorial was an important, even historic, advance in American architectural criticism, he had some justification. As he wrote Wurster in January 1954, "Even Lewis [Mumford] is compelled by *The New Yorker* to work very carefully around such situations." Indeed, despite Haskell's caution, Gateway Center's developer subsequently contacted *Forum*'s executive editors, indicated previous talks with their lawyers, and expressed the "unmistakable suggestion that we lay off him."[56]

Jacobs returned to Gateway Center in *Death and Life* in part because it was a memorable project from her work at *Forum*. In the book, she described Gateway Center more or less as Haskell had done—as "a Radiant City office and hotel project with the buildings set here and there in empty land"—although for her this was exactly what was wrong with it. Based on a better understanding of how cities worked, Jacobs would see Gateway Center in a very different way from the way Haskell did. Quoting Richard Nelson, whose studies of urban behavior preceded Holly Whyte's similar work, she observed that on a typical September afternoon, Nelson counted only three people using Gateway Park: "one old lady knitting, one bum, one unidentifiable character asleep with a newspaper over his face." Contrasting Gateway Park with downtown Pittsburgh's Mellon Square, where there were too many people to count, she concluded, "City park users simply do not seek settings for buildings. They seek settings for themselves. To them, parks are foreground, buildings background, rather than the reverse."

Gateway Center, in other words, would become emblematic of Jacobs's own "paradigm shift," which, as Thomas Kuhn described it, was a new way of looking at the same thing, like "a change in visual gestalt [where] the marks on paper that were first seen as a bird are now seen as an antelope, or vice versa." However, it took time to resolve the image, and although Jacobs has received well-deserved praise for her powers of observation, in 1953, she did not see things as clearly as she did later in that decade.[57]

CHAPTER 5

"Seeds of Self-Regeneration" for City Deserts

And still the deserts of the city have grown and still they are growing, the awful endless blocks, the endless miles of drabness and chaos. A good way to see the problem of the city is to take a bus or streetcar ride, a long ride, through a city you do not know. For in this objective frame of mind, you may stop thinking about the ugliness long enough to think of the work that went into this mess. As a sheer manifestation of energy it is awesome. It says as much about the power and doggedness of life as the leaves of the forest say in spring. Hundreds of thousands of people with hundreds of thousands of plans and purposes built the city and only they will rebuild the city. All else can only be oases in the desert.
—Jane Jacobs, 1955

ON AUGUST 2, 1954, President Eisenhower signed the U.S. Housing Act of 1954 into law, creating the federal Urban Renewal program. Three months later, in November 1954, the U.S. Supreme Court ruled unanimously on the constitutionality of the police power that was necessary to make "urban renewal" a reality.

City rebuilders like Robert Moses had been waiting since the early 1930s for developments like these. Whereas the U.S. Housing Act of 1949 had provided for slum clearance and "urban redevelopment," the new act, which introduced the term "urban renewal," inaugurated a sweeping

160

approach to the problems of slums and blight. Whereas the previous objectives had been clearing slums and redeveloping the razed areas, the act now granted local governments the power to attempt to prevent the spread of urban blight and the "cancerous growth" of new slums through conservation, rehabilitation, modernization, and razing—a much more ambitious, subjective, and constitutionally questionable set of tasks.[1]

Nevertheless, *Berman v. Parker*, a case stemming from a slum clearance master plan for Washington, DC, cleared away the remaining obstacles in the path of the nation's city planners and rebuilders. According to a news story in the November 1954 issue of *Architectural Forum*, just a few weeks before the Supreme Court's ruling, "cities in the past few years have been challenged repeatedly on the constitutionality of their slum clearance laws. . . . As of last month, in 21 of 23 states where the question has been put to test, the laws have been validated." *Berman v. Parker* put the question to rest at the federal level by achieving a ruling against the plaintiff, whose viable and nonblighted department store was slated to be taken through eminent domain and razed as part of the District of Columbia Redevelopment Land Agency's blight-fighting plan. In a unanimous decision, the Court declared on November 22, 1954, "It is within the power of the legislature to determine that the community should be beautiful as well as healthy, spacious as well as clean, well-balanced as well as carefully patrolled." It followed, the Court argued, that urban renewal "need not, by force of the Constitution, be on a piecemeal basis—lot by lot, building by building." Even sound structures could be taken and destroyed if they fell within the determined urban renewal area.[2]

Thus, *Berman v. Parker* upheld the ambitions of federal and state urban renewal programs, as *Forum*'s writer (perhaps Jacobs herself) anticipated, and it "cut back an undergrowth of litigation that is hampering . . . efforts." Disentangled from the understory of grassroots resistance, beginning in 1955, the number of urban renewal projects in planning and construction rose dramatically each year through the early 1960s.[3]

Although the Housing Act of 1954 accepted compromises that had precedents in the Housing Act of 1949, the historian Richard Flanagan characterized the new act as a historic turn in national urban policy. Before 1954, he wrote, "New Deal politicians and liberal interest groups struggled against conservatives to expand federal sponsorship of public housing construction. Liberals argued that federal aid was needed to replace slum housing and meet potential housing shortages for the poor and working class.

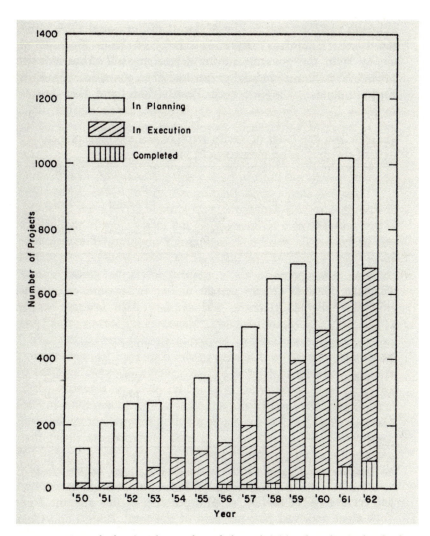

FIGURE 29. A graph showing the number of planned, initiated, and completed urban renewal projects between 1950 and 1962—the same years during which Jacobs wrote about the subject in *Amerika, Architectural Forum,* and *Death and Life*. Relatively few projects were executed following the passage of the Housing Act of 1949, but numbers climbed after the 1954 act, which enabled a more aggressive approach to "urban renewal." Drawn from data from the 1962 annual report of the Urban Renewal Administration, the graph is included in Martin Anderson, *The Federal Bulldozer: A Critical Analysis of Urban Renewal, 1949–1962* (Cambridge, MA: MIT Press, 1964), 43, which cited *Death and Life*. Courtesy of Martin Anderson.

Conservatives retorted that public housing was expensive, unnecessary, and socialistic." However, the Housing Act of 1954 "transcended the acrimonious divide between liberals and conservatives, forging a new consensus that emphasized commercial redevelopment instead of public housing as the answer to central city decline. . . . The Eisenhower administration sought to satisfy moderates in both parties with urban renewal, a policy intended to revitalize the commercial prospects of downtown business districts and increase the size of the urban economic pie."[4]

Thus, despite the fact that urban renewal, and its theorists and practitioners, was later vilified by Jacobs and others, its federal policies initially received sustained and broad social support. And, in this context, Jacobs's own early acceptance and even advocacy of urban renewal were not surprising, especially at a time when completed Title I redevelopment projects were few in number.

What distinguished Jacobs from others was how quickly she not only perceived the failures of urban renewal, but also developed a new vision of the city. Within ten months of the passage of the housing act, her idealized view of city planning began to dissipate. In this, she was not alone and not the first. In April 1955, Jacobs, Lewis Mumford, and her colleague Walter McQuade (also a Greenwich Village resident) joined an ongoing battle with Robert Moses in order to save Washington Square from reconstruction. Shirley Hayes, the Greenwich Village Community Planning District parks committee director, led the charge. By then in its third year, Hayes's Committee to Save Washington Square Park organized a petition and letter-writing campaign to oppose Moses's continued attempts to widen the roads through the park. In its latest incarnation, the road would take the form of a depressed expressway, a miniature version of the Cross Bronx Expressway, which had recently resumed construction a few miles to the north after overcoming lawsuits and protests.

The petition, signed by Jacobs on April 30, 1955, marks the start of her Greenwich Village activism. It read: "I am opposed to the proposed plan for a depressed four-lane roadway, or any other highway through or around Washington Square Park. I am for the Alternate Plan to close Washington Square Park to all vehicular traffic with a bus turn-around back of the Arch." Handwritten at the bottom was Jacobs's personal note to Hayes: "Thanks for your good work. I've written the Mayor and Borough President, each, the attached letter. Please keep me informed of any other effective action that can be taken."[5]

Jacobs's short letter to Mayor Robert F. Wagner Jr. and the borough president Hulan Jack is revealing of not only changes in her frame of mind, but also her shock. Jacobs, the person perhaps most closely associated with opposition to urban renewal today, and at the time an architectural journalist, seems to have been unaware, at the time, of the plans for her own neighborhood. "I have heard with alarm and almost with disbelief, the plans to run a sunken highway through the center of Washington Square," she wrote.[6]

Moreover, although the letter reveals her love of the city, it suggests that perceptions about slums infiltrated even her thinking. She recognized that transforming a storefront building into a family home, as she and her husband had done, was considered eccentric at a time when developments like Stuyvesant Town and Levittown were the popular middle-class choices for dwelling. "My husband and I are among the citizens who truly believe in New York," she continued, "to the extent that we have bought a home in the heart of the city and remodeled it with a lot of hard work (transforming it from slum property) and are raising our three children here." The Jacobses' daughter, Mary, their third child, had recently been born.

But, at the same time, Jacobs's letters to the mayor and borough president reveal the unraveling of her idealism, which, by the time she finished writing *Death and Life*, had turned close to cynicism. "It is very discouraging to try to do our best to make the city more habitable," she concluded, "and then to learn that the city itself is thinking up schemes to make it uninhabitable."[7]

By contrast, Mumford's contribution to Hayes's Washington Square campaign—a letter to the editor of *The Villager*, also in April 1954—was far less polite. Foreshadowing Jacobs's later rhetoric, Mumford's letter (which may have inspired hers) sanctioned public outrage and protest. "The proposed plan to connect West Broadway with Fifth Avenue, by means of an open-cut speedway running through Washington Square is almost too inept to be taken seriously," he wrote. "If there were any general planning intelligence among those responsible, it would have been laughed out of existence long before this." Alluding to his prevailing belief in the functional zoning of the city, Mumford argued that "to preserve Fifth Avenue for display and business, and to preserve the Washington Square district for residence are both more important than to provide a traffic link to the downtown tunnels and bridges, only to clog these passages even worse than they are now clogged." The Washington Square viaduct, he concluded, "is a masterpiece of mis-planning; and those who oppose it are serving the public interest."[8]

Although Mumford had not altered his views about the need to rebuild South Greenwich Village from the ground up, he was now less assertive about Village renewal than in his editorial of February 1952, in which he had proposed a rebuilding plan even more extensive than Robert Moses's. The once-favorable public opinion of Moses for city redevelopment had begun to change, and this just when his "blockbusting" approach was determined to be both reasonable and legal. Following an eye-opening visit to East Harlem in early 1956, Jacobs would become convinced that urban renewal was doing more harm than good and that her hopes for city planning had been misplaced.

Philadelphia's Redevelopment

After three years of writing about the city indirectly, Jacobs wrote her first major city feature, "Philadelphia's Redevelopment: A Progress Report," for *Architectural Forum*'s July 1955 issue. It was a transformative moment for which she had been preparing in various ways for almost twenty years, since her first essays on the city. Moreover, in Philadelphia, she would encounter new ideas about the city and its redevelopment, conceived by Ed Bacon and Louis Kahn, that were very different from the approach in New York and that resonated powerfully with her own sensibilities. She assimilated many of Kahn's and Bacon's ideas into her own understanding of the "ecology of the city," as she later described it.[9]

As a first assignment on urban redevelopment, "Philadelphia's Redevelopment" was an ideal assignment. Jacobs knew Philadelphia well as a native Pennsylvanian, from her parents' connections to the city, and from her assignments for *The Iron Age* and *Amerika*. She already served as *Forum*'s Philadelphia liaison. Moreover, "Philadelphia's Redevelopment" had the advantage of being a follow-up story to "The Philadelphia Cure: Clearing Slums with Penicillin, Not Surgery," which, a few years earlier, had prepared a foundation of praise for a noninvasive approach to urban redevelopment.

At liberty to write about the city at last, Jacobs's familiar voice and many of her characteristic ideas came to the fore. Having recently come to believe that city planners were thinking up schemes to make the city less habitable, the scales had, for the most part, fallen from her eyes. Thinking of the plan to run a road through Washington Square, she was prepared, in

FIGURE 30. "Philadelphia's Redevelopment," published in July 1955, was Jacobs's first major feature on urban redevelopment. In it she praised Kahn and Bacon's master plan proposal, and she admired Kahn's Mill Creek housing project. The article reproduced this plan by Kahn and his partners. The Mill Creek project is in the lower right. Kahn Collection, University of Pennsylvania and Pennsylvania Historical and Museum Commission.

the opening sentences of her essay, to dismiss a half-century of city planning movements with a recognizable skepticism for simplistic slogans and unrealistic solutions. "Once upon a time the general problem of the City Chaotic looked so simple. Boulevards and civic monuments were going to create the City Beautiful," she wrote. "After that proved insufficient, regional plans were to create the City Sensible. These proved unadoptable and now we are struggling, sometimes it seems at the expense of everything else, to improvise the City Traversible."[10]

After idealized hopes for city planning and urban redevelopment, "Philadelphia's Redevelopment" gives the distinct sense that Jacobs cast all that aside. As in Plato's allegory of the cave, Jacobs ascended out of the cave of shadows, in her case on a bus ride through Philadelphia, and saw the city anew. And, as she would do again in the opening pages of *Death and Life*, she recommended that others do the same. With the landscape of the city unfolding block after block, as the bus drove on, she came to realize that the parts of the city redeveloped and renewed without public participation could only be "oases in the desert."[11]

Despite her recognition of these truths, Jacobs's ascent, to follow Plato's parable, was not yet complete; she accepted shadowy half-truths that she would later reject. She still saw the city as an ugly and chaotic "mess" and the redeveloped parts as "oases." Moreover, she described the idea that "people with hundreds of thousands of plans and purposes built the city and only they will rebuild the city" as an "appalling fact." Philadelphia, she wrote, "is a city, perhaps the only US city thus far, that has looked at this appalling fact and begun to deal with it."

A likely reason for this choice of words is that, in 1955, the city's dogged and awe-inspiring life force was still a mystery to her. While Jacobs observed in Philadelphia an "unprecedented display of public-spirited, private rebuilding" and praised the work of individuals and citizen's groups, she could point to no particular reason for the collective effort. "What is happening in Philadelphia," she related, "is of such scope and involves so many people there is no neat and easy explanation for what started it or why. Physical rejuvenation of the city seems to be related to a booming hinterland, dissatisfaction with long do-nothing, a surge of municipal reform and citizen activity, the jolt of the war years."[12]

What Jacobs did understand, and what made a great impression on her, was that Bacon and Kahn respected the city's history, its neighborhoods, and democratic, grassroots rejuvenation. "Philadelphia's abrupt embrace of the new, after long years of apathy, has by some miracle not meant the usual rejection of whatever is old," Jacobs wrote. "When a city can carry on a love affair with its old and its new at once, it has terrific vitality."

Moreover, Jacobs understood that Kahn and Bacon's idea of redevelopment was to create catalysts, not "oases" or "spectacular" architectural projects. Anticipating ideas she would repeat in *Death and Life*, she wrote, "In Philadelphia, a redevelopment area is not a tract slated only—or necessarily—for spectacular replacements. In short, it is not simply to be an oasis. . . . Some of Philadelphia's redevelopment money is to be spent very thinly and very, very shrewdly in interstices of these areas to bring out the good that already exists there or play up potentialities. . . . Whether a new oasis is public or private, Philadelphia's planners look at it not simply as an improvement, but as a catalyst." Anticipating what is today called "urban acupuncture" and "tactical urbanism," she concluded, "Philadelphia's inexpensive devices toward the enormous gain of restoring the neighborhood to the desert may be its greatest contribution to city planning."[13] (In *Death and Life*, Jacobs also used the "oasis" metaphor in a discussion of the use of neighborhood parks, and she wrote at length about the effects of urban redevelopment funding in the chapter titled "Gradual Money and Cataclysmic Money," in which she compared catalyzing versus revolutionary city change to the difference between life-giving irrigation and a torrential, eroding flood.)[14]

Jacobs also greatly appreciated Bacon's and Kahn's personal and intimate understandings of the social life and physical fabric of city neighborhoods, especially the fragility of poorer ones. Kahn himself was a native of Philadelphia's "slums"; his understanding of city life was not theoretical. In the 1952 article "The Philadelphia Cure," Kahn was quoted as stating that "a slum is the most closely knit social neighborhood of all. There is more kindness and more natural behavior than anywhere else. There has to be. So you have got to make any redevelopment a product of the neighborhood, or it fails. You have got to search for the things which give the neighborhood its patriotic unity, and retain them. The amateur quality of the building should not be a consideration." Similarly, Bacon had been shown to be a keen observer of what Jacobs later described as the "unslumming" process and was quoted as observing that the city had the "latent capacity" to restore itself. Bacon was quoted in the same article as saying, "In almost any neighborhood in Philadelphia it is a shock, as one wanders about decaying sections, suddenly to come upon three or four houses, a half-block or a whole street where each property owner has kept his home in fine condition, all of the houses painted, new fronts, and sometimes even a whole street with the same colored awnings. . . . These cells have within them the latent capacity to restore themselves."[15]

Although Jacobs later saw the flaws in Kahn's Mill Creek redevelopment project, in 1955 she saw it as an example of the latent capacity for unslumming. She praised the "wonderfully clever and practical devices for jacking up the district, almost by its own bootstraps." Among these were Kahn's reinforcement of important local institutions and landmarks such as churches, schools, and playgrounds. Quoting Kahn, the Mill Creek plan sought to "bring out, instead of burying, the things built by unselfish effort."[16]

Although Jacobs also complained of promenades with no promenaders in *Death and Life*, she also wrote favorably in 1955 of Kahn's metaphorical "city of movement"—where expressways were like rivers, parking garages were harbors, through-streets were canals, and stopping places were docks—and the Philadelphia's "greenways" plan. "Philadelphia is a long way from becoming Kahn's city of movement, but the seeds of this thinking are germinating and a few of their tender sprouts can even be seen in the pages that follow," she wrote, using a familiar organic metaphor.[17]

Developed with the landscape architect Christopher Tunnard, the greenways plan was a historically important work. Tunnard, who was associated with the British Townscape movement, which, as discussed later, captured Jacobs's and her *Forum* colleagues' attention and admiration around this time, had founded what was perhaps the earliest manifestation of the revived civic design discipline in the United States at Yale in 1949. Similar to Townscape ideas, what was groundbreaking about the greenways plan was its restraint in ground breaking and its attention to city fabric, texture, and landscape. As Jacobs explained, the greenways were an effective alternative to imposing large-scale order through architectural means, especially by a single architect. It was a landscape approach that worked "as a unifier of new projects, as a unifier of time, as a unifier of scale." As she explained,

> The greenway is conceived as a strong, clear system of grove-shaded walks, patterned and textured pavements, little open squares and vistas. The vistas focus mainly on the older significant institutions of the neighborhood, creating a sense of depth in time. Commonly these institutions are visually overpowered and lost behind new construction. Curiously, the problem of unifying a variety of new projects by different architects is an even more difficult problem than reconciling old and new. . . . Nor is giving a large area over to one architect usually satisfactory; without the variety of differing minds and viewpoints, urban scale and texture are sacrificed. Planning Director Ed Bacon thinks that the new

greenway device will go far toward solving this problem by making most of the problem disappear.[18]

In other words, as compared to the typical redevelopment plan, the greenways constituted a new infrastructure of public space, "a new kind of Main Street, primarily for pedestrians." It was additive, not subtractive. Despite her subsequent criticism, it was city building.[19]

In *Death and Life*, Jacobs wrote that Philadelphia's planning department was probably the best in the country, although her most memorable nod to Bacon was to repeat the anti–urban renewal slogan "Fry Bacon!" Having become disappointed with things he did later, this was clearly too delicious for her to resist repeating. (Although Bacon's redevelopment plan for Philadelphia's Society Hill was meant to attract middle- and upper-income earners back to Center City, and was ultimately effective for that purpose, it also involved evicting about one thousand families from their homes, permanently tarnishing his reputation.) Despite the remark, and although Kahn's and Tunnard's names are absent from her book, their influence on her cannot be easily dismissed. The enthusiasm with which she described their ideas in 1955 is clear. She was certainly moved by Bacon's assertions that the balance between top-down and bottom-up decision making would be tipped in favor of the latter. She quoted Bacon as stating, "The efficiency and order which the planner desires is less important than the preservation of individual democratic liberties and, where the two are in conflict, the demands of the democratic process must prevail." It was an idea very close to her heart.[20]

Moreover, her understanding of the city as a complex and dynamic organism, ideas of its "death and life" through the process of "unslumming," and even the words that she used to describe the process, were similar enough to theirs as to suggest that she owed Kahn and Bacon a certain debt. Bacon's description of the city at the 1956 Harvard Urban Design Conference, which Jacobs also participated in, could easily be mistaken for her own words when he said, "We developed [in Philadelphia] a hypothesis: neighborhoods are dynamic organisms which have within themselves the seeds of self-regeneration. They consist of pockets of decay intermixed with substantial sections, which with proper stimulus can be induced to fix themselves up." In the concluding sentence of *Death and Life* Jacobs would repeat the regenerating seed metaphor when she wrote

that "lively, diverse, intense cities contain the seeds of their own regeneration, with energy enough to carry over for problems and needs outside
themselves." Similarly, in a two-part profile of Kahn cowritten and edited
by Jacobs—"Architect Louis Kahn and His Strong-Boned Structures "
(October 1957) and "Louis Kahn and the Living City" (March 1958)—
Kahn was celebrated for his appreciation of the city's concentration and
diversity of uses and for his advocacy for the "twenty-four-hour city," com-
monplaces later attributed to Jacobs. Kahn's theory of "the living city"—
that "if you give the city the right and capability to live, the living city will
inevitably solve its own problems—creatively, colorfully, humorously, and
ever changingly; that planning serves only to *initiate* life, not dominate
it"—became very much her own.[21]

Diversifying Cleveland

Jacobs's experiences in Philadelphia show that it is a mistake to associate her exclusively with New York, let alone Greenwich Village. From the
mid-1950s, her experiences in other cities show a diversity of her influences,
in terms of places, people, and cultural issues, and a continuity of development of her ideas. Indeed, the month after "Philadelphia's Redevelopment"
was published, Jacobs's article about redevelopment in Cleveland echoed
some similar themes. As in her discussion of Philadelphia, she remained
optimistic about city planning. "City planning, per se, is not a problem in
Cleveland," Jacobs wrote in "Cleveland: City with a Deadline," "because it
is being done so well. . . . The city has some of the finest slum clearance
and low-income housing in the country." This was because, as in Philadelphia, the planning process was not wholly top-down. "Most important,
planning has a real democratic foundation under it; every step of the way
Cleveland's planners work with a remarkable local institution, the neighborhood 'area councils' which cover most of the city, poor and well-to-
do both," Jacobs wrote admiringly. "In effect, they are active, grass-roots
planning bodies. They are a bright omen for success of the city's program
of rehabilitation under the urban renewal law."[22]

In "Cleveland," however, Jacobs focused on different problems of city
planning than in her Philadelphia article, namely social and racial dynamics, and particularly the problems of segregation and what became known
as "white flight." Anticipating similar themes in *Death and Life*, she argued
that Cleveland needed to "diversify [its] central city population." No great

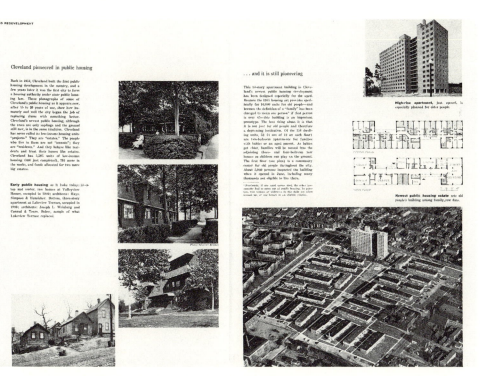

FIGURE 31. In "Cleveland: City with a Deadline," Jacobs wrote, "No big city can afford to allow its heart to become a ghetto for the underprivileged, surrounded by prosperous suburbs." *AF* (Aug. 1955), 130–31.

city, she wrote, "can afford to allow its heart to become a ghetto for the underprivileged, surrounded by prosperous suburbs."[23]

Jacobs also described an urban phenomenon that was typical of American cities in "Cleveland": the migration of well-to-do city dwellers from aging city center neighborhoods to newer rings of development. As city residents' economic status improved, she wrote, "they moved further out, sometimes renting the old house to the next comer, sometimes selling. The next wave of inhabitants moved on, and the next and the next, with the housing progressively deteriorating." This sociogeographic evolution had broken down, however, because African Americans were denied access to the suburbs. Beginning in the 1920s, she continued, African Americans moved in but "they have not moved on, because the suburbs will not let them in. Today 98% of the Cleveland metropolitan area's 207,000 Negroes live in the city proper, many in this central city area." The area she was referring to was considered a slum.

As a means of improving deteriorated conditions, Jacobs was already searching for an alternative to slum clearance. Echoing Bacon's observations about neighborhoods' "latent capacity to restore themselves" and anticipating her own idea of unslumming, she noted that the residents of Cleveland's central city slum "who can afford to own homes, have upgraded the rundown districts they inherited." But it was clear to her that even if the neighborhoods could be physically improved, an enormous problem would remain. In another generation, she wrote, "All of eastern Cleveland might well become a giant Negro ghetto backed up against white suburbs—a financial and social catastrophe."

Reintegration of the city and society was essential. "The solution is not simply to replace the ghetto housing with better housing," she concluded, "but to break up the ghetto pattern itself by bringing some of the suburb back into the central city." By "bringing some of the suburb back into the central city," Jacobs meant white, middle-class residents, and, to this end, she went on to describe and commend a mixed-income Cleveland redevelopment project called Garden Valley.

Jacobs described Garden Valley as "one of the boldest and most imaginative redevelopment jobs conceived by any city." She had high hopes for Cleveland's city planning department, and she later described Ernest Bohn, the director of Cleveland's Housing Authority, and James Lister, the director of its Planning Commission, along with Bacon and a few others, as among the country's best city planners. "Out in Cleveland, a supposed tour by car with Planning Officials Ernest Bohn and James Lister actually amounts to a series of short automobile hops and long exploratory stops."

She had high hopes for Garden Valley's mixed-use and mixed middle- and low-income housing development, which she believed "will permit families hitting hard times, or those graduating out of low-income housing, to move without breaking ties"—a common problem in typical urban renewal. "Green Valley could turn out to be city-rebuilding in a profound sense," she wrote, "because, as one observer of the [nonprofit Cleveland] Development Foundation has said, 'Here are a group of topflight business and industrial leaders learning their way around in city planning, in urban renewal, in race relations and in housing financing. . . . If Garden Valley can stimulate the city's powerful men to look at Cleveland again with the vision of what can be built, it will indeed be a key to rejuvenation.'" The city was the key to social transformation and reintegration. Jacobs concluded that "only in the city proper can middle-income relocation housing be built without restriction of the color of residents."

Jacobs's hope for Green Valley was buoyed by Cleveland's public housing history. She remarked that after fifteen to twenty years of use, public housing in Cleveland showed "how humanely and well the city began the job of replacing slums with something better." Moreover, its directors respected those they served: "Cleveland has never called its low-income housing units 'projects.' They are called 'estates.' The people who live in them are not 'tenants'; they are 'residents.' And they [accordingly] behave like residents and treat their homes like estates."[24]

Unfortunately, like Philadelphia's Mill Creek, Green Valley—which was then called "the community of the future" and a "model neighborhood for all of Cleveland"—did not live up to the high hopes Jacobs and others had for it. Within two years of the construction of the first units in 1957, Garden Valley was already considered run-down and undesirable, and its bad reputation grew and deepened with time. Designed by a young Cleveland native, Allan Jacobs—who had just graduated from the City Planning program at the University of Pennsylvania, where he studied with William L. C. Wheaton, Lewis Mumford, and Martin Meyerson (all of whom Jacobs herself would cross paths with in the years ahead)—the development could not overcome the larger problems: poor management; failure to follow through with the plan to foster a diverse housing demographic, resulting in de facto segregation; and failure to complete key design elements such as landscaping and a transit line in the wake of the city's economic downturn.[25]

Allan Jacobs (no relation of Jane or Bob) would later blame some of Green Valley's problems on a lack of public participation in the design process, despite Jane Jacobs's hopes for its "grass-roots" approach. He also later saw flaws in his own design. In his Greenbelt-influenced, superblock master plan, where both single-family homes and row houses were ruled out in favor of apartment blocks surrounding open space, connections to the surrounding urban fabric were minimal. Later known as the champion of "Great Streets," Allan Jacobs came to believe that the development's street design was inappropriate and that the placement of buildings and roads "fostered neither a sense of publicness nor a feeling of ownership and responsibility." He described how, at the time, it was virtually impossible for city planners to imagine keeping or re-creating the inherited city fabric.

There was no way to design "a street pattern like the existing neighbor-hoods. The mindset of decision-makers was so different. They had in mind places like Radburn and Greenbelt," he said in 2005. But he also remarked that it was unlikely that *any* physical design could have significantly miti-gated the problems of poverty and racism faced by many of Garden Valley's residents.[26]

Allan Jacobs learned from his experiences as Jane Jacobs did from hers. In *Death and Life*, Jacobs would call segregation and racial discrimination "our country's most serious social problem." She would describe urban renewal as a segregating process. "Look what we have built with the first several billions," she observed. "Low-income projects that become worse cen-ters of delinquency, vandalism, and general social hopelessness than the slums they were supposed to replace. Middle-income housing projects which are truly marvels of dullness and regimentation, sealed against any buoyancy or vitality of city life. Luxury housing projects that mitigate their inanity, or try to, with a vapid vulgarity." Moreover, her overarching thesis about city complexity and diversity can be regarded as the exact opposite of such segre-gating mechanisms. However, at the time, Jacobs still believed in urban renewal. She praised a promising redevelopment plan that would "transform a desolate industrial wasteland and an enormous, steep, barren ravine into a neighborhood . . . [and] integrate it with an existing neighborhood which will be rehabilitated under the urban renewal law." Although her ideas about this changed by the time she wrote *Death and Life*, like others at the time, Jacobs believed that breaking up "the ghetto pattern" and bringing back mid-dle-class residents into the central city was the right thing to do, even if this meant suburbanizing the city with a superblock redevelopment plan.[27]

The "Old Pattern" of Washington, DC

Published in *Architectural Forum*'s January 1956 issue, "Washington: 20th Century Capital?" was Jacobs's first bylined article. Around that time, the magazine's policy regarding bylines for staff changed; she was therefore indicated as a staff writer, while Carl Feiss (an itinerant architect and plan-ning consultant) and Frederick Gutheim (a Washington-based city planner) served as editorial consultants. The twenty-four-page feature on a variety of architectural and planning projects in "exploding Washington"—a descrip-tion that anticipated "The Exploding Metropolis" series to which Jacobs con-tributed two years later—was Jacobs's public debut as an architectural critic;

Within the figure image, the text reads:

The city that belongs to all Americans is on the verge of a mighty surge of government building and private redevelopment. It is a battleground of city planning, of architecture, of ideas that will determine for America—what kind of a 20th century capital?

WASHINGTON

We think of it as a special city. But it is everyman's city. Each year more than 4½ million Americans come to look at it—to look at a city. Half a million are high school students. They come because they love the idea of Washington and they want to leave with the belief, "This is how a grand city should be; this is it." A little of the standard of Washington, the standard of a city to inspire man, goes back inside the heads (especially the young heads) to Akron and Atlanta and Albuquerque. Washington has influence beyond the ken of lobbyists.

BY STAFF WRITER JANE JACOBS

CARL FEISS
AND FREDERICK GUTHEIM,
CONSULTANTS

As a 20th century city, Washington is beset with the same problems as every other booming city—choked downtown, haphazard suburban sprawl, blight at the heart—with the exception that its downtown streets are lined with trees, the air is clean and there are many little downtown parks, assets becoming recognized in other cities.

But as a 20th century capital, Washington is a thing unto itself. It is not only an expanding universe. It is an exploding one. Its scale of growth is so swift that dispersal is carrying great chunks out into the greater metropolitan area; decentralization is throwing other huge agency-sized chunks to Denver, Battle Creek, St. Louis; still other chunks—these, in effect, regional subcapitals of the nation—are landing in Atlanta, San Francisco, Chicago, New York, New Orleans. Inside the exploding capital, the "temporaries" now account for as

much space as four Empire State buildings, with 47,000 workers. Cars, moving and parked, have exploded into a problem of such dimensions that both they and the L'Enfant plan for Washington must adjust. Soon a government building program, the first for Washington since the war halted building, will explode into about $250 million of new construction.

Exploding Washington simply cannot avoid remaking itself as a 20th century capital *of some kind or other*.

What kind? Here it is appalling to discover that while time has been moving at such a tremendous pace, time has also been standing stock still in the brains of many of the men who will have much to do with shaping the 20th century capital. Thus among the would-be shapers of the Capitol building itself, we have an attitude that has become fixed upon an outmoded textbook criticism

FIGURE 32. "Washington" was Jacobs's first bylined feature. In it she discussed redevelopment and urban design proposals in the capital city at length. She regarded it as symbolic of the various problems facing the nation's cities. *AF* (Jan. 1956), 92–93.

it came after more than three years of writing for *Forum*, but at a time when thinking about urban redevelopment, as suggested by the title of Jacobs's article, was at a turning point. In June 1955, *The Architectural Review* had published a special issue titled "Outrage," which blasted redevelopment practices in England and made a significant impression on both Douglas Haskell and Jacobs; Haskell had just extended a "warm handshake" to their counterparts at the *Review* in a December 1955 editorial, and, as discussed in the next chapter, Jacobs would collaborate with the *Review* writers Ian Nairn and Gordon Cullen and acknowledge them in *Death and Life*. Thus, with "Washington," Jacobs made good on Haskell's invitation to push architectural criticism into the realm of urban design.[28]

As a collection of redevelopment proposals and critiques, Jacobs wrote about the proposed National Air Museum (which she argued should not be located on the Mall, but at Bolling Field, a defunct military airport); the new façade for the Capitol (of which Haskell had been a staunch opponent for many years); the preservation of historic buildings, including Robert Mills's Patent Office (which was threatened by a proposed parking garage); the city's parking problem (which prompted Jacobs's description of Washington as "the city of magnificent parking lots" because of the way parked cars "greedily devour[ed] the grand spaces"); and the city's recent neoclassical architecture (which she described as a "failure" and a "dead end" as an architectural style, another example of her intellectual preference for modern architecture). The remainder focused on Washington's urban renewal and rehabilitation projects.[29]

As the nation's capital, Washington represented the threatened livability of America's exploding cities. It was poised for gigantic change—$250 million in new construction with a "dominance of overpass and underpass, cloverleaf and ramp" highway building—likely to overwhelm L'Enfant's city plan. And although change was coming at a rapid pace, Jacobs remarked that time had "been standing stock still in the brains of many of the men who will have much to do with shaping the 20th century capital," anticipating a similar barb in *Death and Life*. "The emerging 20th century capital will become a miserable hodge-podge instead of the inspiring city Americans deeply desire, unless thought catches up with event," she affirmed. Washington had an inheritance to work with—"its downtown streets are lined with trees, the air is clean, and there are many little downtown parks, assets becoming recognized in other cities." But it was also beset with the same problems as every other booming city. A "choked downtown, haphazard suburban sprawl, blight at the heart" made it emblematic of cities and city planning during the mid-twentieth century. Its inheritance, like a natural resource, was being similarly depleted. "Exploding Washington simply cannot avoid remaking itself as a 20th century capital *of some kind or other*," Jacobs stated. But "what kind?" she asked.[30]

Her optimism still intact at this crossroads, Jacobs did not yet believe that city planners, decision makers, or larger forces were conspiring to destroy the city. In fact, although she was increasingly apprehensive, she held out hope for the kind of city that Washington could become through urban renewal. In this regard she quoted Supreme Court Justice William Douglas's decision in *Berman v. Parker*: "It is within the power of the legislature to determine that the community should be beautiful as well as healthy, spacious as well as clean, well-balanced as well as carefully patrolled." This idea, she opined, "has always been the idea behind Washington; this is why George Washington commissioned from L'Enfant a grand plan, why Washington has its temples and columns and memorials, its parks and its wealth of trees. It is something that must not be lost." Still believing in urban renewal's potential, Jacobs saw signs of hopeful change in the Justement-Smith plan for Southwest Washington and an urban design proposal by Frederick Gutheim and Willo von Moltke for "a new heart" at the Washington Monument end of the Mall.[31]

Whereas Mary Mix Foley had criticized the Justement-Smith plan in "What Is City Redevelopment?," Jacobs saw things differently. Regarding the part of the plan for the section called Area B—the "national testing ground" where the department store at the center of *Berman v. Parker* had since been razed—Jacobs supported Chloethiel Woodard Smith's opinion that design decisions should not be predetermined by the Federal Housing Administration (FHA) and zoning overlays. In practice, Jacobs observed that such regulations meant the difference between isolating an apartment building on a "sacrosanct high-rise block" or allowing it to be surrounded by row houses and increasing overall density. "Architect Chloethiel Smith (co-author of the Justement-Smith plan, forerunner to current plans for the Southwest, as well as architect on this project)," Jacobs wrote, "thinks that a simple, over-all density and utility-access specification . . . should be the only operative land-use regulations for a project like Area B." Part of Jacobs's subtitle for this section of her article expressed her opinion: "Who shall draw the site plan—FHA, local zoners, or the men who know the subject best?"[32]

For the overall Southwest plan, Jacobs sided with the architects, I. M. Pei and Harry Weese, and the developer William Zeckendorf of Webb & Knapp. "Whatever goes on in the [planning] committee's head, planning does not," she chided. "Planning implied, at the least, a sense of progression and enlightenment of the public, while the committee runs in secret circles." By contrast, she praised the "architecture of city space" created in Pei and Weese's plan for the "South Mall," a new monumental axis that would run perpendicular to the Mall along 10th Street, for being "brilliantly and harmoniously suited to [its] local, citywide, and national functions, each aspect supporting the others and the whole adding up to a genuine architecture of city space."[33]

Representative of her ability to appreciate modern architecture and traditional urbanism at the same time, what most appealed to Jacobs in the designers' "civic planning" was their "break with recent planning practice by returning to an old pattern." Where the South Mall was in keeping with the formality and monumentality of the old L'Enfant and McMillan plans, Pei and Weese's designs for so-called Area C, like Gutheim and von Moltke's design for the Great Plaza, were similarly sympathetic with inherited city patterns. In Area C, Pei and Weese broke with the superblock planning typical of renewal projects in order to propose modern "town or row houses . . . built to the street line." The advantage of the old pattern, Jacobs observed, was that "the street becomes an interesting architectural space, instead of a road between ends of buildings." Other advantages included gardens and interior courts that were really private; parking directly off-street under the houses; the preservation of existing streets, trees, and historic buildings; and an economy of city utilities.[34]

Jacobs similarly praised Gutheim and von Moltke's design for the Great Plaza at the west end of the Mall for its reinterpretation of old city patterns. She admired how their "new park squares and the related plaza would all be treated in the great tradition of urban squares, not as transplanted suburbia. They would make an exciting complex of vista and grand enclosure." Moreover, this would be done without mimicking traditional architecture. Their modern parking structure, for example, "would be handsomely clothed, respecting its monumental neighbors in the essentials of mass, skyline, color, materials and scale, but not attempting to imitate their renaissance details." "Neo-classicism," she wrote, "is a failure. When the supposed non-essentials of the classic styles are removed, all the subtle, complex play of light and shadow depart too. Gone is the sense of softness against hardness, and this turns out to be vital to the style. What remains is hardness against hardness."[35]

A new conception of urban design was thus taking form in Jacobs's mind. Learning from the work of Pei, Weese, Gutheim, and von Moltke, she recognized that city design could return to "an old pattern," without either reviving "traditional" architecture or resorting to suburban models.

Kahn's Poetry Made Practical in Fort Worth

Some months after Jacobs reviewed Gruen's Northland shopping center, the *Harvard Business Review* published "Dynamic Planning for Retail Areas," a November 1954 essay in which Gruen proposed applying the lessons of shopping malls to cities. The article, which cited such diverse sources as *The Heart of the City* and *Women's Wear Daily*, was read by a Texas businessman, who commissioned Gruen to develop a plan for Fort Worth. Jacobs, who knew Gruen and his work well from covering his shopping center projects, was a natural to cover the story for *Forum*. Indeed, she may well have encouraged him to apply the lessons of Northland, which reminded her of historic market towns, to downtown America, and, since she knew them both well, may even have suggested that Gruen study the work of Kahn, who had made a similar proposal to "stimulate more imaginative development of our [Center City] shopping areas along the lines of the new suburban shopping centers" for Philadelphia.[36]

Gruen opened his 1954 essay with an analysis that Jacobs would have found compelling. He argued that the positions staked out by both "decentralizers," the city-hating advocates of suburbia, and the "downtowners," those who regarded "the regional trend as a satanic device," were both wrong for being mutually exclusive. He argued that the city, with its concentration of commerce, finance, and industry, "cannot escape fulfilling its role as a social and cultural center." At the same time, it was a "fantasy" to believe "that somehow people will stop building in the suburbs." Thus, while he thought that there was "no choice but to accept the establishment of outlying shopping centers," he felt that the time had come for urban redevelopment "on a broad scale: slum clearance, creation of green areas within our city cores, provision of parking areas, improvement of traffic arteries, and enrichment of our social, cultural, and civic life." He made the case, in other words, for urban renewal.[37]

Gruen's thinking was paradoxical. He had pioneered and continued to design the regional shopping centers that were contributing to downtown's decline, but he wanted to save the city and its downtown shopping core. His malls were surrounded by parking lots, but he hated cars. He championed private enterprise, the diversity of consumer choice, and "a *democratic* responsibility for the condition of our urban environment," but he designed "*planned*" centers "under the control of a single owner." Nonetheless, Gruen's "organic solution" to the centralization/decentralization question clearly appealed to Jacobs, who praised his Fort Worth plan in *Forum* and *Death and Life*.[38]

The full headline and hook of Jacobs's May 1956 article read, "Typical Downtown Transformed: The Fort Worth Plan; The architects who designed today's most successful shopping center have come up with a plan for bringing similar success to the dense heart of the city." Jacobs described

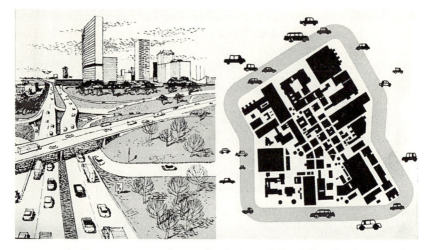

FIGURE 33. Jacobs was a strong advocate for Gruen and Contini's redevelopment plan for Fort Worth, Texas, in "Typical Downtown Transformed" (May 1956) and in *Death and Life*. This diagram shows their proposal for preserving the city from the car and for the pedestrian by locating parking garages on the downtown's perimeter.

the plan as "brilliant," "realistic," and "less authoritarian than the alternative of a car-infested downtown."[39]

Indeed, at the heart of the plan, and Jacobs's praise for it, was the problem of cars, which is why she discussed it at length in chapter 18, "Erosion of Cities or Attrition of Automobiles," of *Death and Life*. Like in Kahn's plan for Philadelphia, ring roads provided access to downtown, visitors parked in peripheral garages, and the city center (like a shopping center) was reserved for pedestrians; only buses and electric carts, "like those used at world's fairs," would be permitted in the pedestrian zone. However, as compared to Kahn's metaphorical plan, which received no mention in *Death and Life*, Jacobs preferred the realism and research methods employed by Gruen and his associate, the city planner Edgardo Contini. "The way the traffic problem was *posed*" was of the essence. "This seems to be the first city for which actual dimensions of the problem have been calculated and faced," she wrote. "The method shows up usual traffic 'planning' for what it is—pursuit of expedients to solve an unmeasured problem." Given various rates of population growth, Gruen and Contini calculated how much space in roadway and parking would be required by a given number of cars. The figures were staggering, suggesting that the city center would have to expand physically just to accommodate the cars, and this in turn would increase the distances between things, making cars even more necessary. The effect, as Jacobs indicated in *Death and Life*, was a "positive feedback" loop: a self-increasing or accelerating dynamic.[40]

But Jacobs's praise was not just about methodology. "The way the planner's part is conceived" was even more important. In her estimation, the physical Fort Worth plan respected "the plans of others"—the plans and ambitions of the city's many inhabitants. "Remarkably little of what exists is interfered with," she wrote. "The Plan respects the variety of healthy city growth, and provides for it." As compared to the wholesale clearance of typical urban renewal projects, Jacobs emphasized that "Gruen's planners surveyed every single building in Fort Worth's downtown, noting use, height, structure, age, condition. Thus guided, the plan places garages and roads for minimum destruction. *Not a single major building is touched.*" "The close analysis of the plan's effect on the interests of everyone involved," she claimed, was "something new for city planning."[41]

Unlike "Olympian" planners who repressed all plans but their own, Gruen's team "resisted the temptation of confusing their wishes with the will of the citizenry." Moreover, "there was no attempt to force it over or finagle it backstage"—as Jacobs had seen done in Washington and New York. The result of Gruen's public presentations was that there were probably "more citizens, especially more leading citizens, in Fort Worth who understand what city planning is about than in any other U.S. city—including the largest," she opined. This satisfied her. At that point she believed that "the citizens must assume initiative." As in her analysis of the U.S. Constitution in *Constitutional Chaff*, the plan provided "a strong skeleton . . . [but] fleshing out is left to the city's users."[42]

In an editorial published concurrently with "Typical Downtown Transformed" in *Forum*'s May 1956 issue, Jacobs celebrated the planning approach she observed in Fort Worth, and she praised Contini, along with Bacon, as being among the "pavement pounders." As compared with the "Olympian" planners, who understood their cities only from bird's-eye views, maps, and statistics, pavement pounders knew their cities intimately, having studied them by using their eyes and feet. She recounted how Bacon delighted "in having figured out, by trial and error, a zig-zag route across Philadelphia, from river to river, that never subjects the walker to a dull vista or uninteresting street." Contini, more recently, had walked with her in Fort Worth and they both wore out their shoes. Remarking on the walk, she wrote, "He knew that square mile of downtown, on foot, the way most people know their own block. Between side excursions into back yards, prowls into alleys, sallies into the middle of the street (future domain of the pedestrian), and plunges up stairs (for a different angle of vision), he enthusiastically detailed the history of this store, the activities on that block, the qualities of the restaurant yonder, the potentialities of around-the-corner."[43]

The pavement-pounding city planners, Jacobs concluded hopefully, were "coming up with by far the best planning," and they were "a breed which seems to be on the increase." However, she didn't believe that walking, or the firsthand knowledge gained from it, was exactly the reason for their better ideas. Rather, she saw better planning as the result of a habit of thought that stemmed from a curiosity about the "living city." Walking and good planning, she wrote, "are two sides of the same attitude, two sides of the pavement pounder's fascination, on an intimate level, with all details of city life and city relationships, of his consuming curiosity about the way the city develops and changes, of his endless preoccupation with the *living* city, and—at the bottom of it all—of his affection for the city." As compared to the Olympian planners, who studied statistics and traffic patterns and "then waved their clearance wands," the pavement pounders were those "who want to change and rebuild the city not out of fundamental disgust with it, but out of fascination with it and love for it."[44]

The East Harlem Experiment

Having written stories about urban redevelopment in Fort Worth, Philadelphia, Cleveland, San Francisco, and Washington, Jacobs seems to have known more about urban redevelopment in cities other than in her adopted hometown of New York until 1956. Around the time she prepared her Fort Worth story, however, she had an eye-opening tour of East Harlem with two of its most knowledgeable residents. In early 1956, William Kirk, a community leader and director of Union Settlement Association, showed Jacobs around the neighborhood, while Ellen Lurie, a Union Settlement social worker, described to her a January 1956 research report that explained the damage done to the neighborhood by the creation of ten housing projects. Later, in *Death and Life*, Jacobs credited Kirk with showing her how to see "the intricate social and economic order under the seeming disorder of cities."[45]

Founded in 1895 by the Union Theological Seminary, like other turn-of-the-century settlement houses, Union Settlement offered social services for some of the millions of immigrants arriving in the city and transitioning to a new life in America. Following service at a St. Louis settlement house and his ordination in 1935, Kirk, a reverend, was hired as the director in 1949, and, with his colleagues, he watched East Harlem change as each new housing project appeared. In 1955, he began reaching out to newspapers and magazines to bring attention to the neighborhood's plight. He first contacted *Architectural Forum* in March 1955, at the suggestion of his friend Phil Will of Perkins & Will Architects, wanting to describe to Haskell the changes that had been taking place. "I think fairly recently Phil Will spoke to you concerning a conversation that he and I had about many of the things which are going on here in East Harlem," he wrote. But it was not until January 1956, when Haskell and Jacobs were outlining a major feature on city planning, that the East Harlem story was followed up on. Haskell wrote Kirk that they had become "seriously interested in a study of city patterns, and we recall how explicit you were about the structure of neighborhoods in Harlem and what produces this structure."[46]

As Jacobs later affirmed, Kirk and Lurie had a very good understanding of their neighborhood's intricate social and economic order. A *New York Times* reporter had listened, and in a May 1955 article titled "Shops a Problem in East Harlem," Kirk explained that demolishing storefront buildings to build superblock housing projects was destroying the neighborhood's social and economic sustainability (to use an anachronistic term). Offering an explanation that Jacobs later repeated almost verbatim, Kirk explained that, "in an area where income is depressed, a store is not only a place where articles are vended, but a social center . . . a meeting place. Storefronts are also used for churches and for political and social clubs. None of this is taken into account in the new housing projects."[47]

By the time Jacobs visited East Harlem, ten housing projects—East River Houses, James Weldon Johnson, Lexington, Washington, Carver, Madison, Franklin, Jefferson, Taft, and Wagner Houses—had consumed fifty-seven blocks, more than two-thirds of East Harlem, and more were planned. Lurie and the East Harlem Small Business Survey and Planning Committee documented the eviction of 1,569 small businesses, affecting the employment of more than 4,500 people. Going door to door, storefront to storefront on the five-block site of the Franklin Houses superblock, they documented the elimination of 211 enterprises, including the following:

two appliance stores, four baby carriage storage locations, four bars, eight barbershops, eleven bakery and pastry shops, two beauty shops, one bicycle shop, fourteen candy stores, two carpenters, ten cleaners, eleven clothing and dry goods merchants, five building contractors, three cheese stores, two drugstores, two egg stores, seven fruit shops, two funeral parlors, six furniture and rug stores, one fortuneteller, five parking garages, fourteen grocery stores, two hardware stores, two jewelry stores, six laundries, two law offices, two liquor stores, one loan maker, one luggage store, one mattress store, four meat markets, one moving and storage company, one novelty shop, three paint stores, one stationer, one pet shop, one plumber, one poultry store, four printers, three radio and TV repair shops, one real estate and insurance business, seven restaurants, four shoe repair shops, two toy stores, two travel agencies, thirteen manufacturing businesses, fifteen wholesalers, two union locals, three churches, eight social clubs, and one political club. Kirk remarked that he was skeptical that anything could save the shattered community, but he thought some good might come from it if the results could be told about in time to save other city communities from the same mistakes.[48]

Although the members of the East Harlem Small Business Survey and Planning Committee acknowledged that much of the housing in East Harlem needed improvement, they argued that "real improvement" included the diversity and various community functions provided by schools, public institutions, small businesses, churches, and political and social clubs. It meant "keeping the best of our old housing and our established businesses" and maintaining "a community made up of all peoples, not creating a segregated neighborhood, economically or culturally." In her January 1956 report, Lurie concluded that it was "not desirable to root out and eliminate all owner-occupied dwellings and enterprises," and she urged the city "to carefully review and study all changes made in East Harlem since World War II."[49]

Later, an increasingly frustrated Lurie would describe East Harlem, in an essay edited by Jacobs, as "the world's most extensively experimented public-housing guinea pig." But while she argued that fourteen project housing experiments were far more than was needed to reveal the experiment's failure, within two months of *Berman v. Parker*, the Lower East Side and Harlem had been designated, more or less in their entireties, as urban renewal "areas suitable for development and redevelopment."[50]

At the same time, however, there was an undeniable need for housing, and not all of the experiments had been failures. Harlem River Houses

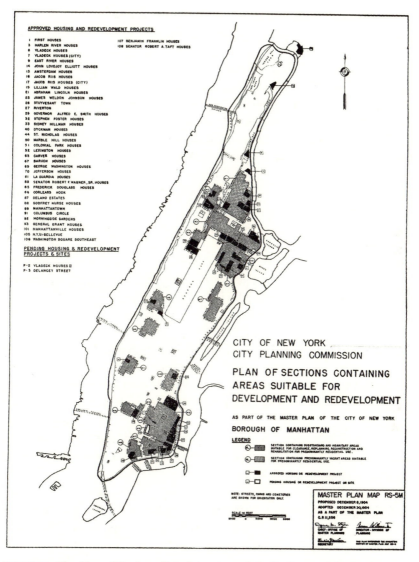

FIGURE 34. The *Plan of Sections Containing Areas Suitable for Development and Redevelopment* (1954) shows the concentration of housing and redevelopment projects (listed in the upper left) in East Harlem and the Lower East Side. Jacobs learned about the impact of the projects built and the proposed project in East Harlem in early 1956. Columbia University Libraries.

(1936–37), the city's first federally funded, owned, and built housing project, was considered a success and among the best-designed public housing anywhere. Moreover, in the 1940s, well before the passage of the housing acts of 1949 and 1954, East Harlem's planning and housing experiment was progressive, locally driven, and apparently so successful that it became the testing ground for the nationalization of urban renewal policy.

In the late 1940s, many of East Harlem's problems had stemmed from the utter lack of building and redevelopment, which led vacant and neglected urban land to become dumping grounds. In a September 1948 exposé, the *New York Times* city columnist Charles Grutzner described the scene that rail passengers traveling through Harlem and the decrepit parts of the Upper East Side saw as they were carried to the downtown train stations. The city's "front door," as this railway entrance to the city was described in words and photographs, was a scandalous mess: "Courtyards were found to be garbage dumps; alleys between buildings were repositories for refuse of all kinds; and lots made vacant by the razing of condemned buildings were covered with piles of junk, some of them afire."[51]

A subsequent *Times* opinion piece took a step toward making "the East Harlem problem" a larger social problem. The editors opined that the neighborhood's plight should "engage the determined attention of the whole city government and, beyond that, the conscience of the people of New York City." They continued: "We, as a city, are not providing decent living conditions in that area—and there are other areas as well, of course."[52]

Nevertheless, consistent with the paternalistic attitude toward slum residents that was a familiar aspect of otherwise well-intentioned housing reform, commentators came to the conclusion that the city's responsibility was to help "remake" East Harlem, physically and socially. Sharing an idea held by many architects and city planners at the time, the *Times* proposed physical rebuilding as the means of remaking the people of East Harlem:

> The basic problem here, of course, is to remake people—the people of East Harlem. We are not at all sure we know how that can be done, but New York, officially and unofficially, cannot rest easy while these people are living up there in that condition and in the frame of mind it helps to produce. . . . We shall, for one thing, have to remodel, rebuild the physical Harlem before we make more sympathetic good citizens out of the Puerto Rican, Spanish,

Italian, Negro, and other families who now live there in such drab and cheerless surroundings.[53]

Just a few days later, in September 1948, another opinion-page piece titled "Rebuilding East Harlem" recommended "a broad, frontal approach" to building new housing and providing new community services. This would "encourage these neighbors of ours in East Harlem to feel that they are accepted as good Americans, that we are genuinely interested in their welfare, and that they enjoy the benefits and have the obligations of all decent Americans."[54]

Despite the patronizing attitude expressed for "these neighbors of ours," the *Times* coverage of the East Harlem story, which continued for three months, resulted in some immediate and positive changes. It caused a shakeup of the Department of Sanitation and the Department of Housing and Buildings, prompted discussions about the conversion of vacant lots into neighborhood playgrounds, and instigated a neighborhood clean-up campaign that spread throughout the city in the following year. It also helped to precipitate the campaign for the wholesale rebuilding of East Harlem, which was, at least initially, a welcome development.

Exemplary of the breadth of belief in the ineffectiveness of "piecemeal" city redevelopment, the idea that East Harlem needed comprehensive rebuilding was shared by local community groups. In December 1948, the *Times* published a letter by the East Harlem Council for Community Planning, which argued that while turning empty lots into playgrounds was a good idea, "a unified plan for the land use in East Harlem" was needed. In agreement with city planners, they wrote, "Piecemeal or patchwork planning for land use will not help. New housing, which is so badly needed, and playgrounds, recreation centers, health clinics, schools and other public services should be integrated into a total plan." They suggested that "the Mayor and the City Planning Commission designate East Harlem as an area in the city in which an experiment in integrated planning should be done."[55]

"Bottom-up" community support started the process, and less than two years later, in August 1950, the East Harlem Council for Community Planning got at least part of its wish. Robert Wagner, then borough president, developed a plan to divide Manhattan into twelve community planning districts. (One of these was the Greenwich Village Community Planning District, of which Shirley Hayes was a committee member.)

Elected mayor in 1953, Wagner saw this structure as a way of involving communities in planning decisions and as the beginning of "a new method for more comprehensive planning of the borough." In a celebrated moment of harmonious thinking among city officials and community leaders, Wagner and the East Harlem council worked together on an experimental redevelopment "pilot project" for a new East Harlem hospital, described by Wagner as "a first-rate example of how neighborhood groups could aid borough officials in important phases of borough planning." To help facilitate the redevelopment process, the council expedited the clearing of the site for a new hospital by assisting with "the removal of tenants from the site and finding new homes for them." At the outset, the redevelopment of East Harlem was exactly the sort of cooperation between a community and city planners that Jacobs advocated at the time.[56]

In fact, the East Harlem "experiment in integrated planning" was so "successful" that, by mid-1955, housing projects had replaced one-third of the seventy-block neighborhood. But with "success" came the unwelcome signs that the experiment was a failure. Just under five years after the city backed the East Harlem council's "pilot project," the *Times* reported that "East Harlem civic leaders are alarmed about the effect that 'a stereotyped approach to housing' is having" upon the area. More widely known by this time as urban renewal, the slum-clearance experiment was degrading the quality of neighborhood life. Paradoxically, "slums" now seemed to be better than new, modern housing. Assisted by Lurie and Kirk, Union Settlement and community groups now tried to reverse the redevelopment process.[57]

As is clear from her comments in *Death and Life*, Jacobs was quickly convinced by Lurie's and Kirk's analyses and arguments. Soon after visiting, in April 1956, she told East Harlem's story to a crowd of distinguished architects and planners at the first Urban Design Conference at Harvard. The combination of events—coming to understand East Harlem's situation and then seeing at Harvard how disconnected practitioners were from consequences on the ground—was a turning point in her understanding of the plight facing cities. And compared with Kirk, Lurie, and many architects and city planners, Jacobs was prepared to understand this plight like few others at the time. Having followed the course of city redevelopment since at least 1949, she understood East Harlem's problems as not unique to the neighborhood or people of East Harlem, as some wanted to believe. Jacobs agreed with Lurie's assessment that East Harlem was "the world's most extensively experimented public-housing guinea pig." She would become a board member of Union Settlement; work with Kirk, Lurie, and Will on developing better housing prototypes for the neighborhood; and refer to East Harlem more than a dozen times in *Death and Life*. But she also saw a larger story: not the failure of urban renewal and project housing in East Harlem, but the failures of urban renewal and project housing at large.

CHAPTER 6

Urban Sprawl, Urban Design, and Urban Renewal

> We are greatly misled by talk about bringing the suburb into the city. The city has its own peculiar virtues and we will do it no service by trying to beat it into some inadequate imitation of the noncity. The starting point must be study of whatever is workable, whatever has charm, and above all, whatever has vitality, in city life, and these are the first qualities that must find a place in the architecture of the rebuilt city.
>
> —Jane Jacobs, 1956

JANE JACOBS'S CAREER as an architectural critic coincided with not only the critical, early years of federally supported suburban development and urban renewal that followed the U.S. Housing Acts of 1949 and 1954, and the Federal Aid Highway Act of 1956, but also the exploding interest in all things *urban*, including the emergence of the field of urban design. As Douglas Haskell, Jacobs's *Architectural Forum* boss, remarked in 1956, "From now on *Forum* will tend even more to be an urban magazine rather than a buildings magazine only."[1]

However, as late as 1958, when Jacobs began writing *Death and Life*, "urban design" was still considered a new term, although it was a postwar modernization of an ancient practice whose twentieth century can be traced back to the "civic art" movement of the turn of the century and the "civic design" movement that emerged in the following decades. Although the term "urban design" was used in the 1930s, and then already associated with urban redevelopment and project housing, urban design was generally seen as a modernization of civic design in the postwar period. As Lewis Mumford stated in his introduction to Clarence Stein's *Toward New Towns for America* (1951), "Except for colonial times, hardly a beginning has been made, up to now, on the history of American city development and urban design." This emphasis on American history emerged from a consciousness about the historical moment and from the opportunities to rebuild U.S. cities after World War II. As Stein wrote in *Toward New Towns*, "As a result of the Redevelopment powers under the Housing Act of 1949, the way is now open for large-scale rebuilding of decaying sections of old cities." In the spirit of Ebenezer Howard, he saw the time as ripe for a new era of nationwide decentralization, with the creation of new towns "widely separated from each other" for the added benefit of Cold War defensive measures and the wholesale rebuilding of great cities.[2]

By 1952, when Jacobs joined *Architectural Forum*, "urban design" appeared with greater frequency. The American Institute of Architects had formed a Committee on Urban Design and Housing in 1951, which, as noted in the article "The Philadelphia Cure," advocated for historic preservation to maintain the "depth in time" (neighborhood coherence in place and time) threatened by large-scale redevelopment. However, urban design remained enough of a new concept that the author (probably Walter McQuade) of "The Philadelphia Cure" felt compelled to distinguish it from "spot architecture" and to make an argument for balancing individualism with civic form. As he wrote, "By pulling in architects skilled in urban design (as distinguished from spot architecture) to co-operate with the various architects hired by separate builders of the separate projects, Philadelphia has evolved remarkable new expedients for *making whole city areas harmonious*. This harmony does not destroy the individual freedom of the individual operator, but it restores the kind of over-all coherence that has all but disappeared from modern city districts."[3]

With the Housing Act of 1954, which transformed the urban redevelopment policies of the 1949 act into much more aggressive urban renewal practices, urban design was seen as a way for architects to expand their role beyond so-called spot architecture. As suggested by an American Institute of Architects (AIA) roundtable titled "The Architect and Urban Design and Urban Redevelopment," held in Washington, DC, around the time that urban renewal legislation was being debated for inclusion in the Housing Act of 1954, urban design aligned itself, and opportunities for architectural work, with the new legislation. (The roundtable was organized by Louis Justement, the codesigner of the Justement-Smith redevelopment plan for Southwest Washington, reviewed by Jacobs.)[4]

The shift from civic design to urban design took a few years. In 1954, Kevin Lynch—a pioneering researcher on cities and the author of *The Image of the City*, which emerged from the same Rockefeller Foundation research initiative as *Death and Life*—was still hesitant to use the latter term. At an American Collegiate Schools of Architecture conference in June that year, Lynch, then a junior professor in city planning at MIT, described his work as "a new look at civic design." Similarly, when the University of Pennsylvania established a civic design program in 1956, its founding director, David Crane, later called it "the progenitor of graduate programs in 'urban design.'" However, in 1958, Crane described urban design as a neologism. "Urban design is a new phrase," he wrote, "at least too new or too ambiguous for any metropolitan classified directories to list any practitioners of the art." Explaining something about the term's nature, he continued, "The phrase has been used in a rather timid reawakening of professional interests in the conscious esthetic choices in city development. Those who use the term have often been careful, self-consciously so, to avoid the pre–New Deal term 'civic design,' which came to have grandiose connotations from its associations with works of Haussmann in Paris, Burnham in Chicago, or Burnham's other associates in the American 'City Beautiful Movement.'"[5]

In this way, urban design was gradually accepted for best reflecting the modernization of the American city that was already under way. At the same time, as suburbia grew, architects, landscape architects, and city planners, whether advocates for cities or for Garden Cities, were concerned about urban sprawl and the urban environment, and urban design was meant to create a forum for their uncoordinated roles in postwar building. As urban designers, they often acknowledged, sometimes explicitly, the mismatch between disciplinary knowledge and the complex needs of the landscapes and cityscapes being rapidly transformed by suburban growth and urban redevelopment.

From her observations of built work in the mid- to late 1950s, Jacobs was among those who were most aware of this mismatch between theory and practice and a simple lack of knowledge. With no hesitancy in saying so, in writing and speeches that increasingly blurred the lines between her work and activism, she made these facts famously public.

More than simply a critic, however, Jacobs contributed significantly to the development of the field of urban design, despite the fact that she didn't like the term "urban design" and never used it in *Death and Life*, preferring "city design" instead. *The Death and Life of Great American Cities* would become a canonical book on cities and urban design, and, in ways little known, developed with Jacobs's thinking about not only urban redevelopment and renewal, but urban sprawl as well.

"Pavement Pounders and Olympians"

In April 1956, a few months after Jacobs came to understand East Harlem's plight, she presented an enthusiastically received paper at the first Urban Design Conference at Harvard University. Although she hated making speeches, the "Harvard Planning Conference"—as those who had not yet embraced "urban design" called it—would make Jacobs's name familiar in architectural and planning circles. "A few years ago, Mrs. Jacobs stepped into prominence at a planners' conference at Harvard," Lewis Mumford recalled in his mostly bitter review of *Death and Life* in 1962. "Into the foggy atmosphere of professional jargon that usually envelops such meetings, she blew like a fresh offshore breeze to present a picture, dramatic but not distorted, of the results of displacing large neighborhood populations to facilitate large-scale rebuilding."[6]

Like other serendipitous events in Jacobs's life, her presence at the conference was a lucky accident. In January 1956, around the time that Jacobs followed up on the East Harlem story, Josep Lluís Sert, the dean of the Harvard Graduate School of Design (GSD), sent Haskell an invitation to be part of a distinguished gathering of planners, architects, and landscape architects who would seek a "common basis for joint work of the three professions in urban design." Although Haskell initially accepted the invitation, after the conference co-organizer and GSD professor Jaqueline Tyrwhitt telephoned to confirm, he sent Sert regrets that he would not be able to attend due to a trip to Europe. In his stead, he recommended *Forum*'s redevelopment specialist. "If another woman beside Miss Tyrwhitt would not be out of place," he wrote, "might I suggest that my substitute be Mrs. Robert Jacobs—Jane Jacobs on our masthead. She has handled more of our redevelopment stories than anybody and will be fresh back from Ft. Worth."[7]

Despite her unanticipated participation in the conference, with her eyes recently opened to the effects of urban renewal "on the ground," Jacobs was one of the most knowledgeable people present. Having no professional training or credentials, she was condescendingly described as Haskell's "assistant" and a "layman," but her talk was nevertheless among the conference's highlights, and the reaction to it testified to both the novelty of her presence and the soundness of her ideas. A conference summary in June 1956 noted among the high points "the warm and direct appeal of Jane Jacobs . . . , who pointed out that a supermarket may replace thirty little stores but doesn't replace thirty little storekeepers and their social place in the community—and a lot of other things that only a layman of considerable feeling could tell a group of planners and architects." In a letter, Victor Gruen told Haskell that Jacobs was the best of the conference's speakers:

> The conference was an interesting one, but it suffered under the weakness of all professional conferences—that too many high-hat words are used which, because they are worn out by now, are ineffective. Everyone was using the expressions "human scale" and "warmth" but Jane was the only one who really talked about it, without ever using any of the big words. She was like a fresh wind in the airless room. It must also be stated that not only what she had to say was excellent, but also the way in which she said it. She's an excellent speaker. Her simplicity and her sincerity and her thoughtfulness swept everybody off his feet. There's no doubt that she was the "star" of the show.[8]

Like new civic design studies and programs in development at Yale, MIT, Penn, Washington University, Virginia Polytechnic Institute, and other places, the Urban Design Conference aimed to serve the need for better education in the wake of the new urban renewal legislation. Like his counterparts at other schools, Sert was aware of the new federal legislation; he was one of the participants at Louis Justement's October 1953 "The Architect and Urban Design and Urban Redevelopment" roundtable, where he delivered a paper titled simply "Urban Design." In 1954, Sert hosted an

American Collegiate Schools of Architecture conference focused on architectural education and civic design, where Lynch observed that "a great
number of individuals, a number of schools, a number of practicing architects have become extremely interested in the subject of the sensuous form
of the city and are beginning to think about it and are beginning to work
on it." Sert agreed that modern architecture and city planning were going
through decisive years and that academic programs needed to change
accordingly. A few months later, a Harvard professor, Siegfried Giedion,
who had also taught seminars on civic design at MIT, renamed his course
"History of Urban Design." These were among the first steps toward the
creation of what was, in name, the first graduate program in urban design,
established at Harvard in 1960.[9]

The first urban design conference in which Jacobs participated was
thus a historic moment for the fields of architecture, city planning, and
landscape architecture. In it, Sert made a definitive break with "civic
design" and made a case for the design professions' participation in urban
renewal. In his opening talk, he explained that the conference "avoided the
term 'Civic Design' as having, in the minds of many, too specialized or too
grandiose a connotation," with its allusions to the City Beautiful movement
and its limited emphasis on civic centers. Criticizing civic design and the
City Beautiful movement as window-dressing the city—a critique Jacobs
later repeated, and expanded, in *Death and Life*—Sert stated to the gathered
crowd, "We cannot screen slums with marble fronts and colonnades, nor
establish balance and harmony in a community [by] developing monumental civic centers, ignoring the living conditions of people in neighborhoods
around those centers."[10]

Sert proceeded to call on design professionals to become more involved
in the urban design practices that had been largely taking place without
their participation. Referring to the "large-scale redevelopment projects"
since 1949, he observed, "Urban design has in the last years, been a no-
man's land that architects, city planners, engineers, and landscape architects
did not invade." After "many years of effort, research, and rediscovery on
an individual basis," he believed that "an era of synthesis" was at hand. But
despite Sert's sincere argument for improving the living conditions of city
dwellers, and his memorable critique of civic centers and beautification
efforts, Jacobs, sitting in the audience, must nevertheless have been shocked
to hear his subsequent "apology" for the city, as he phrased it, and his
unapologetic call to re-shape the city "as a whole" and give it "proper

physical form." She had recently witnessed the results of such ambitions in East Harlem—and would share her observations in her conference presentation.[11]

Suggesting the massive dimensions of the intellectual void that urban design needed to fill, Sert went to great lengths to explain the importance of being "urban-minded"—and Jacobs must have agreed with him in principle. "First of all, we must believe in cities, their importance and value to human progress and culture. We must be urban-minded to get such a position and attitude," he stated, and he went on to contrast this sensibility with prevailing beliefs about the failures of the city and the superiority of the suburbs. "In late years we have heard much talk about the evils of the city, of its being a breeding place for crime, juvenile delinquency, prostitution, diseases of all kinds, traffic congestion, accidents, etc. To leave the city, to live outside it, has become a goal. . . . Everything good and healthy became suburbanite, and to solve the problems of our cities, our city planners turned their back to them."[12]

Despite this argument, Sert was among many of his generation who did not accept the city wholeheartedly. He was the author of a 1944 book originally titled *Should Our Cities Survive?* and, in his Urban Design Conference address, he repeated early twentieth-century ideas about the need to change the city to accommodate the skyscraper. He thus argued that "the solution lies in re-shaping the city as a whole, including the central structures, [and] that "every American city, because of its growth, has to break up into constellations of communities," each with its own center. This combination of Howard's network of Garden Cities and Clarence Stein's New Town proposals with a modernized, Corbusian central city would compose what Jacobs later described as the "Radiant Garden City."[13]

If Jacobs was not already dismayed to hear Sert outline his urban vision, she must have been flabbergasted to hear him define urban design by comparing the walled, well-ordered, and well-landscaped Harvard campus to the surrounding town of Harvard Square. Remarking on their differences, he noted, "In one there is design that results in balance and harmony; in the other, there is no coordination of design elements or harmony whatever." The campus was a well-ordered and parklike setting, while the town outside was a hellish, chaotic, denatured place: "A few steps away, there is a gateway that opens to Harvard Square and like Dante's door to Hell, could carry over it the inscription "Abandon All Hope," meaning all hope of finding these elements that make our environment

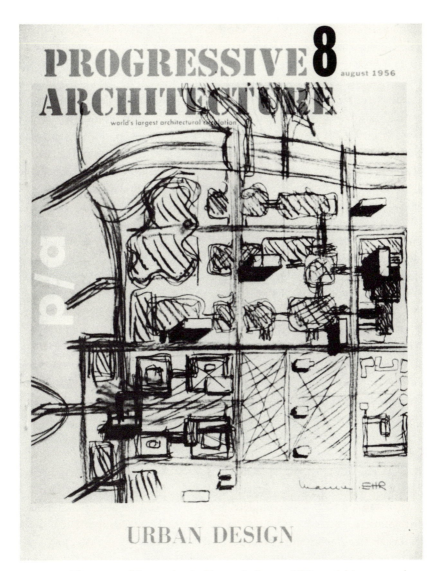

FIGURE 35. The cover of *Progressive Architecture*'s August 1956 special issue on urban design, which reported on the 1956 Harvard Urban Design Conference and included a transcript of Jacobs's speech at the conference.

human, because across the gate there is noise, disorder, lack of visual balance, and harmony. There is naturally no place for trees and you will search in vain for a squirrel."

Sert opined that "on one side of the gate there is design at its best, and on the other it is totally absent." This exemplar of urban design must have struck Jacobs, New Yorker that she was, as motivated by an inherent dislike for the city. Harvard Yard was a gated community, and while Harvard Square may have been noisy and had traffic problems on its winding streets, it was no great city, and it was hardly Hell or even "Hell's Kitchen" (later Clinton) or "Hell's Hundred Acres" (later SoHo), two Manhattan neighborhoods not far from where she lived.[14]

Jacobs's conference presentation offered the inverse of Sert's example. In fact, in the June 1956 issue of *Architectural Forum*, which reprinted her talk, she offered her own comparison. One photograph portrayed a "living neighborhood" in East Harlem, another a well-ordered but "dead" housing project. The caption of the first photograph, of an old Harlem street typical of those destroyed for superblocks, was "The living neighborhood is a complex of little organisms like this East Harlem store-front church and store." The other, next to a photograph of the new Stephen Foster Houses at 112th and Lenox (later renamed the Martin Luther King Jr. Towers), stated "New housing developments like this one in East Harlem, New York City, take into account little beyond sanitary living space, formal playgrounds, and sacrosanct lawns."[15]

While her talk was well received, Jacobs also must have come to realize how deeply entrenched and pervasive the Radiant Garden City model was as a system of thought. This is not to suggest that architects, even among the older generation, were not aware of its shortcomings or that Jacobs's own paradigm shift was complete. During the course of the conference, Sert himself revealed misgivings about the intellectual and physical tools and goals of contemporary practice. "I also have the feeling that a lot of the work being done in architecture and city planning is scale-less. We design things that look very well as models, or blown down to magazine-page size, but very bad when blown up to full size," he commented.[16]

In the meantime, the Congrès Internationaux d'Architecture Moderne (CIAM), the organization that had advocated functionalist city planning principles since the early 1930s, was splintering over this very issue. Undermining two decades of work by the pioneering generation of modern architects, those among the younger generation rejected CIAM's Functionalist

City concept, with its four key functions of dwelling, working, recreation, and circulation. At CIAM's ninth congress in 1953, John Voelcker and Peter and Alison Smithson had presented a project on "urban reidentification" in which they made the iconoclastic argument that the city fabric of slums often succeeded where spacious redevelopment failed. Soon thereafter, they wrote the "Doorn Manifesto," which proposed substituting the narrow functionalism of Le Corbusier and CIAM's Athens Charter with a new understanding of the "ecological" complexity of the city. In 1955, the Smithsons summarized the change in thinking by sharply stating: "We wonder how anyone could possibly believe that in this [the four functions concept] lay the secret of town building." In the face of such discontent, in 1956, Sert stepped down as the president of CIAM, handing over the reins to the "Generation of '56," who would plan CIAM's tenth and final congress, held in Dubrovnik in August of that year. At what Le Corbusier called a moment of "crisis or evolution" for modern architecture, the movement's charismatic leader admitted that only the younger generation was "capable of feeling actual problems, personally, profoundly, the goals to follow, the means to reach them, and the pathetic urgency of the present." A generational shift was under way.[17]

Nevertheless, soon after the Urban Design Conference, Jacobs observed in her May 1956 editorial "Pavement Pounders and Olympians" that ways of looking at the world were deeply ingrained. Although Sert, for example, lamented the scalelessness of contemporary architecture and the lack of contact with "the man in the street" in his introductory remarks, he celebrated the Olympian view of the city. "In late years we have developed a new view of the city, one that only birds could enjoy before," he observed. In the same year that Brasilia, a city both planned from the air and given the form of an airplane or a bird, was being built, Sert described "Cinerama views" of American cities as "more convincing than hundreds of pages of statistics," recalling Le Corbusier's similar arguments for using the airplane to study and plan cities in *Aircraft* (1935), as well as Le Corbusier's enthusiastic endorsement in *The City of To-Morrow and Its Planning* (1929) for using statistics. Le Corbusier claimed, in a particularly Olympian metaphor, that statistics were "the Pegasus of the town planner." Jacobs would reject both tools—bird's-eye views and statistical analysis—in "Pavement Pounders and Olympians" and later writing.[18]

Having assimilated East Harlem's lessons into more widely applicable principles, Jacobs realized that this system of thought needed to be changed.

While echoing the research on East Harlem done by Ellen Lurie and William Kirk, she expanded on the specific case of East Harlem to emphasize structural relationships between the built environment and human practices.

In contrast with decades of antagonism toward the historic city and the concept of separating city functions, she urged the Urban Design Conference audience—and soon thereafter her *Architectural Forum* readership in an article titled "The Missing Link in City Redevelopment"—to look at the relationships between city street, sidewalk, stoop, storefront, and dwelling. Ground-level relationships, she emphasized, were essential. "Look at some lively old parts of the city. Notice the tenement with the stoop and sidewalk and how that stoop and sidewalk belong to the people there," she said. "A living room is not a substitute; this is a different facility."[19]

These relationships, she emphasized, were *functional*. Whereas functionalist zoning and urban renewal projects destroyed the public spaces of the street, the subtle in-between space of the stoop, the flexible functionality of the storefront building, and complex social life all took place in multifunctioning public and semipublic spaces. As Jacobs explained, "A store is also often an empty store *front*. Into these fronts go all manner of churches, clubs, and mutual uplift societies. These store-front activities are enormously valuable. They are the institutions that people create, themselves." And, extending Lurie's social survey data into other principles, Jacobs recognized the city's self-organized and overlooked institutions, invisible to statistics, as spaces of appearance for civil society. She observed, for example, that "most political clubs are in store-fronts" and that, "when an old area is leveled, it is often a great joke that Wardheeler so-and-so has lost his organization." But, she continued, "This is not really hilarious. If you are a nobody, and you don't know anybody who isn't a nobody, the only way you can make yourself heard in a large city is through certain well defined channels. These channels all begin in holes in the wall."[20]

While Jacobs recognized that "the charm, the creative social activity, and the vitality shift over to the old vestigial areas because there is literally no place for them in the new scheme of things," she still had not completely rejected typical project planning or the idea of a "rebuilt city." Thinking like a planner or architect, she saw the old city as offering lessons for new planning and architectural ideas. In an uncharacteristically removed turn of phrase, she said, "We do not suggest these units [parts of the city] be copied, but that you think about these examples of the plaza, the market place, and the forum, all very ugly and makeshift but very much belonging to the inhabitants, very intimate and informal." She went on to suggest that planners and architects should be more careful about how they zoned, where they located stores, and how they designed gathering places and out-door spaces. "The outdoor space should be at *least* as vital as the slum sidewalk," she stated. "It is not enough that unallocated space serve as a sort of easel against which to display the fine art of buildings. In most urban plans, the unbuilt space is a giant bore." She listed three projects that she was familiar with and had written about—Stonorov, Gruen, and Yamasaki's Gratiot plan for Detroit; I. M. Pei's plan for Southwest Washington; and Louis Kahn's Mill Creek in Philadelphia—as "unusual exceptions" to the typical project.

Jacobs would later regret her praise for these projects. But, by mid-1956, the shift in her thinking had begun. She no longer saw the city from the viewpoint of the debate over the shopping mall versus central business districts. She recognized the difference between pavement pounders and Olympians. The latter, as she wrote in the 1958 essay "Downtown Is for People," had "become fascinated with scale models and bird's-eye views. This is a vicarious way to deal with reality, and it is, unhappily, symptom-atic of a design philosophy now dominant." She recognized the threat of suburbanizing the city. And, most important, although she did not yet fully understand the city's "chaos," she had begun to recognize "weird wisdom." "Unless and until some solution for them can be found," she wrote in "The Missing Link," "the least we can do is to respect—in the deepest sense—strips of chaos that have a weird wisdom of their own not yet encompassed in our concept of urban order."[21]

"Man Made America"

After her participation in the 1956 conference, Jacobs turned her atten-tion back to the initial reason for her visit to East Harlem, which was *Archi-tectural Forum*'s "big planning issue," as Haskell called it.[22] While East Harlem was critical to her understanding of cities, larger issues concerning the built environment were also on her mind. The monumental choice of centralization and the preservation of cities, or decentralization through suburbanization, remained a pressing social question.

As Jacobs knew from her early essays on New York City, the desire to escape the city was an old one. But by the 1930s, not long after the model automobile suburb of Radburn was built, the term "sprawl" came into use to describe unplanned and unattractive urban growth. In the postwar period, a whirlwind of factors—car ownership, urban housing conditions and shortages, public policy and financial instruments, highway construction and the automobile industry, and home builders marketing single-family homes with yards for the kids—all conspired to make the suburbs look much more attractive than old and crowded cities to the Baby Boomers' parents. This willful middle class, an important character in *The Death and Life of Great American Cities*, was voting with its wheels.[23]

Postwar suburbanization and exurban growth was not without its critics, however, and, for Haskell and Jacobs, among the most influential were their counterparts at *The Architectural Review* in London. Founded in 1896, the *Review* described itself as the first British architectural publication to depart from a primary concern with the business side of architectural production to focus on architecture's aesthetic and conceptual qualities. In 1927, Hubert de Cronin Hastings—known to his colleagues as "H. de C." and to readers by the penname "Ivor de Wolfe"—assumed the position of editor. Ten years later, Hastings pulled the historian Nikolaus Pevsner and the architectural critic J. M. Richards from the *Review*'s sister publication *The Architect's Journal*. With Pevsner and Richards, the magazine quickly developed a distinctive approach to architectural criticism, which combined a deep respect for architectural history with an understanding of modern architecture's roots in functional vernacular architecture, a sophisticated approach to tradition and modernization much needed in rebuilding cities after the war.

In December 1950, while Haskell was in the midst of reorganizing *Forum*, the *Review* published a remarkably biting special edition. "Man Made America" was devoted exclusively to studying "the mess that is man-made America." Pulling no punches, the *Review*'s editors observed that the United States had "rejected a visual ideal, in favour of a laissez-faire environment—a universe of uncontrollable chaos sparsely inhabited by happy accidents." The result was "a combination of automobile graveyard, industrial no-man's land, and Usonian Idiot's Delight . . . a visually scrofulous waste-land [characterized by] vast areas that fill the interstices between the suburbs and the city centers, not to mention the highways between cities, where not anarchy but visual chaos reigns." For the British, "Man Made America" was a critical cautionary tale and also an opportunity to develop a new approach to the built environment that the *Review* described as "Townscape."[24]

Originally articulated by H. de C. Hastings in December 1949, Townscape was at first a reaction to poor British town planning practices. Although Parliament had enacted the Town and Country Planning Act of 1947, dramatically consolidating the government's control over development and town planning (or city planning, in American usage) in the interest of rebuilding and modernizing London and other parts of the country damaged in the Blitz, postwar rebuilding still frequently resulted in sprawling, low-density housing and industrial areas insensitive to the landscape and of low aesthetic quality. In a country that cherished its landscapes, these developments were particularly troubling: They reminded British observers of the ugly and sprawling landscapes of roadside America. They worried that America was squandering its own utopian potential and that Britain was importing this disregard for the landscape along with its laissez-faire industrialism through the Marshall Plan, which demanded the adoption of American values in exchange for reconstruction dollars. With its "symptoms of infantilism and arrested development," the state of the U.S. urban landscape, the *Review*'s editors wrote, was evidence of the questionable nature of these values.[25]

Despite the powerful Town and Country Planning Act, Hastings and Richards were concerned that the British were just as likely to make a mess of things. "Somewhere inside every Englishman is the original American," they wrote in the introduction to "Man Made America," and these "original Americans" could just as easily create an equally terrible British landscape. Partly to temper their criticism of the United States, they explained that they identified with the American adventure and felt bound up and even personally implicated in its outcome. They believed that Britain's American descendants had learned nothing from the visual fate of England—as though Americans had "no other earthly ambition than to provide a bigger, more general suburbia, to add more wire, to model lovingly still huger areas of industrial and even agricultural scabbery; in the persuasion that the earth's surface . . . is there for no other purpose than to do dirt on."[26]

Reading this anti-American screed in early 1951, Haskell was outraged, and he soon replied with an indignant editorial. "For some years the more recondite among U.S. architects had been quietly enjoying their subscriptions to the *Architectural Review*," he wrote in the April 1951 issue of *Forum*. "But late January these doting Americans received a heavy jolt. The *Review* had set forth on the warpath directly against them. . . . Rarely had a cultural publication, published in a friendly country, issued so wholesale a condemnation of American civilization."[27]

Despite his wounded patriotic pride, Haskell found it difficult to make an effective counterargument. Instead he gave various explanations for the nature of the American landscape. America's scale and tempo lay outside European experience, he offered. Its history was unique: "No European country had its birth at the precise moment of greatest force in the scientific-industrial revolution, in a territory of such boundless resources." Haskell defended the American spirit and underscored his familiar conviction that "there are great reservoirs of vitality even in honky-tonk. Democracy has her victories." And he concluded by expressing hope that the "lightness" of modern American architecture could hold promise: "Our art must favor every invention that permits us to rest lightly on the earth, and *still* not be ramshackle."[28]

But Haskell had to concur that "Man Made America"—which featured essays by Christopher Tunnard, Henry-Russell Hitchcock, and Gerhard Kallmann, and photographs and illustrations by Walker Evans, Saul Steinberg, and the *Review*'s Gordon Cullen—had made a compelling case. He ultimately admitted in his reply that the United States was building a "supremely ugly . . . tin-can civilization" and acknowledged that "thoughtful Americans were unreservedly thankful for the sharp reminder, from an outside source that *some* of the 'mess' is really there."[29] A year later, around the time Jacobs joined his staff, Haskell launched his new editorial agenda, with its renewed focus on architectural criticism and special attention to urban redevelopment. The *Review* had made a deep impression.

Although Haskell recognized that the *Review* had a different readership than *Forum*, by 1955, he could wholeheartedly embrace the *Review*'s lead on Townscape issues. Not only was U.S. sprawl proving the "Man Made America" critique accurate, but the *Review* writers Ian Nairn and Gordon Cullen also directed their critical gaze on England in a special issue titled "Outrage," bravely criticizing everything from signage to the anti-urbanism of British housing estates. This outrage, Nairn wrote, "is that the whole land surface is being covered by the creeping mildew that already circumscribes all of our towns. This death by slow decay we have called Subtopia, a compound word formed from suburb and utopia, i.e., making an ideal of suburbia." This new anti-urban form of urbanization was destroying the fabric of cities and smothering the distinction between town and country. Nairn observed, "Urban sprawl has come to its second stage; with everyone gone to the suburbs the centre has been left to decay. Towns have become half alive: one is where you work, but can't live, the other half is where you live but don't work." Commenting presciently on the consequences of sprawl, he continued, "Half alive towns will produce half alive people, and the most immediate result is that in between working and living there can be up to two hours of limbo, nearly fifteen percent of one's waking hours: forced and frustrating comradeship in public transport or forced and frustrating isolation in private cars."[30]

His own initial outrage further mollified, Haskell prepared for *Forum*'s own "big planning issue," with the inspiration of the *Review*'s example and help from Jacobs, who would serve as its editor. In a preparatory December 1955 editorial titled "Can Roadtown Be Damned?" he extended a warm handshake from the *Forum* editors to their counterparts at the *Review*: "Two paths are open to us. One is to accept Roadtown as a formidable fact and civilize Roadtown, now that it is commanding heavier highway engineering and bigger building capital. The other is to re-examine the very roots of our endlessly shuttling civilization. On both these subjects *Forum* will gladly work with the *Review*." When the "big planning issue" was finally published in September 1956 as "What City Pattern?" Haskell accompanied it with an editorial in which he referred again to "Man Made America." In "Architecture for the Next Twenty Years," he wrote, "Back in 1950, friends of ours across the Atlantic, editing England's *Architectural Review*, cut deeply into our native pride with a complete issue devoted to 'Man Made America.' What they said still rankles—because there was some justice in it."[31]

Jacobs was similarly inspired by Nairn and Cullen's efforts, and she alluded to "Outrage" in her introduction to the feature. She also took Haskell's invitation for collaboration between *Forum* and the *Review* to heart. In the following years she would join forces with Nairn and Cullen on her "blockbuster on the superblock," bring Nairn into the Rockefeller Foundation's urban design research program, and cite their influence in *Death and Life*.[32]

"What City Pattern?"

Forum's special issue "What City Pattern?," one of Jacobs's major writing and editing projects in 1956, included contributions by a number of collaborators. It featured the introductory editorial "By 1976, What City

FIGURE 36. Among the magazine's other influences, *The Architectural Review*'s June 1955 issue, titled "Outrage," made a big impact on Jacobs and her colleagues at *Architectural Forum*. Jacobs cited it in her writing before *Death and Life*, then within the book, and alluded to it again in the introduction to *Death and Life*'s Modern Library edition. Authored by Ian Nairn and illustrated by Gordon Cullen, "Outrage" and the sequel "Counter-Attack Against Subtopia" (Dec. 1956) were reprinted in hardcover in 1956 and 1957. *The Architectural Review* and *The Architectural Press.*

Pattern?" by Jacobs. "First Job: Control New City Sprawl," by Catherine Bauer, an advocate for modern housing, was the lead essay and one that Jacobs ultimately believed required the editorial reply that followed. The next sections were analyses of different aspects of the built environment. First was "Central City: Concentration vs. Congestion," by Jacobs; second, "Fringetown: Just Another Central City?"; and third, "Roadtown: The Great American Excursion" by Walter McQuade and Ogden Tanner. An essay by Victor Gruen, "How to Handle This Chaos of Congestion, This Anarchy of Scatteration," followed, with the whole feature capped off by Haskell's editorial "Architecture for the Next Twenty Years."[33]

As compared to the great city focus of *Death and Life*, "What City Pattern?" and Jacobs's other writing during these years demonstrated her concern for the built environment as a whole—suburban and urban. In her introduction to the collection, for example, Jacobs explained that urban renewal was "only part of an over-all pattern of urbanization taking in spaces far beyond, and between, the old cities." Echoing ideas and rhetoric that she saw in the *Review*, she wrote, "Cities used to be an incident in countryside; now countryside is become an incident in City. The last ten years have given us an unholy mess of land use, land coverage, congestion, and ugliness." The next twenty years would see a crisis, she predicted, as cars, road building, and suburbanization drove the United States into a growth crisis the likes of which had never been seen before. "It is an unprecedented crisis simply because we are an unprecedented nation of centaurs," she wrote. "Our automobile population is rising about as fast as our human population and promises to continue for another generation. . . . And because asphalt will not grow potatoes, the pavement that will be demanded by two cars for every one that we have today will have to come out of [our] other-purpose acreage. There's the rub. For the car is not only a monstrous land-eater itself: it abets that other insatiable land-eater— endless, strung-out suburbanization." She stated that *Forum*'s editors did not have answers: "It is as an eye-opener that this issue is intended."[34]

The next feature was an unexpected eye-opener for Jacobs. Initially, Bauer's lead essay was a great source of hope for Jacobs. When she read the draft in May 1956, she was ebullient, enthusiastically reporting to Haskell that Bauer's essay was "a turning point" and "the start of a new direction" for both architectural criticism and urban theory. "If the next generation's equivalent of the Steins and Mayers and Mumfords can begin to follow the line of thought started here, and show what can be done with the different type of planning it implies, Americans may well end up liking cities," she wrote him in a long memo. Summarizing Bauer's apparent intent, since "the great planning ideas, both inside and outside the city, have been stimulated and intellectually fertilized by city-rejectors," she continued, "how could less imaginative planners and the unimaginative body of citizenry help but take their cue? What and who was there to lead them in any other direction? In this article of Catherine Bauer's is the start of a new direction and I think it is very exciting."[35]

In her piece Bauer had written a devastating critique—a wholesale rejection of generations of city planning theory as anti-urban, utopian, and unworkable—and one Jacobs later repeated in abridged form in *Death and Life*. While Jacobs famously criticized the Radiant Garden City model, Bauer criticized not only Howard's Garden City and Le Corbusier's Radiant City, but also Frank Lloyd Wright's Broadacre City and Buckminster Fuller's "nomadic noncity." Illustrated with photographs of the original concepts and the versions created by less imaginative minds, Bauer's essay critiqued these planning concepts as utopias, a motif that Jacobs also repeated in *Death and Life*. Of the illustrations, "Utopia No. 1" was the Garden City, the model for Clarence Stein and Henry Wright's Radburn and thereafter vulgarized across suburban America. "Utopia No. 2" was Frank Lloyd Wright's Broadacre City, whose "principle has been perverted everywhere, as the typical suburb shows." In the vulgarized version, Wright's sense of organization was gone: "What is left is neither city nor country, only aimless scatteration, congestion, and needless waste." Lastly, "Utopia No. 3" was Le Corbusier's Radiant City, illustrated by what became a familiar juxtaposition of the Voisin plan with housing projects from Manhattan's Lower East Side. "Almost every big city today has vulgarized this concept," the caption read. In the Corlears Hook housing project, for example, "the towers are dropped helter-skelter, the green space around them is shapeless, and there is no sign of relief that Corbu built into his plans with lower buildings that formed semicourts." As in Jacobs's memo to Haskell, the illustrations and captions, written by Jacobs, emphasized the difference between the model and its inevitable interpretation.[36]

Despite Jacobs's initial praise for Bauer's critique, her hopes were soon dashed. Encouraged by Bauer's promising start, Jacobs was sorely disappointed by the conclusion of the final draft. As Jacobs saw it, Bauer's proposal to "control new-city sprawl" was ultimately not so different from the utopias she condemned. Jacobs went to Haskell in a near panic. As Haskell

Utopia No. 3: At the opposite pole from Wright and the decentrists is Le Corbusier with his model for the Super City. His "voisin" plan for Paris (circa 1930; picture, right) was an early stage in his thinking. But it embodied many of the principles he later refined: the skyscraper dwelling; the surrounding park; the separation of pedestrian and auto. Almost every big city today has vulgarized this concept. In Manhattan, for instance, the towers of Corlears Hook are set in a green (picture, below). But the towers are dropped helter-skelter, the green space around them is shapeless, and there is no sign of the relief that Corbu built into his plans with lower buildings that formed semicourts.

FIGURE 37. In September 1956, *Architectural Forum* published a special on city planning and design titled "What City Pattern?," which Jacobs contributed to and edited. "First Job: Control New City Sprawl," by Catherine Bauer, included a critique of prevailing "utopias," and their vulgarizations, as initially proposed by Ebenezer Howard, Frank Lloyd Wright, Buckminster Fuller, and Le Corbusier, as seen here, in a comparison of the Radiant City concept and the Corlears Hook housing project built on the site once proposed for the River Gardens project in the Lower East Side. *AF* (Sept. 1956), 111.

later related to Bauer in July 1956, "Jane Jacobs was in here worried almost sick with fear lest I jump completely into new city planning problems. Her greatest concern: we don't have the political apparatus nor the economic leverage to create the greenbelts. 'In the United States nothing gets done until the situation is desperate; only because the central city situation is desperate does anything get done about it now and we have the instruments. Don't you go escaping out into the country on paper!'" Jacobs scolded him.[37]

Bauer's interpretation of population growth and demographic trends over a twenty-year horizon suggested to her that central cities could not absorb the anticipated growth of fifty million people and their fifty million automobiles, and this led Bauer to propose an updated New Towns program that would control sprawl while accommodating the new population. The result would be compact, transit-oriented satellite cities. Although transit-oriented design is an idea still valid decades later—if no easier to achieve than in 1956—Jacobs interpreted Bauer's proposal as stemming from a preference for new towns outside of the old cities. Thus before it was printed, an editorial caption, written by Jacobs, was appended to the article. It said, "This novel argument says 'forget the old city' because 1976 will see new cities of up to a million people in today's countryside. This provocative concept sets off *Forum*'s discussion of the city pattern to come." However, "forget the old city" was not a message she wanted *Architectural Forum* to support or broadcast. She saw the message as at odds with both the larger pro-cities editorial position that *Forum* had been pursuing and her own interest in working for the magazine.[38]

To Jacobs's apparent dismay, Haskell was responsive to the facts of Bauer's essay, if not sympathetic with her argument. Typical of his approach, he was inclined to seek common ground even between apparently mutually exclusive propositions, whether it was Jacobs's focus on the city center or Bauer's on the region. He agreed with Bauer that "we couldn't duck the fact that so large a part of the problem will in fact be out in the country, whether we yet know of anything we can do about it or not." However, for Haskell, this did not mean giving up on "the old city." As he explained to Bauer, "I don't need to tell you that we don't ourselves agree that urban renewal should be forgotten and our whole energy put on new cities." He reassured Jacobs that *Forum* would keep its focus on the city, but not to the neglect of other issues. As he wrote Gruen on the same day, "We shall argue with [Bauer's] conclusion that you decide between redoing downtown and taking care of the new outlying growth. We shall demand that both things be done." According to Haskell, attention needed to be paid to "the continuity of America's entire 'human habitat' problem, embracing both 'new-towns' and renewal," country and city. The editorial that followed Bauer's essay articulated this argument.[39]

Jacobs was not so compromising. When the preservation of cities was at risk, she rejected the "decentrist" position. Rather than stand with Bauer in what she believed was the quixotic cause of regional planning, she would side with urban renewal. In an editorial reply shaped and partly written by Jacobs and appended to Bauer's essay, *Forum*'s editors wrote that they "promptly acknowledge the problem of giving decent shape to America's scatteration, but will not for that reason surrender their deep concern with urban renewal for today's central city."[40]

Jacobs's other contribution to "What City Pattern?" briefly examined a number of important aspects of the city: the central city itself, central city freeways, central city traffic, and central city housing. Unsurprisingly, "The Central City: Concentration vs. Congestion" discussed the difference between concentration and congestion and made a case for the city. In a few sentences, Jacobs summarized much of what she would elaborate in *Death and Life*—that the very essence of the city was the "intense concentration of people and activities." Concentration meant "exchange, competition, convenience, multiplicity of choice, swift cross-fertilization of ideas, and variety of demand and whim to stimulate variety of skill and will." And from this she concluded, "The suburbs may be incubators of people, but the city stands supreme as the incubator of enterprises," economic, social, and cultural.[41]

Concentration often led to congestion, but, using her favored geographic metaphors, she explained that they were not the same thing. Reminiscent of her essay on the city's infrastructure from fifteen years earlier, and Kahn's more recent plan for Philadelphia, she drew an analogy between cities and ecological systems. "Geologists have a saying that rivers are the mortal enemies of lakes, because the feeder streams tirelessly seek to clog, and the outlet streams to drain," she explained. "Just so, once the rivers of congestion are out of hand, as they are in our towns and cities today, they become the mortal enemies of pooled urban concentration. The elements of the city are clogged and eventually sundered from one another by the rivers of traffic, moving and still. . . . Even more serious, the rivers of congestion insidiously drain away those less visible urban strengths of convenience and swift, easy human interchange—and with them drains the historic, fruitful meaning of the city."[42]

In the next sections of her essay, Jacobs thus questioned whether urban freeways were the answer to congestion and argued for the need to understand various transportation needs. The question Jacobs thus posed was how to "manage the streams of traffic so they feed and nourish instead of choke and kill?" Her answer was to have faith that the city would offer up solutions to its own problems. "The city itself is an invention—a quite marvelous invention," she wrote. "Fundamentally it is an invention in specialization. And the time has come to apply that urban talent for specialization to traffic." Alluding to Kahn's ideas for Philadelphia and Gruen's proposal for Fort Worth, which she described as the most promising of present models, Jacobs offered that we "have begun the first (often fumbling) experimental inventions in sorting out the different local traffics of the central city." Anticipating problems with Kansas City's new beltway and Boston's new elevated highway and proposed Central Artery, she admired Gruen's plan for eliminating congestion at the destination as well as en route and for its openness to invention and adoption by cities of greater size and complexity.[43]

Although Jacobs's admiration for the Fort Worth plan continued in *Death and Life*, her ideas were still evolving at this time. Observing that half of the national $33 billion highway program was earmarked for expressways in and around cities, she wrote that the related "possibilities for good (traffic relief, blight-clearance, and blight protection) are magnificent; the possibilities for ill (new Chinese walls comparable to the old bisecting, blighting railways, more downtown floods of cars with nowhere to park them) are appalling." Later, in *Death and Life*, she did not express any such hope for the good possibilities of highway construction. And while she believed at this time that passenger cars, pedestrians, delivery vehicles, and mass transit all needed different accommodations "suitable to their different natures," in *Death and Life* her argument was more complex for synthesizing Bauer's critique of planning utopias with the automobile problem. "We blame the automobile for too much," she wrote in *Death and Life*. "Automobiles are hardly inherently destroyers of cities." Moreover, since "the point of cities is the multiplicity of choice," she could not reasonably argue for the complete elimination of automobiles, which, realistically, would not go away. The problem, she concluded, was not the car but the planning. While the Radiant City may have been designed for the car, it would have been equally void of city life if dependent on mass transit (and, as an urban interpretation of Howard's rail-enabled Garden City, it originally was). Many years before city center congestion charges were implemented, she reasoned that the problem of cars was not their conflict with other uses but their number: When choked by their own redundancy, cars don't move faster than the horses they replaced. Ultimately, for their own good and for the good of the cities that they would ultimately overwhelm through a positive feedback loop, she recognized the choice as the attrition of automobiles *or* the erosion of cities.[44]

Even as Jacobs proposed her city traffic solution in "What City Pattern?" the larger problem of sprawl and suburban settlement would nevertheless have remained unanswered. And she knew this. As she wrote in her introduction, "As a people, we are not too well prepared for physical planning to these dimensions: we are short on a philosophy for it, on laws, effective agencies, techniques. . . . It would be presumptuous of *Forum*'s editors to pretend they had answers." Nevertheless, Gruen's concluding essay, "How to Handle This Chaos of Congestion, This Anarchy of Scatteration," was meant to offer some ideas. "What is needed," Jacobs wrote in introducing it, "is a *working method* for contending with a situation that stops at none of the old boundaries. Could anybody come up with an approach that embraces concentration, dispersion, and scatteration—and brings order into all three? Because of Architect Victor Gruen's planning against congestion in Fort Worth and against scatteration in suburbia, *Forum* asked him for a working approach, to start off the thorough discussion that must follow."[45]

Gruen's tactics may have intrigued Jacobs. Building on his mall designs and plan for Fort Worth, he elaborated a concept of "cluster planning" that used walking distance as its basic unit of measurement and design. His proposal was also realistic for recognizing the need for some walking distance from a parking space to a final destination, and it was praiseworthy for not recommending residential slum clearance in urban areas. Referring to the Fort Worth plan, Gruen reported that, "without demolishing a single structure of value, and hardly touching anything of more than two stories, we could get enough space for the encircling belt highway, enough space for green areas on both sides of it, enough space for garages, enough space for expansion for fifteen years—and when we were through we had enough left over for new cultural and civic areas."[46]

It is unlikely, however, that even the best ideas for handling sprawl would have satisfied Jacobs's expectations for the collective will, laws, agencies, and techniques necessary to make a difference. Gruen admitted as much: "A solution is only possible if we attack the problem of the entire fabric of urban organization." Although his proposal avoided the anti-urbanism and heavy-handed design ideas of Howard, Wright, and Le Corbusier, it was an admission that revealed his strategy as perhaps no less utopian. As Jacobs had warned Haskell, she did not believe anything would get done until the situation was desperate. Although she would remain concerned about sprawl, Jacobs's strategy would ultimately be to focus her energies on the city and to attack the forces of anti-urbanism, even including friends, like Bauer, whom she branded in *Death and Life* as a "decentrist" for escaping to the country rather than standing with the city.

"The Dreary Deadlock of Public Housing"

Forum's issue on "city patterns" was not two weeks old when, in early September 1956, Haskell wrote Bauer to ask if she would help them with another big feature issue, a "major re-evaluation" of public housing. Apart from the "gosh-awful repulsiveness and institutionalism" of New York City's public housing, he offered a list of questions that might be asked of public housing at large, among them the roles of land reuse and racism, whether housing projects should be smaller and more integrated with their communities, and the place of subsidies toward homeownership. He mentioned a list of people with whom he had discussed the subject, including Vernon DeMars, Charley Abrams, Ernie Bohm, Dorothy Montgomery, Juan O'Gorman, and, of course, Jane Jacobs. After many trips to Harlem, Jacobs reported that public housing in the project model made "altogether a life less pleasant than the less comfortable life in adjacent slums."[47]

A two-part series, "The Dreary Deadlock of Public Housing," published in May and June 1957, thus became one of Jacobs's major writing projects in that year, and it was an important one for her preparation for *Death and Life*, where she referred to it. Although Jacobs's contribution, apart from editing, was a one-page introduction, others' contributions resonated with her. In addition to Bauer, who wrote the essay for part 1, many of the authors of the shorter pieces of part 2's "symposium"—James Rouse, Ellen Lurie, William L. C. Wheaton, Charles Abrams, Henry Churchill, Stanley Tankel, Dorothy Montgomery, Elizabeth Wood, Vernon DeMars, Lee Johnson, and Carl Feiss—later made appearances in *Death and Life*. Beyond her work for *Forum*, however, "The Dreary Deadlock" was a segue to Jacobs's increasing activism in her own neighborhood as a member of the Greenwich Village Study group, chaired by Tankel, a New York city planner.[48]

Like her criticism of planning utopias in "What City Pattern?," Bauer's essay was hard-hitting when it came to public housing and more even-handed when it came to discussing urban and suburban housing issues. She presciently anticipated both the migration of lower-income and minority families to the suburbs and the need for "better balanced communities with a wider variety of homes." But turning to the city, she attacked public housing's creation of an "extreme form of paternalistic class-segregation [manifested] architecturally in the name of 'modern community planning'"—ideas originating, she explained, "from British garden city planners and . . . rationalized by the Bauhaus school of modern architects." As Jacobs would also do, Bauer accepted the early experiments but rejected settling for the results. Among other failures, while Federal Housing Administration policy was creating a "lily-white suburbia," the early success of "nondiscrimination and mixed racial occupancy in northern public housing projects" was giving way to more and more projects "virtually all-Negro."[49]

Others made similarly "Jacobsian" remarks, many of which appeared indirectly or in quotation in *Death and Life*'s seventeenth chapter, where Jacobs referenced the article. Jacobs quoted the developer James Rouse's point that public housing was not an end in itself. "Clearing pockets of slums and replacing them with new housing, public or private, does little to correct the basic conditions which cause slums," he wrote. The ultimate goal, Rouse offered, must be "self-contained neighborhoods which have a soul, a spirit and a healthy pride—neighborhoods which people will vigorously defend against the forces of decay." Public housing often created just the opposite.[50]

Tankel made similar remarks, also quoted in *Death and Life*. "Why is it just occurring to us to see if the slums themselves have some of the ingredients of a good housing policy?" he asked. "We are discovering suddenly that slums are human in scale; that slum families don't necessarily move when their incomes go up; that independence in slums is not stifled by paternalistic management policy; and finally (incredible!) that slum people, like other people, don't like being booted out of their neighborhoods. We are coming to realize that it is not people and social institutions which are properly the subject of attack, but their housing conditions."[51]

The architect Henry Churchill agreed, adding, "We need an amendment to the [1954 Housing] Act, declaring the use of the word 'project' not only unconstitutional but wicked." Expressing a shared sentiment about public housing design, particularly tower blocks, he stated that there was no reason subsidized housing should be in any way distinguishable from private housing "in looks, location, color, method of construction, or anything else except for the subsidy necessary to make it available to those who need it."[52]

Finally, Ellen Lurie, a social worker at East Harlem's Union Settlement House, whom Jacobs invited to contribute, offered a list of ideas that Jacobs would later reiterate in *Death and Life*. Her essay also received Jacobs's decisive hand as an editor. Lurie's original essay began in this way: "New York City's East Harlem is probably the world's most extensively experimented public-housing guinea pig. In this proportionately small section of some 200 square blocks, fourteen public housing projects have already been or soon will be constructed. Actually, no self-respecting laboratory technician would dare subject one guinea pig to fourteen identical tests in order to discover the efficacy of a method. . . . Yet public housing did not bring neighborhood renewal to East Harlem." In editing it, however, Jacobs cut all this to a simple statement: "Public housing has not brought neighborhood renewal." She removed all references to East Harlem, leaving the edited essay an indictment of urban renewal and public housing *at large*, and she presented Lurie's key observations as general principles. "Too much of the cultural richness inherent in the slum neighborhood was destroyed," Lurie wrote, although with Jacobs's edits this loss of richness referred to all affected groups. Now emphasizing the vitality and intelligence of poor city neighborhoods everywhere, Lurie indicated that their complexity must be better understood by many contributors to city building, including city dwellers themselves. "There must be a real understanding of the neighborhood and the people who live there. Planners are needed—and not only architects. Sociologists, psychologists, clergymen, educators, and the people of the neighborhood themselves must study the social as well as the physical needs of the community," she said. "Those who do this must be humble, for even among the poorest, most unsavory-appearing community has elements of unique vitality which must be recognized, ferreted out, and saved."[53]

Lurie's conclusion for the failures of public housing, repeated by Jacobs in "Subsidizing Dwellings" (chapter 17 of *Death and Life*), was the subsidization of private housing. Lurie offered, "There is something basically

FIGURE 38. This photo of the Stephen Foster Houses in East Harlem accompanied Jacobs's June 1956 article "The Missing Link in City Redevelopment," a version of her Urban Design Conference talk. She wrote, "New housing developments like this one in East Harlem, New York City, take into account little beyond sanitary living space, formal playgrounds, and sacrosanct lawns." *AF* (Jun. 1956), 132.

impossible about public landlordship." In her book, Jacobs explained the sentiment as a societal one: "Because we lack any ideology that puts government as the landlord and owner of public housing in context with the rest of our national life, we have no sense about how to contend with such a thing." It was at odds with the "meaning of home as it has evolved otherwise in our tradition." She concluded that "the best that can be said of the conception is that it did afford a chance to experiment with some physical and social planning theories which did not pan out." As others had suggested in "The Dreary Deadlock," it was time to experiment with financial incentives that would correct market failures such as blacklisted districts, provide guarantees for private landlords, and channel public-supported private development into unslumming. In *Death and Life*, Jacobs would also similarly emphasize the need to enact public policies that were truly public. "Separate but equal makes nothing but trouble in a society where people are not taught that caste is a part of the divine order," she wrote.[54]

At this time, however, Jacobs was thinking about architectural alternatives to typical high-rise project housing in "Row Houses for Cities," which accompanied the first part of "The Dreary Deadlock of Public Housing." "Row Houses" was actually the second time Jacobs examined the virtues of this quintessential urban housing type in a *Forum* article. The first was the last piece of her "Central City" feature for "What City Pattern?" in September 1956, where, in a short, four-paragraph essay titled "Central City Housing: Return to the Outdoor Room," she succinctly described a number of the advantages of row houses, particularly when they were mixed with high-rises.

Still characteristic of her writing at this time, Jacobs's essay included some ideas that she would later reject, such as the separation of traffic. New row-housing developments, she wrote, for example, separated "the street and all that belongs to it from the dismounted inhabitant and all that belongs to him, carefully disposed to create outdoor rooms, carefully punctuated with what the British, in their excellent experiments with mingled low and high rise housing, call 'point' buildings."[55]

In "Row Houses for Cities," she elaborated on this point. "The big rediscovery is that a basic scheme dating from pedestrian days in Pompeii and carriage days in Philadelphia, turns out to be an excellent answer to the automobile," she wrote. "If the row houses are placed close along the street (or along an enlargement of the street for parking), and all vehicles are kept to the street side, then all the land for yards, garden and play can be concentrated on the other side of the houses, and the old vehicular alley can be converted to a pedestrian walk or commons. This pattern," she continued, "effectively segregates vehicles, protects other activities and creates a kind of walled space with delightful possibilities."[56]

Apart from issues of the car, Jacobs extolled the virtues of their semi-private spaces. "No other city land serves such a fantastic variety of digging, gardening, repairing, playing, chattering, and plain sitting, or can be so subtly responsive to the needs of children and neighborhood as the row-house yard," she wrote. To this she added the architect Henry Whitney's arguments that row houses naturally cut the costs not only of land but also of infrastructure, and they made walking distances that much shorter. Moreover, row houses seemed to answer the desires and needs of the willful middle class. "The middle-income flight to the suburbs," he said, "results primarily from a simple human necessity—the need for closer relationship between the indoors where the mother is doing the housework and the outdoors where her children and the neighbors' are playing. High rise apartments cannot do this; row housing can."

In "Row Houses for Cities," case studies included I. M. Pei and Harry Weese's designs for Southwest Washington; Wright, Andrade & Amenta's Eastwick development for the Philadelphia Redevelopment Authority; and Henry Whitney's design for the Baltimore Housing Authority. Eastwick was praised for the close relationship of interior planning to exterior land use, while the Baltimore project, which offered individual, fenced yards, gave the tenants the status and responsibilities of normal householders and did not "set them off in outlandishly different quarters from their nonproject neighbors."[57]

Despite being better in some ways than high-rise housing, these suburban projects—which had densities of twenty-one and thirty-five units per acre—were not praised in *Death and Life*. But Jacobs would not forget Whitney's research on housing. In "Row Houses for Cities," Jacobs reproduced Whitney's chart of dwelling density per acre in various combinations of low- and high-rise units. In *Death and Life*—where she observed that Greenwich Village had 125 to more than 200 dwellings per acre, and Boston's North End up to 275—she referred to his research again, although to support her own arguments for density and diversity. "Mr. Whitney found that no matter how you slice it, it is physically impossible to get above low city densities (40 to an acre or thereabouts) without standardizing all but a minute token of the dwellings—*unless ground coverages are increased*, which is to say unless open space is decreased," she reasoned.[58]

Jacobs—who lived in a number of city homes with small backyards—did not give up on the idea of row houses. Among her activist projects after *Death and Life* was a ten-year fight for the West Village Houses, a cooperative housing project of five-story row-house "walkups," put forward as an alternative to a typical renewal housing project for her neighborhood. Though West Village Houses would not be built until many years later, she started thinking about housing in her own neighborhood during these years. At the time of the "Dreary Deadlock" series, Jacobs became a member of the Greenwich Village Study, which formed in early 1957 and included thirty-four professionals—thirteen in city planning (including Tankel), eight in architecture, eleven in social sciences, and one each from engineering and real estate—to consider the future of the neighborhood, particularly its housing, zoning, schools, traffic, and opportunities for youth. By this time, part of Robert Moses's massive Washington Square South project—now known as Washington Square Southeast (and NYU's University Village)—was moving forward, although in mid-1957 Jacobs did not address it directly, seemingly unaware of the details at the time.[59]

In May 1957, Jacobs remained primarily concerned about the Washington Square traffic problem, and, speaking at an early Greenwich Village Study forum at Cooper Union, she offered a parable about "Dr. Moses." In the parable, a man with a cold went to the doctor, demanding a cure. When told there was no cure for the common cold, the doctor advised sleeping with the windows open, though it was winter, and letting the cold air rush through. The patient retorted, "I might get pneumonia!" "Exactly!" the doctor replied, and, glancing at his medicine cabinet, said, "We know how to cure that!" In the punch line, Greenwich Village is told to let traffic rush through the park, but retorts, "I might get blight!" Dr. Moses replies, "Exactly!" and, glancing at his bulldozer, says, "We know how to cure that!" Continuing the medical analogy, and riffing on another simile—that blight and slums were like cancer—Jacobs stated, "In the traffic for Washington Square, we see how neatly a cancer can be planted." Then, picking up Lurie's metaphor, she punched again: "Unfortunately, these doctors seem to be confusing their guinea pigs with their patients."[60]

In her talk, Jacobs then expanded on previous statements she had made about city planning with regard to Washington Square. "The outrageous plan for Washington Square is a vital issue in itself," she stated. "But it is important for another reason. It shows us so clearly something we must understand and face: This city either is not interested, or does not know how, to preserve and improve healthy neighborhoods." Alluding again to her parable, she continued: "City fathers worry because formerly stable neighborhoods deteriorate, because middle-income families move out, because Manhattan is becoming a place of only the very rich, the very poor, and the transient." Therefore, their only solution was redevelopment. "The best you can say for redevelopment is that, in certain cases, it is the lesser evil," Jacobs offered, with some ambivalence. She qualified this by observing that, "as practiced in New York, it is very painful." Side effects included

FIGURE 39. A 1957 proposal for Washington Square showing a roadway through the park and a pedestrian bridge connecting the bisected halves. *NYT*.

"catastrophic dislocation and hardship to tens of thousands of citizens," slum-shifting, destruction of business, great expenditure of public funds and diminished tax revenue, and great dullness.[61]

"The great virtue of the city, the thing that helps make up for all its disadvantages, is that it is interesting," Jacobs explained, making her case for Greenwich Village. Here, she observed, was "an area of the city with power to attract and hold a real cross-section of the population, including a lot of middle-income families. An area with a demonstrated potential for extending and upgrading its fringes. An area that pays more in taxes than it gets back in services. . . . Wouldn't you think the city fathers would want to understand what makes our area successful and learn from it?" Real estate developers too had observed the area's appeal, but they threatened it. Alluding to the "self-destruction of diversity" concept that she would explore at length in *Death and Life*, she noted that developers had said the Village was "fated to become largely an area of high-rent apartments with a transient population." This, Jacobs replied, "is one of the classic steps toward deterioration."[62]

Jacobs concluded her talk with four points for preserving and improving the Village, along with a mantra for community activism. Repeating points made by some other committee members, she advocated, first, "zoning to retain our scale, our variety, and the wonderful flexibility which make the Village so successful as an incubator of the arts and business." Second, there needed to be "traffic control to keep us from being destroyed by traffic plans gone completely antisocial." Constructive, "creative use" of zoning and traffic control, she emphasized, were "more important to our future than everything else put together." Third, there had to be "judicious rebuilding to mend the wear and tear of time and use," and, fourth, "careful siting and design of public facilities to make most sense for the community." All of these points would find their way into *Death and Life*, where, in her chapter "The Self-Destruction of Diversity," she referred to the work of Greenwich Village civic groups and advocated "zoning for diversity"—a concept that required intimate local knowledge of a neighborhood. Her mantra for civic activism, borrowed from one of her opponents, also endured, and offered the means to the end: "Agree on what you want, and use every pressure, rational and emotional, to get it. There is no other recipe."[63]

Scatteration Versus Concentration

Although Jacobs is so closely associated with cities, before dedicating her energies to the work that led to *Death and Life*, she was preoccupied with questions of land use and suburban sprawl. After "What City Pattern?" *Forum* published a series of articles on land use, some of them authored by Jacobs, including an editorial titled "Our 'Surplus' Land" and an article titled "New York's Office Boom," both published in March 1957. Almost a year later, in January 1958, while she worked on her important April 1958 essay "Downtown Is for People," *Forum* published her article "The City's Threat to Open Land."

As she would later reiterate in *Death and Life*, in which she noted the loss of three thousand acres per day to sprawl, in these early essays Jacobs argued that land was a finite and precious resource. "Everybody is using land and more land, as if the reservoir of open land were inexhaustible," she warned in "Our 'Surplus' Land." Among sprawl's other problems—she later included pollution and the loss of countryside and wilderness—she

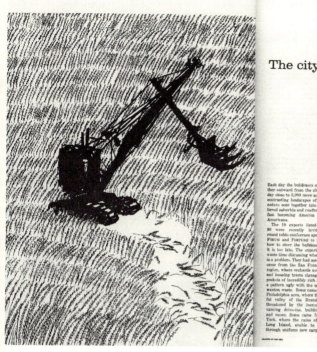

The city's threat to open land

The aimless sprawl of suburbia is destroying
a precious asset. How can we preserve
vital breathing space in our explosively growing
metropolitan areas? A round table report

Each day the buildozers munch farther outward from the cities. Each day close to 3,000 more acres of the contrasting landscapes of man and nature ooze together into the unrelieved suburbia and roadtown that is fast becoming America for most Americans.

The 19 experts listed on page 90 were recently invited to a round table conference sponsored by FORUM and FORTUNE to figure out how to steer the buildozers before it is too late. The experts did not waste time discussing whether there is a problem. They had seen it. Some came from the San Francisco Bay region, where orchards are toppling and housing tracts zigzagging over pockets of incredibly rich topsoil, in a pattern ugly with the ugliness of wanton waste. Some came from the Philadelphia area, where the beautiful valley of the Brandywine is threatened by the inexorably advancing driveins, building tracts and neons. Some came from New York, where the rains of western Long Island, unable to percolate through uniform new carpetings of

roofs and roads, are now scant guard against intrusion of salt water. Some came from the national capital area, where whole counties of rolling land are being swallowed in repetitive suburbia, with not even the equivalent of Washington's Rock Creek Park saved out. Some came from New England, where the subdivision signs are going up on the Truro moors within sight of the last magnificent stretch of pristine beach on the Atlantic mainland. Furthermore, they all came well aware that these despoilings of the great American inheritance are not exceptions. They are painful symbols of the rule of the unloosed buildozer in Chicago-Detroit-Cleveland or Albany-Troy-Schenectady or Norfolk-Newport News-Portsmouth or Houston or Los Angeles-San Bernardino-San Diego or any of several dozen other vast city sprawls in the making.

Is the cliché true that this is progress, and you can't stop progress? The round table participants thought that endless sprawl was no more progress than erosion is progress and that sprawl must be con-

trolled. Because by 1975, 42 million more people, a staggering increase of 44 per cent, will pile into the metropolitan areas. Most of them will move into what is now this suburbia or rural fringe or breathing space between separate cities. Even to grasp the fact of this 44-per-cent metropolitan population increase does not convey a picture of the added sprawl it represents. For example, the New York Regional Plan Association estimates that the New York-Connecticut-New Jersey metropolitan region, which now contains 15.5 million people and 1,100 square miles, will increase 25 per cent in population by 1975, but because the current pattern of growth is sprawl, the increase in area will be a huge 64 per cent—another 700 square miles.

State responsibility

The problem seemed "insoluble" to some participants at the opening of the discussion. It is so staggeringly big, it involves so many people, so many interests, so many kinds of land and enterprises. Intellectually,

FIGURE 40. In "The City's Threat to Open Land," published while Jacobs was working on her canonical essay "Downtown Is for People," Jacobs discussed the problems and consequences of urban sprawl. *AF* (Jan. 1958), 89–90.

was especially worried that there would not be enough farmland to feed an ever-growing population. Comparing the automobile to the locomotive, she offered the near extinction of buffalo in the wake of the intercontinental railroad as an analogy for the destruction of a food supply and a civilization, a concern reminiscent of those she later expressed in *Dark Age Ahead*.[64]

For the good of cities and the countryside, Jacobs offered that underused urban land was the better reservoir to tap. "The first step is to realize that unlimited land is not where we think it is," she stated, "but that a wealth of it lies almost unnoticed where we think it isn't." City halls and renewal agencies have been overly focused on slum clearance and residential development, she argued. They needed to make an inventory of their land reservoirs, much of it abandoned, underused, or undeveloped industrial, commercial, and interstitial land standing derelict and empty. Referring to the example of Gruen's Fort Worth plan (and to her May 1956 article), which utilized such land and thereby also avoided demolition, she argued, "Even in inner city cores, supposedly the most intensively used areas on the map, pools of surplus and underused land abound." And Fort Worth was not unique, she said. A map of Cincinnati's half-vacant downtown offered another example.[65]

Examining Manhattan's new forty million square feet of office space and forty-one new office buildings, "New York's Office Boom" offered an extreme illustration of the utilization of urban land, among other important points. Architecturally, she was not impressed, with a few exceptions; Lever House and the Seagram, Pepsi-Cola, and Union Carbide buildings were described again as masterpieces in *Death and Life*. "Esthetically, this boom is pretty much a bust," she wrote, critiquing the form-dictating zoning envelopes, the simple-minded use and scalelessness of repetitive industrial materials, and contextual conflicts. From there, she went on to discuss urban design and, in a rare use of the term, wrote, "The few proud buildings of this boom make it clear that a new and urgent problem in urban design accompanies beneficial opening up of ground space." Considering the case of the Seagram Building (1957) and its neighbor, the Astor Plaza Building (1959)—which she also alluded to in *Death and Life*'s chapter 19, "Visual Order: Its Limitations and Possibilities"—the problem was the addition of the Astor Plaza Building's plaza, which "cancelled out" the welcomed *first* interruption in the street wall created by the Seagram's setback. Buildings did not exist in isolation and therefore architects and clients needed to consider their work also as "town planning" or such coincidental plazas would "total up as happenstance, blobbed-together meanders."[66]

Ultimately Jacobs was less interested in these "proud buildings," as she called them, than in the "many-sided, enduring value of prideful building." Puns aside, as she had done with many a writing assignment, she took the opportunity to write about important and enduring issues. In "New York's Office Boom," it was why all of these corporations would choose to concentrate in the "most chokingly congested" parts of Manhattan. "What has happened to those sensible-sounding postwar catchwords, 'dispersal' and 'decentralization'? What has happened to the vision of the happy file clerks eating sandwiches on the grass far from the maddening crowd?" she quipped. "What has happened to the theory that modern magical communication makes constant shoulder-rubbing unnecessary?"[67]

Anticipating her arguments for the necessity of mixed primary uses and concentration in *Death and Life*, Jacobs presciently argued that technology would not replace physical presence. Apparently referring to the then-futuristic Tonotron videophone, Jacobs wrote that "person-to-person (even with video added) is no substitute for face-to-face, for the peek at figures not to be broadcast, the shared Martini, the subtle sizing up, the chance to bring the full weight of personality to bear." Invoking the Garment District, the subject of one of her earliest essays, she wrote, "Face-to-face business and gossip, famous phenomenon of garment district sidewalks, is just as important although more cloistered on Park Avenue." Sidewalks, she continued, were essential because concentration demanded short walking distances. In an early version of today's "creative class" argument, she explained that the young seventeen-to-twenty-five-year-old demographic, then in short supply, was attracted to Manhattan for "air conditioning, 'glamor,' adjacent shops and lots of them, and location in the throbbing center of things"—all of these forces contributed to the office boom. Adding to and anticipating her ideas about self-organization and the self-destruction of diversity, she described a self-reinforcing process. Also anticipating Rem Koolhaas's argument for the "culture of congestion" in *Delirious New York* (1978), Jacobs made what was, in the late 1950s, a truly radical argument. "Office district congestion is not visibly sowing the seeds of its own destruction, as reason says it should be. It is visibly sowing seeds of proliferation." She continued, "The most striking result, and perhaps the most significant, is that without planning or policy—based on nothing but pragmatic, separate decisions by thousands of tenants—office-Manhattan is sorting out, consolidating, and densely populating" its pedestrian-scaled working districts. Taken together, "Our 'Surplus' Land" and "New York's Office Boom" were arguments for density. The question left unanswered was how to make this happen.[68]

Jacobs's subsequent August 1957 article "Metropolitan Government" was a topical departure for her at the time, although she would return to the problem of great city governance years later. At the moment, however, she began to think about some structural possibilities for addressing the overarching land-use questions she had raised. Contrary to later stereotypes that arose in reaction to *Death and Life*, Jacobs did not believe that market reactions or the collection of individual decisions were enough. Although she was not optimistic about its institution, she called metropolitan government "the complicated instrument the cities must design before they can redesign themselves."[69]

On account of the automobile, Jacobs continued, metropolitan areas faced an unprecedented crisis of massive and complex problems— "monstrous traffic, missing or bankrupt transit, incompatible land uses, unbalanced tax structures, transformation of old core cities into racial and economic ghettos, pollution of air and water, and a host of others"— requiring coordinated thinking and planning. The obstacles, she realized, were tremendous. The nation's 174 metropolitan areas were a "weird mélange of 16,210 separate units of government." And despite having become "a nation of metropoli," the federal government had yet to come to grips with the fact of cities. Reminiscent of Henri Pirenne's histories of cities, and anticipating ideas she would explore in *Systems of Survival* and other books, she wrote, "Our states, divided into their revealingly named *counties*, are an organizational heritage from feudal territorial warlords who fitted the city into their scheme of things as a special, chartered 'exception.'" She further observed that, although some states had authorized regional planning activity and drafted master plans, there was no plan or power to affect those plans. Quoting Charles M. Haar—a Harvard law professor whom she had met at the Urban Design Conference and whom she would cite again in *Death and Life*—she wrote, "Without such clarification [of enforcement], there is small hope for a reconciliation of divergent interests, without which planning becomes simply a pleasant intellectual hobby."[70]

As for federal intervention, Jacobs also harbored little hope. Assuming that the federal government could miraculously coordinate its own agencies involved with cities and the suburban development, it was impossible to imagine Washington filling a planning role satisfactorily for the metropolitan area. Jacobs bluntly observed that the policies of the Federal Housing Administration and the Public Housing Administration, whether deliberately or not, "probably had more to do with the progressive ghettoizing of core cities, the class segregation of the suburbs, and the form of metropolitan scatteration than any other factors." The new federal highway program, she predicted, would have an even more profound impact.[71]

Thus, in the short term, regional planning was politically inconceivable and potentially destructive as a distraction from more immediate matters. By the time the metropolitan governmental structures were in place, it was possible that both the countryside and city would have been destroyed. The

Metropolitan government

by JANE JACOBS

The complicated instrument the cities must
design before they can redesign themselves

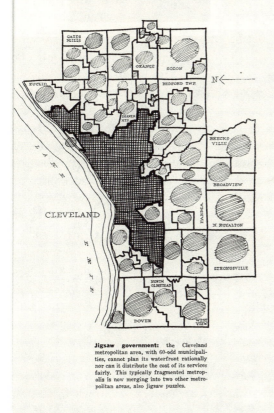

Jigsaw government: the Cleveland
metropolitan area, with 60-odd municipalities, cannot plan its waterfront rationally
nor can it distribute the cost of its services
fairly. This typically fragmented metropolis is now merging into two other metropolitan areas, also jigsaw puzzles.

In spite of a potent grass-roots-and-
town-meeting folklore, the US has
become a nation of metropoli; very
peculiar metropoli with problems
that are something new—at least in
degree—under the sun. Sprawling
over municipal lines, township lines,
school district lines, county lines,
even state lines, our 174 metropolitan areas are a weird melange of
16,210 separate units of government. The Chicago metropolitan
area, one of the prize examples of
fragmentation, has about a thousand
contiguous or overlapping local government units. But the problem is
similar everywhere: how does the
metropolitan area (which lacks governmental entity) contend with urgent and massive problems of a
metropolitan nature, armed with a
cross-purpose jackstraw heap of
local sovereignties representing genuinely clashing interests?

The metropolitan problems—monstrous traffic, missing or bankrupt
transit, incompatible land uses, unbalanced land uses with their sequel
of unbalanced tax structures, transformation of old core cities into racial and economic ghettos, pollution
of air and water, and a host of
others—are not new in kind. But
they have become abruptly massive
and urgent during the past ten
years because we have had a phenomenal growth of metropolitan
population and this has coincided
with the phenomenal scatteration
made possible by the automobile.
These problems will become still
more massive as the present metropolitan area populations of about 96
million increase by an estimated 54
million in the next 18 years.

Cumulatively, the number, size,
and complexity of the metropolitan
problems add up to a metropolitan
crisis, as set forth in last month's
FORUM ("The Hundred Billion Dollar Question"). Looked at another
way, they also add up to one of
the greatest adventures in inventive
self-government that any people has
ever had a chance at.

Governmentally, we have never

Figure 41. In "Metropolitan Government," Jacobs wrote about the chaotic layers of city
and county government and also the need for a coordinated approach to city planning
problems. *AF* (Aug. 1957), 124.

number, size, and complexity of metropolitan problems already created a metropolitan crisis.[72] As she had explained to Haskell during their work on "What City Pattern?," it was only because the central city situation was desperate that it received some attention.

On a more positive note, Jacobs offered that the very idea of metropolitan government was young, not much older than the eponymously titled book *Metropolitan Government* (1942) by the political scientist Victor Jones. Drawing on the work of Jones, Haar, the Regional Plan Association director Henry Fagin, and others, she outlined possibilities for creating state-level agencies and the federation of metropolitan governmental units, as had been established in Toronto (the city, probably not coincidentally, that would later become her home). Such new layers of government would be controversial, far from perfect, and would take many years to establish. However, they would be "one of the greatest adventures in inventive self-government that any people has ever had a chance at." Calling up her deeply held belief in U.S. democracy, she quoted the architect Henry Churchill as stating that those who despair that self-government can ever be worked out with neatness and certitude should remember that, "within the broadest possible framework of the general good, disorder must be allowed for, lest the people perish. Any form of initiative is disordering of the status quo and so needs encouragement, not suppression, if democracy is to retain vitality."[73] Taking Churchill's idea a step further, Jacobs related it to another of her deeply held beliefs: the importance of trial, error, and experimentation. "The first thing to understand about metropolitan government is that it is going to be dealt with not by abstract logic or elegance of structure, but in a combination of approaches by trial, error, and immense experimentation in a context of expediency and conflicting interests," she wrote. "Whatever we arrive at, we shall feel our way there."[74]

In "The City's Threat to Open Land," published in January 1958, Jacobs offered some similar ideas, negative and positive. The essay was Jacobs's summary of an "Open Land" roundtable co-moderated by Haskell and Holly Whyte, who was then organizing a series of articles about the built environment for *Fortune* (later reprinted as *The Exploding Metropolis* in 1958). Whyte's essay for the series—"Urban Sprawl"—spun out of the "Open Land" roundtable, which he mentioned in the essay. Other participants included Catherine Bauer (who read and commented on Jacobs's draft summary), Charles Abrams, Ed Bacon, Charles Haar, Henry Fagin, and Carl Feiss.

In her article, Jacobs described the sprawl debate as already well developed and well understood (even by contemporary standards). Panelists "did not waste time discussing whether there is a problem." It was clear that "whole counties of rolling land are being swallowed in repetitive suburbia" and "vast city sprawls" were growing between the "megalopolises" and "supercities." Scenic landscape was being destroyed and precious Class I farmland was being consumed. Impervious surfaces abounded with rain "unable to percolate through uniform new carpetings of roofs and roads." Streams were being polluted and watersheds fouled. Although the terms were different, this was the early age of environmentalism. For the built environment, the waste of "scatteration" left in its wake and at its flanks an astonishing amount of open space that counted for nothing and bore "no relationship to soils, water, topography." What was left over was "too random, too formless, too inefficient" to amount to anything. "It is too blighted even to retain its attraction as a place to fill in," she wrote.[75] The only question was "how to steer the bulldozers before it is too late."

Jacobs's answer offered some insight into her approach to planning (or lack of it). She emphasized the necessity of the immediate acquisition of open land. Her prescription was "action first" to avoid "paralysis by analysis." As Jacobs put it, "Set aside open land before it is too late; rationalize its use later." "There is no such thing as 'unused' open land," she remarked. Conversely, "To remain open may be by far the highest use of a piece of land in both the public and private interest," she continued. "Scatteration . . . had outdated the old concept of 'developed' versus 'undeveloped' land—the concept that a favor is done for any land when it is built on."[76]

Ad hoc preservation was thus a necessity and "no betrayal of the cause of regional planning." On the contrary, each ad hoc "incident of improvement" could "accelerate *de facto* regional planning as nothing else could." This tactical urbanism, she anticipated, could be the focus of action and the realistic, informed, and intelligent pressure of activists. "Open land amid sprawl is tangible, it is understandable, its benefits to a huge cross-section of population and interests can be made obvious," Jacobs wrote hopefully. "And the dismaying truth about its desperate urgency is already registered in the brain of anyone with eyes to see what has happened to the metropolitan countryside of five years ago."[77]

Jacobs's conception of "action first" for open-land preservation also had its counterpart in her approach to preserving the city. The situation was desperate; there was no more time for "escaping into the country on paper" with comprehensive plans that would take years to be drawn up and debated than there was for New Towns. While sprawl and the loss of farm and open land were problems for civilization, if metropolitan government was impractical and "de facto regional planning" ultimately inadequate, perhaps cities could be saved.

"Downtown Is for People"

Although Jacobs later denied being associated with the Greenwich Village Study, in late 1957 she remained engaged in neighborhood activism through the group as she worked on the "Open Land" symposium and pitched a story that Haskell would describe as "the first comprehensive piece" on the subject of urban redevelopment. The article that became "Downtown Is for People" was Jacobs's prelude to *Death and Life*.[78]

In November 1957, Cooper Union hosted another forum for the Greenwich Village Study to present its preliminary findings, and, in December, the NYU Law School hosted a third presentation with an audience of three hundred persons and speakers, including Tankel, Jacobs, Gruen (evidently invited by Jacobs), and local politicians, including Carmine DeSapio and Bill Passannante (a state assemblyman). Passannante and DeSapio, the leading figure of Tammany Hall (the New York Democratic party) and the Greenwich Village District (and a Washington Square resident), had the power to challenge Moses's plan but made ambiguous remarks about their support for closing the square to all traffic. Behind the scenes, as Jacobs later described, he and Passannante were the targets for local pressure in a game of Machiavellian politics. The Joint Emergency Committee to Close Washington Square to All but Emergency Traffic, led by Shirley Hayes and the local economist and consultant Ray Rubinow, had collected ten thousand signatures, which they delivered to DeSapio.[79]

At both presentations, Tankel spoke about Village demographics and the Washington Square roadway, arguing—possibly after Jacobs's coaching —that it did not make a difference if the road was fifty feet wide, as Moses wanted, or thirty-six feet wide, as compromisers proposed. But he did not make clear demands for the closure of the square to all but emergency traffic.

Jacobs, now recognized as the chair of the Study's housing committee, at last addressed the Washington Square Southeast housing project, but she recognized in it the much larger problems of urban renewal that she would

address in her forthcoming article and in *Death and Life*. "We do not consider community destruction as progress, no matter how shiny or clean it
looks," Jacobs stated, likely thinking of East Harlem. New housing, though
it might be needed, should not be built at the expense of the neighborhood,
and it should not be in the now-familiar form. Segueing from Tankel's
remarks that Village demographics revealed a replacement of families for a
"transient population with little interest in community welfare," Jacobs
argued for housing that catered to a diverse community and respected its
physical nature. "There should be some low-income public housing. But—
and this is a big *but*—any new building, whether for middle or low income
groups, should not be in the form of 'projects' such as we are accustomed
to see elsewhere in New York and as we shall soon see rising in the Washington Square Southeast high-income project," she said. "Aesthetically, the
approach is out of keeping with the Village. Furthermore, its implicit economic class segregation is socially undesirable and retrogressive from the
situation now being found in the Village." She argued that the needed alternative was a program of "spot redevelopment" (later called infill housing)
for low- and middle-income families on a scale compatible with the Village.

Apart from the social and class segregation of project development,
Jacobs also objected to the underlying premise, or excuses, of slum-
clearance urban renewal. "She defended the Villager's right to his cold-
water flat if he wants it," *The Village Voice* reported. "Many Villagers, especially a great many artists and writers, as well as simply old, established
communities of families make out pretty well in what, objectively considered, is substandard housing," she stated. Likely thinking again of East Harlem, she added that low rents and neighborhood social networks are more
important than new apartments. She concluded, "It would be authoritarian, and a disservice to the community to take the attitude that this sense
of values is wrong and that all tenement dwellings are, by definition, bad."[80]

The day after Jacobs's talk was reported in the *Voice*, Haskell told his
colleagues and superiors—Ralph "Del" Paine (the publisher of *Forum* and
Fortune), Joe Hazen (the managing editor of *Forum* and *House & Home*),
Paul Grotz (the art director for *Forum*), and Lawrence P. Lessing (the assistant managing editor of *Fortune* and a science writer)—about a big story
idea. Jacobs was prepared to attack the project concept. Jacobs, he told
them, "has been talking about an approach to city pattern which I think
we should discuss very seriously with her because it just might make an
impression in *Forum* as strong as our September 1956 ["City Patterns"]

issue."[81] Although he had been taken aback by her ideas at first, she had convinced him.

Haskell explained that Jacobs was prepared to take on generations of city planning theory. First, she would attack the idea of the large-scale, top-down planning approach: "Jane is moving right with the times because the ideas she is talking about do not require large-scale land acquisition, large-scale project planning, large-scale bureaucracy, etc., etc. Nevertheless, Jane is quite dauntlessly going in the face of some seventy-five years of tradition in city planning derived out of the original Garden City concept."

Next, she would attack the superblock, and superblock thinking, and argue for small blocks and more streets. Haskell explained: "The super-block has been one of the main pillars of this concept, along with the green-belt idea and the satellite town. What Jane is saying is that we do too much super-block thinking and, if anything, we need to cut our present blocks still smaller because the nervous system of the city is the street system."

Lastly, she would argue for more ground coverage and a more fine-grained and intimately scaled city fabric. "As I understand it, we would have a great deal of individual action on tightly packed small parcels by individual owners and no great dedications of land immediately contiguous to the houses, to space, light and air," Haskell concluded. "This space, light, and air would be brought in to the fabric by municipalities through condemnation of a great many more little squares for outright park use. So the kids of the vicinity could jump from their tightly-packed houses right into an open space the way my nephew used to be able to run down into Gramercy Park."[82]

Like few others, Haskell knew the extent of Jacobs's expertise. Even as she worked on the "Open Land" piece, she was preparing a summary of urban renewal projects that would be published in the April 1958 issue as "Redevelopment Today." In this unbylined feature, Jacobs wrote, "After nearly a decade of federal aid to urban redevelopment, only 17 Title I projects are now in use." However, among the completed projects—in New York City (Corlears Hook, Kingsview Homes, Delano Village, Columbus Circle Coliseum, Morningside Gardens); two projects in Manchester, New Hampshire; Baltimore, Maryland (Waverly, Johns Hopkins–Broadway); Philadelphia (Spring Garden Homes, Cambridge Plaza Homes, Penn Towne, Harrison Plaza); Syracuse, New York; Norfolk, Virginia; Providence, Rhode Island (Willard Street); and Chicago (Lake Meadows)—she saw "much material for a serious reevaluation of redevelopment." The elimination of urban "decay and squalor which these first 17 projects have achieved is heartening," she admitted, "but it is sobering to scrutinize the architectural results of the rebuilding. Is this indeed the city of the future, the hope of redevelopment? Architecturally or socially the results do not match the political ingenuity that made them possible."[83]

With this work in mind, Haskell recommended Jacobs's feature for further discussion at the next executive editors' meeting and that she should be allowed to elaborate her argument, despite the hostile reaction that they might receive at first from architects and city planners. He told his colleagues, "I think there is enough content in this to rate a serious go-around in our next editorial discussion to weigh giving Jane a big hunk of space for exposition and debate. I can imagine it would make many an existing planner furious at first, just as my own temptation was to be furious, but it is likely to rouse a very unexpected enthusiasm and give a new point for leverage in thinking and action about the city."[84]

Two months later, in January 1958, the last editorial board member finally gave his affirmative vote, and Jane was given the go-ahead for her "blockbuster on the superblock." It would lead her, by the end of the year, into writing *The Death and Life of Great American Cities*.[85]

CHAPTER 7

A New System of Thought

> This book is neither a retelling in new form of things already said, nor an expansion and enlargement of previously worked out basic ground, but it is an attempt to make what amounts to a different system of thought about the great city.
> —Jane Jacobs, 1959

WHEN JACOBS FIRST outlined a book on American cities in the summer of 1958, the time was ripe for a new way of thinking about cities, and people knew it. As Douglas Haskell said of her "blockbuster on the superblock" in 1957, Jacobs's criticism of large-scale land acquisition, large-scale project planning, and large-scale bureaucracy was "right with the times." After "Downtown Is for People" was published, Catherine Bauer expressed a similar sentiment. "Your piece was absolutely knockout, also splendidly timed, I think, to make a major dent. A couple years ago would have been too much on the up-tide . . . and you would only have sounded sentimental," Bauer wrote. But "now that the South Side of Chicago really looks like the City of the Future of 1930, however, and many other cities are visibly on the way, there are some tremors of doubt . . . though less in architectural offices for the most part than elsewhere."[1]

Jacobs admitted as much to Bauer. She dated her change in thinking to around 1956 and suggested that "Downtown Is for People" and a follow-up writing project that she had in mind—which would become *Death and Life*—were both "a symptom of the times":

I wish I could take credit for wisely judging the time was ripe for the viewpoint in the downtown article; but the fact is I am just a symptom of the times. These ideas have just been stewing around in me for the past two years or so, not before. Wish I could claim more foresightedness and forbearance, but it wouldn't be true. Right now I am just dying to do a series for *Forum* on what we can learn from the existing city about what is right, and the implications of this both for city rebuilding and new, fresh building. I believe they think I am kind of nuts, but sooner or later I will get permission to do it, and I know it will be interesting.[2]

The late 1950s were a time of great change. The years when Jacobs wrote *Death and Life* saw breakthroughs and momentous events in space exploration, geopolitics, desegregation, medicine, technology, literature, and the arts. The revolutions of the 1960s were just over the horizon, and criticism of all sorts, from angry young men and women, had blossomed by the time she started writing her book. As Jacobs admitted, she was not alone in recognizing the need for new thinking about the city and the built environment. Civic design and urban design programs were revived and created at American universities throughout the 1950s. Kevin Lynch was at work on "Form of the City" studies at MIT and, in 1954, he published an eponymous article in *Scientific American* in which he considered such basic city characteristics as size, density, grain, shape, and pattern. In 1956, Bauer wrote her broad critique of twentieth-century city planning in "What City Pattern?," and Ian Nairn and Gordon Cullen published the "Outrage" special edition and "Counter-Attack Against Subtopia" in 1956 and 1957. At the University of Pennsylvania, the chair of the new department of landscape architecture, Ian McHarg, was, like Lynch, working on fundamental research in his field, and, in 1957, he wrote "The Humane City: Must the Man of Distinction Always Move to the Suburbs?," an argument that landscape architects needed to shift their focus from horticulture to the design of cities. In New York, and elsewhere, opposition to Robert Moses's "blockbusting" approach to urban renewal grew each year. By 1958, Shirley Hayes's Committee to Save Washington Square, then six years old, had evolved into the Joint Emergency Committee to Close Washington Square Park to Traffic. Although Lewis Mumford had previously advocated the redevelopment of the area, his understanding had also changed; he described Moses's plan to run Fifth Avenue through the park as a "piece of unqualified vandalism." And by 1959 Grady Clay—the real estate editor for the Louisville *Courier-Journal* and associate editor of *Landscape Architecture* —published "Metropolis Regained," a Townscape-inspired essay admired by Jacobs for its thorough criticisms of city planning and advocacy of city life. Indeed, by the time she started writing *Death and Life*, there was ferment, even competition, in Jacobs's circle. McHarg wrote Clay to say, "I enjoyed the *Fortune* article by J. Jacobs, but I hope that this has not usurped your projected article."[3]

Architecture culture, meanwhile, remained in crisis but was also starting to move in new directions. Le Corbusier's chapel of Notre Dame du Haut (1954), in Ronchamp, France, heralded change. With Ronchamp, the master abandoned the very tenets and dogmas of modern architecture that he had defined, an act some younger architects considered so heretical that they accused Le Corbusier of causing a "crisis of rationalism." However, Le Corbusier's abandonment of the machine aesthetic of the 1920s was just one example of postwar disillusionment with the ideology of modernism that was broadly shared by architects young and old. By the mid-1950s, new ideas, and points of view previously suppressed, came to the fore. As Reyner Banham, a British critic, wrote in his 1955 essay "The New Brutalism," new movements—such as New Empiricism, New Traditionalism, New Regionalism, and New Palladianism—were appearing right and left. "The use of phrases of the form 'The New X-ism'—where X equals any adjectival root became commonplace in the early nineteen-fifties in fourth-year studios and other places where architecture is discussed, rather than practiced," he quipped. With this explosion of new ideas, the tenth meeting of the Congrès Internationaux d'Architecture Moderne (CIAM), held in 1956, would be the last official gathering of the organization that had championed modern architecture. In 1959, while Jacobs worked on *Death and Life*, "Team 10" (named for their role in organizing that last conference), which included the British architects John Voelcker and Alison and Peter Smithson and the Dutch architect Jacob Bakema, decided to disband the organization and no longer use its name. Bakema declared that young architects, like CIAM's founders, must renew their relationship with the present. To this end, and to "intensify the attempts for finding a new architectural language, individuals and groups must work in their own way." Indeed, Bakema went so far as to make a case against the use of the term "modern architecture." He explained that "in our Dutch circumstances we no longer like the word *l'Architecture Moderne*," and he went on to give a

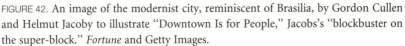

FIGURE 42. An image of the modernist city, reminiscent of Brasilia, by Gordon Cullen and Helmut Jacoby to illustrate "Downtown Is for People," Jacobs's "blockbuster on the super-block." *Fortune* and Getty Images.

rather Jacobsian reason: "Why don't we like it? Because we think that after the war, towns have been built, streets have been built, in a way that makes them look like what people associate with *l'Architecture Moderne*: we have mass repetition of blocks, [and] houses are placed in these blocks in military fashion."[4]

Thus, orthodox modern architecture—as previously conceived—was all but dead by the time Jacobs started *Death and Life*. However, the paradigm shift was not immediate. The rhetoric and images of the 1930s were extraordinarily powerful, and many among the Generation of '56 were not ready to part with them. As Banham wrote in 1966, the "vision of the Radiant City survived everything, and continued to dominate the minds of the Team 10-Brutalist connection even after the Athens Charter had been declared obsolete." Thus, while some modern architects were critical of CIAM modernism and sought ways to engage the particulars of place and time in their work, others remained committed to a more utopian project of "total architecture." Characteristic of paradigm shifts, new and old ideas coexisted in a confused state. Despite their criticisms of CIAM urbanism, Team 10 members and others advanced the metabolist and megastructural movements of the 1960s and 1970s with a persisting ambition for "total architecture." As Bakema put it, "If we don't work for an architecture expressing three-dimensional human behavior in total life, architects will lose their natural function in society, and they will end as decorators of mechanization-administration schemes. If we don't realize total architecture, we will end in no-architecture." Peter and Alison Smithson may have argued for replacing the functional hierarchy of modernist city planning with a hierarchy of human associations, but their London Roads Study of 1959 sought to give a wholly "new pattern" to the city—one that privileged the efficient movement of automobiles. When asked about their plan for the Soho district, Peter Smithson answered, "In the end we would probably destroy everything."[5]

The "Blockbuster on the Superblock"

Jacobs's proposal for *Death and Life* was published in *Fortune* in April 1958 as "Downtown Is for People." To Haskell's disappointment, the editors of Time, Incorporated, decided to divert her feature to *Fortune*, where it would have more space, gain greater exposure, and become the capstone of William Whyte's series of articles on cities and urban sprawl. They hoped to repeat the success that Whyte recently achieved with another series—a sequence of interviews with corporate executives that led to his best-selling book *The Organization Man* (1956).[6]

It was a good decision for *Fortune* and, ultimately, for Jacobs. Illustrated with a "photo essay" by Nairn and Cullen (who made drawings from Nairn's photographs) titled "Scale of the City" and accompanied by a heavily edited sidebar "What Makes a Good Square Good?" by Clay, Jacobs's feature garnered one of the strongest responses of any article published by the magazine. Whyte sent Haskell a transcription of thirty glowing letters from mayors, city planning directors, academics, real estate developers, and urban renewal consultants, including Raymond Vernon, a New York planning director; James Rouse; Frank Zeidler, the mayor of Milwaukee, Wisconsin; Richard Dilworth, the mayor of Philadelphia; Raymond Tucker, the mayor of St. Louis, Missouri; James Gardner, the mayor of Shreveport, Louisiana; James McCarthy, a city planning director in San Francisco; Francis Violich, a city planning professor in Berkeley, California; J. B. Jackson, the editor of *Landscape*; György Kepes, an MIT professor; and Ellen Lurie and William Kirk, Jacobs's acquaintances. "Look what your girl did for us!"

FIGURE 43. A sketch of San Francisco's Union Square drawn by Gordon Cullen from a photograph by Ian Nairn. Based on Cullen and Nairn's "Townscape" design philosophy, a series of pedestrian-eye views of real cities illustrated Jacobs's "Downtown Is for People." *Fortune* and Getty Images.

Whyte penciled on the top of the memo. "This is one of the best responses we've ever had!"[7]

Haskell was delighted with Jacobs's success but disappointed that it was *Fortune* rather than *Forum* that was receiving the recognition. The relationship between *Forum* and *Fortune* was somewhat strained, at least from Haskell's perspective. As he wrote Bauer in October 1957, "We are working with Whyte and *Fortune* in a highly cooperative spirit, but on the other hand, it is quite natural for *Fortune* people to need material they have in hand." After Jacobs's article was published, Haskell was similarly keen to point out that Whyte was their "student," not the other way around, and that Jacobs, one of his best writers, had been "lent" to *Fortune*. In a letter to Nairn in May 1958, he acknowledged that *Fortune* deserved praise for being ahead of most writing about architecture and urbanism in the United States, but "they got their cram course from *Forum*, and, alas, they got the first comprehensive piece on this subject by *Forum*'s own best writer [Jane Jacobs]. Since it will travel farther in *Fortune*, we can only be happy that

Holly Whyte was so brilliant a student. Moreover, the work he is doing under his own steam, and with no help from us, on open space, is quite wonderful."[8]

For Jacobs, "Downtown Is for People" was an opportunity to rearticulate, synthesize, and expand on points she had made in previous essays: the significance of the city's concentration and centrality, and the need to protect it from the automobile; the need to study it on foot and to design it at the eye level and for the human horizon, not for viewpoints from cars or airplanes; the collaborative process of city making; and the flaws of statistical design techniques and urban renewal projects like the "ersatz suburb" of Gateway Center. Anticipating points that she would elaborate in whole chapters of *Death and Life*, Jacobs argued that the street, not the block, was the city's essential formal and functional element, and that the multiple functions of the public space of the street needed to be respected and augmented, as in the example of Rockefeller Center. She argued the need for old buildings and short blocks, compact public spaces, focal points in city design, and the variety and function of a mixture of old and new. New buildings, she observed, invited chain stores and restaurants, not the marginal and exceptional enterprises that only a city could support. She argued in favor of mixed uses, multiple functions, a twenty-four-hour city, and the public spaces and planning that would facilitate these interactions and relationships. She argued for thinking beyond the limits of a redevelopment site: "Look at the bird's eye views published of forthcoming projects," she remarked, "if they bother to indicate the surrounding streets, all too likely an airbrush has softened the streets into an innocuous blur." And she argued for designing with the "peculiar combinations of past and present, climate and topography, or accidents of growth." She explained, in a Townscape-like fashion, that "a sense of place is built up, in the end, from many little things too, some so small people take them for granted, and yet the lack of them takes the flavor out of the city: irregularities in level, so often bulldozed away; different kinds of paving, signs and fireplugs and street lights, white marble stoops." Cities, Jacobs argued, were physical and perceptual topographies, and city building needed to be a collaborative affair, an activity of common senses, not of single plans and perceptions. "The remarkable intricacy and liveliness of downtown can never be created by the abstract logic of a few men," she affirmed.[9]

Among those captivated by Jacobs's article was Chadbourne Gilpatric, the associate director of the Humanities Division of the Rockefeller

Foundation and a champion of the foundation's urban design research initiative. In fact, Jacobs was already on his radar before "Downtown Is for People." In February 1958, Gilpatric had contacted Haskell, who suggested he speak with Jacobs about issues of cities and critical thinking about their renewal. In his notes on this conversation with Haskell, Gilpatric noted, "Haskell deplores the paucity of critical thinking about new demands for architecture and design in city planning. One of the few able and imaginative people concerned with this domain is Jane Jacobs, on his staff. She has just completed a long piece for the next issue of *Fortune* on the problem of the overloaded central city, i.e., congested downtown areas in American cities. (Jay Gold of *Fortune* will send an advance copy of this issue.) She might be a person worth talking to soon."[10]

By this time, the Rockefeller Foundation's ten-year urban design research initiative was halfway through its run. Launched in 1952, the initiative was the inspiration of Wallace K. Harrison, a new Rockefeller Foundation executive and trustee and also the lead architect of Rockefeller Center, the 1939 World's Fair, and the United Nations headquarters. Harrison, who was then working on plans for Lincoln Center with the architect Pietro Belluschi, also the dean of MIT's School of Architecture and Planning, had recommended MIT for the foundation's support. As part of the emergent interest in urban design, in 1952, Belluschi was considering the establishment of a new civic design program, and two of his faculty members, Kevin Lynch, assistant professor of city planning, and György Kepes, professor of visual design, had recently begun collaborative research on the form and experiential qualities of the city in a graduate seminar named "The Form of the City." Following up on Harrison's recommendation, Charles Fahs, the director of the foundation's Humanities Division, began a series of conversations with Lynch, Kepes, and John Ely Burchard, the MIT dean of Humanities and Social Sciences, to discuss possible research initiatives for funding.[11]

Burchard pushed the idea further. With a background in liberal arts and architectural engineering, Burchard was a passionate proponent of developing programs for the study of art in conjunction with general education, with a special interest in architecture and its education for both majors and nonmajors. He was also an amateur urbanist who would later write "The Urban Aesthetic" (1957) for the *Annals of the American Academy of Political and Social Science*, where he made observations about the phenomena, experience, and life of the city in terms later associated with

Jacobs. At the time that the Rockefeller Foundation was considering supporting research on urbanism, Burchard felt that city planning had
neglected "aesthetic elements to concentrate largely on technical ones of
communication, hygiene, and economics." He therefore supported faculty
and research projects that sought to develop more holistic approaches to
the study of the city. He wanted to "get a more humanistic element into
planning," with greater concern for the aesthetic and intellectual problems
of dwellers in the communities being planned.[12]

Burchard's comments pointed to the often-overlooked fact that, in
1953, city planning was still a relatively young field. The first city planning
degree program had been established at Harvard, with the support of the
Rockefeller Foundation, in 1929, but approximately half of the degree programs that existed by the early 1950s had been established during the postwar years. For MIT, a new Center for Urban and Regional Studies, directed
by the planner Louis Wetmore, was a step toward Burchard's goals; it would
become the institutional home for urban design research, "a means of
bringing together architecture and planning." Belluschi believed that
"architecture could not flourish without connections with its application
in planning, and also that city and regional planning needed architecture,
with particular emphasis on the visual element."[13]

By September 1953, MIT faculty had outlined three possible research
initiatives: (1) the study of the relationship between economic activity and
city structure; (2) the value of decentralization in response to the threat of
enemy attack; and (3) visual aspects of the physical environment. The first
topic was of particular interest to Wetmore, whose work concerned urban
economics and industrial location; the second was of interest to the city
planning chair-elect Gordon Stephenson and the architecture department
head Lawrence Anderson. Ultimately, it was the third topic, a study of the
phenomenological characteristics of the urban environment, that was of
interest to the foundation, and it led to the first urban design research grant
to Lynch and Kepes in 1954 and to Lynch's *Image of the City* in 1960—work
that would influence Jacobs's in various ways.[14]

As a collaborative project between an architect/city planner and an artist who was oriented toward environment, science, and visual design, Lynch
and Kepes's proposal to study the visual aspects of the urban environment
was fundamentally concerned with the human experience of the city, and
it helped to lay the groundwork for the foundation's support of Jacobs's
work. Building on their "Form of the City" research, in which they sought

FIGURE 44. As shown in Kevin Lynch's *Image of the City*, the Central Artery in Boston was a problematic edge urban condition. It was characteristic of new urban features that affected the "imageability" of modern cities. Photo by Nishan Bichajian, 1956. MIT Libraries.

to analyze effects on the city landscape from new buildings, like Boston's John Hancock Building (the first tower, built in 1947, now known as the Berkeley Building), which some had regarded as destroying the "aesthetic skyline." Through urban analysis they hoped to develop techniques to anticipate such effects. More broadly, they were interested in light, color, and other phenomenological qualities of the urban landscape, as well as in developing a "grammar of visual features" that was similar to the Townscape research being done by Cullen during the same years and to which it was later compared.[15]

In the fall of 1953, as Lynch and Kepes drafted their first grant proposal, they made explicit the association between urban design and urban redevelopment, and they also discussed the urban growth and sprawl that would be "dominant for many decades to come." They recognized, however, that "little systematic research has been done which has the three-dimensional city as its core." Anticipating Jacobs's criticism and research of a few years later, they wrote, "We possess several fragmentary concepts of desirable urban form: density relations, neighborhood organization, superblock design, specialization of traffic ways, standards for public facilities and housing, greenbelts, and so on. Currently useful in city planning practice, they are partly based on intuition and are the centers of controversy. Architects and planners, although centrally concerned with this subject, are only now beginning to turn to research to provide the desperately needed information, criteria, and techniques." They wanted to know answers to the following questions: "What are the effects of urban design from the point of view of the citizen? What is the meaning which such design has for people? What is the relationship of form to individuals? [How could urban design provide] a sense of location so that the resident both knows his way around and feels at home?" Burchard summed up the problem this way: "It is only once in a while that a Corbusier has a chance to build an [entire] city, and the cost of empirical experiment of this sort is large. Surely something can be achieved by rational analysis and laboratory experiment."[16]

While their framing objectives had the character of academic research, of particular interest to Lynch and Kepes were the "psychological and sensuous effects of city form on the individual." Their final grant proposal was accordingly titled "The Perceptual Form of Cities." From their study, they intended to learn how to build "a rich sensuous world out of the urban environment, one capable of generating new forms, new values, new imagery." They wanted to know what effects "the total visual environment of the city have on the inhabitants, and what would be the effects of various changes in the visual environment?" And they wondered if "the loss of unity in the architectural designs in modern cities produces unhappiness in the population, and how can happiness be restored by improving the unity of urban design?"[17]

To find answers, their starting point was the study of "the nature of the sensuous effects themselves," with an analysis of the urban environment with the goal of developing descriptions of significant visual elements such as spaces, surfaces, silhouettes, masses, scale relations, color, detail, time, and patterns. Phenomenological research would thus "concentrate on the sensuous impact of the physical city by sight, smell, sound, and touch; on the interactions of these sense data as they combine with each other in place and time and with the preconceptions of the observer; and on the decisions or outside influences that have created such particular sensations in the physical setting." Influenced by Gestalt theory, and the Gestalt-influenced Townscape theory, they believed that "a high level of meaning in the physical forms of parts and whole, expressive of their particular natures and functions, allow[s] the user to 'read' the city easily and to feel that it is 'warm,' stimulating, that it has character, or is well adapted to human ends." When awarded in 1954, the Rockefeller Foundation's grant to Lynch, Kepes, and MIT helped to establish the field of urban design, which the foundation's directors described as an effort to correct "the relative neglect of aesthetic aspects in connection with city planning during the last few decades."[18]

In the following years, the foundation's attention turned to the University of Pennsylvania. Under G. Holmes Perkins's leadership, in 1954, the school had reestablished its landscape architecture program, which had ceased instruction during the war, with Ian McHarg as director, and it launched a new civic design program in 1956 under William L. C. Wheaton. Perkins, McHarg, and Wheaton were initially unsuccessful in convincing the foundation to support their work, largely because it was so nascent. As Perkins observed in 1956, "There is little which can be described as research in the school, or, in fact, in other architectural schools." But Edward D'Arms, the foundation director, understood the matter quite clearly. In response to an unsuccessful proposal by McHarg, he remarked, "McHarg, by implication at least, seems to regard landscape architecture as something different and distinct from architecture or city planning. Actually, it seems to me that the examples he has given of landscape architecture (parkways, expressways, municipal parks, play fields, playgrounds) should be regarded as part of the total urban or rural scene and, hence, can hardly be considered separately from either architecture proper or urban design and suburban planning." It was a telling observation about the poor articulation of landscape architecture theory in the mid-1950s.[19]

Likely influenced by this feedback, McHarg would go on to revolutionize landscape architecture and write the seminal book *Design with Nature* (1969). However, the foundation's second grant went to Erwin Anton Gutkind, a University of Pennsylvania faculty member and architect and historian, for his ambitious history of Western planning and urbanization, with a small line item to McHarg as project administrator. Gutkind's eight-volume *International History of City Development*, published between 1964 and 1972, fulfilled the humanities department's basic mission, while Gutkind was seen as a successor to his friend Lewis Mumford, who was then also teaching at Penn.[20]

While valuable undertakings, the primary research project at MIT and the major historical project at Penn left the foundation looking for someone to answer the "almost complete absence of critical writing about the design of cities in the American popular and professional press." This is what led Gilpatric—a Rhodes scholar, former professor of philosophy, and polymath with an interest in literary criticism—to Haskell in February 1958.[21]

Indeed, there was so little writing of its kind that when Gilpatric read the draft of "Downtown Is for People" a few days later, he remarked to a colleague that Jacobs had drawn heavily on Lynch and Kepes's research. Although Jacobs had indeed referenced their work in her article, it was an overstatement that was ultimately to her credit, for the article appeared to Gilpatric to be on par with work from academics at a major research institution. Moreover, at a time when Mumford's "Sky Line" column in *The New Yorker* and Clay's articles in the *Courier Journal* were regarded as "the only regularly published criticisms of urban design appearing in any American [magazine or] newspaper," the success of her *Fortune* piece put her in the national spotlight. As Gilpatric put it a few months before Jacobs was awarded her first grant, "One form of the question was where there were to be found other Lewis Mumfords, who could bring his critical, philosophical and historical background to bear on problems of urban planning." She would be another Lewis Mumford, and perhaps more.[22]

A Book on "What the City Is"

Following the success of "Downtown Is for People," Jacobs gave a talk at a symposium on the future of New York at the New School for Social Research in April 1958. Moderated by Raymond Vernon (later cited in *Death and Life*), other speakers included Victor Gruen, Charles Abrams, and the developer Robert Dowling. In her talk, Jacobs's research, writing, and activism wove together ever tighter. She explained, "New York's basic material is its enormous variety of activities and people, and the intricate relationships among them." Anticipating similar arguments in *Death and*

FIGURE 45. Chadbourne Gilpatric at his home in White Plains, New York, ca. 1955. Marguerite Gilpatric.

Life, she went on to observe that the new Lincoln Center project and Moses's revived project to run a road through Washington Square Park were two examples of how, "at great expense, we are systematically building rigor mortis into our city." For its own sake, Lincoln Center needed urbanity—restaurants, bars, flower shops, studios, music shops, and all sorts of interesting places—as well as for its neighbors' sake. "The project is so placed, and so bounded, that there will be no possible place where urbanity can work itself in," she predicted.[23]

Just five blocks from the New School, the Washington Square project, she continued, represented another way to destroy a community, but one that would be stopped. "Because we are an effective, functioning community," she stated, "we are going to defeat that piece of vandalism and get Washington Square Park closed to all but emergency traffic. We have to." Echoing her 1955 letter to Mayor Wagner, she declared, "This is a chips-down test of the whole question of whether human values can survive in the city." Such projects must be stopped, and the thinking behind them must be changed.[24]

Among those who attended the event were Mumford and Jason Epstein, the senior editor of Doubleday, who was turning "The Exploding Metropolis" series into a book. Her talk made a big impression on them. Soon thereafter, Mumford wrote her and said she needed to reach a larger audience: "You stated, with such refreshing clarity, a point of view that only a few people in city planning circles, like Ed Bacon, even dimly apprehend. Your analysis of the functions of the city is sociology of the first order. . . . You ought to reach a wider audience for your ideas. Have you thought of the *Saturday Evening Post*? They seem in a mood for serious contributions these days. At all events, keep hammering: your worst opponents are the old fogies who imagine that Le Corbusier circa 1922–25 is the last word in urbanism." Undoubtedly encouraged by this, Jacobs presented the first outline for her project to Gilpatric a few days later.[25]

In a long conversation on May 9, Jacobs and Gilpatric talked about her recent trip to Baltimore to visit the new Charles Center redevelopment project. In "New Heart for Baltimore," published in *Forum*'s June 1958 issue, Jacobs reiterated that the project, although large in scale, was currently the best of its kind because many city departments and civic groups had been involved; because the streets and public spaces would be city property, not private property; and because numerous developers would be involved. With such an organization, "There would be no overall developer who could impose design and the kind of objectionable features typical of many big development projects." She admitted that Charles Center, "like all urban redevelopment, will cause hardship and perplexing injustices to some people now on the site." Despite the hardship to businessmen like Isaac Hamburger, a third-generation men's wear store owner, however, Jacobs praised Charles Center for drawing on more than a decade of "trial-and-error experience" with city redevelopment; for site planning that made the redevelopment less "a 'project' than an integral, continuous part of downtown"; and for creating "undiluted urbanity" through "architecturally designed and architecturally organized [open] spaces," which she associated with a scale and tradition closer to public spaces from medieval and renaissance times. "The open spaces," she observed, "are not simply places left without buildings."[26]

When next asked how the Rockefeller Foundation could best support the design and planning of cities, Jacobs told Gilpatric that she would like to see the foundation "give opportunities for observation and writing to some first-rate architectural critics who could develop helpful new ideas for the planning of cities." She recommended Ian Nairn (possibly "the best man there is on cityscapes"), Grady Clay ("the best man she knows at the present time" in the United States), and Catherine Bauer (who "is far ahead of her time and full of ideas"). She also recommended Nathan Glazer, an associate professor of sociology and social institutions at Berkeley, who had recently submitted the essay "The Great City and the City Planners" to *Architectural Forum* (published as "Why City Planning Is Obsolete" in July 1958)—which Jacobs would later cite in *Death and Life*.[27]

Finally, Jacobs indicated to Gilpatric that she also had an idea for a project of her own. She was interested in making an intensive three-month study of New York, focused on the city's public sphere. She had four studies, and articles, in mind: first, the city's streets and their sociological function; second, the scale of neighborhoods and the relationship of the size of social groups to their function as neighborhoods or communities; third, the city's social mixture and interaction, which she believed was "the essence of urban life"; and fourth, the implications of these scales and mixtures on the city's public streets and places. As she first imagined them, these articles would probably be published in *Architectural Forum*, but she needed a few months' leave from her other editorial responsibilities to write them.[28]

Jacobs and Gilpatric would not talk again until early June. By that time, her thoughts about writing a series of articles had changed to writing a book, the subject of which would be "what is the city" or "what should the city be for people." Referring to Henri Pirenne's *Medieval Cities*, the primary theme of the book would be showing the flaws of the contemporary planning concept of the city "as a castle where the overall plan is subject to a single or collective mastermind." In contrast to this top-down approach, Jacobs would explain her understanding of a "highly pluralistic concept of the city which allows for many forces and chance factors." A book, she added, would give her the opportunity to expand her research beyond New York, to other cities, including Baltimore, Pittsburgh, and Philadelphia.[29]

In mid-June, Jacobs followed up on their conversation with a revised proposal, the first outline of her book. Such a book, she reiterated, was needed because "we are now planning for our cities with very little idea of what the city is, what works well in it, and what does not." Anticipating the introduction to *Death and Life*, she stated that most city planning and rebuilding ideas, since the time of Ebenezer Howard, had been based on rejection of the city, in favor of small towns and suburban values. In the meantime, she continued, enough experiments based on such ideas had been built to show their failures. As she similarly remarked in *Death and Life*, "Our cities have gone through an enormous amount of unplanned trial-and-error experimentation. If we will only look for this and try to understand what it means, we can learn much from it to guide our treatment of the city and stimulate our imagination about ways to improve the city."[30]

The outline of Jacobs's book now included five sections—street, park, scale, mixture, and focal centers—and she went on to discuss each. "The street is the most important organ of the city; we need to know what jobs it does, how people try to use it, when and how it works as a unifier and a social control, what distinguishes the streets of socially or economically successful parts of the city, what has been past experience with superblocks and other street variations in the city," she explained. Parks, she went on, were a specialized extension of the street, with similar principles of social safety and informal use, and a better understanding of what distinguishes parts that "do a good job" was also needed. Scale included the "characteristic sizes of things in the big city, and ranges of sizes, and also the frequency with which similar things occur. We need to know the characteristic scale of different kinds of commercial and cultural enterprises, the scale of big-city neighborhoods and communities, the scale of the kinds of institutions that have grown most spontaneously or have been most responsive to needs."[31]

Mixtures, she continued, were related to scale, but there was much that is interesting about them. Anticipating her critical discussions of diversity in *Death and Life*, mixtures indicated "the sort of mixtures occurring in business areas that have shown the best survival value, the kinds of mixtures of people and activities that occur in areas which fight political battles for community survival or improvement most successfully, what happens to areas of extreme sorting-out of people or activities, and why, what opposing forces are at work for mixing and sorting." Lastly, focal centers were the places within a city community, large or small, that are "important out of all proportion to their size." Anticipating a number of chapters in *Death and Life* about city form and public space, she wrote, "We need to know what kinds of things are in the places where big-city communities come to a focus, what kind of effect they exert, and what relation they have to a sense of community. Related to this is the question of 'borders' and edges of areas within the city. The borders are much less significant than the centers, but present planning has pretty well overlooked the importance of centers and concentrated on defining borders, often with ridiculous results because what looks like a border in orthodox planning theory may, in reality, be a vital center." Jacobs wrote that she would conclude her book by analyzing the implications of all this for planning in cities, and she would suggest suitable aims and means for big city planning and rebuilding. She would also discuss the limitations of planning: "the things in the city that must be left to happen, that no planner can do for people, but that will be done well or ill or not at all, partly depending on whether the general framework hampers the functioning of the city or fosters it."[32]

In the remainder of her letter, Jacobs wrote about her focus, method, time frame, and other comments about what, other than her five elements of study, would be at the heart of the book. She would draw primarily on Manhattan, she explained, because she knew it well, and within Manhattan most on "East Harlem, Greenwich Village (a big range is presented among these two), and the series of downtowns which Manhattan has grown from south to north." However, she would test her observations against other parts of the city, and against a number of other cities entirely, to avoid taking things for granted in places she knew well, to reveal superficial irrelevancies, and to concentrate on the widest applicability for her findings.[33]

In writing her book, Jacobs remarked, "I would aim at the general interested citizen, rather than writing for the specialist. But I hope (and think) that the book would interest specialists." On account of the subject matter, moreover, she would avoid abstraction. "I plan to make my points and describe the city mainly by means of specific instances and examples. I would include examples embracing, in each section, commercial life, residential life, cultural and institutional life, because one of the very important characteristics of the big city is the inextricable interdependence among all these aspects of life; we have already been led much astray by arbitrary attempts to deal with these as isolated and independent entities," she wrote.

In conclusion, she wrote, "My bias, in general, is that of a person who is on the side of the big city. . . . I want to see it work well and fulfill its potentialities." And then, underscoring her lifelong interest in the relationship of cities to civilizations, she affirmed, "The most valuable thing about it [the big city], in my view, is that it is a marvelously intricate, constantly adjusting network of people and their activities. This network makes all the unique and constructive contributions of the great city possible; it also makes possible the social controls that have to be effective on people, communities and enterprises within the big city if we are to maintain a high standard (or even a decent standard) of civilization." The project, she now estimated, would take about nine months—three for research, five for writing, and one for editing. "I know it's a tight schedule," she admitted, but "I do my best work when I am under pressure that I have to do my utmost to meet. It is not very comfortable, but it works."[34]

A few days later, Jacobs asked Mumford's opinion about writing a book. In a letter, she thanked him for his kind words about her New School talk and praised his recent article in *Architectural Record* on the highway-building boom following the Federal Aid Highway Act of 1956. With characteristic interest not just in criticism, but in the underlying principles of flawed ideas, she wrote, "Your article on highways in the *Record* was splendid. It was so good to read not just a criticism of the way highway planning is being done, or an exhortation to do it better, but an analysis of the destructive and lopsided premises on which the very existence of the program, as it stands, is based. You made a statement I've never seen before, and that I think is terribly important: about the relationship between the cost of feeding this automobile way of life, and the poverty of our public standard of living, schools, libraries, and the like." Mumford responded with great enthusiasm and generous encouragement. "Though I can't guess how the public would take to it, you have a duty to produce the book!" he exclaimed. "There's no one else who's had so many fresh and sensible things to say about the city—and it's high time these things were said and discussed."[35]

"Relations of Function to Design in Large Cities"

Early support for Jacobs's book project was invigorating. Epstein, who would become her lifelong editor, offered her an advance on a book contract. However, Gilpatric and his colleagues still had questions about the scope and content of the work. In July 1958, Jacobs addressed these indirectly in an editorial in *Forum* and directly in a series of letters to Gilpatric. In "What Is a City?," published in *Forum* in July 1958, Jacobs explained much of her project and many of her ambitions. A city, she explained, "consists of an intricate living network of relationships, and is made up of an enormously rich variety of people and activities. . . . [C]onsider the thousands upon thousands of pieces, most of them quite small, which make a big city. Consider the interdependence, the constant adjustment, and the mutual support of every kind which must work in the city, and work well. This network of human relationships is, in fact, all that the city has which is of unique value." The idea of a city as a network of human relationships echoed similar ideas in "Downtown Is for People," "Philadelphia's Redevelopment" from a few years earlier, and her first essays on the city.[36]

Jacobs continued by admitting that cities needed help. "The average US city does need rebuilding, to be sure; in some portions it needs wholesale clearance." But this did not excuse the need to criticize current thinking, programs, and practices. To support her case, she quoted from Harrison Salisbury's recent series of articles on the "shook-up generation" in the *New York Times*. "When slum clearance enters an area," Salisbury wrote, "it does not merely rip out slatternly houses. It uproots the people. It tears out the churches. It destroys the local businessman. It sends the neighborhood lawyer to new offices downtown and it mangles the tight skein of community friendships and group relationships beyond repair." Resonant with her analysis of East Harlem in her 1956 Urban Design Conference talk, "The Missing Link in City Redevelopment," Jacobs quoted the same passage from Salisbury again in *Death and Life*. She agreed with his criticism of the flawed premises of redevelopment as well—in fact, she originally titled one of *Death and Life*'s chapters "Redevelopment—The Shook Up City."[37]

Shifting her focus to the related economic impacts, and anticipating *Death and Life*'s chapters "Gradual Money and Cataclysmic Money" and "Subsidizing Dwellings," Jacobs argued that urban redevelopment rested on the flawed premise that subsidized improvement would catalyze further spontaneous improvement. "Unfortunately, things are not working that way in most cities," she observed. "Living communities, portions of living commercial districts, are so ruthlessly and haphazardly amputated that the remnants, far from improving, often develop galloping gangrene." Social and economic segregation, moreover, went hand-in-hand. "We do not need to be prophets to see that we are creating an urban monster—a pseudo-city composed of economically segregated islands, of large, repetitive, separated, monotonous buildings," she contended.[38]

Jacobs concluded "What Is a City?" with a list of ideas that she would reiterate both in her follow-up proposals to Gilpatric, written soon after, and in *Death and Life*. "We must begin to examine and nurture what is good about the city to find the wisdom and practicality imbedded in them, such as how a great city, full of strangers, informally polices itself, and why various enterprises locate where they do." In an early formulation of her "eyes on the street" idea, she added, "We may find the old city was not so stupid in orienting all its eyes and activities toward the street." She went on to discuss why various enterprises locate, thrive, and fail in certain locations and of the consequent need to be astute about locating schools, health centers, welfare offices, shopping areas, and parks, so that facilities strengthen communities and reinforce "the living network of relationships." Alluding to the counterexample of Lincoln Center, she observed that downtown theater owners had traditionally located where the city was lively and would become livelier for their presence. To build strong communities, she offered that we must avoid fostering communities composed only of the transient—"either the publically housed transient poor, or the childless, transient rich." For the frequently dislocated poor, this meant searching for economic ways of rehabilitating structurally sound buildings without evicting "old, well-rooted communities."[39]

In a letter to Gilpatric on July 1, Jacobs added to these foundational ideas her conceptions of complexity and emergent order. This order, she explained to Gilpatric, underlay the city's network of relationships:

> Within the seeming chaos and jumble of the city is a remarkable degree of order, in the form of relationships of all kinds that people have evolved and that are absolutely fundamental to city life— more fundamental and necessary to safety, to convenience, to social action, to economic opportunity, than anything conceived of in the image of the rebuilt city. Where it works at all well, this network of relationships is astonishingly intricate. It requires a staggering diversity of activities and people, very intimately inter- locked (although often casually so), and able to make constant adjustments to needs and circumstances; the physical form of the city has also to be full of variety and flexibility for people to accom- modate it to their needs.[40]

Appreciation of the existence of this ordered complexity, and Jacobs's goals of understanding and communicating it, would distinguish her approach from others. She offered that there were presently two "dominant and very compelling mental images of the city" that had come to shape the thinking of both citizens and city planners. One was "the image of the city in trouble, an inhuman mass of masonry, a chaos of happenstance growth, a place starved of the simple decencies and amenities of life, beset with so many accumulated problems it makes your head swim." The other image was of "the rebuilt city, the antithesis of all that the unplanned city represents, a carefully planned panorama of projects and green spaces, a place where functions are sorted-out instead of jumbled together, a place of light, air, sunshine, dignity, and order for all." Echoing Bauer's, Glazer's, and others' criticisms of the suburbanism of Howard's low-density Garden City and of Le Corbusier's high-density garden city, she argued that city planners and theorists had replaced city problems with a patterns of design better suited for suburbs and small towns. Jacobs proposed to offer a different image of the city, "not drawn from mine or anyone else's imagination or wishes but, so far as this is possible, from real life; an image more compelling to the reader than the abstractions, because he is convinced it is truer." Her goal, moreover, was not just presenting a new image of the city, but opening "the reader's eyes to a different way of looking at the city for himself and understanding what he sees."[41]

Later criticized for her empirical approach, Jacobs, in her letters to Gilpatric, was thoughtful and deliberate about her approach to writing *Death and Life*. To convince readers of her ideas about the city, she deliberately built up "a pointed accumulation of examples, illustrations, and explanations of cause and effect" and pursued an incremental organization of her argument. Her goal was "to present this accumulation of facts, and inferences from facts, so it really adds up for the reader and persuades him of its significance, instead of overwhelming or confusing him." Referring to the structure of her book, this would be achieved by "taking up certain aspects of the city, one at a time, without evading the intricacy of each aspect, but by choosing the sequence of subjects so that an understanding of each illuminates the next one and leads into it." She explained that in her book—as in the city—"complexity is thus of the essence, but it won't do to throw these intricacies at the reader like a basket of leaves."[42]

Once again, Jacobs reiterated her initial outline and sequence of topics: the street, park, scale, mixture, centers and edges (originally "focal centers"), and then "the implications of all of this for the physical city and its people." But what was becoming increasingly clear to her was the notion of *use*. She admitted that there were quite a number of people today looking at the city in the same way: "hunting for evidence of how people use it." She mentioned William Kirk, the head worker of Union Settlement, as she did again in the introduction to *Death and Life*. But she explained that many others did not understand the issue. In East Harlem, $250 million had been spent on redevelopment, but no one seemed to understand what was being destroyed or what was being created. She gave another example from her Harvard talk from 1956, also influenced by her experiences in East Harlem, about her observations of the use of storefronts. "A few years ago I gave a talk about the great importance of stores and storekeepers in city neighborhoods, and also the important non-commercial ways in which city people use storefronts," she wrote. "Since then, I have been distressed at the way this observation has been simplified into a gimmick, 'the corner grocery store,' by many people who were apparently moved by what they heard, but who have fixed in their heads so formalized an image of the 'residential' city that they are unable to assimilate contrary data from real life, except by modifying it into a pretty meaningless gadget."[43]

Jacobs's report of the influence of her 1956 Harvard talk was not exaggerated. Mumford and others had been impressed by her thinking then, and they continued to be as she pursued her book project. A week later, Jacobs showed Gilpatric a recent letter from Mumford and also mentioned that the architect Henry Churchill had offered to help her with research in Philadelphia. In fact, everyone she had discussed her proposal with was enthusiastic. A few weeks later, Hans Simons, the president of the New School, enthusiastically agreed to sponsor and administer her project, and he wrote Gilpatric that Jacobs's unusual qualifications for researching and writing her book would be assisted by the school's faculty and staff resources. Mumford, Bauer, Whyte, and others, she told him, would likely endorse her as well.

At the end of July 1958, Gilpatric wrote Mumford, Bauer, Whyte, and Epstein, as well as the Yale professor Christopher Tunnard; Martin Meyerson, the director of the Harvard-MIT Joint Center for Urban Studies; and Holmes Perkins for their comments. In their letters, sent in August, Mumford and Bauer, whom Jacobs would later criticize in *Death and Life*, were very enthusiastic. Mumford wrote that "there is no one among the younger generation whose work, in housing and planning, seems to me more promising. Indeed, she has already opened various fresh lines of investigation on matters that have been singularly ignored or misinterpreted by both planners and urban sociologists." Bauer concurred: "I'd back Jane Jacobs if I were you. She's already proven her effectiveness in promoting what has been a highly unfashionable viewpoint on the brutalities and banalities of present-day large-scale civic design. She's a good writer, sensitive and imaginative, with real personal concern for the qualitative visual and social aspect of modern American cities." Whyte was equally admiring and stated, "I believe the result may prove to be one of the great contributions to the whole field of urban planning and design." Epstein affirmed that he had offered her a contract. Meyerson questioned whether she could finish a book of real substance within eight months, but he described her as a very stimulating writer of great ability. Perkins, who was later alienated by the rhetorical attacks on city planners in her book, similarly wrote, "Her interest in the subject and her enthusiastic way of tackling the problem have truly brought new life into the discussion of the city. On these counts she is deserving of all the possible support that can be given her. She is a keen observer and to my mind a good writer."[44]

The only respondent who was not enthusiastic was Tunnard, who implied that she was an amateur. He wrote, "Studies of the city and of urbanization and urban aesthetics are suffering because they are being done in an amateur fashion by people who think it's an exciting new field. Her project sounds grandiose and vague, from the sub-headings you gave me. Perhaps I am underestimating her capabilities."[45]

With otherwise overwhelming support, on September 8, the Rockefeller Foundation awarded $10,000, the first of a series of grants to cover Jacobs's research and secretarial, travel, and living expenses while on leave from *Architectural Forum*, to the New School for Social Research and Jane Jacobs for a study of "relations of function to design in large cities."[46]

"A Book on American Cities"

In October 1958, Jacobs began her leave, intending to return to her job when her project was completed less than a year later. Her research phase began in early October with an appropriate and stimulating start at the University of Pennsylvania Conference on Urban Design Criticism, held at the Westchester Country Club, in Rye, New York. This event had emerged from her suggestion that the foundation support architectural critics who could develop helpful new ideas for the planning of cities, and she had praised the University of Pennsylvania as being "the most productive and influential center" in the United States for architectural and city planning research.[47]

As orchestrated by the city planning chair, William L. C. Wheaton (whom Jacobs knew as a consultant on the Baltimore Charles Center project); David Crane, who circulated an extensive working paper in September; and Gilpatric, the purpose of the conference was to discuss "the low state of present urban design" and, with a few exceptional writers in attendance, the "almost complete absence" of critical writing about the design of cities in America. Anticipated outcomes were articles on the philosophy of urban design, suggestions for foundation program development, and possibly specific proposals for foundation support. In a sense, *The Death and Life of Great American Cities* would be its most significant outcome.

The conference was organized into three presentation sessions on Friday, slideshows on Thursday and Friday evenings, and working sessions on Saturday. Overarching topics concerned "some philosophical views," with Gilpatric on "The Meaning of Depth in Criticism," Ian McHarg on "New and Old Attitudes in Urban Environment," and Edward Weeks, the editor of the *Atlantic Monthly*, on "The Intangibles." A second session focused on "efforts, inhibitions, and failings in the urban design press," with presentations by Gordon Stephenson, then the chair of the Department of Town and Regional Planning at the University of Toronto, on "Design and City Planning as Seen in the Press"; Frederick Gutheim, an architect, planner, author, and journalist (whom Jacobs knew from her January 1956 article on Washington, DC), on "Efforts of the Working Press"; and Jacobs on "Inhibiting Factors in Criticism." The third group reflected on "idea and form in urban design criticism," with talks by Kevin Lynch on "Idea-building and the Instruments of Communication," Grady Clay on "Form and Method in Design Criticism," and Catherine Bauer on "Professional Introspection and Extroversion." Mumford spoke on cities during lunch. Presenting slideshows were J. B. Jackson on "Ecology and Values in Environment"; Leslie Cheek, the Virginia Museum of Fine Art director, on "The Virginia Town Exhibit"; Bauer on "Asian Vernaculars in Urban Design"; and Clay on "Ruminations on European Townscapes." On Saturday evening, the architect Arthur Holden read "Sonnets for My City" and Louis Kahn discussed "Ideas of the City."[48]

When Gilpatric first mentioned that her idea for supporting architectural or urban design criticism might take the form of a conference, Jacobs had warned him that it would be successful only if it was focused. Her

FIGURE 46. The attendees of the 1958 University of Pennsylvania Conference on Urban Design Criticism included William L. C. Wheaton, Lewis Mumford, Ian McHarg, J. B. Jackson, David Crane, Louis Kahn, G. Holmes Perkins, Catherine Bauer Wurster, Edward Weeks, Kevin Lynch, Gordon Stephenson, and I. M. Pei. Jacobs is seen here speaking with Weeks. Grady Clay was the photographer. Grady Clay.

talk was accordingly to the point. Jacobs discussed three factors inhibiting criticism.

First was the journalist's conflicted relationship with his sources. It is difficult, she pointed out, "for an architectural editor to be simultaneously both an all-purpose diplomat in the profession and a major critic. One or the other must suffer." Second was the problem of the journalist being influenced by parties involved in a project and their description of the extenuating circumstances of the project's deficiencies. "If these were generally nice people who had been doing their best, and for whom the critic could not help but feel sympathy once he understood their difficulties, you can see how it would affect his review and how far off it might be as information on the worth of the work itself," she said. "It takes an extremely tough-minded person not to be unduly influenced." Third, and most significant, was the lack of willingness on the part of publications and writers to criticize, for various reasons. One of these, as Haskell had observed around the time Jacobs joined *Forum*, was the fear of libel suits and the resulting habit to "print only the work you can praise and discuss only those aspects of the work that are laudable." Anticipating *Death and Life* and her future activism, Jacobs offered that "getting either quality or quantity of urban design criticism, and hopefully both, is the problem of getting publications to understand that intelligent criticism—in some cases very destructive criticism—can be of more real help to a community in its aims at improvement than is automatic applause, and so much more help that it is actually worth the real and unmistakable trouble it causes." *Death and Life*'s criticism and her activism would prove her right.[49]

After the conference, Jacobs told Gilpatric she thought it had been an exciting and promising event. She mentioned being "most interested in the advice of I. M. Pei and Arthur Holden, both leading architects who were trying to see architectural needs in light of existing laws and regulations, but also for the social consequences of architectural schemes and development projects." They talked about continuing the conversation together during an evening later in October or November. In fact, Jacobs continued to participate in discussions about urban design hosted by Gilpatric during the next few years, while she wrote *Death and Life*, although she shared with Gilpatric her dislike for the terms "urban design" and "urban design criticism." She told him that as a description for "the complex field of city development, in which architectural planning corresponds with an adequate philosophy of city life," she preferred the phrase "city design criticism," "partly because the terms 'urban' and 'planning' have objectionable connotations at this point."[50]

Perhaps still believing that she could complete the research for her book in three months, Jacobs compiled a list of people involved in renewal and development she wanted to meet. First on her list was James Rouse, whom she knew from writing about shopping centers in 1953 and more recently from her work on "A New Heart for Baltimore." Second was William Slayton, a colleague of Pei and the director of the Webb and Knapp/William Zeckendorf development project in Southwest Washington. Slayton, not mentioned directly in *Death and Life*, worked for the Housing and Home Finance Agency before being selected by President Kennedy to be the commissioner of the Urban Renewal Administration in 1961, wherein he prohibited racial and cultural discrimination from developers involved in urban renewal housing.[51]

Amid these visits and making plans for others to Philadelphia and Boston, Jacobs remained involved in the fight to save Washington Square, which came to a head in 1958. As she had said in her New School talk, the neighborhood *had to* prevail, and it eventually won a trial period in which the square, which previously admitted buses, would be closed to all but emergency vehicles. In September 1958, Jacobs spoke at a public hearing at City Hall, as did Shirley Hayes, Eleanor Roosevelt (who had lived in

Washington Square after FDR's death), Margaret Mead (another Village resident), Haskell, Stanley Tankel, Charlie Abrams, and some of the other thirty thousand petitioners. In November, she gave a longer talk to the New York State Motorbus Association, explaining that "down in Greenwich Village we are as progressive as anybody. Sometimes we are accused of being too progressive. But we concluded that piling in more cars, to the detriment of every other city value—and as a mere stopgap measure at that—is no more progress than erosion is progress." Her thoughts having changed significantly since her early writing about shopping centers, she added, "The greatest menace to downtown today comes not from suburban shopping centers; nor from decentralization of offices. . . . The greatest menace comes rather from well-meant attempts at traffic stopgap expediencies." She went on to list the effects of widened streets, parking lots and garages, and the parking requirements of stadia and similar venues on city life—ideas repeated today. She remarked that citizens can make their stands here and there but that, for the sake of cities, advocacy was needed by many—including the Motorbus people in the audience—in order to support better policies about public transportation. She urged them to be better advocates for their own industry.[52]

On November 1, Tankel drove the last car through the Washington Square arch and Jacobs's daughter, Mary, helped tie a ribbon to mark the "closing" ceremony. Although the closure was temporary, and buses continued to drive through the square until the permanent and complete closure in 1963, Jacobs reported on the "human victory" of Washington Square in a short editorial in the December 1958 issue of *Forum*. Anticipating her chapter on governing and planning districts, she wrote that effective political pressure had won the day. She concluded that the park, despite its deliberate neglect by the Parks Department, was full of people, with gangs and juvenile delinquents conspicuously absent. People came to play music or checkers, sing and dance, read and "have a genuine 'village' good time." She wrote, "All this is heartening to see in a great modern city. It proves that city neighborhoods too can be human, and it deserves its victory."[53]

In the meantime, Jacobs had been to Philadelphia, where she visited various redevelopment projects and spoke with the journalist Joseph "Mack" Guess, who encouraged her to take especially hard looks at the widely touted Morningside Gardens project in New York and Lake Meadows in Chicago. She had been to Cincinnati, where she participated in a conference on the relationship of cities and suburbs with Charlie Farnsley, the former mayor of Louisville, Kentucky; Gruen; Clay; and others. While there, she toured the city and observed its downtown, parks, and housing projects. And she had also been to Boston, where she had notable and extensive conversations with Edward Logue, the director of the Boston Redevelopment Authority, and his staff and where she visited the city's North End.[54]

Just a few months into her research, the North End made a big impression on her—and she told Gilpatric of her experiences in much the same way as she related them in the introduction to *Death and Life*. "With no sights of big building projects," she told him, "the residents have undertaken to improve their homes, stores, so that outside and inside there is new and attractive decoration, as with awnings, painting, benches put out. The streets and alleys are full of quite evidently happy and communicative people who, in response to odd questions now and then, expressed immense joy in their life and the situation." Redevelopment Authority officials, she related, "partly from lack of firsthand acquaintance, view this area with something close to horror and feel that it should really be razed and some ambitious new housing project undertaken, with the usual highrise buildings and big open plazas." She noted the low rates of crime and high level of public health but admitted that its density of two hundred residential units per acre was high. Nevertheless, she admired the residents for "taking care of themselves, with a sense of social solidarity and social values, and resisting 'big projectism' as it might be launched by municipal government or real estate speculators." Similar to her descriptions of Greenwich Village and Chicago's Back-of-the-Yards in *Death and Life*, she said, "There is a zest, friendliness, social responsiveness and responsibility which one would like to expect in certain city areas."[55]

In early January 1959, Jacobs planned a trip to tour San Francisco and Los Angeles, armed with maps and materials from the American Society of Planning Officials lent to her by Clay and Bauer, as well as their suggestions for things to see and people to meet. She looked forward to visiting Bauer in Berkeley and talking over some ideas. "Many, many thanks for the notes. You are wonderful," Jacobs wrote her. "I am getting some very iconoclastic notions about density and open space (in cities) from what I see on my travels. Would love to have a chance to talk with you about them."[56]

At the last minute, however, Jacobs delayed these travel plans in order to attend a meeting in East Harlem, where she remained involved in neighborhood issues as a board member of Union Settlement. She was disappointed that she would not see Bauer, who was leaving for India soon after their planned get-together in San Francisco. "The reason I have to postpone the trip," she wrote, "is that the East Harlem Housing Council, to which I belong by virtue of being on the board of a settlement up there, has persuaded the NYC Housing Authority to put a 30-day stop on two horrid projects well along in the planning for East Harlem while we see if we can't come up with something better that can still get approval in Washington." She explained that the two housing projects would be home to about a thousand families. "If we can shake up some of the miserable old stereotypes here it will not only matter to those thousand, but also might make a difference in the authority's approach to others, so we sure don't want to miss the chance for lack of trying." As her collaborator on the "Dreary Deadlock" series, Bauer must have appreciated both this and the challenge ahead. So, Jacobs concluded, "I need to be here during the earlier stages of it, or so the council thinks, more for moral support than anything else I guess, because I am no architect. But we have a good firm of architects putting their all into it, strictly as a public service! Since I helped instigate the whole thing, I can't just leave at the crucial moment."[57]

"Salvaging Projects"

Perhaps self-conscious about talking about housing with an expert such as Bauer, Jacobs was modest about her role in trying to improve housing in East Harlem. In early December 1958, she addressed the United Neighborhood Houses of New York, a federation of settlement houses founded in 1919 (and still a lively organization), where she spoke about the planner's need to hear from residents and the virtues of institutions like Union Settlement to serve as the voice of the residents. She also spoke on a familiar theme: the perpetuation of outdated housing principles and formulas established by an earlier generation of planners that thwarted creative exploration.[58]

Though Jacobs's work in East Harlem would delay progress on her book, it provided direct and practical experience with the types of housing projects and planning concepts that she would criticize—and offer alternatives to—in Death and Life. The DeWitt Clinton housing project, the focus of her efforts at this time, was approved by the city's Board of Estimate in 1956 and was one of the proposed redevelopment projects that first led Kirk to contact Haskell in 1955. She had since become a board member of Union Settlement, and by the end of 1958, she had become one of the

leaders of the housing committee of the East Harlem Council for Community Planning.

In early January 1959, shortly before her trip to California, Jacobs,
Kirk, and Lurie; Mildred Zucker, the director of the James Weldon Community Center; and four architects from Perkins & Will, including Phil
Will, met to discuss alternatives to the proposed DeWitt Clinton housing
project. The project would evict approximately nine hundred families and
destroy sixty stores, a number of small factories and warehouses that
employed more than one hundred people, and five small churches between
104th and 110th streets (east of Park Avenue) and then replace them with
twenty-one-story apartment towers. The group had won an opportunity to
present the Housing Authority with an alternative project that would provide not only bedrooms, but also ones in which the residents could "live
completely." As they discussed in their meeting, they wanted to see shops
and resident amenities (not apartments) at the ground floor, for neighborhood streets to remain as active gathering places—to "bleed street life into
our project!"—and to replace the towers-only scheme with a mix of walk-
up and high-rise apartments that would serve children, parents, and the
elderly. Details included niches and irregularities in the building lines to
create "door step living" (as Jacobs later described in the use of sidewalks
in *Death and Life*), active open spaces with small play areas and gathering
places, and bike paths and storage. In the bigger picture, their goal was to
critique prevailing ideas and replace them with a mixed-use, mixed-
building housing model.[59]

In February 1959, after her trip to California, the group met with
twenty-five tenants and representatives from East Harlem housing projects
to get direct feedback that might improve their proposal. Lurie noted that
the attendees "derived status by being asked to be critical of a plan drawn
up by a group that proposes to represent them." A few days later, Jacobs
presented their alternative scheme to the Housing Authority.[60]

In her presentation, Jacobs spoke about the evidence of flaws in the
East River, Johnson, and Washington housing projects, where there was
high turnover and no evidence of improvement to the surrounding neighborhoods. "We are convinced," she affirmed, "that a great part of the poor
social showing of East Harlem's projects is owing to the physical design of
the buildings themselves and their grounds." Dwelling density, she offered,
was not the problem. While DeWitt Clinton might have more than 130
apartments per acre, she reported that otherwise similar projects in St.

Louis and Philadelphia, with densities of only 60 dwellings or less per acre, had proved to be no better than New York's high-density projects and in some cases had appeared to be worse. However, while likely thinking of Boston's North End, she observed that socially successful neighborhoods with even higher densities could be found in low-rent, "non-project areas" of New York and other cities.[61]

In the initial draft of her presentation, Jacobs planned to discuss the conceptual reasons behind the failures of project housing. Although she edited much of this out of her final copy, the draft included a critique of eight planning and design theories, outlined in conversation with her housing committee collaborators, that she would make again in *Death and Life*: the theory of "neat beauty" (large neat buildings, inhuman in scale, surrounded by lots of grass and unused open space); the theory of improvement (that such projects would improve their surroundings); the theory of safety (that closing streets and isolating housing from the street would make them safer); the theory of elevators, aka "streamlined progress" (that using elevators was better than walking up stairs); the theory of rebuilding old community (replacing diverse family types with "homogenous child-bearing, acceptably composed families," eliminating stores, and destroying the "social heart along streets of heterogeneity" to create a "totally new kind of community"); the theory of streamlined recreation (the idea of open space as a quiet oasis and the elimination of the places of "informal non-structural life"—corner stores, sidewalks, stoops, landings, and lobbies); the theory of small sites (the scalar irrelevance of tower schemes to their sites, whether large or small); and the theory of regulations and codes (where "planning [was] almost the same as the final plan," where rules came first and family, people, and community came last).[62]

In Jacobs's presentation, much of this material was refined to a single statement:

The design trouble in East Harlem's projects goes much deeper than the accommodation of high densities. The trouble is rooted, rather, in public housing's disregard of the social structure of city neighborhoods, particularly poor neighborhoods. The projects are designed for a kind of sophisticated family individualism, which is beyond the inner resources and the financial resources of their tenants, and which is the opposite of the highly communal and cooperative society among families in the old slums. The projects

are designed not to include, but to exclude the constant informal
social controls which are needed by every society, including that of
the poor.[63]

Soon after the meeting with the Housing Authority, Jacobs wrote up a
press release that spoke of "what can be accomplished when interested citizens and public spirited private specialists take the initiative of cooperating
with official agencies toward the solution of a common problem." In the
five-page document, Jacobs outlined the various problems with public
housing and noted that the loss of some 2,500 stores and storekeepers in
East Harlem due to the housing project clearance had destroyed the vital
community role played by the shop owners and their enterprises. Speaking
for her committee, she also criticized the federal public housing policy that
limited walk-up apartments to three stories, while up to six floors were
permitted in the city of New York. Advocating for local decision making
and greater housing diversity, she wrote, "We think the walk-up restriction
of the federal code is unrealistic; like many federal housing restrictions it
has apparently been framed with the 'average' city in mind." Taking a long
view to reframe the argument in historical terms, she concluded, "We suspect that future generations of Americans will regard the deliberate dead-
ness of low-income housing as unnecessary and will attempt to introduce
into it again the vitality of city neighborhoods. . . . A project built today
will probably stand for sixty or seventy years. Ideas and neighborhoods
have changed since 1895 and presumably they will change as much by the
year 2025."[64]

In April 1959, *Forum* published an article called "Public Housing . . .
for People," written by Jacobs's colleague Richard Miller, about the committee's proposal for DeWitt Clinton. The article described "the need for
overhauling US public housing policies and dropping the shackles and shib-
boleths that encumber project design." Illustrated with sketches of Perkins & Will's scheme and some of the same photographs of Harlem street
life used to illustrate Jacobs's 1956 article "The Missing Link in City Redevelopment," the article quoted at some length from Jacobs's press release,
referred to Jacobs's other ideas and writing on the subject (including a nod
to Ernest Bohn of Cleveland), and would have had her approval, if not her
hand in it. Described as a hypothetical design solution, the article explained
that the purpose of the design was to demonstrate the major faults of public
housing that could be corrected without a significant change in the number

of dwellings provided or cost. Miller noted, however, that the designers could not satisfy the committee's objectives while simultaneously satisfying "the myriad mandates of setback, interspace, and site-planning which have been heaped upon public housing design by bureaucrat after bureaucrat." Their violations of the regulations—four-and-a-half-story walk-ups, court-yards, and the provision of retail and workshop space below the ground-level *piloti*, among others—were therefore described as "premeditated" and the design as something of an act of protest. Miller concluded the article by stating, "Perkins & Will, like many other architectural firms, will not accept actual public housing commissions until design requirements, fee sched-ules, and contract provisions established by the PHA [Public Housing Administration] in Washington are reformed."[65]

Unsurprisingly, the committee's proposal for DeWitt Clinton was rejected by the Housing Authority, which had little choice but to comply with federal regulations. In her chapter on "salvaging projects" in *Death and Life*, Jacobs briefly described the proposal, giving full credit to Per-kins & Will. She made no reference to her extensive involvement, allowing a paragraph-long anecdote to stand in for, and indeed belie, her direct experience working in public housing regulations and design.[66]

Writing *Death and Life*

In the midst of her work in East Harlem, in February 1959, Jacobs wrote her friend Grady Clay a funny letter:

> I am now the proud possessor of a hide-out in which to work, just
> a few short blocks from home. My husband found and rented it
> for me under false pretenses—that it was for him—because it is in
> a men's rooming house. However, the other denizens, who seem
> to run mostly to musicians and magicians, seem to have accepted
> my odd presence tolerantly and to have made the further tolerant
> assumption that I have some sort of relationship with Mr. Jacobs
> which I do not wish to advertise. I have not disillusioned them.
> Ah, the city is a wonderful place.[67]

She also offered some quips about her visit to California, which included San Francisco, Berkeley, Los Angeles, and Disneyland. "Los Angeles didn't surprise me as much as I'd expected," she wrote, "because

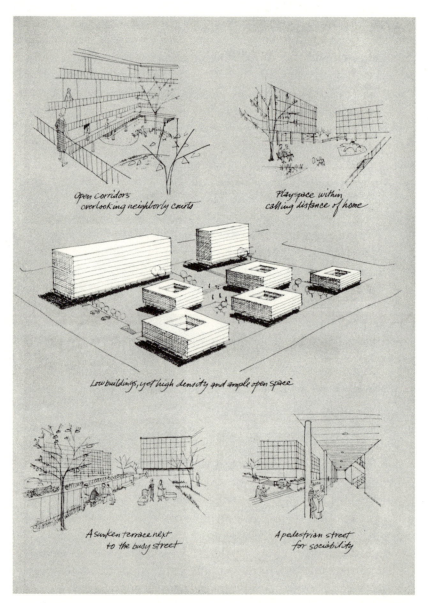

FIGURE 47. In early January 1959, while at work on *Death and Life*, Jacobs worked with architects from Perkins & Will and Ellen Lurie and William Kirk from Union Settlement House (Jacobs served as one of its board members) on trying to improve the designs of an East Harlem housing project. Jacobs's colleague Richard Miller wrote about their unsuccessful proposal in "Public Housing . . . for People." *AF* (Apr. 1959), 134.

I've seen so much of it, we all have, in other cities." But there, she went on, "there's nothing else but Los Angeles. . . . A great big bag of sticky hard candy; the more different the pieces try to look, the more the whole bag looks the same. Just the same it interested me tremendously, and so did Disneyland which Catherine Bauer told me not to miss and she was right!"

Jokes aside, Jacobs was worried about her book. "Despite the hide-out, I am almost two months behind schedule from when I thought I'd be writing, which makes me feel fairly desperate. Now I'm only in the process of sorting out my notes and glop, a vast and gruesome task, but one that I find I can't evade. Do you think I will ever get this thing done? I'm really dying to start writing although I know that when I do I will frequently wonder why." Jacobs and Clay's correspondence continued over the next few months. He provided her with information about Louisville, which found its way into her book, and she praised his "Townscape" columns and encouraged him on his new essay. "It's great that you're writing the *Horizon* piece," she wrote, "and you will do it much better than I ever possibly could."[68]

They traded ideas about street life and safety, and, continuing the discussion, she shared anecdotes about neighborhood parks from her Baltimore friend Penny Kostritsky (later retold in *Death and Life*) and went on to remark that in rebuilt cities a "buffer principle" was being deployed that was in direct conflict with the fact that strangers are an essential part of daily city life. "The buffer principle—keep the strangers out—seems to be the motif of the rebuilt city generally from Stuyvesant Town on, and it is engendering enormous hostilities and insecurities, not only in New York but also in Chicago, Baltimore (where the Johns Hopkins Title I job has a 9-ft. cyclone fence around it!), and Los Angeles," she wrote. "Boston will have a lulu with its West End redevelopment because it is built to be unsafe unless the strangers are kept out, although the designers don't mean it that way. They never do. But that's what they get."

Then, in response to questions from Clay's previous letter, Jacobs went on to explain the evolution of her thinking, saying that she had been shocked at seeing early redevelopment and housing projects when they were completed and that she felt guilty about, and implicated in, having written about them favorably. She related her early experiences in East Harlem with Kirk in much the same way as in the first chapter of *Death and Life*, but with even more feeling. She told Clay, "I began to see that the most important thing in life in East Harlem was relationships of all kinds among people—that these relationships, many of them very casual, were the means of keeping the peace, of assistance in time of trouble, of squeezing some fun and joy out of the slum, of avenues to opportunity and glimpses of different choices in life, and of any sort of political participation. I saw that many people in East Harlem were of true importance in their circles and had the dignity that comes of having some influence and mastery, however little, on their environment." In urban renewal projects, she "saw that these relationships were wiped out in the projects, drastically built out of them, and so was the dignity and the responsibility." From this, she explained, "I began to get a glimmer of the idea that the workings of the city were based on mutual support among a great variety of things, and that this principle was totally missing from the rebuilt city."[69]

Jacobs went on at length, discussing the city-hating tradition in "orthodox town planning," and repeated the half-joking remarks made by planners about the great fire or several hundred sticks of dynamite that would make the work of transforming their cities into suburban shopping centers that much easier. As far as knowledge was concerned—again rehearsing passages from *Death and Life*—she compared city planning, "and its creatures redevelopment and renewal," to medical science in the age of bloodletting. "There is no bedrock of knowledge about how the city works, and this leaves even those with affection for the city in a relatively helpless position," she concluded.

Creating a foundation of knowledge about how the city works was ultimately her mission, but she lacked confidence in her contribution. She explained that the functions of the city—how it was used and how it worked—were her focus and that the lack of knowledge about them in planning literature motivated her. When she wrote in the "Illustrations" page of *Death and Life* "please look closely at real cities . . . and think about what you see," she was describing her own method and experience:

> I began getting very curious about how the city worked as well as how it looked. And I'm sorry to say that I got mighty little help from the writings on planning. In fact, the more I looked at how the city worked, the more I saw that a great many of the planning rules were outright hokum, abstractions that had nothing to do with real life. I also became more and more struck with the sheer sentimentality of town planning. I decided the only way to find out what is good planning for the city is to start looking at the city

itself, notice what is working well and what is not, and try to find out why, and to forget about the theory because it only stands in the way of seeing, in this case.[70]

Rebuilding twentieth-century planning theory from the ground up was an ambitious task, and, as the scope of her project grew, Jacobs fell further behind her expectations and into despair about completing the book. She had no hope of finishing it before October 1959, when her grant expired, and she could not afford, and did not want, to lose her job at *Architectural Forum*. After a lunch with her in June 1959, Gilpatric noted his disappointment. Jacobs had run into many unexpected problems and had completed less writing than he had expected.[71]

In a letter in July, Jacobs explained two of at least three reasons for her delays. First and foremost, she had overestimated her understanding of the city:

[A]s I proceeded with my research and traveling during the initial months, I found that I needed to go into a good many aspects of the behavior of cities which I had either not previously thought about, or had not understood as significant. For instance, I had given no thought, until I bumped into it hard in the course of my research, to what actually occurs and why when a city area spontaneously unslums itself; I had given very little thought to the intricate connections of city density with city safety and attractiveness, nor to the paradox that decay and over-crowding today are more apt to be associated with relatively low city densities than high ones; I had not realized a good many of the economic ramifications involved in city success and deterioration; on almost everything I had thought about, in fact, I found relationships I had not taken into account but that must be taken into account.[72]

Second, not only was she learning about her subject as she went, but she was learning how to write such a book. "I did not anticipate the difficulties I was going to get into in organizing and writing. It is far different from writing and organizing articles, and how different I had no conception until I waded in. In retrospect, how over-optimistic I was about the writing! Well, I have been going through considerable trial, error and bafflement, but . . . I have been learning by doing," she told him. The transformation from a series of articles to a field-changing book had caught up with her.[73]

Third, although she didn't mention this to Gilpatric, some of her time had been consumed with neighborhood projects in East Harlem and Greenwich Village. Robert Moses fought back against the closure of Washington Square to cars with proposals to make Fifth Avenue a one-way street and to widen the roads around the park to facilitate traffic flow toward the southern bridges and tunnels. Jacobs assumed the role of leader of the fight against making Fifth Avenue a one-way. It would not be the only battle she would have while writing the book. Later in the year, she would form the Save the Sidewalks Committee to stop the widening of Hudson Street.[74]

The good news that she could share with Gilpatric was that she now had a good sense of her project, and she sent him an outline for what she called simply a "book on American cities." In structure, it had already begun to resemble the four parts and many of the chapters of *The Death and Life of Great American Cities*. It took this form:

1. Introduction
Part I—The Nature of Cities
2. The peculiar jobs of the city street
3. The meaning and uses of city neighborhoods
4. The nature of city parks
5. The uses of variety
6. The uses of concentration
Part II—The Knack of Mutual Support
7. The importance of primary and secondary mixture
8. Incubation of enterprises and culture
9. Physical centers vs. physical edges
10. The pitfalls of too much success
Part III—Decay and Rejuvenation
11. Slumming and unslumming
12. The blight of dullness
13. Gradual money for gradual change
14. Redevelopment—The shook-up city
Part IV—How to Change Our Ways
15. Where and why thinking about cities got off the track
16. Planning by diagnosis
17. Attrition of the automobile

18. Municipal organization for proper planning
19. The basic practical problem—public money vs. flexibility
20. Visual order for the city—its possibilities and limitations

The bad news was that there was much, much more to be done. She had a draft of a number of chapters for part I, but these were going to require extensive rewriting. She still needed to write first drafts of at least fifteen chapters. She would need another year at least and additional foundation support. Her hair was turning white from the stress.

Gilpatric did not reply to Jacobs with much encouragement. "I am reluctant," he told her, "to take up your request with others until I have something more to show on the content and ideas of your book." This made her a bit desperate. "Without further help, the problem and decision I will have to face is whether I ought to go back to work at my job for a period of time, probably a year, save up as much as I can and finance as much as possible of the continuation of the book later by this means, or whether I ought to attempt to borrow the necessary money from some source and pay it back in the years after the book is completed," she explained.[75]

The idea of postponing the book was almost as repugnant as the idea of abandoning the project, which she had decided she would not do. Her past years of covering urban redevelopment for *Forum*, her initial research and writing, and her recent fights with City Hall all contributed to her sense of her book's importance.

"Without wishing to sound immodest about it," she wrote Gilpatric, "I feel very deeply that it is important for this book to get finished and published, because I think it is needed. City rebuilding, and plans for rebuilding, for renewal, for civic facilities and for traffic and highways are going ahead very fast, to say nothing of the speed with which unplanned development is also occurring." She explained, "We are copying failure, in new architectural and planning dress, and we are creating city which is, more and more, composed of mutually hostile or non-interacting islands, city which at worst lacks even such primitive necessities as built-in safety for humans from one another in its public spaces, and which at best is inhospitable to urban variety, vitality, and experimentation. We are doing this, not because we have to, but from lack of the understanding required to do better." The results of current planning theories and practices—homogeneity, insularity, paucity of eyes and activities on the streets, lack of varied and well-designed open spaces, elimination of urban density, and resistance to change, adaptation, variety, vitality, and experimentation— were creating demonstrably unsuccessful cities. The theory needed to change.[76]

Jacobs explained how she had struggled with understanding the project and her subject matter. She was learning as she wrote. She told Gilpatric, "The necessities of what must be done to the prior work continually come clearer to me, and this is a process which has to be continued through the whole book. . . . Some of my earlier troubles came from not understanding this, and attempting to do it in article-sized chunks, alternating basic creative writing and organization with rewriting and reorganization. It was a waste and a frustration." She now knew she needed to work through the whole book and argument because, she explained, "the logic of every part is a portion of the logic of the whole [book], done in the light of the whole."

Ultimately making a case for the foundation's continued support, she sought to assure Gilpatric that the result would be worth the effort. She knew that she was creating new and important knowledge about city life and design. "If this sounds esoteric or something, and not the way all books are written, which I know, I can only lay it to the fact that this book is neither a retelling in new form of things already said, nor an expansion and enlargement of previously worked out basic ground," she wrote.

Jacobs's goal was nothing less than synthesizing a new system of thought about the great city to create a new foundation for the understanding of cities:

> In my book, I am not rehashing old material on cities and city planning. I am working with new concepts about the city and its behavior. Many of these concepts are quite radically opposed to those accepted in orthodox and conventional planning theory. I think I am proving the validity of these new concepts and giving evidence, from experience in the city itself, which shows that the alternative to ignoring them is not the rebuilding of some improved type of city but, rather, the social, economic, and visual disintegration of the city. I am trying to get the theory and practice of city planning and design started on a new and different track. . . . The times, intellectually speaking, are ripe for understanding and accepting these ideas. . . . My contribution is the organizing of these observations and ideas into workable systems of thought

about the city, and in indicating the new aims and tactics which planning must adopt to catalyze constructive and genuinely urban city behavior.

She summed up her argument simply: "This is the kind of thing I am up to, and it is hard work, but I cannot think of anything I could do which might be more useful to my times."[77]

In the following weeks, Gilpatric sought renewed support for Jacobs's project. Holly Whyte wrote Gilpatric a very supportive note on her behalf, stating, "I believe Jane Jacobs has a great contribution to make and quite frankly I was happy to hear that she wants to spend more time on the book. . . . I wholeheartedly recommend the additional assistance for the extra time she wants to give the book. I believe a great and influential book is in the making."[78]

Other letters and comments of support for Jacobs's continued work on her book came from Kirk, the writer Eric Larrabee, W. N. Seymour (a member of the Committee to Save Washington Square), Charlie Farnsley, and the planner Barclay Jones. Kirk wrote, "Other than Jane Jacobs, there have been few individuals who have been interested or aware of the successes and failures that have accompanied these vast changes [in East Harlem]." Larrabee stated, "She has somehow managed to free herself from the layers of preconception which surround [study of the city], and looks at cities as they are with a clear and sympathetic eye. What she sees is that the city functions in ways we have only dimly begun to understand; and she is making what seems to me a first rate effort to convert her perceptions into usable generalities." In a related conversation, Farnsley (mentioned in *Death and Life*'s acknowledgments) congratulated the foundation on its support for "the one promising author on the subject of urban problems," adding that "Lewis Mumford hates the city while Ms. Jacobs loves it." Remarking on the impact of Jacobs's work even before *Death and Life* was published, Jones, whose research—including attendance at the third Urban Design Conference at Harvard—was also supported by the foundation, observed that the impact of Jacobs's presentation at the 1956 conference had not been forgotten. He told Gilpatric, "The first question with respect to criticism of current urban design was raised by Jane Jacobs at the first of these conferences. Since that time, an increasing amount of criticism of current urban design has been appearing in both the professional and the popular press. Articles by Jane Jacobs, Grady Clay, William H. Whyte, Jr.,

Nathan Glazer, and others have all appeared since Mrs. Jacobs' original speech. The format of this, the third Conference, seems to reflect this growing criticism."[79]

The last of these letters had not yet been received when Gilpatric wrote his colleagues a memo approving the extension of Jacobs's grant to support her book on " 'a new system of thought' for bringing improvement to large cities." In October 1959, the Rockefeller Foundation renewed her grant until May 1960, allowing her to continue her leave from *Architectural Forum*, which Haskell also graciously renewed, although she had recently caused him some trouble with remarks in the *New York Times*. In July, as she was making her renewed case for the importance of her book, she was quoted in an article on slum clearance and housing as saying, "Title I in its very nature is a track for the gravy train. It hands great chunks of the city over to officially anointed barons, makes city rebuilding and city commerce into a monopolistic set-up for the favored few." After reading this, Haskell told her, "I believe you really should not have sounded off in the *New York Times* without making a check because you are identified there as an editor of *Forum* and not as an individual." He had refrained from commenting himself because *Forum*'s publisher had indicated that they should tell their own story in the magazine. He explained furthermore, "We don't see the urban renewal situation as black and white as you do, and are having a meeting today to decide what attitude *Forum* should take." But he promised, "I shall keep as quiet as possible around the shop hoping that this one will blow over. . . . Of course you know I appreciate your having strong concerns and convictions."[80]

When Jacobs wrote to Gilpatric later in October 1959 to thank him for his continued support, she was happy to tell him that the writing was going well. "I'm averaging a chapter a week, instead of the slow and discouraging chapter a month of the spring and summer," she said. However, to others, like her friend Saul Alinsky, who shared with her knowledge about Chicago, she admitted continuing struggles. In correspondence with Alinsky, who was also at work on a book, she wrote, "My problem with the book is not lack of immediacy. It is anything but remote, aloof, etc. from the current political, social and economic fix. You expressed my difficulties exactly when you wrote about your writing problem, 'I've got so damned much to say and everything is so interrelated with everything else.' Isn't it the devil!" But she was by this time, in August 1959, cautiously optimistic. "I've had fundamental messes of organization that blocked me completely. Now I think I've got them combed out (maybe) and have relatively minor messes of organization, but many of them. I'm only half way in the first draft, but think I'm making progress. Still a long way to go, but I can't imagine stopping. It is like some kind of limbo," she told him.[81]

By the time Jacobs's second grant was about to expire in May 1960—a third grant extension would carry her to May 1961—she had the book's title and was ready to share a number of chapters with Glazer and Epstein. She told Gilpatric that she was gratified to report that Glazer thought the book would make a real contribution to the understanding of cities. Epstein estimated a publication date of August or September 1961. She tentatively offered a few chapters to Gilpatric as well, with a caveat that still applies to today's readers: "There are (or I hope there will be) advantages to reading it all at once, for of necessity many avenues of thought get opened up in the early part that must be traveled one by one later on." Nevertheless, she felt obliged to show him something and offered that "enough is completed to show the general pitch and direction, as the book will not turn into a different kind of book at any point."[82]

Two weeks later, Gilpatric replied, "I think the title is excellent and the beginning superb. I was fascinated, exhilarated and informed by Chapter 1." He also gave her some suggestions, such as using the term "togetherness" less frequently and quoting the first line of E. B. White's *Here Is New York* (1949) during her discussion of privacy in cities. His most notable piece of advice, which he repeated when he read the full manuscript in March 1961, was to make the book shorter: "In what follows, there is a great deal of insight and constructive observation but I do have the strong feeling that rewriting in quite a few places, particularly compression, is called for."[83]

Jacobs disagreed with some of his comments but noted that others were right as soon as she read them. She also agreed that "the whole thing needs considerable trimming and pruning, which I'll do at the end, in a good cold-blooded mood. I'm now a little beyond what I think is the halfway mark in pages, a little under it in number of chapters. All the hardest part is done, I believe. A few more months' work and it should be finished."[84]

Jacobs finished the manuscript at the end of January 1961 and returned to *Architectural Forum* on February 1. In the end, *The Death and Life of Great American Cities*, Jacobs's study of the relation of function to design in large cities, took two years and four months, three times longer than she had expected.

Ultimately, it was a book of twenty-two chapters. Remaining focused on function, Jacobs retitled chapters in Part I to emphasize "use" and split the preliminary chapter on "The Peculiar Jobs of the City Street" into three chapters on "The Uses of Sidewalks." Other chapters were reordered and a separate chapter on "The Need for Small Blocks" was added, emphasizing the four conditions for city diversity (previously "mutual support") in Part II. Other chapters were retitled, including "Redevelopment—The Shook-Up City" and "Planning by Diagnosis," sometimes making less obvious Jacobs's inspirations and intentions. Perhaps most significant, in her initial conception, the book had concluded with the chapter "Visual Order for the City," in which she emphasized that *a city cannot be a work of art.* As Jacobs explained to Gilpatric, "I draw my reasoning on esthetics from reasoning about the structure of cities—I think esthetics ought to express structure and explain order among other things—and structure depends in its turn upon function." She ultimately summed it up this way: "A city's very *structure* consists of mixture of uses, and we get closest to its structural secrets when we deal with the conditions that generate diversity."[85] The final draft, however, had a new concluding chapter, "The Kind of Problem a City Is," which transcended considerations of the function of design and, with the help of a long extract from an essay by Warren Weaver, the Rockefeller Foundation's former director of life sciences, proposed a new epistemology and methodology of design and planning. Perhaps including material from the previous chapter 15, "Where and Why Thinking About Cities Got Off the Track," the new conclusion closed the book by framing the problems and possibilities of cities in an environmental context shaped by the suburban impulse, the sentimentalization of nature, and the destruction of irreplaceable human habitat including the city.

When Gilpatric read the final version, he argued that Jacobs should cut the 669-page manuscript by half. He described the book as "thoughtful and thought-provoking, vividly and constructively concrete (with many illuminating cues to problems of city life and building), powerful in its effect, and most timely." However, he doubted that it would "hold the interest it should if it remains as long and as discursive as the draft." Specific suggestions included eliminating much of the anecdotal material that served as data for Jacobs's theses, in favor of more focus on tactics. He recommended cutting extended references to Kevin Lynch's *Image of the City.* Some months earlier, after reading the book, Jacobs had written Gilpatric with enthusiasm about Lynch's book, the first to emerge from the foundation's urban design research program, with enthusiasm. She told him that Lynch's book "is reassuring to me, and I have learned from it too." She was "fascinated to discover that the five elements of city design he has signaled out—paths, edges, districts, nodes, and landmarks—are the same ones I have figured out as basic for expression of the functional (social and economic) aspects of city order, although I have called them streets, borders, districts, centers of activity, and focus points. . . . In so many instances, we have gotten to the same place by following entirely different lines of reasoning." In *Death and Life*, Jacobs took his suggestion and cut the discussion of Lynch back to three relatively minor references.[86]

Gilpatric also recommended cutting back on her quotation of Warren Weaver's essay on complexity science, which served as the keystone for her conclusion, in favor of more criticism. He wrote her, "I was sorry to note that you didn't include in this chapter a critique of some of the governing images of city organization and physical layout, which are out-dated. This is more than made up, perhaps, by the lambasting you give the Garden City planners and addicts of the Radiant City."[87]

No doubt shocked by Gilpatric's suggestion to cut her book in half, Jacobs did not reply to his letter for some six weeks, by which time the manuscript was being set in type. She told him that she had done some editing, but nowhere near the extent of his suggestions. To do so, she told him, would have "pulled supporting beams out of the structure of the book," and other readers had confirmed her belief that "the detail, in its cumulative effect, is what makes the book convincing." She added that "this country is full of digesters, reviewers, and summarizers, and those who do not care to read a book as long as this will get some of the drift of its ideas through those means anyhow." She concluded by saying that she had edited her quotation of Weaver's essay from the Rockefeller Foundation's *1958 Annual Report* somewhat but that it was still long enough to require permission to use it.[88]

Given the intensity of Jacobs's caustic remarks, it was rather ironic that Gilpatric wanted an even more critical tone, and less emphasis on such theoretical content as Weaver's essay, although he admitted that her application of complexity science to cities had merit. A serendipitous discovery, Weaver's essay "Science and Complexity" was published as a modest festschrift, in honor of his retirement from the foundation, in the same volume that reported Jacobs's first grant for *Death and Life*. However, the essay ultimately galvanized Jacobs's ideas about the complexity of the city and provided the theoretical conclusion for the sequential and cumulative observations of the preceding twenty-one chapters. Applying Weaver's concepts, Jacobs argued that the city was like other living things, a system of interrelated and interdependent variables, or "organized complexity." In making this leap, she was among the first people to recognize the significance of complexity science outside of scientific circles, and she was perhaps the first person to recognize complexity's significance to cities.[89]

The Death and Life of Great American Cities was published on October 1, 1961, but as early as June, Epstein, who was immensely pleased with the book, had arranged for excerpts to be published in various magazines. In September, Haskell published an excerpt in *Architectural Forum* and welcomed her return to the magazine—which would be brief. She had become an author, fulfilling a childhood ambition to make an important contribution, and already knew that she had other books to write.

Later in October, Jacobs sent Gilpatric a brief note with an attachment, a copy of three blurbs from William Whyte, Harrison Salisbury, and the writer Martin Mayer that praised the book. She thought he would like to see them. "I was naturally very pleased when I saw the comments," she wrote, "even though I know I'm not as good as that." She signed off by commenting that she had seen her first review of the book the day before and that she was already getting some less favorable feedback. She wrote, "As an antidote to the praise, I am getting a spate of furiously angry and denunciatory letters from planners and housers who seem to have me tabbed as an irresponsible, if not vicious, demagogue!"[90]

A different system of thought about great cities had emerged, but it was not the work of a demagogue or an amateur. *The Death and Life of Great American Cities* was not a book that Jacobs had planned at the outset; she learned about cities by writing it. But she had been writing it for almost thirty years, since her first essays on the city and through her work for *Architectural Forum*.

A *Vita Activa* and *Contemplativa*

> Any usefulness that this image of the city will have will depend first, on
> how true it is (on this I will try my best), and second, on whether it exerts
> any influence on the things that are done deliberately to shape the city
> and its life. I hope it will, but of course I do not know.
> —Jane Jacobs, 1958

ON FEBRUARY 21, 1961, three weeks after she sent off the manuscript
for *Death and Life* and returned to *Architectural Forum*, Jacobs opened the
New York Times to find that her neighborhood and another in the East
Village were the first two "anchor points" of a cross-island urban renewal
area proposed to include as many as fifteen project sites. Walter Fried, the
vice chairman of the city's Housing and Redevelopment Board—an organization formed in 1960 to replace Robert Moses's Committee on Slum
Clearance—was quoted as saying, "We've asked the Planning Commission
to make a study of the entire area between Fourteenth and Canal Streets,
river-to-river, to determine what it should look like forty years from now."
Other project sites, the *Times* reported, would not be announced "until
plans are firmer, it was explained, since a mere announcement sometimes
causes great anxiety in the affected neighborhoods."[1]

The anxiety was warranted, and Jacobs's fight to save her neighborhood
began immediately. Within two days of the announcement, the Housing
and Redevelopment Board—which had made a preliminary study in

advance of the City Planning Commission's direct public involvement—would request $350,000 from the city's Board of Estimate for a formal survey of the neighborhood and additional planning. From her work covering urban redevelopment, Jacobs understood that renewal plans initially presented to the public as "studies" were well developed and that the survey and funding request was a standard step in a typical Title I urban renewal project. A few days later, she was quoted in the *Times* as the chairman of the Committee to Save the West Village, stating, "The aim of the committee is to kill this project entirely because if it goes through it can mean only the destruction of the community. Then we will look for an alternative. We want enforced conservation of the buildings, not their destruction." Jacobs devoted most of 1961 to fighting the renewal plan, later observing, "The city's selection of the area and its schemes for converting it into inane anticity were about as neat a case study as could well be imagined of the intellectual idiocies and ignorance of city workings that I had been writing about."[2]

The Save the West Village organization, spearheaded by Jacobs, her husband, her close friend Rachele Wall, Gloria Hamilton (an owner of the local White Horse Tavern), and others, fought back with every tool at their disposal: petitions, leaflets, newspaper advertisements, letters to the editor, press conferences, publicity stunts, technical and legal strategies, art auctions, Christmas wreath and book sales for fundraising, politicking, and coalition building. They quickly learned that the opposition was steps ahead of them. The Housing and Redevelopment Board had requested the Board of Estimate's hearing as early as February 15, preempting the mayor's announcement, and a select group of individuals and local organizations had already been prepared, in advance of the public announcement, to support a West Village renewal project. These included the Citizens Housing and Planning Council (directed by Roger Starr, who wrote a scathing review of *Death and Life* in January 1962) and a number of other important city and civic organizations, including a local settlement house, a charitable organization, a church and pastor with personal connections to Moses, local politicians, and a number of what Jacobs and others called "fronts" or "puppet" organizations. "Mi-Cove," the Middle Income Co-Operative Village, Jacobs later explained, was "what we came to know as a puppet organization set up by the City . . . created by the City to be, in effect, the representative of the citizens of the West Village." Others were the "Neighbors Committee" and "West Greenwich Village Site Tenants' Council."[3]

With support from Bill Passanante, a local assemblyman, the Board of Estimate's vote was postponed until March. Soon thereafter the Manhattan borough president Edward Dudley requested a postponement until April, although he predicted that "virtually all of Manhattan would eventually be studied for urban renewal action." After the March meeting, when no action was taken, the *Times* reported that "a group of militant residents of Greenwich Village" was unsuccessful in persuading the board to kill outright the proposed urban renewal project.[4]

In the meantime, Rachele Wall had convinced another friend, Lester Eisner, the regional director of the federal Urban Renewal Administration, to visit the neighborhood, and his advice and information about Title I procedures, process, data, and law helped the neighborhood shape a counterattack. Despite Jacobs's knowledge of urban renewal from her work at *Forum* and in East Harlem, she did not have the procedural knowledge necessary to fight a specific renewal project. From Eisner and their own research, the group learned to avoid citizen participation in the planning process (a legal requirement), and they produced their own door-to-door questionnaire and slum designation survey, which documented every building in the fourteen-block subject area and included such aspects as comparisons of soot and noise pollution (from sound recordings) in the West Village with those in areas not considered slums. "We all had jobs and some of us who were working mothers had two jobs," Jacobs later recalled. "Everybody was in on this. Either their second job or their third job was saving the neighborhood." Working late into many nights, they produced a remarkable neighborhood study. Eisner told them it was an extraordinary job, one that would have cost the government $50,000. "It showed that, by all the legal criteria, the West Village was not a slum—could not legally be designated for urban renewal," Jacobs said later. "But that made no difference to the City Planning Commission. It wasn't interested in our information. It had already—they had already made up their minds. They totally disregarded it." Despite Eisner's help, massive forces were aligned against them.[5]

In early April, the *Times* discussed the West Village renewal proposal in the context of a larger congressional effort to increase federal funding for urban renewal by $2.5 billion over four years and "for a broader range of urban renewal projects than has so far been attempted." The paper reported that, by the end of the month, James Felt, the chairman of the City Planning Commission, would make public a comprehensive proposal of middle-income housing and renewal projects throughout the city and that all projects before the Board of Estimate, including the controversial West Village proposal, would be referred to the City Planning Commission for review and inclusion in its master proposal. Mayor Wagner was quoted as stating that "1961–62 will be a banner year in our continuing battle to turn back blight and deterioration and to create wholesome, productive communities."[6]

A few weeks later, around eight hundred people attended the twelve-hour-long Board of Estimate hearing on April 27, where an attorney for Save the West Village served a court order to Mayor Wagner. The order claimed that the commission had failed to hold public hearings and make its case for designating the neighborhood for renewal, and it ordered the mayor, the planning commission, the Board of Estimate, and the Housing and Redevelopment Board to show why they should not be restrained from designating the area as blighted. As spokesperson, Jacobs charged that city authorities were using Mi-Cove as a puppet organization to give the impression that residents approved of renewal and had practiced deception in their procedures. She asserted that the West Village was in the process of private rehabilitation and was not a slum.[7]

In May, Felt countered with his own public relations campaign. He admitted that the housing board's attempt to shortcut a hearing had been a mistake, but he argued that Jacobs and the Save the West Village group were "fighting the ghost of Robert Moses." Seeking to allay fears about a new package of eighteen urban renewal projects, Felt reiterated that there would be public hearings on each one and that the "backbone of renewal is in conserving and improving our existing structures and relating new developments to the character and needs of the community." At a time when New York had no preservation laws, Felt promised to establish a "Committee for the Preservation of Structures of Historic and Esthetic Importance," and he asserted that the commission had renounced Moses's "bulldozer approach." Within the West Village battle, Jacobs later explained, could be found the origins of the city's historic preservation movement: "We in the West Village were supposed to be thrown to the wolves, so to speak, as a sacrifice for the city giving people the preservation measure." But Jacobs and her allies were delighted about this, she recalled, because the neighborhood believed in the preservation measure and they were pleased that their efforts had pushed Felt into it.[8]

With each postponement of a hearing, the Save the West Village membership grew and its organization strengthened. Active members organized into subgroups that studied the legal issues related to urban renewal or the workings of city government, while others translated documents into Spanish or handled public relations. Children collected signatures for petitions and delivered leaflets to shopkeepers who allowed their storefronts to be used as bulletin boards for the quick dissemination of information. Although the organization put forth some theoretical arguments—such as the writer Erik Wensberg's criticism of the functionalist city planning belief in the segregation of industrial and residential land uses in a *Times* editorial—in order to unify diverse interests, the message was kept simple: Kill the proposal.[9]

In early June, as the City Planning Commission met, Jacobs and other committee leaders delivered a petition to the mayor's office demanding the removal of Felt as commissioner and Clarence Davies as chairman of the Housing and Redevelopment Board. Although this did little more than fragment sympathetic forces who didn't support the tactic, by August, with his reelection looming, Mayor Wagner began to signal his opposition to the Village renewal proposal. In mid-August, Wagner declared that the "bulldozer approach" was off the table. With his mayoral opponents promising to scrap the project if elected, on September 6, on the eve of the primary election, Wagner spoke the words Jacobs and others were waiting to hear. The *Times* reported that Mayor Wagner "would ask the City Planning Commission to kill the highly controversial plan for renewing a fourteen-block section of Greenwich Village."[10]

Nevertheless, on October 18, 1961, the City Planning Commission determined that the West Village was suitable for urban renewal. Coming just a few days after "How City Planners Hurt Cities," the first widely read excerpt of *Death and Life*, was published in the *Saturday Evening Post*, the commission declared the neighborhood "a substandard area by reason of the large number of structures therein that are deteriorating or dilapidated, the mixture of incompatible land uses, the lack of open space for active and passive recreation, the unsatisfactory traffic conditions," and other factors. While recognizing the "charm of diversity . . . so typical of Greenwich Village," the commission stated that the West Village's "kind of mixture, however, is of an entirely different quality from mixtures of residential uses with industrial warehousing and automotive uses, which have a completely different physical aspect—the creation of noise, dirt, traffic and other conditions incompatible with residences."[11]

The West Village battle was ultimately about more than the West Village neighborhood—it was a struggle for the enterprise of city planning. In its formal report, the commission argued that public intervention for renewal was not necessarily destructive or harmful and that it absolutely did not believe in "the *laissez faire* theory of urban renewal"—the idea that "local residents, if left to their own efforts without the interference of government, can bring about the renewal of the City." The commission rejected the pressure to stop trying to renew cities. "The problems of the 20th century urban revolution will never be solved by a modernized version of *laissez faire*. To accept this is to abandon our cities to the very process which created the slums of the past and necessitated housing and urban renewal programs to bring about their elimination." Thus, despite recognizing that a substantial majority of the local community was opposed, the commission determined that it would be "derelict in its responsibility if it blindly accepted the argument that community opposition to a proposal was by itself sufficient grounds for rejecting that proposal." It ordered that the city's master plan be changed to show that West Village was "characterized by blight and suitable for clearance, replanning, reconstruction or rehabilitation for predominantly residential use."[12]

A "near riot" ensued. The *Times* reported that the "Villagers, led by Mrs. Jane Jacobs, chairman of the Committee to Save the West Village, leapt from their seats and rushed forward. They shouted that a 'deal' had been made with a builder, that the Mayor had been 'double-crossed' and that the commission's action was illegal." They shouted "Down with Felt!" and "Felt made a deal!" Policemen escorted several from the room and carried one man out by his feet.[13]

Interviewed after the meeting, Jacobs declared, "It's the same old story. First the builder picks the property, then he gets the Planning Commission to designate it, and then the people get bulldozed out of their homes." She reported, moreover, that in a meeting with Mayor Wagner a few days before, she and five other West Village committee members were offered a "deal" where, if they acquiesced, the mayor would kill the project a week after its designation. They rejected the deal, threatening legal action. Moreover, she claimed to have "documentary proof" that a deal had been made with a developer prior to the public announcement in February.[14]

On the following day, October 19, Jacobs held a press conference at the Lion's Head coffee shop—a neighborhood institution mentioned in Jacobs's "Hudson Street ballet"—where she presented documents showing that an architect had been hired as early as October 1960 by a construction company's urban renewal department to produce schemes for the redevelopment of the West Village. Other documents, studied by a forensic analyst,

FIGURE 48. Jacobs at the Lion's Head coffee shop, where she held a press conference to present evidence showing that schemes to redevelop her neighborhood had been prepared before the required public hearings had taken place. (On Jacobs's right is Erik Wensberg.) Getty Images.

showed that the same typewriter that had been used by the architect and the construction company was also used to create petitions and other documents for the neighborhood organizations that worked with the developers and city officials. "We have all turned into detectives, and are finding out amazing facts about relationships between the builders and the Planning Commission and the Housing and Redevelopment Board," she wrote the editor of the *Saturday Evening Post*. On October 24, the Housing and Redevelopment Board announced that it would drop its West Village renewal proposal.[15]

Whether or not the renewal project was dropped because of Jacobs's revelations of corruption, the news coincided with the release of *The Death and Life of Great American Cities*. In addition to the excerpts in *Forum* and the *Saturday Evening Post*, other excerpts, and reactions to them, were published in *Columbia University Forum* ("City Planning: The Victory over Vitality," October 9), *The Reporter* ("How Money Can Make or Break Our Cities," October 12), and the *Wall Street Journal* ("Plans Against People," October 19). The first reviews of the book appeared within days of the Housing and Redevelopment Board's announcement.[16]

In November, with the release of *Death and Life*, stories of Jacobs's battles against Moses over Washington Square Park and with the City Planning Commission over the West Village spread across the country and overseas. Felt held his ground against Mayor Wagner and the wayward Housing and Redevelopment Board, but, following a leak of letters between him and the mayor, the planning commissioner finally capitulated, announcing on January 16, 1962, that, at its next meeting, the commission would remove the "blight" designation from the West Village neighborhood. With the designation removed, Jacobs was quoted stating, "Our sympathy goes out to other areas that are now being victimized by the Planning Commission."[17]

In February 1962, on the one-year anniversary of the West Village renewal announcement, Jacobs spoke at the University of Pittsburgh, giving the first of many talks that year. She spoke of the recent fight and what she had learned from it with a paper entitled "The Citizen in Urban Renewal: Participation or Manipulation?" She spoke at length about the tactics used to satisfy urban renewal legal requirements for citizen participation. That provision, she explained, is "partly an acknowledgement that the cooperation of the people concerned is needed, and it is partly an acknowledgement that the United States is a democracy. It goes against the national conscience not to observe the forms of democracy—and perhaps most so when the substance itself is authoritarian."[18]

Jacobs detailed the way "the city officials were, to all intents and purposes, manufacturing citizens' organizations to rubberstamp its plans," not only in Greenwich Village, but also in East Harlem and the Lower East Side, where the fabricated groups were sometimes called "cuckoo committees" after birds that take over others' nests. She told of a "citizens' meeting" where planning officials ran the slide projector in a room containing only one neighborhood resident, the appointed neighborhood committee chair. "We learned that if the cuckoo committee or its successors had succeeded only slightly, had gotten together so much as a presentable handful of membership, the city officials could have chosen to consult with this creature of their own purposes, and to recognize it as the 'responsible citizens' organization' of the area," she said. Adding that private firms were also enlisted to this end, she related, "We learned that non-governmental organizations were frequently the middlemen for this operation of participating the citizens into urban renewal, courtesy of urban renewal money." As she later described it in *Systems of Survival*, urban renewal was a "monstrous hybrid."

Apart from direct manipulation, Jacobs remarked on the subtler but incessant sales pitch for urban renewal that was being broadcast to the public. Taking up questions of whose plans were being served in city planning and urban renewal, from *Death and Life* and earlier writing like "Philadelphia's Redevelopment," Jacobs argued that citizens were being exhorted to serve interests that were detrimental to them. "At bottom," she declared, "the urban renewers try to cry up citizen participation to save *their* programs and solve *their* problems, not solve the citizens' problems."[19]

Ideologies and Utopias

Despite objections from those invested in the urban renewal regime and critiques of her arguments and implications of who and what was to blame for city problems, Jacobs's vision of the city was quickly and widely discussed. Or, stated more accurately, parts of Jacobs's inclusive vision of the city were quickly embraced by an ideologically broad spectrum of readers. Both conservatives and liberals could find ideas in *Death and Life* that resonated with their points of view.

Based on their particular local experiences, New Yorkers, whether liberal or conservative, were especially inclined to agree with Jacobs, familiar as they were with the fights against Moses, the failures of mass housing, and the corruption of urban renewal. William F. Buckley Jr.'s New York City–based *National Review* praised the book in December 1961; the columnist Ernest van den Haag, an ex-communist turned conservative and public advocate for segregation, praised Jacobs's advocacy for cities that were being "planned to death by the people supposed to preserve and renew them." Despite van den Haag's politics, this was a point many people could agree with by 1961. As Eric Larrabee, who worked as an editor at *Harper's Magazine* before becoming editor at *Horizon*, put it, "The clearing of slums, and their replacement with aseptic modern structures, is no longer the liberal's utopian objective that it once was. Urban renewal, beginning as a banner of enlightenment, has become a watchword for a mixture of destructiveness and exploitation, mildly flavored with profiteering." As noted in a May 1962 review in *American City Magazine* (also based in New York), "It is the only book that we know of which is quoted in context both by liberals and conservatives."[20]

In 1969, around the time Jacobs's next book, *The Economy of Cities*, was to be published, Jacobs's friend Leticia Kent wrote, "*The Death and Life of Great American Cities* was first panned by liberals, then hailed by liberals and conservatives alike." Kent's statement about a broad rejection by liberals is an exaggeration. Charles Abrams, who is credited with the expression "Socialism for the rich and capitalism for the poor," celebrated *Death and Life* as "an abattoir for sacred cows"—including some liberal sacred cows. In this regard, economic and social conservatives found immediate validation in Jacobs's writing, especially the rural and suburban conservatives who had never seen any reason to support federal funding for urban redevelopment and other conservatives who saw federal funding for public housing as socialistic or collectivist. For liberals, abandoning well-intentioned social aspirations was a more difficult process, partly because it required admitting that those who had opposed liberal policies, for whatever reasons, had been right. Within a few decades, in *All That Is Solid Melts into Air* (1982), a book that drew its title from Marx and Engels's *Communist Manifesto*, Marshall Berman (a New Yorker whose neighborhood was partially destroyed by Moses) could hold out *Death and Life* as the "one work that perfectly expresses the modernism of the street in the 1960s." Some years after that, the Marxist critic Fredric Jameson offered similar praise, noting that Jacobs's observations about the productive capacities of cities, particularly "handicraft" cities, "is comparable only to that of Marx himself." It took some decades of the proliferation of what Jacobs described as "suburban" chain stores, and the monopolization of cities (and suburbs) by corporate retail, for Jacobs's enthusiasm for the local mom-and-pop store and nonprofit storefront organizations to be understood as a radical critique of the new economy.[21]

Around 1961, however, commentators had difficulty seeing beyond prevailing wisdom, and, in this regard, the reaction of the architect-planner Percival Goodman was perhaps characteristic. Goodman—who had worked in East Harlem on plans for slum clearance and designs for public housing, imagined a new *Master Plan for New York* (1944), and cowrote the utopian book *Communitas: Ways of Livelihood and Means of Life*, with his brother

Paul in 1947 (revised in 1960)—said of Jacobs, "When she is right, she is very, very right; but when she is wrong, it is horrid."[22]

In *Communitas*, Goodman also criticized Moses, Ebenezer Howard's and Le Corbusier's Garden Cities, the dull suburbs and their petite bourgeoisie, and the planner's ideal of "fitting the man to the plan," as well as Frank Lloyd Wright's anti-urban Broadacres and Buckminster Fuller's "Universal Architect" uber-planner concept, both of which had escaped Jacobs's wrath in *Death and Life*. Goodman was also a critic of the notion of "housing," which he called "the *reductio ad absurdum* of isolated planning" for the practice of excluding all other city functions. Already in 1947, he had criticized "housers," in Jacobsian terms, for being more concerned with "sociological abstractions" than with local interests, as well as housing projects that resulted in hygienic ghettos with "the segregation of income groups, in government and subsidized projects." In 1960, after the passage of the federal housing acts, he added that connecting housing to slum clearance was a dubious social policy and, perhaps with a nod to Jacobs and her neighborhood battles, he added that "housers do not inhabit 'housing,'" they live in "technically substandard" homes in places like Greenwich Village. Such critiques led Goodman to other points of agreement, including a philosophy of "neofunctionalism," in which he criticized, just as Jacobs later did, the streamlined "machines whose operation is not transparent," in favor of a deeper and more humane understanding of modernist functionalism. Neofunctionalists, Goodman wrote, "take exception to much that is universally accepted, because it doesn't add up; they stop to praise many things universally disregarded, such as the custom of sitting on slum stoops and sidewalks, with or without chairs." Goodman's emblem was the ailanthus, the elegant weed that sprouted from many New York City backyards, and his Camillo Sitte–inspired proposal for a prototypical town square also wove together living and working spaces in a tight orbit with a similar combination of dignity and informality. "Everything is mixed up here," he wrote. His ideal city had much in common with Jacobs's.[23]

However, Goodman, like others, interpreted Jacobs's attack on flawed social policies and her respect for local knowledge and decision making as a laissez-faire approach and a tacit defense of the status quo. Similar to Commissioner Felt's comment that quitting current efforts at urban renewal and housing development was a capitulation to the *laissez faire* theory of urban renewal, Goodman observed, "Jane Jacobs's book suggests we leave everything pretty much as it is except we paint the walls." Like

Felt and other critics, Goodman threw back at Jacobs charges of wishful thinking. According to Goodman, Jacobs's city was one where "slums in [her] ideal city 'unslum' themselves" and landlords don't raise the rent. Her "essential weakness is in her anti-utopianism," he said, explaining that "she believes only what is in front of her nose. So, no planning is required, just the strategy and tactics involved in immediate situations. The problem is to win the battle not the war. In rough and tumble politics such a method applies and in fact is the statesmanship of our time. Thus this book [*Death and Life*] is bound to be popular."[24]

In a stunningly condescending review, "Mother Jacobs' Home Remedies," Lewis Mumford made similar comments about Jacobs's "mingling of sense and sentimentality, of mature judgments and schoolgirl howlers," and her praise for the city's "higgledy-piggledy unplanned casualness," "mishmash of functions and activities," and "random community." Unable to accept her idea that "a city cannot be a work of art," Mumford asserted, "Mrs. Jacobs has no use for the orderly distribution of [social and civic] activities or the handsome design of their necessary structures; she prefers the hit-and-miss distribution of the present city. . . . Mrs. Jacobs' most original proposal, then, as a theorist of metropolitan development[,] is to turn its chronic symptom of disorder—excessive congestion—into a remedy, by deliberately enlarging the scope of the disease." Seeing great cities themselves as a symptom of a disease caused by cataclysmic technical and financial powers, Mumford argued that "order-making forces, not the dynamic ones," needed cultivation and, to that end, reaffirmed, "If our urban civilization is to escape progressive dissolution, we shall have to rebuild it from the ground up."[25]

At the same time, advocates of a truly laissez-faire approach argued that Jacobs was not liberal enough, and they would go so far as to hijack her ideas to support the opposite of what she endorsed: suburban automobility and greenfield suburban development. Following Jacobs's analysis of cities as organized complexity, in 1964, around the time that the architect Robert Venturi was writing *Complexity and Contradiction in Architecture* (1966), the planner Melvin Webber observed, "We have mistaken for 'urban chaos' what is more likely to be a newly emerging order whose signal qualities are complexity and diversity." Seeing the advocacy for dense, centralized cities as an "ideological campaign" (and helping to turn it into one), Webber made the case that personal mobility and telecommunications enabled "community without propinquity" and rendered "the unitary conceptions of urban places" as anachronistic. "We would do well," he argued, "to accept the private vehicle as an indispensable medium of metropolitan interaction—more, as an important instrument of personal freedom." His example was Los Angeles, which was then building its free-way system. Webber concluded that the task of the planner was not to defend open space or city form against the evils of urban sprawl: "This is a mission of evangelists, not planners. Rather, and as a barest minimum, the task is to seek that spatial distribution of urban populations and urban activities that will permit greater freedom for human interaction."[26]

Echoing Webber's argument, in 1969, the British critics Reyner Ban-ham and Paul Barker, the geographer Peter Hall, and the architect Cedric Price observed, "The irony is that the planners themselves constantly talk— since the appearance of Jane Jacobs's *Death and Life of Great American Cities*—about the need to restore spontaneity and vitality to urban life. They never seem to draw the obvious conclusion—that the monuments of our century that have spontaneity and vitality are found not in the old cities, but in the American West." In "Non-Plan: An Experiment in Free-dom," they made a case for an experiment in laissez-faire development inspired by Los Angeles, Las Vegas, and the American commercial strip, and they argued that "physical planners have no right to set their value judgment up against yours" and that "people should be allowed to build what they like." They concluded, "The notion that the planner has the right to say what is 'right' is really an extraordinary hangover from the days of collectivism in left-wing thought, which has long ago been abandoned elsewhere." Exactly twenty years after *The Architectural Review* launched the Townscape movement, "Non-Plan" became "Man Made America's" countermanifesto, soon followed by Venturi, Scott-Brown, and Izenour's *Learning from Las Vegas*.[27]

Despite its different geographical and political manifestations, the non-planning movement, in which *Death and Life* played a part, can be traced to ideological debates of the 1940s and 1950s. As a world war against fas-cism turned into a cold war against communism, antitotalitarian philosophies—such as those of the libertarian political philosopher and economist Friedrich Hayek and Hayek's friend and debating partner, the philosopher of science Karl Popper—sought to explain the roots of totali-tarian thought and defend against its proliferation. In an epoch defined by George Orwell's *Nineteen Eighty-Four* (1949), people on both the left and the right were increasingly repelled by the repressions of Marxist-Leninist states, fearful of their imitation in Western welfare states, and generally suspicious of social engineering. Jacobs, who was intimately involved in the war efforts of the Office of War Information (OWI) and the State Department, was unquestionably affected by these debates, and she found intellectual allegiances and sympathies among their spokesmen.

In this context, there are indeed many points of agreement between Jacobs and Hayek. Both were drawn to basic principles of Western liberal thought and the ideals of a broad base of social powers. Hayek's *The Road to Serfdom* (1944), whose title was a reference to de Tocqueville's *Democracy in America*, shared themes with Jacobs's *Constitutional Chaff*, her writings for the OWI and *Amerika* about the American ideals of tolerance and local self-government, and the spirited defense of her beliefs in response to accusations of un-American activities. Both were suspicious of nationalism and aware that democracies could suppress minorities through majority rule. Both opposed top-down, paternalistic, utopian, and statistically driven social and economic planning, and both broadly criticized "planners" of all kinds. In contrast, both favored smaller-scale organizations where local knowledge of the particular circumstances of time and place could be respected and leveraged, arguing that modern society was characterized by multifarious individual efforts, complex interrelationships, and unpredictable outcomes that no individual or groups of politicians and planners could completely survey, understand, or anticipate.[28]

A shared lack of faith in the rational powers of an individual or group to design complex social systems, including cities, led Hayek and Jacobs—and others in the 1950s and 1960s—to see complex systems as the evolutionary results of the trial and error of human actions. This, in turn, led both to an interest in complexity science's explanations of spontaneous order and its relevance to social science and economics. In a 1964 essay, "The Theory of Complex Phenomena," Hayek presented a discussion of complexity theory similar to Jacobs's in the last chapter of *Death and Life*, with similar points about the difficulty of planning and predicting outcomes in complex systems. In *The Nature of Economies*, Jacobs extended the discussion to parallels between the complexities of ecosystems and economic systems, expanding on her ideas in *Death and Life*.[29]

Hayek and Jacobs also shared some similar ideas about the city, city planning, and housing. In *The Constitution of Liberty* (1960), Hayek wrote, "Civilization as we know it is inseparable from urban life," while recognizing that, due to its density and complexity, the price mechanism was "an imperfect guide" for solving the interrelated problems and allocating the communal costs of city life. Like Jacobs, Hayek deferred to individual decision making wherever possible in housing decisions. "The issue is therefore not whether one ought or ought not to be for town planning, but whether the measures to be used are to supplement and assist the market or to suspend it and put central direction in its place," he wrote. "The practical problems which policy raises here are of great complexity, and no perfect solution is to be expected." To this end, both recognized the need for zoning regulations, but also advocated performance zoning as an alternative to use zoning and specification codes.[30]

Despite these points of agreement, Jacobs rejected the libertarian ideology and label for various reasons and in various ways. Whereas Hayek described "social justice" as being equivalent to socialism, Jacobs did not follow his slippery-slope logic. Hayek's contradictory rationalism led him to warn against the "'middle way' between 'atomistic' competition and central direction," but Jacobs was less dogmatic. In *Death and Life* and her prior work, she attended to a far wider range of planned and unplanned failures of the market and self-segregation, including, for example, racism, sexist wage discrepancies (the primary reason for her union organizing and support of the Labor Party in the 1940s), social segregation, economic redlining and blacklisting, the problems of private car ownership and use, and the consumption of rural land. She recognized the virtues of the public realm, including public education and public transportation, and the larger social significance, beyond market value, of public sidewalks, streets, and city spaces. She saw that a city required flourishing public and quasi-public institutions. Public life was an important element of civilization and liberty, according to Jacobs, and it required a spatial infrastructure to thrive. The self-policing eyes on public streets were an anti-panopticon, the urban opposite of an architecture of institutional control, providing resistance to the police state, but only with the cooperation of a society and government embodying these values.[31]

A robust public realm was, in turn, essential to a free and open society through its diversity. In ways that Hayek ignored, Jacobs understood that the spontaneous self-organization was not always positive. She associated "price-tagged populations" with planned lower-income and middle-class housing projects, but she also observed that self-segregated urban and suburban "turfs" were also unplanned. As compared to the suburbs, however, cities were naturally more diverse, and the public realm of the city was therefore vitally important in breaking down turf psychology. She observed, "Sidewalk public contact and sidewalk public safety, taken together, bear directly on our country's most serious social problem—segregation and racial discrimination."[32]

As early as 1945, when she wrote a very honest propaganda piece on the history of the United States for the OWI, Jacobs was concerned about these issues. In her essay's conclusion she observed, "The nation's 13,000,000 Negro citizens do not yet have full economic equality and opportunity. Under the leadership of the national government and of many private organizations their position is being improved but much progress must still be made. . . . Though Americans have built a united and productive country with a great degree of freedom, education and economic opportunity for its people, there are still many ways in which it can be improved." Years later, housing projects—particularly in private projects, where racial discrimination was commonplace prior to the Civil Rights Act of 1964—not only exacerbated segregation, but also literally destroyed the public space of the street, compounding the city's segregation. "Overcoming residential discrimination comes hard where people have no means of keeping a civilized public life on a basically dignified public footing, and their private lives on a private footing," she wrote. She added that, if African American slums were prevented from unslumming by redlining and segregation, "the damage to our cities might be the least of our worries; unslumming is a by-product of other kinds of vigor and other forms of economic and social change." If not corrected, Americans' "tendencies toward master-race psychology" would destroy the country.[33]

Pragmatism and the Polis

Years later, in 1987, Jacobs explicitly distanced herself from "libertarianism." By this time libertarianism was associated, as it remains today in the United States, with a capitalistic free-market ideology and a critique of state powers. By comparison, Jacobs stated that she was "highly in favor of helping the poor and giving everyone as good an education as they want and can use—not what they can *pay* for." She continued, "I think health care, not tied to money, is terribly important. One of the reasons I care about a developing economy is that it can underpin things like this." She similarly questioned the anarchism of abandoning laws in favor of an ideal of personal responsibility, stating, "Libertarians would say, 'Look, we shouldn't even have laws about drugs. That's up to people to be responsible about themselves. We shouldn't have lots of laws about things that aren't harmful to people.' I'm not so sure about that. I think people do need help of various kinds." For Jacobs, "social capital"—a term she popularized in *Death and Life*—and various forms of "abeconomic" behavior (like love and friendship) were more important than financial capital and economic behaviors. As she remarked in an interview about economics and moral philosophy, "We must recognize that the best things in life have nothing to do with economics."[34]

Jacobs understood the destructive power of capital. Her theory of the "self-destruction of diversity" recognized that the demand and competition for popular business and residential districts would eventually destroy them. Giving examples in *Death and Life* of the gentrification of Eighth Street in Greenwich Village and the monopolization of the four corners of a "100 percent location" by four banks in Philadelphia, Jacobs showed how capital and competition could destroy the diversity of cities. Describing the destructive forces of spontaneously leveraged capital, not just those of large privately and publicly held capital, she explained, "The cataclysmic effects in such cases arise, not from vast wholesaling of credit at all, but from the aggregate of many individual transactions which happen to be heavily concentrated in one locality in one period of time. Society has produced no deliberate stimulants to this destruction of outstanding city success." But, unlike free-market libertarians, Jacobs did not believe that this spontaneous process be left to its own devices. She continued, "But neither has society done anything to hamper or divert this form of city-destroying money flood. Private investment shapes cities, but social ideas (and laws) shape private investment. . . . If and when we think that [a] lively, diversified city, capable of continual, close-grained improvement and change, is desirable, then we will adjust the financial machinery to get that." Borrowing the idea of "feedback" from cybernetics and new discoveries in biology (such as DNA), she argued, "In creating city success, we human beings have created marvels, but we left out feedback." While she didn't believe that a true or perfect feedback system could be created, regulations and incentives were imperfect but necessary substitutes to maintain diversity and prevent cities, or parts of cities, from destroying themselves. To further counterbalance such market effects, Jacobs proposed regulation in the form of "zoning for diversity," the use of public policy to strategically locate public facilities and incentivize the location of private ones, and urban

FIGURE 49. Jacobs with her husband (right foreground) and son (standing) at the Lion's Head coffee shop at a planning meeting for West Village Houses in May 1963. On the table behind them are brochures for the proposed low-rise, subsidized housing development, which was designed in place of a massive urban renewal project with apartment towers for middle- and upper-income tenants. Courtesy of Bob Gomel.

development, ostensibly through both public and private means, to get "the supply of vital, diversified city streets and districts into a saner relationship with demand."[35]

These anti-laissez-faire ideas were consistent with Jacobs's activism in the West Village, where the focus of the fight, apart from the designation of her neighborhood as an urban renewal district, was against the middle-class and luxury housing projects that were eliminating and being planned to replace the affordable housing and mixed uses of Greenwich Village and her neighborhood. Another endeavor, which built on Jacobs's experiences in working to improve public housing in East Harlem, was her ten-year fight for West Village Houses, a 420-unit low-income and middle-income housing development developed by a nonprofit corporation with public funds, completed in 1974, which also sought to push back against the forces of gentrification.[36]

If, in these ways, Hayek's antiplanning ideas can be seen as a more extreme model than Jacobs's, a better comparison might be found in Karl

Popper's *The Open Society and Its Enemies* (1945) and *The Poverty of Histor-icism* (1957). In these, Popper also analyzed the overestimation of abilities to predict the outcomes of planning in complex systems and rejected wholesale "utopian social engineering" with arguments that ranged from the practical need to keep imperfect systems in place while they were being improved to the desire to avoid violence. Just as Jacobs attacked utopianism and spoke of her idea that a city cannot be a work of art because of the heavy-handed authorship or homogeny that this requires, Popper criticized the utopian's and aestheticist's aggressive tabula rasa approach. Similar to Hayek, Popper observed, "The view that society should be beautiful like a work of art leads only too easily to violent measures," and he argued that planners and engineers of this kind "will not start work on a city nor on an individual, nor will they draw up laws, unless they are given a clean canvas, or have cleaned it themselves." However, while Hayek acknowledged that "everybody who is not a complete fatalist is a planner," Popper—like Jacobs—had a higher tolerance for incremental "piecemeal engineering" based on experience, induction, trial and error, and improvisation. Pop-per's critique limited planning in scale and to contexts where it was openly discussed, where it could be criticized, and where failed plans could be acknowledged and ended. Thus, as compared to the cataclysmic approach of urban renewal—whether by idealists or profiteers—Jacobs, following Popper, advocated an incremental approach to city change. She wrote, "City building that has a solid footing produces continual and gradual change, building complex diversifications."

Popper's "piecemeal engineering," in other words, was like piecemeal redevelopment, the approach once advocated in "The Philadelphia Cure"—before the approach was effectively overruled by *Berman v. Parker*, which explicitly stated that urban renewal, enabled by eminent domain and police powers, "need not, by force of the Constitution, be on a piecemeal basis, lot by lot, building by building." Following *Berman v. Parker*, Jacobs was, of course, not alone in her criticism of the wide use of state powers to take private property. Like Popper, she argued that revolutionary effects could result instead from an evolutionary process. Although a policy's "cumulative effects should be revolutionary, like any strategy aimed at keeping things working, it has to be engaged in as a form of evolution." In contrast to Hayek's Darwinian emphasis on competition, Jacobs empha-sized the mutual support found in nature and the cooperation found in human societies, which she saw as the foundation of law and trade. The ideas of mutual aid and symbiosis, which can be found throughout her work, were also a foundation of her activism, where she understood the need to develop broad, bipartisan alliances to advocate for local concerns.[37]

Like Popper, Jacobs was criticized for being anti-utopian, insufficiently utopian, and for being utopian in the wrong way. In a review of *The Economy of Cities*, the socialist Michael Harrington wrote, "The future will be unlivable unless it incarnates the values and passion of a Jane Jacobs." But, he noted, "To think that local organization, even with risk capital, can accomplish these sweeping changes is utopian in the worst sense of the word." In terms of local organization, Harrington was ostensibly alluding to Jacobs's work as an activist and implicitly to her admiration for her friend Saul Alinsky, author of *Reveille for Radicals*, and for planner-organizers like Chester Hartman, author of *Between Eminence and Notoriety: Four Decades of Radical Urban Planning*, for which Jacobs wrote the foreword. Harrington was also critiquing the limits of localism in terms of political and financial power, which could be overcome by nonlocal governmental intervention, and he was right to point out these issues. One of the great dilemmas of *Death and Life* is Jacobs's simultaneous love for the great city and her recognition of how difficult a great city is to govern properly. In *Death and Life*, in the chapter "Governing and Planning Districts," Jacobs discussed the failures of the democratic system—the ignorance and disinterest of politicians and planners, and the time wasted by citizens valiantly arguing the fates of predetermined decisions. But in a passage of notable graciousness to the officials she was fighting, she wrote, "Their energy, wits, patience and human responsiveness are, on the whole, creditable. I see no reason to expect great improvement from finding better. These are not boys sent on a man's errand. These are men sent on a superman's errand."[38]

The underlying problem of our cities, Jacobs concluded, "is a most understandable failure by our society to keep abreast of demanding historical changes." These historical changes, she explained, "are not only an immense increase in the size of great cities, but also the immensely increased responsibilities—for housing, for welfare, for health, for education, for regulatory planning—which have been taken on by the governments of great municipalities." New York, she added, was "not unique in failing to match such profound changes in circumstances with appropriate functional changes in administrative and planning structure. Every great American city is at a similar impasse." Here she acknowledged the social criticism of Lewis Mumford, whose first book was a treatise on utopias.

"When human affairs reach, in truth and in fact, new levels of complica-
tion, the only thing that can be done is to devise means of maintaining
things well at the new level," she wrote. "The alternative is what Lewis
Mumford has aptly called 'unbuilding,' the fate of a society which cannot
maintain the complexity on which it is built and on which it depends."
Despite her other criticisms of Mumford, she believed that he was right
about this. Not only could "supermen" not manage the great city, planners'
acts of "unbuilding" were an almost inevitable outcome of societies' inabili-
ties to maintain complexity in the face of massive, historical change.
"Insensibly and gradually, as city administrative organization has failed to
evolve suitably along with city growth and complexity, city 'unbuilding'
has become a destructive but practical necessity for planning and other
administrative staffs, whose members are also being sent on supermen's
errands," Jacobs reasoned. "Routine, ruthless, wasteful, oversimplified
solutions for all manner of city physical needs (let alone social and economic needs) *have* to be devised by administrative systems which have lost
the power to comprehend, to handle, and to value an infinity of vital,
unique, intricate and interlocked details."[39]

Jacobs went on to explain that, to cope with new realities and new
complexities, planning needed a new focus and a new mantra—"planning
for vitality"—a phrase she repeated six times to emphasize points made in
Death and Life's previous chapters. Recognizing that institutions and their
systems had not evolved in ways that were up to the task, she acknowledged
that this new form of planning would require the reinvention of systems.
Although planning for vitality required specific knowledge of the precise
and unique places in a city with which they are dealing, planners should
gain knowledge and learn only from "the people of the place, because
nobody else knows enough about it." She admitted that city planners "do
not even have the means of gathering and comprehending the intimate,
many-sided information required, partly because of their own unsuitable
structures for comprehending big cities, and partly because of the same
structural inadequacies in other departments." As a consequence, she
acceded, "It is futile to expect that citizens will act with responsibility, verve,
and experience on big, city-wide issues when self-government has been rendered all but impossible on localized issues, which are often of the most
direct importance to people."[40]

Jacobs's solution to this daunting problem was a substantial horizontal
and decentralized restructuring of municipal administration and governmental intelligence that cynics might call wishful, utopian, and well beyond

piecemeal engineering, though not anarchistic. In fact, she went on to propose that a broader metropolitan government, which was necessary for addressing such nonlocal matters as pollution, major transportation problems, and land and water conservation, could be built on the foundation of a reorganized and decentralized municipal government. Repeating points from her 1957 article "Metropolitan Government," Jacobs offered that "there is great need for common and coordinated action (and financial support) on many metropolitan area problems, and still more need for localized coordination here and there among different governmental units within a metropolitan area." Her solution to the governmental "crazy quilt" was to federate local polities "into a super-area government which would have extensive planning powers and administrative organs for carrying the plans [for addressing metropolitan concerns] into action." Taxes would fund the work of metropolitan government and spread out the expenses of great city amenities. She explained, "Part of the taxes from each locality would go to the Metropolitan Government, thus helping also to relieve great cities of part of the financial burden they carry, unrecompensated, for major central city facilities used by the hinterland." In this scheme, great cities would work more closely with the "welter of overlapping, duplicating, strangulated, town, county, small-city and township governments" and "barriers to joint planning and joint support of common metropolitan facilities, would thus, it is reasoned, be overcome."[41]

Jacobs recognized that the idea of metropolitan government was politically unpopular and that "voters sensibly decline to federate into a system where bigness means local helplessness, ruthless, oversimplified planning, and administrative chaos." In making a case for planning at this level, she understood that people should wonder, "How is helplessness against 'conquering' planners an improvement over no planning? How is bigger administration, with labyrinths nobody can comprehend or navigate, an improvement over crazy-quilt township and suburban governments?" However, Jacobs believed the answer was within great cities. "We already have governmental units which cry out for new and workable strategies and tactics of big metropolitan administration and planning, and these are the great cities themselves," she wrote. "If great cities can learn to administer, coordinate, and plan in terms of administrative districts at understandable scale, we may become competent, as a society, to deal too with those crazy quilts of government and administration in the greater metropolitan areas. Today we are not competent to do so."[42]

If one of the great paradoxes of *Death and Life* was that planning and administration were needed despite the fact that great cities might be too big to govern and beyond the capacities of planners and experts, another was that, despite Jacobs's criticisms of theoreticians, a new vision and theory of the city was needed. While well aware that there were "pavement-pounding" planners, she nevertheless saw the need for a new intellectual framework, one that would replace ideas borrowed from the physical sciences with a life science–oriented approach to cities. As she explained in the book's last chapter, a methodology—a new scientific method—would include thinking about processes, working inductively, and being attentive to "unaverage clues." Once again, despite her criticisms, she understood that planners of Howard's and Le Corbusier's generations, and even those of younger generations, could not have been aware of and had not yet recognized what recent advances in the human and life sciences, such as Warren Weaver's complexity science, suggested for cities. "These advances have, of course, filtered from the life sciences into general knowledge; they have become part of the intellectual fund of our times. And so a growing number of people have begun, gradually, to think of cities as problems in organized complexity—organisms that are replete with unexamined, but obviously intricately interconnected, and surely understandable, relationships." Reflecting on her own contribution, she explained, "This book is one manifestation of that idea." However, complexity theory did not necessarily make cities easier to plan or administer—perhaps the opposite. Complexity theory confirmed what Jacobs already knew: that planners' predictive capacities were greatly challenged by the many interconnected variables embodied in cities.[43]

While working on *The Economy of Cities*, Jacobs went so far as to question the nature of New York City as a great city. Thinking about the discrepancies between great cities as productive economic units but problematic administrative units, she observed, "Take New York. Back before the turn of the century, it was five cities. It was probably a mistake to consolidate them into one. Five autonomous city governments are probably not enough for New York now." With the premise of *Cities and the Wealth of Nations* already in mind, she was equally ready to question the idea of nations for similar reasons: "I think it is also questionable that large nations are really viable governmental units any longer. They may be obsolete—like dinosaurs. The viable nations of the future may be on the scale of Sweden or Holland, rather than on the scale of the United States, China or the Soviet Union."[44]

FIGURE 50. Jacobs at her typewriter, ca. 1961. Jacobs Papers.

These comments came soon after Jacobs left the United States. In 1967, she was arrested during a Vietnam War protest march at the Pentagon, and, in January 1968, while still at work on *The Economy of Cities*, she was a signatory of an advertisement published in New York newspapers protesting the war and supporting a proposed war tax. The protestors, all well-known writers and public intellectuals, quoted Henry David Thoreau, the author of *Civil Disobedience* (1849), who said then of America's war with Mexico, "If a thousand men were not to pay their tax bills this year, that would not be a violent and bloody measure, as it would be to pay them and enable the States to commit violence and shed innocent blood." Less than four months later, in April 1968, Jacobs was arrested again and charged with disorderly conduct, inciting to riot, criminal mischief, and obstructing government administration during a public hearing about plans for the Lower Manhattan Expressway. A few months after that, she and her husband moved their family to Toronto in protest of the war and to protect their sons from the draft.[45]

In an interview in 1972, Jacobs was asked if she felt any regret or guilt about leaving New York. "None at all," she replied. "I did the best I could for twenty years. I fought as long as I could, but I've had enough. There's no virtue in fighting battles and losing. In Toronto you have a chance of winning." In fact, Jacobs had won all of her major battles, including one against Toronto's Spadina Expressway only the year before, but she was weary of activism, stating, "It's absurd to make your life absurd in response to absurd governments." Her critiques of nationalism in *The Question of Separatism: Quebec and the Struggle over Sovereignty* and *Cities and the Wealth of Nations: Principles of Economic Life* would follow. Despite her frustrations with government (which she saw as "forever susceptible to barbaric actions"), in *Systems of Survival* Jacobs would nevertheless seek to understand the symbiosis and mutual support of the exchange and guardian mentalities. "The guardian-commercial symbiosis," she wrote, "combats force, fraud, and unconscionable greed in commercial life—and simultaneously impels guardians to respect private plans, private property, and personal rights." Inspired by Plato's *Republic*, "the city-state as an allegory of how the virtuous individual should conduct his life," Jacobs sought to contribute to the great philosophical dialogue about civilization.[46]

In *Systems of Survival*, Jacobs observed, "Most of us after our formative years resist revising our views of how the world works." She did not—even when this took her from "pavement pounding" to "Olympian" heights. On one hand, Jacobs recognized that practical changes would be incomplete without corresponding intellectual changes. On the other, whether she was thinking about city sidewalks or the moral systems of civilizations, Jacobs remained deeply connected to the phenomena and human experiences of the city. "Theories and other abstractions are powerful tools only in the limited sense that the Greek mythological giant Antaeus was powerful," she wrote. "When Antaeus was not in intimate contact with earth, his strength rapidly ebbed." As a theorist and activist, this was equally true of Jacobs herself.[47]

SOURCES AND ABBREVIATIONS

JACOBS'S MAJOR WORKS, IN CHRONOLOGICAL ORDER

Constitutional Chaff: Rejected Suggestions of the Constitutional Convention of 1787, with Explanatory Argument (New York: Columbia University Press, 1941).

The Death and Life of Great American Cities (New York: Random House, 1961).

The Economy of Cities (New York: Random House, 1969).

The Question of Separatism: Quebec and the Struggle Over Sovereignty (New York: Random House, 1980).

Cities and the Wealth of Nations: Principles of Economic Life (New York: Random House, 1984).

Systems of Survival: A Dialogue on the Moral Foundations of Commerce and Politics (New York: Random House, 1992).

A Schoolteacher in Old Alaska: The Story of Hannah Breece (New York: Random House, 1995).

The Nature of Economies (New York: Random House, 2000).

Dark Age Ahead (New York: Random House, 2004).

A NOTE ABOUT JANE BUTZNER JACOBS'S EARLY WRITING
AND NONBYLINED WRITING FOR *ARCHITECTURAL FORUM*

In July 1958, Jacobs prepared a résumé in support of her Rockefeller Foundation grant and listed her major writing projects and publications to date (RF 1.2 200R, New School, 390:3380, Rockefeller Archive Center). She highlighted, for example, freelance writing for *Vogue*, *Cue*, the *New York Herald Tribune*, and *Harper's Bazaar*, as well as her book *Constitutional Chaff* and articles completed for *The Iron Age*, *Amerika Illustrated*, and *Architectural Forum*. Some of these writings, discussed in this book, are saved in her papers at Boston College's Burns Library; some are reprinted in *Ideas That Matter: The Worlds of Jane Jacobs*, edited by Max Allen; and I identified others by way of archival notes and clues and by searching magazines, microfilm, and newspaper archives. As for Jacobs's work at *Architectural Forum*, her résumé included the important statement that she had "written articles appearing in almost every issue beginning with May of '52." The following articles, she continued, "are most relevant to my present interest in writing about the nature of cities":

"New Thinking on Shopping Centers," Mar. 1953
"Good-by Neighborhood Schools?," Apr. 1953
"Philadelphia," Jul. 1955
"Cleveland," Aug. 1955
"Washington," Jan. 1956
"The Fort Worth Plan," May 1956
"Pavement Pounders and Olympians" (editorial), May 1956
"The Missing Link in City Redevelopment," Jun. 1956
"By 1976 What City Pattern?" (editorial) and City Pattern sections on "Central
   City" (concentration; ring freeways; traffic; housing), Sep. 1956
"Why Aren't There More Good Shopping Centers?," Dec. 1956
"Our 'Surplus' Land" (editorial), Mar. 1957
"New York's Office Boom," Mar. 1957
"Row Houses for Cities," May 1957
"Symposium on what to do about public housing," Jun. 1957
"Metropolitan Government," Aug. 1957
"The City's Threat to Open Land," Jan. 1958
"Round-up of redevelopment projects," Apr. 1958
"New Heart for Baltimore," Jun. 1958
"What Is A City?" (editorial), Jul. 1958
"Housing for the Elderly," Aug. 1958
Also, "Downtown is for People," *Fortune* magazine, Apr. 1958

Following the standard editorial practice, for most of the time she worked at *Architec-tural Forum* many of her articles were not bylined. This policy was discussed in the mid-1950s—her colleague Walter McQuade advocated a change to bylines or author initials in October 1954—but the policy did not change until some years later. As such, the articles that Jacobs listed were only some of the articles that she wrote or collaborated on for *Forum* between May 1952 and October 1958, when she went on leave to write *Death and Life*. Although I have identified many more written for and before her work at *Forum*, her complete bibliography may never be known.

ABBREVIATIONS

AF	*Architectural Forum*
Alinsky Papers	Saul Alinsky Papers, Briscoe Center for American History, University of Texas at Austin
AI	*Amerika Illustrated*
AR	*The Architectural Review*
CBW Papers	Catherine Bauer Wurster Papers, Bancroft Library, University of California, Berkeley
CC	*Constitutional Chaff: Rejected Suggestions of the Constitutional Convention of 1787, with Explanatory Argument*
CPR	Civilian Personnel Records, National Personnel Records Center, St. Louis, MO
CWN	*Cities and the Wealth of Nations: Principles of Economic Life*
D&L	*The Death and Life of Great American Cities*

DAA	*Dark Age Ahead*
EOC	*The Economy of Cities*
FBI	Federal Bureau of Investigation Archives
Haskell Papers	Douglas Haskell Papers, Avery Architectural and Fine Arts Library, Columbia University, New York
Hayes Papers	Shirley Hayes Papers, New-York Historical Society, New York
IA	*The Iron Age*
ITM	Max Allen, ed., *Ideas That Matter: The Worlds of Jane Jacobs* (Owen Sound, Ontario: Ginger, 1997)
Jacobs Papers	Jane Jacobs Papers, John J. Burns Library, Boston College, Boston, MA
LGWA	La Guardia and Wagner Archives, La Guardia Community College, City University of New York
NYCHA	New York City Housing Authority
NYHT	*New York Herald Tribune*
NYT	*The New York Times*
RAC	Rockefeller Foundation Archives, Rockefeller Archive Center, Sleepy Hollow, New York
RF	Rockefeller Foundation
Sert Papers	Josep Lluís Sert Papers, Loeb Library, Special Collections, Harvard Graduate School of Design, Cambridge, MA
SOS	*Systems of Survival: A Dialogue on the Moral Foundations of Commerce and Politics*
USAR	Union Settlement Association Records, Rare Book and Manuscript Library, Columbia University, New York
VV	*The Village Voice*

NOTES

INTRODUCTION

The epigraph for this chapter is from Jane Jacobs, letter to Grady Clay, Mar. 3, 1959, courtesy of Grady Clay.

1. William H. Whyte Jr., "Preface: C. D. Jackson Meets Jane Jacobs," in *The Exploding Metropolis* (Berkeley: University of California Press, 1993), xv. Two of Jacobs's four New York "working districts" essays and Jacobs's first book, *Constitutional Chaff: Rejected Suggestions of the Constitutional Convention of 1787, with Explanatory Argument* (New York: Columbia University Press, 1941), were "lost" and not incorporated into Jacobs's historiography until 2007. See Peter L. Laurence, "Jane Jacobs Before *Death and Life*," *Journal of the Society of Architectural Historians* (Mar. 2007), 5–15. The anthology mentioned is Max Allen, ed., *Ideas That Matter: The Worlds of Jane Jacobs* (Owen Sound, Ontario: Ginger, 1997). Although Jacobs's work before the late 1950s receives only a few pages, *ITM* is a valuable collection of primary and secondary sources; it was coedited by Mary Rowe with Jacobs's assistance around the time that Jacobs established her archive at Boston College.

2. Douglas Haskell, memo to Jane Jacobs, Jul. 2, 1959 (Haskell Papers, 79:6).

3. Jacobs, letter to Clay, Mar. 3, 1959.

4. The first headline is from the *Saturday Evening Post* (Oct. 14, 1961); the second is from *Harper's* (Nov. 4, 1961).

5. Peter L. Laurence, "Contradictions and Complexities: Jane Jacobs' and Robert Venturi's Complexity Theories," *Journal of Architectural Education* (Feb. 2006), 49–60.

6. A complete bibliography of writing about Jacobs, *Death and Life*, and her other books would include many thousands of citations. However, important books and edited collections include Marshall Berman, *All That Is Solid Melts into Air: The Experience of Modernity* (New York: Simon and Schuster, 1982); James C. Scott, *Seeing Like a State: How Certain Schemes to Improve the Human Condition Have Failed* (New Haven, CT: Yale University Press, 1999); Alice Alexiou Sparberg, *Jane Jacobs: Urban Visionary* (New Brunswick, NJ: Rutgers University

Press, 2006); Tim Mennel, *Block by Block: Jane Jacobs and the Future of New York* (New York: Princeton Architectural Press, 2007); Glenna Lang, *Genius of Common Sense: Jane Jacobs and the Story of "The Death and Life of Great American Cities"* (Boston: David R. Godine, 2009); Anthony Flint, *Wrestling with Moses: How Jane Jacobs Took on New York's Master Builder and Transformed the American City* (New York: Random House, 2009); Stephen Goldsmith and Lynne Elizabeth, *What We See: Advancing the Observations of Jane Jacobs* (New York: New Village, 2010); Roberta Brandes Gratz, *The Battle for Gotham: New York in the Shadow of Robert Moses and Jane Jacobs* (New York: Nation, 2010); Samuel Zipp, *Manhattan Projects: The Rise and Fall of Urban Renewal in Cold War New York* (New York: Oxford University Press, 2010); Christopher Klemek, *The Transatlantic Collapse of Urban Renewal: Postwar Urbanism from New York to Berlin* (Chicago: University of Chicago Press, 2011); Tim Mennel and Max Page, *Reconsidering Jane Jacobs* (Chicago: Planners Press, 2011); Sonia Hirt and Diane Zahm, *The Urban Wisdom of Jane Jacobs* (New York: Routledge, 2012); and Dirk Schubert, *Contemporary Perspectives on Jane Jacobs: Reassessing the Impacts of an Urban Visionary* (Surrey, UK: Ashgate, 2014). I was also a contributor to *Reconsidering Jane Jacobs*; see Peter L. Laurence, "The Unknown Jane Jacobs: Geographer, Propagandist, City Planning Idealist," 15–36, which outlines some of the ideas described here.

7. Lewis Mumford, "Mother Jacobs' Home Remedies," *NY* 38 (Dec. 1, 1962), 149; *D&L*, 51.

8. *D&L*, 3, 371, 435 (emphasis in the original).

9. Peter L. Laurence, "The Death and Life of Urban Design: Jane Jacobs, the Rockefeller Foundation and the New Research in Urbanism, 1955–65," *Journal of Urban Design* (Jun. 2006), 145–72.

CHAPTER 1

The epigraph for this chapter is from Jane Butzner, "Flowers Come to Town," *Vogue* (Feb. 15, 1937), 113–14.

1. *Death and Life* was also dedicated to her husband, Bob; her sons, Jim and Ned; and her daughter, Mary.

2. *D&L*, 348, 376.

3. Bonnie Yochelson, *Berenice Abbott: Changing New York, the Complete WPA Project* (New York: New Press/Museum of the City of New York, 1997), 85. I learned of Jacobs's friendship with Abbott from a family member. After being introduced by their mutual friend Leticia Kent, the Jacobses visited Abbott in Maine during the summers.

4. "New York of the Future: A Titan City," *NYT* (Nov. 2, 1924), XX7.

5. E. B. White, *Here Is New York* (New York: Harper and Bros., 1949), 9.

6. Regional Plan Committee, *The Regional Plan of New York and Its Environs*, vol. 1 (Philadelphia: Wm. Fell Printers, 1929), 111–12; vol. 2, 581, 583. Le Corbusier's *The City of To-Morrow and Its Planning* (Mineola, NY: Dover, 1987) was originally published as *Urbanisme* in 1925 and first published in English (in New York) in 1929.

7. The phrase "the pathology of public housing" comes from Richard Plunz, *A History of Housing in New York City* (New York: Columbia University Press, 1990), 247, but Jacobs, citing Herbert Gans, used the term "pathological" to describe flawed housing projects in *Death and Life* (272). See also Max Page, *The Creative Destruction of Manhattan, 1900–1940* (Chicago: University of Chicago Press, 1999), 69–109.

8. *D&L*, 271.

9. Jacobs, letter to Ms. Talmey, Nov. 22, 1961 (Jacobs Papers, 13:12), 1. A slightly different version of Jacobs's autobiographical account in this letter is republished in *ITM*, 3. For Jacobs on Scranton and the Depression, see *DAA*, 54.

10. James Howard Kunstler, interview with Jane Jacobs, Sept. 6, 2000, *Metropolis* (Mar. 2001), accessed Oct. 24, 2007, http://www.kunstler.com/mags_jacobs2.htm.

11. Jacobs, letter to Talmey, 1; Jane Butzner Jacobs, applications for federal employment, Nov. 27, 1943, Oct. 26, 1946, and Sept. 8, 1949, CPR. See also *DAA*, 53.

12. *CWN*, 124–25.

13. "It Happened in Brooklyn," oral history, Jul. 12, 2000 (Jacobs Papers, 1:1).

14. Civil Service Commission application, Jan. 5, 1950 (NPRC), 2.

15. Jane Butzner Jacobs, application for federal employment, Sept. 8, 1949, Attachment H, CPR. Before he became a writer, Hemphill was an inventor, the creator of equipment used in commercial ice plants, and a former utilities company executive in South Carolina. See "Robert Herman Hemphill" obituary (*NYT*, Apr. 24, 1941), 21. Hemphill is cited in "Ask Central Bank, No Interest Bonds; Sixteen Groups in National Monetary Conference Adopt Inflation Program," *NYT* (Jan. 17, 1935), 4.

16. Jacobs, application, Sept. 8, 1949, attachments F and G.

17. Le Corbusier, *When Cathedrals Were White* (New York: McGraw-Hill, 1964), 55. *Cathedrals* was originally published in 1937 and translated into English in 1947. See also Mardges Bacon, *Le Corbusier in America* (Cambridge, MA: MIT Press, 2001), 52. Jacobs admired Rockefeller Center, where she worked from 1952 to 1961, for the way it worked with the existing city block structure. In *D&L*, she referred to it on some six occasions (cf. 89, 104, 110, 181, 386, 439) and opined that "none of today's pallid imitations of Rockefeller Center is as good as the original" (439). See also *D&L*, 377.

18. Kunstler, interview; Henry I. Brock, "Le Corbusier Scans Gotham's Towers; the French Architect, on a Tour, Finds the City Violently Alive, a Wilderness of Experiment Toward a New Order," *NYT* (Nov. 3, 1935), SM10, 32; Le Corbusier, "The Street," in *Le Corbusier, Oeuvre complète, Vol. 1, 1910–29* (Boston: Birkhäuser, 1995), 112, 118. See also Le Corbusier, *Cathedrals*, 40; Bacon, *Le Corbusier in America*, 158.

19. Rockefeller Foundation, *1958 Annual Report* (New York: Rockefeller Foundation, 1958), 291; *D&L*, 376, 377; Jonathan Karp, "Jane Jacobs Doesn't Live Here Anymore," *ITM*, 15.

20. Jane Butzner, "Where the Fur Flies," *Vogue* (Nov. 15, 1935), 103; "Leather Shocking Tales," *Vogue* (Mar. 1, 1936), 139; "Diamonds in the Tough," *Vogue* (Oct. 15, 1936), 154; "Flowers Come to Town," 113–14. "Flowers" and "Diamonds" were reprinted in *ITM*, 35–37; I found the missing "Fur" and "Leather" essays in 2005 in microfilms of the magazine.

21. *EOC*, 11.

22. "Leather," 139.

23. "Diamonds," 154.

24. Le Corbusier, *Cathedrals*, 34; "Fur," 103.

25. *D&L*, 376.

26. Caroline F. Ware, *Greenwich Village, 1920–1930: A Comment on American Civilization in the Post-War Years* (Boston: Houghton Mifflin, 1935), 124.

27. *Christian Science Monitor*, Aug. 29, 1927, quoted in Ware, *Greenwich Village*, 21; *D&L*, ch. 15, "Unslumming and Slumming," and 271, 290.

28. Jan Seidler Ramirez, "Greenwich Village," in *The Encyclopedia of New York City*, ed. Kenneth T. Jackson (New Haven, CT: Yale University Press, 1995), 508. The reference here is to Richard Florida's Jacobs-inspired "creative class" theory and book *The Rise of the Creative Class* (New York: Basic Books, 2002).

29. Federal Writers' Project of the Works Progress Administration in New York City (1939), *The WPA Guide to New York City* (New York: Pantheon, 1982), 126; Eric Homberger, *The Historical Atlas of New York City* (New York: Henry Holt, 2005), 134; Ramirez, "Greenwich Village"; *D&L*, 275.

30. *D&L*, 273.

31. Ibid., 273, 290.

32. Ibid., 274. See also Joel Schwartz, *The New York Approach: Robert Moses, Urban Liberals, and Redevelopment of the Inner City* (Columbus: Ohio State University Press, 1993), 26.

33. Homberger, Historical Atlas, 84; Plunz, History of Housing, 9–10; Henry James, quoted in Peter Hall's *Cities of Tomorrow: An Intellectual History of Urban Planning and Design in the Twentieth Century*, 3rd ed. (Malden, MA: Blackwell, 2002), 36. See also Kenneth Jackson, *Crabgrass Frontier: The Suburbanization of the United States* (New York: Oxford University Press, 1985); John Stilgoe, *Borderland: Origins of the American Suburb, 1820–1939* (New Haven, CT: Yale University Press, 1988); and Robert Bruegmann, *Sprawl: A Compact History* (Chicago: University of Chicago Press, 2005).

34. "Slumming in This Town; a Fashionable London Mania Reaches New-York; Slumming Parties to Be the Rage This Winter; Good Districts to Visit," *NYT* (Sept. 14, 1884), 4.

35. Homberger, *Historical Atlas*, 110. See also NYC Department of City Planning, Population Division, "New York City Total and Foreign-Born Population, 1790–2000"; "A Plea for More Parks; Reasons Why We Should Have Them and Cheap Fares on the Elevated," *NYT* (Nov. 27, 1891), 5.

36. "Mulberry Bend as a Park; Property Owners Want the City to Pay the Whole Cost," *NYT* (Jan. 21, 1893), 9. See also Plunz, *History of Housing*, 52, 73–78, and Page, *Creative Destruction*, 2–5.

37. "Queer Foreign Quarter; Mulberry Bend Park and Its Curious Inhabitants; Glimpse of Italy in the Midst of New-York; Language, Manners, Dress and Customs All Strange; Transformation of a Wretched Quarter; Chinamen Near By in Pell and Mott Streets; What Trees and Grass Mean to These People," *NYT* (Jul. 12, 1896), 32; "Plea for More Parks," 5. See also Ebenezer Howard, *To-Morrow: A Peaceful Path to Real Reform*, ed. Peter Hall, Dennis Hardy, and Colin Ward (New York: Routledge, 2003), 157–58, 163.

38. Schwartz, *New York Approach*, 26.

39. Stewart Chase, "A Suburban Garden City for the Motor Age," *NYT* (Jun. 24, 1928), XX4; "City Planning Aid Asked of Realtors; John Nolen of Mass. Commission Urges National Association to Research; 'Super Block' City Viewed," *NYT* (Jun. 28, 1929), 15; Regional Plan Committee, *Regional Plan of New York*, vol. 2: 5, 219. See also Clarence Stein, *Toward New Towns for America* (1951; Cambridge, MA: MIT Press, 1989), 21. In *D&L*, Jacobs described Radburn and other Greenbelt towns as "incomplete modifications" of Howard's "Garden City." See Le Corbusier, "What Is the Problem of America?," in *Oeuvre complète, 1934–1938*, 2nd ed., trans. A. Dakin (Zurich: Les Editions d'Architecture, 1947), 66–67; Lewis Mumford, *The Culture of Cities* (New York: Harcourt, Brace, 1938), 459.

40. *D&L*, 287, 406.

41. Bacon, Le Corbusier in America, 160–61.

42. "First Houses Open, Roosevelt Hails New Slum Policy; East Side Block Thronged for Dedication of the City's Low-Rent Project; First Step, Officials Say," *NYT* (Dec. 4, 1935), 16.

43. Ibid. See also Plunz, *History of Housing*, 210.

44. Lee E. Cooper, "City Speeds Work on Three Public Housing Projects; First City Houses Ready for Opening; Families from the East Side Slums Soon to Occupy Modern Suites," *NYT* (Nov. 24, 1935), RE1.

45. "First Houses Assailed; Kings Associated Builders See Extravagance in Project," *NYT* (Dec. 19, 1935), 8; Charles Abrams, "Letter to the Editor: Mr. Moses on Housing; Commissioner's Views on Federal Program Meet with Criticism," *NYT* (Jul. 1, 1936), 24; "First Houses Cost Held $10,000 A Room; Total Expenditure $1,155,649, Against $328,621 Estimated, Survey Discloses," *NYT* (Sept. 25, 1936), 25; Robert Moses, "Slums and City Planning," *Atlantic* (Jan. 1, 1945), n.p. (accessed online).

46. Roland Wood, "Vast Housing Plan Envisaged for City; Post Sees First Houses as Proving Ground for Program to Provide Homes for 500,000 Families," *NYT* (Dec. 8, 1935), E10. See also Christopher Mele, *Selling the Lower East Side: Culture, Real Estate, and Resistance in New York* (Minneapolis: University of Minnesota Press, 2000), 110.

47. Rem Koolhaas, *Delirious New York: A Retroactive Manifesto for Manhattan* (New York: Monacelli, 1994), 10. Written in 1978, a low point for New York City, Koolhaas's argument for "Manhattanism," and its pro-urban, hyper-dense "culture of congestion," came more than two decades after Jacobs's similar arguments about the virtues of congestion (discussed later), but it marked an important generational shift toward urbanism in architecture culture. See also Robert A. M. Stern, Gregory Gilmartin, and Thomas Mellins, *New York 1930: Architecture and Urbanism Between the Two World Wars* (New York: Rizzoli, 1987), 439–40.

48. "Great White Plague in City's Tenements; Report of the Charity Organization Society's Committee," *NYT* (Feb. 7, 1904), 11; Henry J. Rosner, "The RFC Subsidizes Fred F. French," *Nation* 136 (Apr. 19, 1933), 438; "Asking Aid of the RFC," *NYT* (Feb. 8, 1933), 18; Stern et al., *New York 1930*, 418.

49. Rosner, "RFC Subsidizes Fred F. French," 438; U.S. Department of Housing and Urban Development, "HUD Historical Background," www.hud.gov/offices/adm/about/admguide/history.cfm, accessed Mar. 26, 2007. See also Richard Pommer, "The Architecture of Urban Housing in the United States During the Early 1930s," *Journal of the Society of Architectural Historians* 37 (Dec. 1978), 235.

50. Robert Moses, letter to Dorothy Pratt, Apr. 17, 1933 (Haskell Papers, 34:9).

51. Plunz, *History of Housing*, 139, 210.

52. Douglas Haskell, "New Mayland," *Nation* 134 (Mar. 9, 1932), 292.

53. "Backs Housing Plan for Chrystie Area," *NYT* (Mar. 3, 1932), 21; Stern et al., *New York 1930*, 443.

54. "File a New Plan for Slum Housing," *NYT* (Jul. 30, 1933), 126; "East River Housing Favored by O'Brien," *NYT* (Jul. 13, 1933), 21; Le Corbusier, *City of To-Morrow*, 173, 184, 288.

55. "Rutgerstown," *NYT* (Aug. 1, 1933), 16; Plunz, *History of Housing*, 190–91.

56. "East Side Housing Not for the Poor," *NYT* (Jul. 8, 1933), 13.

57. "Ickes Bars Loans to Two Projects Here for Lack of Funds," *NYT* (Jun. 13, 1934), 1; "War on Slums Proceeds Steadily," *NYT* (Jun. 17, 1934), XX2.

58. Bacon, *Le Corbusier in America*, 164–65; Plunz, *History of Housing*, 219–21; Paul Emmons, "Diagrammatic Practices: The Office of Frederick L. Ackerman and 'Architectural Graphic Standards,' " *Journal of the Society of Architectural Historians* 64 (Mar. 2005), 4–21; "Brooklyn Slum Clearance," *NYT* (Oct. 15, 1936), 26.

59. "Brooklyn Slum Clearance," 26; Lewis Mumford, "The Sky Line: The New Order," *New Yorker* (Feb. 26, 1938), reprinted in Robert Wojtowicz, *Sidewalk Critic: Lewis Mumford's Writing on New York* (New York: Princeton Architectural Press, 2000), 209.

60. According to Betty Butzner and Jonathan Karp, Jane and Betty visited one of "the first public housing" projects in Brooklyn in the late 1930s or early 1940s. "She began thinking about whether these houses were imaginatively enough designed and how people would like them," Betty recalled. Quoted in Karp, *ITM*, 16. See also Catherine Mackenzie, "120 'First Families' Get New Homes," *NYT* (Dec. 1, 1935), E10; "25,789 Apply for Suites in Williamsburg Housing," *NYT* (Jul. 9, 1937), 35.

61. R. L. Duffus, "What Modern Housing Means and Why It Is Delayed," *NYT* (Dec. 23, 1934), BR3; Albert Mayer, "Garden Cities Within a City: A Large Scheme of Rehousing," *NYT* (May 6, 1934), XX3.

62. Lewis Mumford, "The Sky Line: Old and New," *New Yorker* (Jan. 11, 1936), in Wojtowicz, *Sidewalk Critic*, 151.

63. Mayer, "Garden Cities Within a City," XX3; "New Colony Urged as Slum Solution," *NYT* (Jul. 25, 1937), 33. The Slum Clearance Committee of New York was formed in 1933 and prepared a book of maps and charts of fourteen "special study areas" that was presented to the NYCHA in April 1934. This committee was different from the Mayor's Committee on Slum Clearance, created by New York City mayor William O'Dwyer in 1948 and chaired by Robert Moses.

64. Le Corbusier, "A Noted Architect Dissects Our Cities," *NYT* (Jan. 3, 1932), SM10; Frederick Etchells, introduction to Le Corbusier, *City of To-Morrow*, xiv.

CHAPTER 2

The epigraph for this chapter is from *D&L*, 221.

1. SOS, 20–21.

2. Jane Jacobs, letter to Chadbourne Gilpatric, Jul. 23, 1959 (RG 1.2, series 200R, 390:3381, RAC).

3. See, for example, Thomas Kuhn, *The Structure of Scientific Revolutions* (Chicago: University of Chicago Press, 1962), 85. In *D&L*, Jacobs used the term "orthodox [city] planning" about twenty times, usually as a shorthand for "orthodox modern city planning and city architectural design" (17). It is worth noting that she used the word "modern" about the same number of times. Sometimes it had a negative connotation, as in "orthodox modern city planning," but it was generally not negative for her. She never used the term "modernism" in *D&L* and was not antimodern per se. See *D&L*, 6.

4. Jacobs, letter to Ms. Talmey, Nov. 22, 1961, 1. A slightly different version of Jacobs's autobiographical account in this letter is republished in *ITM*, 3. Columbia's Extension program was reorganized as the College of General Studies in 1947.

5. Information about Jacobs's coursework at Columbia University is from Jane Butzner [Jacobs], applications for federal employment, Nov. 27, 1943; Oct. 26, 1946; and Sept. 8, 1949, CPR; FBI, Jane Butzner Jacobs, NY File no. 123–252, Jul. 20, 1948, 2. Jacobs took classes

during the day and night for two years for a total of sixty-five credits. See also Kunstler, interview with Jacobs, part 1, 6.

6. "News Items: Columbia University, Department of Geography," *Economic Geography* 2 (Apr. 1926), 332; Harlan H. Barrows, "Geography as Human Ecology," *Annals of the Association of American Geographers* 13 (Mar. 1923), 1, 3 (emphasis in the original).

7. *DAA*, 177–78. Jacobs indicated here that Mumford's "obtuse" foreword to the 1956 paperback edition of Pirenne's *Medieval Cities* was another source of disagreement between them. See also *EOS*, 131; *CWN*, 241; and *SOS*, 219.

8. Chadbourne Gilpatric, interview with Jane Jacobs, Jun. 4, 1958 (RF RG 1.2, series 200R, 390:3380, RAC).

9. *D&L*, 13, 436; Laurence, "Contradictions and Complexities," 49–60.

10. Jacobs, letter to Ms. Talmey, 1–3. See also Kunstler, interview with Jacobs, part 1, 6.

11. The extent of Hemphill's involvement in Jacobs's *Constitutional Chaff* is unclear. He was certainly an influence on the project, both in terms of "wisdom and enthusiasm" for which Jacobs thanked him in the acknowledgments and indirectly through the legal research that Jacobs did for him in 1935 and 1936. Others who knew Jacobs (FBI informants in the late 1940s) believed that he was a collaborator on the book or vice versa, although this is unlikely because Hemphill had retired to Florida by the late 1930s and died there in 1941. Her key source for *Constitutional Chaff* was *Documents Illustrative of the Formation of the Union of the American States*, 69th Congress, 1st Sess., House Doc. no. 398, ed. Charles C. Tansill (Washington, DC: Government Printing Office, 1927). As Jacobs notes in the preface, this document made available to the general public all of the known notes on the proceedings of the Constitutional Convention for the first time.

12. Jacobs, application for federal employment, Standard Form no. 57, U.S. Civil Service Commission, Sept. 8, 1949, Attachment K, 1.

13. Max Farrand, "Constitutional Chaff: Rejected Suggestions of the Constitutional Convention of 1787, with Explanatory Argument" (book review), *American Historical Review* 47 (Oct. 1941), 197–98; E. Wilder Spaulding (book review), *New York History* (Jul. 1941), n.p.

A more recent citation can be found in Douglas D. Heckathorn and Steven M. Maser, "Bargaining and Constitutional Contracts," *American Journal of Political Science* 31 (Feb. 1987), 166. Thanks to Glenna Lang for sharing the Spaulding review.

14. Jane Butzner, "Caution, Men Working," *Cue: The Weekly Magazine of New York Life* (May 18, 1940), 24.

15. *The Death and Life of Great American Cities* (New York: Modern Library, 1993), xvi (hereafter cited as *D&L*, Modern Library edition).

16. *CC*, 2, 4 (emphasis in the original).

17. Henri Pirenne, *Medieval Cities* (1925; Princeton, NJ: Princeton University Press, 1946), 193.

18. Hannah Arendt, *The Human Condition* (Chicago: University of Chicago Press, 1958), 194–95. Jacobs cited Arendt in *SOS*, 200, 233. Also see *CC*, 2, 4; Jacobs, "A Lesson in Urban Redevelopment: Philadelphia's Redevelopment, a Progress Report," *AF* 103 (Jul. 1955), 118; *D&L*, 405–6; Jane Jacobs and Mary Rowe, introduction, in *Toronto: Considering Self-Government*, ed. Mary Rowe (Ontario: Ginger, 2000), xv–xxi.

19. *SOS*, 205.

20. *D&L*, 406, 407; *CC*, 1.

21. *CC*, 2.

22. Ibid.

23. *CC*, 153.

24. Jacobs was registered as a Republican in 1936, suggesting that she voted against Roosevelt (a Democrat) in 1936; as a Democrat in 1937, suggesting she voted against La Guardia (Republican) in 1937; and as a Republican in 1938, 1939, and 1940, suggesting she voted against Governor Lehman (a Democrat) in 1938 and again against Roosevelt in 1940, for his unprecedented third term. She registered with the ALP from the early 1940s until 1949. See FBI, "Jane Butzner Jacobs, Special Inquiry—State Department," Form 1, NY File no. 123–252, 10; Jacobs, "Interrogatory," Mar. 25, 1952 (Jacobs Papers, 12:8), 6.

25. There may be some contradictions in Jacobs's support for Willkie. Unlike his primary contestants, in 1940, Willkie advocated support for allies in World War II, although not necessarily for entering the war. However, Jacobs was a strong isolationist until the attack on Pearl Harbor. Thus, it seems that her opposition to FDR's third term and other policies outweighed this.

26. *SOS*, xi–xii.

27. J. I. Butzner, "Non-Ferrous Metals," *IA* 151 (Jan. 7, 1943), 140, 236 (emphasis in the original).

28. Ibid., 290.

29. J. I. Butzner, "Silver Alloy Brazing with High-Speed Localized Gas Heating," *IA* 152 (Sept. 23, 1943), 38.

30. Jane Butzner Jacobs, FBI NY File no. 123–252, Jul. 20, 1948, 4–5.

31. Jane Butzner, "Women Wanted to Fill 2,795 Kinds of Jobs," *NYHT* (Oct. 18, 1942), n.p.; Jane Butzner, "Waves and Waacs Go Through the Assignment Classification Mill," *NYHT* (Mar. 28, 1943), n.p.

32. Jane Jacobs, "Answers to Interrogatory for Jane Butzner Jacobs," Jul. 22, 1949 (Jacobs Papers, 12:8), 1.

33. Butzner Jacobs, FBI NY File, 4–5.

34. Jane Butzner, "Trylon's Steel Helps to Build Big New Nickel Plant in Cuba," *NYHT* (Dec. 27, 1942), n.p.

35. [Jane Butzner], "30,000 Unemployed and 7,000 Empty Houses in Scranton, Neglected City," *IA* 151 (Mar. 25, 1943), 94.

36. Butzner, "30,000 Unemployed," 95.

37. Butzner, "Waves and Waacs," n.p.

38. Jane Butzner, "Daily's Effort Saves City from 'Ghost Town' Fate: *Scranton Tribune* Leadership Converting Mining Town into Manufacturing Center Because of Vanishing Coal Veins," *Editor & Publisher* (Sept. 4, 1943), 12.

39. "Ex-Scranton Girl Helps Home City: Miss Butzner's Story in *Iron Age* Brought Nationwide Publicity," *Scrantonian* (Sept. 26, 1943), reprinted in *ITM*, 37. The story of Jacobs's Scranton campaign is told well in Lang, *Genius of Common Sense*, 31–32, 115.

40. George Stratemeyer, letter to Jane Butzner, Jul. 11, 1943 (Jacobs Papers, 23:5).

41. OWI, "Justification for Rapid Promotion" for Jane Butzner, Oct. 3, 1944.

42. *SOS*, 23–24, 28, 215.

43. Ibid. Regarding Jacobs's affiliation with the trader moral system, see Fred Lawrence, ed., *Ethics in Making a Living: The Jane Jacobs Conference* (Atlanta: Scholars Press, 1989), 5.

44. Butzner Jacobs, FBI NY File, 3.

45. "Jane Butzner, Robert Jacobs to Wed Today," *Scranton Tribune* (May 27, 1944), reprinted in *ITM*, 37. The last store at 555 Hudson Street sold candy, soda, and cigars. For descriptions of the Jacobses' home, see Eric Larrabee, "In Print: Jane Jacobs," *Horizon*, reprinted in *ITM*, 50; Gin Briggs, "Crusader on Housing: Jane Butzner Jacobs Wrote Controversial Book," *NYT* (May 6, 1963), 42. See also *D&L*, 50–53.

46. Leticia Kent, "Jane Jacobs: An Oral History Interview Conducted for the GVSHP Preservation Archives, Toronto, Canada, October 1997" (New York: Greenwich Village Society for Historic Preservation, 2001), 5–7. Jacobs said, "You know I've gotten a lot of credit—first, last and in between—for being astute politically. But I don't think I was astute politically at all in comparison with Bob" (7).

47. J. L. Moreno, "Foundations of Sociometry: An Introduction," *Sociometry* 4 (Feb. 1941), 15; J. L. Moreno, "Reflections on My Method of Group Psychotherapy and Psychodrama," in *Experimentation and Innovation in Psychotherapy*, ed. Harold Greenwald (New Brunswick, NJ: Transaction, 2010), 133.

48. J. L. Moreno, "Sociometry in Relation to Other Social Sciences," *Sociometry* 1 (July–Oct. 1937), 207.

49. J. L. Moreno, ed., "Sociometric Ballot of Research Projects," *Sociometry* 8 (May 1945), 229–30.

50. Jane Butzner Jacobs, application for federal employment, Sept. 8, 1949 (CPR), Attachment D, 1.

51. Moreno's conception of interpersonal relationships shares something with the philosopher of phenomenology Edmund Husserl's concept of intersubjectivity. Jacobs's interest in Moreno's ideas, including his thoughts about the city, provides part of an intellectual foundation for such a phenomenological interpretation of her work as has been explored by David Seamon in "Jane Jacobs's *Death and Life of Great American Cities* as a Phenomenology of Urban Place," *Journal of Space Syntax* (Aug. 2012), 139–49.

52. Jacobs and her colleagues were terminated from their positions at the OWI in December 1945, and they were apparently unaware that the State Department would take over some of the OWI's foreign affairs roles and New York publications offices. They were also unaware that they would have the opportunity to be rehired in positions similar or identical to those that they had held during the war. Jacobs was required to reapply for her position with the State Department and to undergo a new background check. However, once rehired, her federal employment record was effectively continuous, despite the gap in employment and shift in departments.

53. Jane Butzner Jacobs, application for federal employment, Sept. 8, 1949 (CPR), Attachment C.

54. Ibid. *The Coast Watchers* was reprinted by Oxford University Press in 1959, by Bantam Books in 1979, and by Doubleday in a Book Club edition. In 1946, Jacobs also discussed writing a memoir for Tania Manooiloff Cosman, who eventually self-published *My Heritage with Morning Glories: A White Russian Growing Up in China* in 1995.

55. Howard Oiseth, "The First Magazine," in *The Way It Was: USIA's Press and Publications Service (1935–77)* (Washington, DC: U.S. Information Agency, 1977), 56. See also "Amerika for the Russians," *Time* (Mar. 4, 1946), Time Archive, http://www.time.com, accessed Feb. 7, 2007. I am indebted to Martin Manning of the Department of State for a related history of State Department and U.S. Information Agency publications.

56. "Amerika for the Russians"; Oiseth, "First Magazine," 56–57. *Amerika Illustrated* outlived the USSR, which was dissolved in 1991, and it continued to be popular in Russia until it ceased publication in 1994.

57. Quoted in Oiseth, "First Magazine," 57. See also Creighton Peet, "Russian 'Amerika,' A Magazine About U.S. for Soviet Citizens," *College Art Journal* (Fall 1951), 18.

58. U.S. Civil Service Commission, "Classification Sheet," Nov. 5, 1946, 1–2. Among Jane's colleagues at *Amerika* was Bob Jacobs's cousin John Jacobs, who joined the magazine in 1948, a few years after her. After the New York office closed in 1952, he moved to Washington, worked for the Voice of America, and joined the magazine's new DC staff, rising to editor in 1959. Arthur Pariente, "USIA Profile: A Philosopher on Overseas Information," *USIA World*, Aug. 1970 (Jacobs Papers, 24:5).

59. Jacobs, application for federal employment, Sept. 8, 1949, Attachment A, 2. See also Peet, "Russian 'Amerika,'" 17; Jennifer Griffin, "US Stops Publishing *Amerika*," Associated Press (Aug. 17, 1994), accessed online Sept. 9, 1997.

60. Jacobs, application for federal employment, Sept. 8, 1949, Attachment A, 6.

61. Ibid., 5; Richard E. Morrissey, "Justification for Promotion," Dec. 21, 1949 (CPR), 2–3.

62. Public Law 80–402, 22 USC 1442–Sec. 1442a, National Security Measures.

63. FBI, Jane Butzner Jacobs, Special Inquiry, Public Law 402, 80th Congress (Voice of America), May 13, 1948, 2. NKVD was the Soviet espionage agency that preceded the KGB.

64. [J. Edgar Hoover,] FBI, Voice of America investigation, Oct. 1, 1948; [J. Edgar Hoover,] FBI, Jane Butzner Jacobs Special Inquiry—State Department, Jun. 18, 1948.

65. Joseph McCarthy, "Major Speeches and Debates of Senator Joe McCarthy Delivered in the United States Senate, 1950–1951," U.S. Government Printing Office, n.p.

66. Ibid.

67. FBI, Jane Butzner Jacobs, Special Inquiry—State Department, Dec. 10, 1951, 2–3.

68. Jane Jacobs, letter to Carrell St. Claire, Jul. 22, 1949 (Jacobs Papers, 12:8).

69. Two of the individuals Jacobs was asked about were Seymour Peck and Sylvia Grovesmith Peck. Sylvia worked with Jacobs in the State Department publications office, but she did not know Seymour Peck, a *New York Times* columnist, who was later subpoenaed by the Senate Security Subcommittee. In 1955, Peck admitted communist affiliations between 1935 and '49, and he was indicted for contempt of Congress the following year for refusing to label others as communists.

70. Butzner Jacobs, FBI NY File, 3; Jacobs, "Interrogatory," I10.

71. Jacobs, "Interrogatory," F2.

72. Ibid., F1–3.

73. Ibid., F2.

74. "Many of Staff Quit Magazine *Amerika*; Resist Move from New York to Washington of Periodical Distributed in Soviet [*sic*]," *NYT* (Apr. 15, 1952), 4; "Propaganda Steps by U.S. Criticized; Publications Chief Quits over Shake-Up Plan," *NYT* (Jun. 1, 1952), 29; "Editorial: *Amerika* Magazine," *NYT* (Jun. 28, 1952), 18.

75. Pirenne, *Medieval Cities*, 177; David Simon, "Foreign Information Program; Proposed Change in Operations Is Opposed as Harmful," *NYT* (Jun. 9, 1952), 22.

76. Jacobs, "Interrogatory," F1, F3, F7–8.

CHAPTER 3

The epigraph for this chapter is from "On Architectural Criticism," quoted in Robert Alan Benson, "Douglas Putnam Haskell (1899–1979): The Early Critical Writings" (Ph.D. diss., University of Michigan, 1987), 233. I am indebted to Benson for an understanding of Haskell's early career and writing.

1. "Organ of Integration," *Time* (Apr. 11, 1932), n.p.

2. Jacobs, letter to Ms. Talmey, Nov. 22, 1961, 2. The first of Jacobs's articles on urban redevelopment for *Amerika* was "Planned Reconstruction of Lagging City Districts," *AI* (no. 25, n.d. [Feb. 1949?]), 1–9. Jacobs's second article on the subject was titled "Slum Clearance," *AI* (no. 43, Aug. 1950), 2–11. *Amerika* no. 43 was rare in having a publication date. Because it could be almost nine months until a Russian reader saw the magazine because of the uncertain amount of time needed to clear Soviet censors, the editors sometimes avoided dating the magazine to extend its shelf life. The copy reviewed was also rare among surviving copies to have an English insert with a summary of the contents, which indicated the English titles of the articles. Translations in this chapter are by Alina Yakubova and Artemiy Zheltov. See also Jacobs, "New Horizons in Architecture," *AI* (no. 29, n.d. [Jun. 1949?]), 2–11; "New Horizons in Architecture, Part II," *AI* (no. 30, n.d. [Jul. 1949?]), 26–35.

3. [Jane Jacobs], "Two-in-One Hospital; Big Double Hospital," *AF* 96 (June 1952), 138.

4. Ibid., 140.

5. Douglas Haskell, memo to Suzanne Gleaves and Perry Prentice, "Why We Publish Modern," Mar. 17, 1952 (Haskell Papers, 57:3).

6. Benson, "Douglas Putnam Haskell," 83. Thanks to Richard Longstreth for related information about the Haskells.

7. Peter Blake, *No Place Like Utopia: Modern Architecture and the Company We Kept* (New York: W. W. Norton, 1993), 163.

8. Douglas Haskell, memo to staff regarding the new editorial policy, Jul. 23, 1952 (Haskell Papers, 57:3), 2 (emphasis in the original).

9. Ibid., 3.

10. Ibid., 4.

11. Ibid., 1.

12. Mary Ferranti and Janet Parks, Finding Aid for the Douglas Putnam Haskell Papers, Nov. 2006 (Department of Drawings and Archives, Avery Architectural and Fine Arts Library), 3.

13. See ch. 3, "Toward an Organic Architectural Criticism," in Robert Wojtowicz, *Lewis Mumford and American Modernism: Eutopian Theories for Architecture and Urban Planning* (New York: Cambridge University Press, 1996). It is especially helpful for understanding Mumford's contributions to architectural criticism.

14. Benson, "Douglas Putnam Haskell," 2, 20.

15. Ibid., 49.

16. Ibid., 67. See also "Shells," cited in Benson, "Douglas Putnam Haskell," 62; Leon Solon, "Modernism in Architecture," *Architectural Record* 58 (Sept. 1925), 215.

17. Benson, "Douglas Putnam Haskell," 84.

18. Ibid., 344. In *Modern Architecture* (1929), Henry-Russell Hitchcock first used the term "international style" to describe the work of the architects he called the "New Pioneers,"

including Le Corbusier. Hitchcock's point was to emphasize the idea that the new architecture was a cross-cultural and transnational phenomenon, but he did not capitalize the term "international style." See Hitchcock, *Modern Architecture: Romanticism and Reintegration* (New York: Da Capo, 1993), 162. The label reappeared the following year, in Hitchcock and Philip Johnson's book *The International Style: Architecture Since 1922* (1932; New York: W. W. Norton, 1997), which accompanied their Museum of Modern Art exhibition. Hitchcock, who thereafter embraced the term, later equivocated. In the foreword to a 1966 edition of the book, he emphasized the fact that it was Alfred Barr who first capitalized the term: "[This] book has for some time belonged to history, and the 'Style' (which Alfred Barr in his Preface to the book capitalized, but which we in our text did not) has been universally recognized" (vii).

19. Douglas Haskell, "The Column, the Gable, and the Box," *The Arts* 17 (June 1931).

20. *D&L*, 371 (emphasis in the original).

21. Douglas Haskell, "What the Man About Town Will Build," *Nation* 134 (Apr. 13, 1932), 441–42.

22. Douglas Haskell, "Is It Functional?" *Creative Art* 10 (May 1932), 373–74.

23. Ibid., 378.

24. Ibid.

25. Benson, "Douglas Putnam Haskell," 233, 488.

26. Douglas Haskell, letter to William W. Wurster, Nov. 4, 1952 (Haskell Papers, 24:6).

27. Benson, "Douglas Putnam Haskell," 234.

28. J. M. Richards, "The Next Step?" *AR* 107 (Mar. 1950), 166.

29. Leicester B. Holland, "The Function of Functionalism," *Architect and Engineer* 126 (Aug. 1936), 25, 32. This article was presented at the sixty-eighth convention of the American Institute of Architects, May 1936, and was also reprinted in *Octagon* 8 (Jul. 1936), 3–10.

30. Ibid., 27–30. This critique of functionalism anticipated Robert Venturi's wry diagrammatic critique of modernism, firmness + commodity = delight.

31. James MacQuedy [J. M. Richards], "Criticism," *AR* 99 (Dec. 1940), 183.

32. Ibid.

33. Philip Johnson and Henry-Russell Hitchcock, "Mr. Oud Embroiders a Theme," *Architectural Record* (Dec. 1946), 80. This article and Oud's reply can be found in Joan Ockman, *Architecture Culture 1943–1968: A Documentary Anthology* (New York: Rizzoli, 1993), 103–6.

34. J. J. P. Oud, "Mr. Oud Replies," *Architectural Record* (Mar. 1947), 18.

35. Hubert de Cronin Hastings, Nikolaus Pevsner, and J. M. Richards, "The Functional Tradition," *AR* 107 (Jan. 1950), 3.

36. J. M. Richards, "The New Empiricism: Sweden's Latest Style," *AR* (Jun. 1947), 199–200. Richards quoted Sven Backström from a September 1943 article in *AR*.

37. Mumford's essay has three sections without headings. The first two sections deal with new architecture in New York and Washington, DC; the third discusses functionalism and "that native and human form of modernism which one might call the Bay Region style." Mumford, "Status Quo," *New Yorker* 23 (Oct. 11, 1947), 104–10. This essay, when discussed today, is usually referred to by the title "The Bay Region Style."

38. Museum of Modern Art, "What Is Happening to Modern Architecture? A Symposium at the Museum of Modern Art," *MOMA Bulletin* 15 (Spring 1948), 9.

39. Ibid., 8–9.

40. Douglas Haskell, "Googie Architecture," *House & Home* 1 (Feb. 1952), 85–86.

41. Henry-Russell Hitchcock, "The International Style Twenty Years After," *Architectural Record* 110 (Aug. 1951), 90, 97.

42. Richards, "The Next Step?," 166, 181.

43. Douglas Haskell, "Criticism vs. Statesmanship in Architecture," *AF* 98 (May 1953), 97.

44. Jane Jacobs and the Rockefeller Foundation, *The Rockefeller Foundation Annual Report, 1958* (New York: Rockefeller Foundation, 1958), 291; *D&L*, Modern Library edition, xiii, 390.

45. J. M. Richards, "Architect, Critic and Public," *Royal Architectural Institute of Canada Journal* 27 (Nov. 1950), 372.

46. Talbot Hamlin, "Criticism Might Help Architecture: Let's Try It," *American Architect* 137 (May 1930), 41.

47. Ibid.

48. Blake, *No Place Like Utopia*, 163.

49. "Enter House and Home," *Time* (Jan. 21, 1952), n.p.

50. Douglas Haskell, telegram to Robert Little, David Runnells, Charles Goodman, and Oscar Stonorov, Nov. 13, 1951 (Haskell Papers, 80:8). "Monsters" contributors included Robert Little of Cleveland, David Runnells of Kansas City, Charles Goodman of Washington, DC, and Oscar Stonorov of Philadelphia. Their suggestions included Kansas City's Starlight Theater; Houston's Shamrock Hotel; U.S. Steel's Fairless Works; airport terminals in Seattle, Pittsburgh, and Baltimore (which looked "hideously gross alongside the elegant planes that they are inevitably seen with"); and Boston's 1947 John Hancock Life Insurance Building. David Runnells and Charles Goodman, telegrams to Douglas Haskell, Nov. 23 and 27, 1951 (Haskell Papers, 80:8).

51. Perry Prentice, memo to Joe Hazen and Douglas Haskell, Nov. 14, 1951 (Haskell Papers, 80:8); Joe Hazen, memo to Douglas Haskell, Nov. 14, 1951 (Haskell Papers, 80:8); Douglas Haskell, memo to Joe Hazen, Nov. 16, 1951 (Haskell Papers, 80:8).

52. Haskell, memo to Hazen, Nov. 16, 1951.

53. Ibid.

54. Ibid.

55. Albert Connelly, letter to Howard Myers, Apr. 26, 1937 (Haskell Papers, 80:8).

56. Blake, *No Place Like Utopia*, 46. *Forum*'s dedication to Wright did not mean that Blake or others accepted Wright's antics without comment. In May 1953, Haskell wrote a letter to George Howe relating a recent episode. "I tried to help keep FLlW from acting like a fool," he wrote, "but it can't be done." The conversation included these highlights: Haskell said, "Frank Wright, I just can't believe God exhausted Himself in creating even you." Wright replied, "I'm not exhausted. I am God." Douglas Haskell, letter to George Howe, May 23, 1953 (Haskell Papers, 57:4).

57. Haskell, "Googie Architecture," 85–86.

58. Haskell, memo to staff, 4.

59. Haskell, "Googie Architecture," 88.

60. Ibid.

61. Jane Jacobs, memo to Douglas Haskell, Jul. 22, 1952 (Haskell Papers, 4–4).

62. Douglas Haskell, letter to Vincent Kling, Mar. 10, 1953 (Haskell Papers, 11:6); [Jane Jacobs], "Hospital for the Well," *AF* 99 (Dec. 1953), 130–35.

63. Jane Jacobs, memo to Douglas Haskell, Mar. 25, 1953 (Haskell Papers, 8:7). For the definitive study on Gruen, see M. Jeffrey Hardwick, *Mall Maker: Victor Gruen, Architect of an American Dream* (Philadelphia: University of Pennsylvania Press, 2004). Gruen had a long-standing relationship with *AF*'s editors, who had published his work since the late 1930s (28, 73). Gruen and his family escaped Nazi-controlled Vienna in 1938. In New York, Gruen first found work drafting designs for the 1939 World's Fair, then returned to store design.

64. Jane Jacobs, memo to Douglas Haskell, Joe Hazen, and Mary Jane Lightbown, May 16, 1955 (Haskell Papers, 10:7).

65. Ibid. Commonly known as the Trenton Bath House, Kahn's swimming center is located in Ewing, New Jersey.

66. Ibid.

67. *D&L*, 227.

68. Jane Jacobs, memo to Douglas Haskell, Joe Hazen, and Mary Jane Lightbown, Dec. 10, 1954 (Haskell Papers, 12:4). See also Rosalie R. Radomsky, "A Viñoly Redesign; Architecture Building at City College," *NYT* (Nov. 3, 2002), sec. 11, 1.

69. Jacobs, memo to Haskell, Hazen, and Lightbown, Dec. 10, 1954.

70. *D&L*, 375.

71. Eve Auchincloss and Nancy Lynch, "Disturber of the Peace: Jane Jacobs (Interview)," *Mademoiselle* (Oct. 1962), 165–66.

72. Ibid., 166–67; *D&L*, 7–8.

73. *D&L*, 374.

CHAPTER 4

The epigraph for this chapter is from [Jane Jacobs], "Rosenfield and His Hospitals: He Approaches His Jobs like a City Planner," *AF* 97 (Sept. 1952), 128.

1. Haskell, memo to staff, Jul. 23, 1952.

2. Merle Travis and Cliffie Stone, "No Vacancy," recorded by Merle Travis, Capitol Single #258, May 1946 (Hill and Range Songs, 1946, 1975).

3. I allude here to *Should Our Cities Survive?*, the original title of Josep Lluís Sert's book *Can Our Cities Survive?* (Cambridge, MA: Harvard University Press, 1944), as well as Eric Mumford's books on Sert and modern city planning theory. His *The CIAM Discourse on Urbanism, 1928–1960* (Cambridge, MA: MIT Press, 2000) is essential for understanding the rise and fall of modern city planning and for tracking the internal doubts and attacks that made Jacobs's attacks less revolutionary than is commonly believed. Also, his *Defining Urban Design: CIAM Architects and the Formation of Discipline, 1937–69* (New Haven, CT: Yale University Press, 2009) is an equally essential history of urban design.

4. Clarence Stein, *Toward New Towns for America* (1951; Cambridge, MA: MIT Press, 1989), 7; Harold Hauf, "City Planning and Civil Defense," *Architectural Record* 108 (Dec. 1950), 99. The idea of decentralization as a defense measure was not new after World War II. After World War I, Le Corbusier had also argued that his Radiant City concept could protect cities from aerial bombardment. Le Corbusier, *The Radiant City* (1933; New York: Orion Press and Grossman, 1967), 60.

5. "The Philadelphia Cure: Clearing Slums with Penicillin, Not Surgery," *AF* 96 (Apr. 1952), 115. The author may have been Walter McQuade.

6. "Redevelopment of Norfolk: Federal Slum Clearance Gets Its First Full Scale Tryout," *AF* 92 (May 1950), 132–37. See also "Modernization by the Block," *AF* 93 (Oct. 1950), 171–80, which examined "slum modernization" in Philadelphia and Baltimore, and Henry S. Churchill, "City Redevelopment," *AF* 93 (Dec. 1950), 72–77, which focused on Nashville, Philadelphia, and Providence.

7. "Redevelopment of Norfolk," 132. I discussed the Stuyvesant Town precedent in "The Death and Life of Urban Design."

8. James Baldwin, "The Negro and the American Promise," interview with Kenneth Clark, WGBH TV, Spring 1963. Baldwin described urban renewal as "negro removal" while relating a conversation that he had with a teenager from San Francisco. Baldwin recalled, "He said, 'I've got no country. I've got no flag.' Now, he's only sixteen years old, and I couldn't say, 'You do.' I don't have any evidence to prove that he does. They were tearing down his house, because San Francisco is engaging—as most northern cities now are engaged—in something called 'urban renewal,' which means moving the Negroes out. It means Negro removal—that is what it means. The federal government is an accomplice to this fact."

9. "Chicago Redevelops," *AF* 93 (Aug. 1950), 99–105.

10. *D&L*, 50.

11. See Charles Jencks, *The Language of Post-Modern Architecture* (New York: Rizzoli, 1977).

12. "Slum Surgery in St. Louis," *AF* 94 (Apr. 1951), 128–36.

13. *D&L*, 77. A few years after *Death and Life*, *Forum* published "The Case History of a Failure," *AF* 123 (Dec. 1965), 22–25, in which James Bailey recanted the magazine's former praise, and he reported on the Public Housing Administration's and the architectural firm HOK's unsuccessful attempts to save the project from the social implosion that preceded the physical one. See also Katharine Bristol, "The Pruitt-Igoe Myth," *Journal of Architectural Education* (May 1991), 163–71; and Chad Freidrich's 2011 excellent documentary film by the same name.

14. "Slum Surgery in St. Louis," 129, 136.

15. Robert Caro, *The Power Broker: Robert Moses and the Fall of New York* (New York: Vintage, 1974), 753, 777. In his redevelopment proposals of the early 1950s, Moses called this group, which he chaired, the Committee on Slum Clearance Plans. Moses also directed the Mayor's Committee on Slum Clearance, which, as noted earlier, was different from the Slum Clearance Committee of New York, which was formed in 1933.

16. "Topics of the *Times*: New Face for the Village," *NYT* (Mar. 13, 1951), 30; Robert Moses et al., "Washington Square South" and "South Village: Slum Clearance Plan Under Title I of the Housing Act of 1949," NYC Committee on Slum Clearance Plans, Jan. 1951. At the time of Moses's proposals, there were already roads bisecting Washington Square. Running south from Fifth Avenue, the road ran through the thirty-foot-wide arch and then split, with one branch connecting to Thompson Street and the other connecting to West Broadway, the two blocks south of the arch. Moses sought to widen this to a divided four-lane roadway more than fifty feet wide and connect this to a widened, four-lane West Broadway called "Fifth Avenue South," which would effectively extend Fifth Avenue to Canal Street, in order to provide access to the Holland Tunnel. While Shirley Hayes, and later Jacobs, campaigned for closing Washington Square to all motor traffic, others groups sought compromise positions that retained the existing connection to West Broadway. See "De Sapio Supports Study

on Village; Advocates 'Minimal Through Roadway' in Washington Sq., Not Expressway," *NYT* (Dec. 20, 1957), 29. In the midst of the battle for the square, Gilbert Millstein wrote a brief history of the park, which included its historical traffic issues in "New Battle of Our Village Square," *NYT* (May 4, 1958), SM32. Showing how history repeated itself, Millstein noted that in 1870 Boss Tweed created a street through the square to connect Fifth Avenue to what was then known as Laurens Street but renamed South Fifth Avenue (before being named West Broadway in the 1890s).

17. Lewis Mumford, "Fifth Avenue, for Better or Worse," *New Yorker* 28 (Aug. 16, 1952), 56.

18. Mary Mix Foley, "What Is Urban Redevelopment? Replanning of Washington's Famous Capitol Slums Poses a Basic Question for Every U.S. Community," *AF* 97 (Aug. 1952), 124–31.

19. Ibid., 128. Chloethiel Woodard Smith (1911–93) was one of the first women to break the glass ceiling in the American architectural profession. The "Robert Moses approach" to urban redevelopment was sometimes also called the "New York approach," as noted in Joel Schwartz, *The New York Approach: Robert Moses, Urban Liberals, and Redevelopment of the Inner City* (Columbus: Ohio State University Press, 1993).

20. "The Philadelphia Cure," 115.

21. Ibid., 113–14 (emphasis in the original).

22. Ibid., 118.

23. Le Corbusier, ch. 14, "Physic or Surgery," in *The City of To-Morrow and Its Planning* (*Urbanisme*, 8th ed.) (1929; New York: Dover, 1987), 253–76. Eric Mumford discusses the Philadelphia cure in *Defining Urban Design*, 74.

24. [Jacobs], "Rosenfield and His Hospitals," 128–34.

25. [Jane Jacobs], "New Hospital Type," *AF* 98 (Jan. 1953), 118–21. Kahn's rocky relationship with Rosenfield is described by David Brownlee in *Louis I. Kahn: In the Realm of Architecture*, ed. David B. Brownlee and David G. De Long (New York: Rizzoli, 1991), 40–41.

26. [Jacobs], "Rosenfield and His Hospitals," 128–29.

27. Ibid., 128.

28. [Jane Jacobs], "New Thinking on Shopping Centers," *AF* 98 (Mar. 1953), 122–45. See also the note about her early writing above.

29. [Jacobs], "New Thinking on Shopping Centers," 122. See also Louis Kahn, "Toward a New Plan for Midtown Philadelphia," *Perspecta* 2 (1953), 11; and M. Jeffrey Hardwick, *Mall Maker: Victor Gruen, Architect of an American Dream* (Philadelphia: University of Pennsylvania Press, 2004), 112–16.

30. From the early 1950s, James Rouse was a strong supporter of the federal urban renewal program and may have influenced Jacobs in this regard at the time. Joshua Olsen, *Better Places, Better Lives: A Biography of James Rouse* (Washington, DC: Urban Land Institute, 2003), 63.

31. [Jacobs], "New Thinking on Shopping Centers," 136, 143.

32. Ibid., 127, 132.

33. Ibid., 122.

34. Ibid., 122–23.

35. Ibid., 125, 132.

36. Stuart Chase, "A Suburban Garden City for the Motor Age," *NYT* (Jun. 24, 1928), 4; [Jane Jacobs], "Northland: A New Yardstick for Shopping Center Planning," *AF* 100 (Jun. 1954), 103.

37. [Jacobs], "Northland," 103, 106, 110–11; Hardwick, *Mall Maker*, 129.

38. [Jacobs], "Northland," 103–4.

39. [Jacobs], "Northland," 103; Hardwick, *Mall Maker*, 165.

40. *D&L*, 4, 71, 192, 454.

41. [Jane Jacobs], "Good-by Neighborhood Schools? The School Village Plan: 'Junk the Neighborhood School,'" *AF* 98 (Apr. 1953), 129–35, 174ff.

42. Ibid., 190.

43. [Jane Jacobs], "Marshall Shaffer: Teacher-at-Large of Hospital Architecture," *AF* 98 (May 1953), 125ff.; *D&L*, 324.

44. [Jacobs], "Marshall Shaffer," 125 (emphasis in the original).

45. Ibid., 164, 168 (emphasis in the original).

46. Douglas Haskell, memo to Perry Prentice, Aug. 25, 1953 (Haskell Papers, 38–11).

47. Douglas Haskell, letter to William W. Wurster, Jan. 14, 1954 (Haskell Papers, 24–6).

48. Douglas Haskell, "Pittsburgh and the Architect's Problem," *AF* 93 (Sept. 1950), 127.

49. Douglas Haskell et al., "Gateway Center: Now, at Last . . . Office Towers in a Park," *AF* 99 (Dec. 1953), 112–16; Douglas Haskell, "Architecture: Stepchild or Fashioner of Cities?" *AF* 99 (Dec. 1953), 117.

50. Haskell, "Pittsburgh and the Architect's Problem," 127; Haskell, "Gateway Center," 113.

51. Douglas Haskell et al., "The Need for Better Planning, and How to Get It," *AF* 98 (Jun. 1953), 146–55.

52. Ibid., 152.

53. *D&L*, 12; Eric Mumford, *CIAM Discourse*, 201–15. See also Jaqueline Tyrwhitt, Josep Lluís Sert, and Ernesto N. Rogers, eds., *The Heart of the City: Towards the Humanization of Urban Life* (London: Lund Humphries, 1952).

54. Haskell, "Architecture: Stepchild or Fashioner of Cities?" 117; Haskell, "Pittsburgh and the Architect's Problem," 127.

55. Haskell, "Architecture: Stepchild or Fashioner of Cities?" 117; Haskell, "Pittsburgh and the Architect's Problem," 127 (emphasis in the original).

56. Haskell, letter to Wurster, Jan. 14, 1954.

57. *D&L*, 106; Kuhn, *Structure of Scientific Revolutions*, 85.

CHAPTER 5

The epigraph for this chapter is from [Jane Jacobs], "Philadelphia's Redevelopment: A Progress Report," *AF* 103 (Jul. 1955), 118.

1. Ashley Foard and Hilbert Fefferman, "Federal Urban Renewal Legislation," in *Urban Renewal: The Record and the Controversy*, ed. James Q. Wilson (Cambridge, MA: MIT Press, 1966), 96. See also B. T. McGraw, "The Housing Act of 1954 and Implications for Minorities," *Phylon* 16 (Spring 1955), 171–82.

2. "Slum Clearance Faces Supreme Court Test," *AF* 100 (Nov. 1954), 120; Martin Anderson, *The Federal Bulldozer: A Critical Analysis of Urban Renewal, 1949–1962* (Cambridge, MA: MIT Press, 1964), 187–88.

3. "Slum Clearance Faces Supreme Court Test," 120; Anderson, *Federal Bulldozer*, 43.

4. Richard M. Flanagan, "The Housing Act of 1954: The Sea Change in National Urban Policy," *Urban Affairs Review* (Nov. 1997), 265, 267.

5. Jane Jacobs, tear-off campaign petition to the Washington Square Park Committee, Apr. 30, 1955 (Hayes Papers, 4:1).

6. Jane Jacobs, letters to Mayor Wagner and Hulan Jack, Jun. 1, 1955 (Hayes Papers, 3:10). With the help of Dr. Jean Ashton and the New-York Historical Society's Shirley Hayes Papers, this letter and the history of Jacobs's early activism were first brought to light in my article "Jane Jacobs Before *Death and Life*."

7. Jacobs, letters to Wagner and Jack.

8. Lewis Mumford, letter to *The Villager*, Apr. 1955 (Hayes Papers, 3:10).

9. Jane Jacobs, foreword to *D&L*, Modern Library edition, xvi. For a full account of Bacon's work and thought, see Gregory L. Heller, *Ed Bacon: Planning, Politics, and the Building of Modern Philadelphia* (Philadelphia: University of Pennsylvania Press, 2013).

10. [Jacobs], "Philadelphia's Redevelopment," 118.

11. Ibid.

12. Ibid.

13. Ibid.

14. *D&L*, 293.

15. "The Philadelphia Cure," 118.

16. [Jacobs], "Philadelphia's Redevelopment," 126.

17. Ibid., 120.

18. Ibid., 127. On the "greenways" plan, see also Heller, *Ed Bacon*, 112.

19. [Jacobs], "Philadelphia's Redevelopment," 126.

20. Ibid., 120; *D&L*, 258, 416.

21. The Bacon quotation is from "Urban Design: Condensed Report of an Invitation Conference, Harvard University, Apr. 9–10, 1956," *Progressive Architecture* (Aug. 1956), 108. Jacobs was a participant at this conference. Compare with *D&L*, 448. "Architect Louis Kahn and His Strong-Boned Structures," *AF* (Oct. 1957), 135–43, carried Walter McQuade's byline, although Jacobs contributed to it. The feature began with Jacobs's review of Kahn's work in May 1955 (Jacobs, memo to Haskell, Hazen, and Lightbown, May 16, 1955), which was followed by a list of works that Jacobs compiled in 1957 for research on the article (cf. Jane Jacobs, list of Louis Kahn's projects, 1957 [n.d.] [Haskell Papers, 10:7]). In June 1957, Haskell wrote Kahn stating that Jacobs would start the article but that McQuade would finish it (Douglas Haskell, letter to Louis Kahn, Jun. 10, 1957 [Haskell Papers, 10:7]). See "Louis Kahn and the Living City," *AF* (Mar. 1958), 114–19. Jacobs may have suggested the title; in her May 1956 editorial "Pavement Pounders and Olympians," Jacobs used the phrase "the living city."

22. [Jane Jacobs], "Cleveland: City with a Deadline," *AF* (Aug. 1955), 131.

23. Ibid., 131, 135.

24. Ibid., 135–38. The term "project" was used to describe public housing developments from the time of their origins in the 1930s. It was in the mid-1950s, when projects proliferated, that the term acquired a negative connotation.

25. Bradley Flamm, "The Garden Valley: Remembering Visions and Values in 1950s Cleveland with Allan Jacobs," *Berkeley Planning Journal* 18 (2005), 101, 112–13.

26. Ibid., 108–9, 114.

27. [Jacobs], "Cleveland," 136; *D&L*, 4, 71, 282. Jacobs's article also included descriptions of both a mixed-use (and therefore unlike the typical urban renewal project) superblock

redevelopment project called Charity Hospital and a more typical public housing project. Contrary to expectations, she did not criticize them for their urban design or planning concepts.

28. Jane Jacobs, "Washington: 20th Century Capital?" *AF* (Jan. 1956), 92–115. Until around 1956, only specially commissioned articles received bylines in *Architectural Forum*.

29. Ibid., 103–113.

30. Ibid., 93, 94, 103 (emphasis in the original).

31. Ibid., 94.

32. Ibid., 100, 101.

33. Ibid., 97.

34. Ibid., 98.

35. Ibid., 114.

36. Louis Kahn, "Toward a New Plan for Midtown Philadelphia," *Perspecta* 2 (1953), 11; Victor Gruen, "Dynamic Planning for Retail Areas," *Harvard Business Review* 32 (Nov.– Dec. 1954), 53. In conversation with a Rockefeller Foundation director in 1958, Jacobs described Kahn as "one of the most fertile idea men in urban design and originator of ideas for which Victor Gruen has become so noted in the Fort Worth Central City Plan" (Chadbourne Gilpatric, interview with Jane Jacobs, June 4, 1958, RF RG 1.2, series 200R, 390:3380, RAC).

37. Gruen, "Dynamic Planning," 57, 62. Jacobs later adopted the "decentralists" versus "downtowner" trope, but she used the term "decentrists" in *D&L*. She attributed the term to Catherine Bauer (19–20).

38. Gruen, "Dynamic Planning," 54, 56, 62 (emphasis in the original); Hardwick, *Mall Maker*, 182. In ch. 7, "Saving Our Cities," Hardwick outlines Gruen's transformation from retail architect to city planner, and he provides a history of the Fort Worth plan.

39. [Jane Jacobs], "Typical Downtown Transformed: The Fort Worth Plan," *AF* (May 1956), 146.

40. Ibid., 147 (emphasis in the original); *D&L*, 351.

41. [Jacobs], "Typical Downtown Transformed," 147, 150 (emphasis in the original).

42. Ibid. In the end, the State Highway Commission and property rights advocates defeated Gruen's plan. The commission rejected Gruen's belt highway; private parking garage owners defeated a bill that would have allowed the city to construct the plan's six municipal parking garages (which they described as vaguely socialistic); and the state legislature rejected, by one vote, the urban renewal legislation that would have allowed the city to tap the federal funds necessary to fund Gruen's plan (Hardwick, *Mall Maker*, 187–89).

43. [Jane Jacobs], "Pavement Pounders and Olympians," *AF* 104 (May 1956), 164. Among city planners, Contini, not Gruen, received Jacobs's praise. Hardwick suggests that, as compared to Contini, Gruen was concerned with the details of a city primarily to make an effective presentation. He reminded himself to "insert local data" because he otherwise delivered the same speech in different cities (*Mall Maker*, 191).

44. [Jacobs], "Pavement Pounders and Olympians," 164.

45. *D&L*, 15–16.

46. William Kirk, letter to Douglas Haskell, Mar. 17, 1955 (Haskell Papers, 22:1); Douglas Haskell, letter to William Kirk, Jan. 17, 1956 (Haskell Papers, 22:1). For more about New York settlement houses, see www.unionsettlement.org and United Neighborhood Houses at www.unhny.org.

47. "Shops a Problem in East Harlem: Only 2 of 9 Housing Projects Provide for Them," *NYT* (May 8, 1955), 46. Storefront churches were of particular important in East Harlem. As indicated in a 1950 *NYT* article, "the area is now the testing grounds for the interdenominational, interracial 'storefront' churches started two and one-half years ago by Mr. Webber and the Rev. Don Benedict." The article also noted that the Rev. George W. Webber, pastor of the East Harlem Protestant Parish, charged that the people of East Harlem were "'treated not as persons but as things' by the police, school officials, and landlords." See "East Harlem People Treated as 'Things,' Pastor of Storefront Church Charges," *NYT* (Dec. 11, 1950), 26.

48. Ellen Lurie, *East Harlem Small Business Survey and Planning Committee Fact Sheet*, Jan. 16, 1956 (USAR, series V, 35:7), 1. Some of the figures quoted in the "fact sheet" were quoted in the May 8, 1955, *Times* article "Shops a Problem in East Harlem," indicating that some of the research had already been done before then. The *Times* reporter Charles Grutzner later returned to East Harlem to see the aftermath of the destruction of these city blocks and buildings. See Grutzner, "Housing Projects Make Bitter D.P.'s; Some Merchants Cite Loss of Business and Savings as City Confiscates Land," *NYT* (Mar. 18, 1957), 29; "Most of Neighborhood Businessmen Uprooted by East Harlem Project Complain of Treatment by City," *NYT* (Mar. 18, 1957), 29. Jacobs related Kirk's skepticism to Grady Clay in a letter on March 3, 1959 (courtesy of Grady Clay).

49. Lurie, *East Harlem Small Business Survey*.

50. Ellen Lurie, draft of essay for *Architectural Forum*, "The Dreary Deadlock of Public Housing" (USAR, series V, 35:7), 1.

51. Charles Grutzner, "City's 'Front Door' Obscured by Litter; Officials Depressed by Dirt and Refuse That Introduce New York to Rail Visitors," *NYT* (Sept. 21, 1948), 29; New York City Planning Commission, "Master Plan Map RS-5M, Borough of Manhattan," *Master Plan of Sections Containing Areas Suitable for Development and Redevelopment* (Dec. 30, 1954), 13. Samuel Zipp relates other important parts of the East Harlem story in *Manhattan Projects*, 258ff.

52. "The East Harlem Problem," *NYT* (Sept. 22, 1948), 30.

53. Ibid.

54. "Rebuilding East Harlem," *NYT* (Sept. 25, 1948), 16.

55. Rita Morgan, Maryal Knox, and Clyde Murray, "Letter to the Editor: For Action in East Harlem, Utilization of Area for Experiment in Integrated Planning Suggested," *NYT* (Dec. 7, 1948), 30.

56. Charles Bennett, "Wagner Advances Borough Planning; Makes East Harlem Hospital 'Pilot Project' for 12 Civic Districts of Manhattan," *NYT* (Aug. 12, 1950), 13.

57. "Shops a Problem in East Harlem," 46.

CHAPTER 6

The epigraph for this chapter is from Jane Jacobs, "The Missing Link in City Redevelopment," *AF* 104 (Jun. 1956), 133.

1. Douglas Haskell, letter to Catherine Bauer, Oct. 5, 1956 (CBW Papers, Correspondence).

2. Influential turn-of-the-century treatises included Charles M. Robinson's *Modern Civic Art, or, The City Made Beautiful* (New York: G. P. Putnam's Sons, 1903), which popularized the City Beautiful movement; Patrick Geddes's essay "Civics as Applied Sociology" (1904; Project Gutenberg, 2004), an argument for the systematic study of cities; Daniel Burnham

and Edward Bennett's *Plan of Chicago* (1909; New York: Princeton Architectural Press, 1993), which promoted the concept of the "civic center"; Thomas Mawson's *Civic Art: Studies in Town Planning, Parks, Boulevards, and Open Spaces* (London: B. T. Batsford, 1911); and Werner Hegemann and Elbert Peets's *The American Vitruvius: An Architect's Handbook of Civic Art* (1922; New York: Princeton Architectural Press, 1988). In these years, the American City Planning movement also emerged, with the First National Conference on City Planning held in Washington, DC, in 1909. In 1917, Frederick Law Olmsted and Flavel Shurtleff founded the American City Planning Institute, later renamed the American Institute of Planners. See Mel Scott, *American City Planning Since 1890* (Berkeley: University of California Press, 1971), 95; Miles Colean, "Economic and Social Significance of Housing Design," *Annals of the American Academy of Political and Social Science* 190 (Mar. 1937), 101; Lewis Mumford, introduction to Clarence Stein, *Toward New Towns for America* (Cambridge, MA: MIT Press, 1989), 11; Stein, *Toward New Towns for America*, 7.

3. "The Philadelphia Cure," 113 (emphasis in the original). Thanks to Nancy Hadley, the archivist for the American Institute of Architects, for historical information about the urban design committee.

4. E. Mumford, *Defining Urban Design*, 102, 233.

5. Kevin Lynch, "Proceedings of the June 1954 ACSA Conference: A New Look at Civic Design," *Journal of Architectural Education* 10 (Spring 1955), 32; Ann L. Strong and George E. Thomas, *The Book of the School: 100 Years of the Graduate School of Fine Arts of the University of Pennsylvania* (Philadelphia: Graduate School of Fine Arts), 141; David Crane, "A Working Paper for the University of Pennsylvania Conference on Urban Design Criticism" (RF RG 1.2, University of Pennsylvania—Community Planning Conference, Oct. 1958–61, series 200, 457:3904, RAC), 6. Google Books Ngram searches (books.google.com/ngrams) show the use of the term "civic design" reaching a peak in print use in the mid-1950s. Replacing it, "urban design" grew dramatically from the early 1950s, peaking in the 1970s, declining, and then rising again. "Urban sprawl" and "urban environment" have similar histories. "Urban redevelopment" peaked in the late 1950s, while "urban renewal" peaked in the late 1960s.

6. L. Mumford, "Mother Jacobs' Home Remedies," 151.

7. Douglas Haskell, letter to Josep Lluís Sert, Mar. 19, 1956 (Haskell Papers, 20:5); Harvard Graduate School of Design Alumni Association, "Urban Design Conference," *GSD Alumni Newsletter* 1, Dec. 29, 1955 (Sert Papers).

8. Harvard Graduate School of Design Alumni Association, "Urban Design Conference Report," *GSD Alumni Newsletter* 2, Jun. 7, 1956 (Sert Papers); Victor Gruen, letter to Douglas Haskell, Apr. 16, 1956 (Haskell Papers, 8:7).

9. Lynch, "Proceedings," 32; Josep Lluís Sert, "Proceedings of the June 1954 ACSA Conference: Welcome Address: The Challenge Ahead," *Journal of Architectural Education* 10 (Spring 1955), 3. See also E. Mumford, *Defining Urban Design*, 102; Eric Mumford, "The Emergence of Urban Design in the Breakup of CIAM," in *Urban Design*, ed. A. Krieger and W. Saunders (Minneapolis: University of Minnesota Press, 2009), 17, 25; Eric Mumford and Hashim Sarkis, eds., *Josep Lluís Sert, the Architect of Urban Design, 1953–1969* (New Haven, CT: Yale University Press and Harvard Graduate School of Design, 2008); and Richard Marshall, "The Elusiveness of Urban Design: The Perpetual Problems of Definition and Role," *Harvard Design Magazine* 24 (Spring/Summer 2006), 26.

10. Josep Lluís Sert, "Introduction," for the Urban Design Conference, Harvard Graduate School of Design, Apr. 9, 1956 (Sert Papers), 3; "Condensed Report of an Invitation

Conference Sponsored by the Faculty and Alumni Association of the Graduate School of Design, Harvard University, April 9–10, 1956," *Progressive Architecture* 37 (Aug. 1956), 97.

11. Sert, "Introduction," 9, 11. In the "Condensed Report" transcript, Sert's "apology for the city" was changed to "a case for the city" (97).

12. Sert, "Introduction," 8–9. See also Sert, "Centres of Community," in *Heart of the City*, 3–4.

13. Sert, "Introduction," 9, 11; E. Mumford, *CIAM Discourse*, 133.

14. Sert, "Introduction," 5–6.

15. Jacobs, "Missing Link in City Redevelopment," 132–33.

16. "Condensed Report," 99.

17. [John Voelcker, Peter Smithson, and Alison Smithson], "Aix-en-Provence 1954: CIAM 9," in *CIAM '59 in Otterlo*, ed. Oscar Newman (Stuttgart: Karl Kramer Verlag, 1961), 14, 16; Jacob Bakema and Aldo van Eyck et al. "Doorn Manifesto," in *Architecture Culture 1943–1968*, ed. Joan Ockman (New York: Columbia Books of Architecture/Rizzoli, 1993), 13–24, 181–83; Max Risselada and Dirk van den Heuvel, eds., *Team 10: In Search of a Utopia of the Present* (Rotterdam: NAi, 2005), 43. See also Volker Welter, *Biopolis, Patrick Geddes and the City of Life* (Cambridge, MA: MIT Press, 2002), 253–4; E. Mumford, *CIAM Discourse*, 248; and Peter L. Laurence, "Modern (or Contemporary) Architecture Circa 1959," in *A Critical History of Contemporary Architecture, 1960–2010*, ed. Elie Haddad and David Rifkind (London: Ashgate, 2014), 9–29.

18. Sert, "Introduction," 4; *Can Our Cities Survive?*, 10; Le Corbusier, *City of To-Morrow*, 107; [Jacobs], "Pavement Pounders and Olympians," 164; *D&L*, 436–37.

19. Jacobs, "Missing Link in City Redevelopment," 133.

20. Ibid., 132.

21. Ibid., 133. Jacobs's speech was also reprinted in *Progressive Architecture*'s "Condensed Report," but the text is not identical to "Missing Link." Jacobs likely edited the latter before publishing it. Jane Jacobs, "Downtown Is for People," *Fortune* 57 (Apr. 1958), 134.

22. Douglas Haskell, letter to Catherine Bauer Wurster, May 28, 1956 (Haskell Papers, 24:6).

23. Bruegmann, *Sprawl*, 119.

24. "Man Made America: A Special Number of *The Architectural Review*," *AR* 108 (Dec. 1950), 339, 343, 415, 414. For the Townscape's influence on urban design history, see David Gosling, *The Evolution of American Urban Design* (West Sussex: Wiley-Academy, 2003), 42; Laurence, "Contradictions and Complexities," 49–60; Laurence, "Death and Life of Urban Design," 145–72; Clément Orillard, "Tracing Urban Design's 'Townscape' Origins: Some Relationships Between a British Editorial Policy and an American Academic Field in the 1950s," *Urban History* 36 (2009), 284–302. See also Erdem Erten, "Shaping 'The Second Half Century': *The Architectural Review*, 1947–1971" (Ph.D. diss., MIT, 2004); and Mathew Aitchison, ed., *Nikolaus Pevsner: Visual Planning and the Picturesque* (Los Angeles: Getty, 2010).

25. "Man Made America," 416.

26. Ibid., 340.

27. Douglas Haskell, "A Reply to: Man Made America, Special Number of *The Architectural Review*," *AF* 94 (Apr. 1951), 158.

28. Ibid., 159.

29. Ibid., 158.

30. Ian Nairn, *Outrage* (London: Architectural Press), i, 381; Douglas Haskell, letter to John Rannells, Feb. 26, 1954 (Haskell Papers, 38:1), 2–3.

31. Douglas Haskell, "Can Roadtown Be Damned?" *AF* 103 (Dec. 1955), 166; Douglas Haskell, "Architecture for the Next Twenty Years," *AF* 105 (Sept. 1956), 164.

32. Apart from citing Nairn and Cullen in *D&L* (390), Jacobs later acknowledged *AR*'s influence in the introduction to *D&L*, Modern Library edition (xiii).

33. [Jane Jacobs, Walter McQuade, Ogden Tanner, and Douglas Haskell], "What City Pattern?" *AF* 105 (Sept. 1956), 103–29. Catherine Bauer married the architect William Wurster in 1940, but went by "Catherine Bauer" in her professional life and in print. Since Haskell knew her and William socially, he sometimes addressed her as Wurster.

34. [Jane Jacobs], "By 1976 What City Pattern?" *AF* (Sept. 1956), 103.

35. Jane Jacobs, memo to Douglas Haskell, May 28, 1956 (Haskell Papers, 24:6).

36. Catherine Bauer, "First Job: Control New-City Sprawl," *AF* 105 (Sept. 1956), 111. There is some evidence that Bauer was not happy with the captions that Jacobs had written. Speaking of her future "Dreary Deadlock of Public Housing" article, in a December 1956 letter, Haskell wrote to Bauer, "We agreed to have you check the captions this time." Douglas Haskell, letter to Catherine Bauer, Dec. 21, 1956 (CBW Papers, Correspondence).

37. Douglas Haskell, letter to Catherine Bauer, July 13, 1956 (Haskell Papers, 24:6).

38. [Jacobs et al.], "What City Pattern?" 105.

39. Haskell, letter to Bauer, July 13, 1956; Douglas Haskell, letter to Victor Gruen, July 13, 1958 (Haskell Papers, 8:7); [Haskell et al.], "What City Pattern? *Forum* Editors Reply," 113. Perhaps unknown to Jacobs, Haskell had in fact initially asked Bauer in February 1956 to "tell the decentralization story for a *Forum* issue on cities." He wrote her, "Could we get you to put the case for a completely decentralized pattern the way you were talking about it here in New York [recently], if you had until July to do it?" Douglas Haskell, letter to Catherine Bauer, Feb. 27, 1956 (CBW Papers, Correspondence).

40. [Haskell et al.], "What City Pattern? *Forum* Editors Reply."

41. [Jane Jacobs], "What City Pattern? The Central City: Concentration vs. Congestion," *AF* 105 (Sept. 1956), 115.

42. Ibid.

43. Ibid.

44. *D&L*, 338, 340, 343, 349–53.

45. [Jacobs], "What City Pattern?" 130 (emphasis in the original).

46. Ibid., 134.

47. Douglas Haskell, letter to Catherine Bauer Wurster, Sept. 12, 1956 (Haskell Papers, 24:6).

48. *D&L*, 337. Jacobs also wrote a summary of the series for New York's *Citizens' Housing & Planning Council Newsletter*. Jane Jacobs, memo to Douglas Haskell, Jun. 3, 1957 (Haskell Papers, 79:6).

49. Catherine Bauer, "The Dreary Deadlock of Public Housing," *AF* (May 1957), 142, 219, 221 (emphasis in the original).

50. James Rouse, "The Dreary Deadlock of Public Housing," part 2, *AF* (Jun. 1957), 140.

51. Stanley Tankel, "Dreary Deadlock," part 2, 222.

52. Henry Churchill, "Dreary Deadlock," part 2, 218.

53. Ellen Lurie, "Dreary Deadlock," part 2, 139–41ff.; Ellen Lurie, "Architectural Forum" (USAR 35:7), 1.

54. *D&L*, 324–25.

55. [Jane Jacobs], "Central City Housing," *AF* (Sept. 1956), 121.

56. [Jane Jacobs], "Row Houses for Cities," *AF* (May 1957), 148.

57. [Jacobs], "Row Houses for Cities," 148–52.

58. *D&L*, 215–16 (emphasis in the original).

59. "Housing Designed by Village Group," *NYT* (May 6, 1963), 1; Peter Freiberg, "Village Wins 10-Year Fight for $23M Housing Project," *New York Post* (Apr. 21, 1972), 10; Judith Lack, "Dispute Still Rages as West Village Houses Meets Its Sales Test," *NYT* (Aug. 18, 1974), 8–1.

60. Jane Jacobs, "Reason, Emotion, Pressure: There Is No Other Recipe," *VV* (May 22, 1957), 4.

61. Ibid.

62. Ibid., 12.

63. Ibid.; *D&L*, 252. In 1957, Jacobs attributed the "recipe" for neighborhood activism to the New York City councilman Stanley Isaacs, a longtime city politician. She later spoke of him in her 1997 oral history in the context of her fight to save the West Village. See Kent, "Jane Jacobs: An Oral History," 36–37. She also mentioned Isaacs in *D&L* (406) in the context of New York City politics.

64. *D&L*, 220, 445; [Jane Jacobs], "Our 'Surplus' Land," *AF* (Mar. 1957), 101–2.

65. [Jacobs], "Our 'Surplus' Land," 102.

66. Jane Jacobs, "New York's Office Boom," *AF* (Mar. 1957), 104–13; *D&L*, 227, 383.

67. Jacobs, "New York's Office Boom," 105.

68. Ibid., 111.

69. Jane Jacobs, "Metropolitan Government," *AF* (Aug. 1957), 124.

70. Ibid., 127.

71. Ibid., 204.

72. Ibid., 124.

73. Ibid., 124, 208.

74. Ibid., 125.

75. [Jane Jacobs], "The City's Threat to Open Land," *AF* (Jan. 1958), 87. See also Jane Jacobs, "Breathing Space for Americans" [a draft of "The City's Threat to Open Land"] (CBW Papers, Correspondence), 2.

76. [Jacobs], "City's Threat to Open Land," 89.

77. Ibid., 90, 166.

78. In her oral history with Kent, Jacobs stated, "I didn't play any part in the Greenwich Village Study." However, newspaper articles cited here, some of which included her photograph, plainly indicate that she was a member and a spokesperson on various issues. In another oral history, Claire Tankel, the widow of Stanley Tankel, affirmed the significance of Jacobs's role in the Study. Although it seems surprising that Jacobs would have forgotten her involvement, she gave many speeches after 1957 and was often in the paper. Moreover, while Claire Tankel felt that the closing of Washington Square was an outcome of the Study, Jacobs did not seem to believe that Tankel or the Study deserved much credit. They also had a major

falling out. Tankel was a compromiser; Jacobs was not. When they worked together, Jacobs had him in tears on account of her criticism of his wording of a press release that was apparently concerned about the closure of Washington Square. Later, during the Save the West Village battle, Tankel was on the Landmarks Commission at a time when Historic District designation for the Village was being debated. Jacobs felt that he and others were prepared to accept a trade of the City Planning Commission's designation of the West Village as a renewal area in exchange for adoption of the Historic Preservation designation elsewhere. Claire Tankel recalled, "Jane was just furious. I mean I don't think they even talked again, she was so angry." See Kent, "Jane Jacobs: An Oral History," 62; and Laura Hansen, "Claire Tankel: An Oral History Interview Conducted for the GVSHP Preservation Archives," Mar. 1, 1997 and Feb. 20, 1998, 34, 54–55.

79. "Greenwich Village Study Wants More Housing, No Projects, Traffic to Bypass Square," *VV* (Nov. 20, 1957), 1; "DeSapio Supports Study on Village; Advocates 'Minimal Through Roadway' in Washington Sq., Not Expressway," *NYT* (Dec. 20, 1957), 29; Daniel Wolf, "Washington Square: Study Calls It Major Asset; DeSapio Stand Causes??? [*sic*]," *VV* (Dec. 25, 1957), 1; Kent, "Jane Jacobs: An Oral History," passim.

80. "Greenwich Village Study," 1, 3; "Washington Square," 1.

81. Douglas Haskell, memo to Joe Hazen, Lawrence Lessing, Paul Grotz, and Del Paine, Nov. 21, 1957 (Haskell Papers, 79:6). Jacobs later stated that Holly Whyte asked her to write the article for *Fortune*. However, it is as likely that she pitched the article to both Whyte and Haskell. See Jacobs, letter to Ms. Talmey, Nov. 22, 1961, 2.

82. Haskell, memo to Hazen et al. Nov. 21, 1957.

83. [Jane Jacobs], "Redevelopment Today," *AF* 108 (Apr. 1958), 108–13. The redevelopment projects included by Jacobs were only a certain subset of redevelopment projects related to the U.S. Housing Act of 1949. Her list did not include earlier redevelopment projects like Stuyvesant Town, many locally funded housing projects, or Pittsburgh's Gateway Center, for example. Martin Anderson later confirmed the relatively small number of completed projects in 1958 and through 1962 in *Federal Bulldozer* (43).

84. Haskell, memo to Hazen et al., Nov. 21, 1957.

85. Lawrence Lessing, memo to Douglas Haskell, Edgar Smith, Joe Hazen, and Paul Grotz, Jan. 24, 1958 (Haskell Papers, 80:1).

CHAPTER 7

The epigraph for this chapter is from Jane Jacobs, letter to Chadbourne Gilpatric, Jul. 23, 1959 (RF RG 1.2, Series series 200, 390:3381, RAC), 3.

1. Catherine Bauer, letter to Jane Jacobs, Apr. 27, 1958 (Bauer Papers, MS 774/163c).

2. Jane Jacobs, letter to Catherine Bauer, Apr. 29, 1958 (Bauer Papers, MS 774/163c).

3. Fred Kaplan, *1959: The Year Everything Changed* (Hoboken, NJ: Wiley, 2009), 1; Kevin Lynch, "The Form of Cities," *Scientific American* (Apr. 1954), 55–63; Ian McHarg, "The Humane City: Must the Man of Distinction Always Move to the Suburbs?" *Landscape Architecture* 48 (Jan. 1958), 101–7; "Lewis Mumford, City Planning Expert and Author Urges Washington Square Park Closed to Traffic," press release of the Joint Emergency Committee to Close Washington Square Park to Traffic, Mar. 1958 (Hayes Papers, 4:6); Ian McHarg, letter to Grady Clay, Apr. 8, 1958 (personal papers of Grady Clay). In "Metropolis Regained," published in *Horizon* magazine in July 1959, Clay criticized such influential conceptions of "the city of the future" as Norman Bel Geddes and General Motors' "Futurama," as well as

Ebenezer Howard's Garden Cities movement and less theoretical motivations for decentralization and suburbanization. He described the essay as a direct result of the Penn Conference
on Urban Design Criticism. In *Wrestling with Moses*, Anthony Flint discusses the battles for
Washington Square at some length (76–88). For much more on the backlash to Moses in the
1950s and 1960s, see also Joel Schwartz, *The New York Approach: Robert Moses, Urban Liberals,
and Redevelopment of the Inner City* (Columbus: Ohio State University Press, 1993); Robert
Stern, Thomas Mellins, and David Fishman, *New York 1960* (New York: Monacelli, 1995);
Robert Fishman, "Revolt of the Urbs: Robert Moses and His Critics," in *Robert Moses and the
Modern City: The Transformation of New York*, ed. H. Ballon and K. Jackson (New York:
W. W. Norton, 2007), 122–29; and Gratz, *Battle for Gotham*.

   4. James Sterling, "Ronchamp: Le Corbusier's Chapel and the Crisis of Rationalism,"
AR 119 (Mar. 1956), 155–61; Newman, *CIAM '59 in Otterlo*, 10, 21, 26. See also my essay
"Modern (or Contemporary) Architecture circa 1959," 11.

   5. Newman, *CIAM '59 in Otterlo*, 10, 12, 68, 77; Reyner Banham, *The New Brutalism:
Ethic or Aesthetic?* (New York: Reinhold, 1966), 72; Alison and Peter Smithson, "The Built
World: Urban Re-Identification," *Architectural Design* (June 1955). See also Jacob Bakema et
al., "Doorn Manifesto," in *Architecture Culture 1943–1968*, 181–83.

   6. William "Holly" Whyte Jr. and Jacobs were contemporaries, almost the same age,
although Whyte joined *Fortune* and Time, Inc., in 1946 and was senior to her within the
organization by six years. As described in this chapter, Whyte's support was important to
Jacobs's career. However, he later overstated his influence on her. In the preface to the second
edition of *The Exploding Metropolis*, he stated that when he met Jacobs, her work at *Forum*
"consisted mainly of writing captions" (xv).

   7. William H. Whyte and Ruth Kammler, "Selection of Letters Received in March and
April 1958 by *Fortune* Magazine Letters Dept. re 'Downtown Is for People' by Jane Jacobs"
(RF RG 1.2, series 200R, 390:3380, RAC). Contributions to the article by Nairn and Clay were
likely at Jacobs's suggestion, because she knew them better than Whyte. However, *Fortune*
underwrote Nairn's travel to six U.S. cities for his contribution and Clay's tour of eleven cities
for his. In the course of these travels, Jacobs hosted Nairn during his visit to New York, and
Clay hosted him in Louisville, Kentucky. Clay later complained that his essay had been cut to
two thousand words from twelve thousand, but he published a series of articles on his travels
in Louisville newspapers and magazines.

   8. Douglas Haskell, telegram to Catherine Bauer, Oct. 19, 1957 (Bauer Papers, Correspondence); Douglas Haskell, letter to Ian Nairn, May 7, 1958, letter to the editors [*AR*], Jan.
7, 1959 (Haskell Papers, 2:3).

   9. Jane Jacobs, "Downtown Is for People," 134, 138–39, 241–42.

   10. Chadbourne Gilpatric, interview with Douglas Haskell, Feb. 22, 1958 (RF RG 1.2,
series 200R, 390:3380, RAC).

   11. MIT School of Architecture and Planning Visiting Committee, Meeting of the Visiting Committee to the School of Architecture and Planning, MIT, Apr. 7, 1952 (Haskell Papers,
34:5), 2. Haskell, then Jacobs's new supervisor, was also a member of MIT's Visiting Committee. In one of the earlier conversations about the Rockefeller Foundation's support for urban
design, Stein and Stephenson sought support for *Town Planning Review*, which was then
struggling. They explained that the publication, which was the only one at the time that
published articles on urban history, was of particular importance to the field. See Charles

Fahs, interview with John Burchard, Clarence Stein, and Frederick Adams, Jan. 6, 1953 (RF RG 1.2, MIT City Planning, series 200R, 375:3330.30, RAC).

12. See John Ely Burchard, "My Worries About the Education of Architects," *Journal of Architectural Education* 10 (Spring 1955), 5. Another aspect of Burchard's influence on architectural education was his service on the Harvard and Princeton Visiting Committees. See Leland Devinney and Edward D'Arms, interview with MIT Architecture and Planning Faculty [Pietro Belluschi, Lawrence Anderson, Louis Wetmore, György Kepes, Lloyd Rodwin, Kevin Lynch, and Walter Isard], Feb. 17, 1954 (RF RG 1.2, MIT City Planning, series 200R, 375:3330.30, RAC), 6; John Ely Burchard, "Metropolis in Ferment: The Urban Aesthetic," *Annals of the American Academy of Political and Social Science* 314 (Nov. 1957), 112–22; and Charles B. Fahs, interview with John Burchard, July 24, 1953 (RF RG 1.2, MIT City Planning, series 200R, 375:3330.30, RAC).

13. Frederick Adams described his studies of education in the field of city planning, and details of the twenty-three U.S. degree programs, the majority of them new, including their disciplinary foundations (ten developed out of architecture programs, five out of social sciences, four out of landscape architecture, one out of engineering, and so on). Charles B. Fahs, interview with Dr. John Burchard et al., Jan. 6, 1953; Devinney and D'Arms, interview, 1.

14. Charles B. Fahs, interview with John Burchard, Lawrence Anderson, Louis Wetmore, Frederick Adams, and Gordon Stephenson, Sept. 18, 1953 (RF RG 1.2, MIT City Planning, series 200R, 375:3330.30, RAC). MIT's Center for Urban and Regional Studies, with Wetmore as inaugural director, preceded the establishment of similar research institutes at Harvard and Penn. As compared to a more "humanistic" direction proposed by the Rockefeller Foundation and Burchard, Wetmore's research focused on urban economics and the "problems of intra-regional industrial location." He left MIT for the University of Illinois at Urbana-Champaign in 1955. (Cf. Wetmore Papers, University of Illinois at Urbana-Champaign.) In 1953, Gordon Stephenson was tapped to succeed Frederick Adams, his former instructor, as chair of the city planning department. However, he was denied a permanent visa, ostensibly because of suspicions aroused by his work for Le Corbusier on the Palace of the Soviets and subsequent trips to the Soviet Union during the 1930s. Gordon Stephenson, *On a Human Scale: A Life in City Design* (South Fremantle, Australia: Fremantle Arts Center Press, 1992), 108, 155.

15. Devinney and D'Arms, interview, 3.

16. MIT Center for Urban and Regional Studies, "The Three-Dimensional Urban Environment," draft research proposal, Oct. 7, 1953 (RF RG 1.2, MIT City Planning, series 200R, 375:3330.30, RAC), 1–2; Fahs, interview with J. Burchard et al., Sept. 18, 1953, 2. The first MIT proposal, an amalgamation of research interests, was submitted by the Center for Urban and Regional Studies while Kevin Lynch was in Florence, Italy, studying city form and the experience of the city. Lynch and Kepes were also not present at some of the early meetings. It appears, however, that their research agenda was presented by the Center for Urban and Regional Studies.

17. MIT Center for Urban and Regional Studies, Kevin Lynch, and György Kepes, "Proposed Study: The Perceptual Forms of Cities," Dec. 23, 1953 (RF RG 1.2, MIT City Planning, series 200R, 375:3330.30, RAC), 1. To understand "psychological reactions to the city," Lynch and Kepes indicated that they would consult with a social psychologist about interviewing a "well-selected but relatively small sample, perhaps twenty to thirty persons, in order to investigate their attitudes toward the city, their perception and grasp of it, the elements most

important in giving them pleasure or displeasure, and their history and memories in relation
to the city." This aspect of the research, more so than their critical theories, eventually dominated the analytical and objective sensibility of Lynch's book *Image of the City*. See Devinney
and D'Arms, interview, 3.

18. MIT Center for Urban and Regional Studies, "The Three-Dimensional Urban Environment," 2, 4, 10; Rockefeller Foundation Humanities Division, grant report for MIT Lynch-
Kepes city planning study (RF 54034), Apr. 7, 1954 (RF RG 1.2, MIT City Planning, series
200R, 375:3330.30, RAC), 2.

19. Edward F. D'Arms, interview with University of Pennsylvania School of Fine Arts
Faculty, Mar. 16, 1956 (RF RG 1.2, University of Pennsylvania—Community Planning, series
200, 456:3899, RAC); Edward F. D'Arms, memo to Humanities Officers of the Rockefeller
Foundation, Oct. 19, 1955 (RF RG 1.2, University of Pennsylvania—Community Planning,
series 200, 456:3899, RAC).

20. Gutkind's research project was believed to be an opportunity to balance the "social
science or social engineering" direction of Penn's School of Fine Arts. The Gutkind project,
he wrote, "will tend to balance this tendency and at the same time to provide materials which
will make it possible to introduce historical perspectives and materials into the field of urban
studies"; to "restore a humanistic balance to the program of the School of Fine Arts"; and to
build "historical depth into the school." The first Penn grant also included a smaller amount
for Ian McHarg's research on pedagogy in the field of landscape architecture. D'Arms, interview, Mar. 16, 1965; D'Arms, memo to Humanities Directors of the Rockefeller Foundation,
Apr. 6, 1956 (RF RG 1.2, University of Pennsylvania—Community Planning, series 200,
456:3899, RAC).

21. William L. C. Wheaton and the University of Pennsylvania Institute for Urban Studies, "A Proposal to the Rockefeller Foundation for a Conference on Criticism in Urban
Design," Jun. 12, 1958 (RF RG 1.2, University of Pennsylvania—Community Planning, series
200, 457:3904, RAC).

22. Lynch published parts of his research prior to the publication of *The Image of the
City* in 1960, including "Some Childhood Memories of the City," *Journal of the American
Institute of Planners* 22 (1956), 142–52, with Alvin K. Lukashok. However, an early version of
"The Image of the City" was circulated in February 1958, and this is likely what she was
referring to in "Downtown Is for People." See Wheaton et al., "Proposal to the Rockefeller
Foundation"; Chadbourne Gilpatric, "Critical Viewpoints in City Design," visit to Institute
for Urban Studies, University of Pennsylvania, May 7, 1958 (RF RG 1.2, University of
Pennsylvania—Community Planning, series 200, 456:3900, RAC); Chadbourne Gilpatric,
interview visit to Institute for Urban Studies, University of Pennsylvania, May 7, 1958 (RF
RG 1.2, University of Pennsylvania—Community Planning, series 200, 456:3900, RAC).

23. "Excerpts from a Speech by Jane Jacobs," New School for Social Research, Apr. 17,
1958 (Hayes Papers, 4:6).

24. Ibid.

25. Lewis Mumford, letter to Jane Jacobs, May 3, 1958 (Jacobs Papers, 13:11).

26. Chadbourne Gilpatric, interview with Jane Jacobs, May 9, 1958 (RF RG 1.2, series
200R, 390:3380, RAC); Jane Jacobs, "New Heart for Baltimore," *AF* (Jun. 1958), 88–90. The
Charles Center project director, George Kostritsky, was later the "K" in the architectural firm
RTKL. Jacobs cited him and her friend Penny Kostritsky in *D&L*. Before the Charles Center,

Baltimore had pursued a less destructive approach than seen, for example, in New York. Although Moses had been hired by the city in 1944 to recommend a route for a downtown expressway, opposition was immediate: "Baltimoreans made it clear that they weren't going to have their communities plowed under for a Moses-type expressway. They were speaking Jane Jacobs' thoughts before she wrote them down." Gwinn Owens, "How the Great Moses Was Wiped Out by Jane Jacobs," *Baltimore Sun*, Aug. 6, 1981 (reprinted in *ITM*, 99).

27. Gilpatric, interview with Jacobs, May 9, 1958.

28. Ibid. Jacobs also offered that the New School for Social Research would likely host her and administer a foundation grant; she knew that Arthur Swift, the school's dean, whom she knew from the Union Settlement's board of directors, would be interested in such research.

29. Gilpatric, interview with Jacobs, Jun. 4, 1958.

30. Jane Jacobs, letter to Chadbourne Gilpatric, Jun. 14, 1958 (RF RG 1.2, series 200R, 390:3380, RAC).

31. Ibid.

32. Ibid.

33. Ibid.

34. Ibid.

35. Jane Jacobs, letter to Lewis Mumford, Jun. 17, 1958 (unlocated). Jacobs referred to Mumford's April 1958 article "The Highway and the City" in *D&L* (358). The article was republished in Mumford's book *The Urban Prospect* (New York: Harcourt, Brace & World, 1968), 92–107. See also Lewis Mumford, letter to Jane Jacobs, Jun. 18, 1958 (Jacobs Papers, 13:11).

36. Chadbourne Gilpatric, interview with Jane Jacobs, Jun. 26, 1958 (RF RG 1.2, series 200R, 390:3380, RAC). Later that year, Jason Epstein and his editorial staff moved to Random House, which published *The Death and Life of Great American Cities*. Epstein was Jacobs's longtime editor. She dedicated *Cities and the Wealth of Nations: Principles of Economic Life* (1984), her fourth major book, to him.

37. [Jane Jacobs], "What Is a City?" *AF* (Jul. 1958), 63; Harrison Salisbury, "'Shook' Youngsters Spring from the Housing Jungles," *NYT* (Mar. 26, 1958), 1.

38. [Jacobs], "What Is a City?"; Salisbury, "'Shook' Youngsters," 1; *D&L*, 137.

39. [Jacobs], "What Is a City?"

40. Jane Jacobs, letter to Chadbourne Gilpatric, Jul. 1, 1958 (Jacobs Papers, 13:11).

41. Ibid.

42. Ibid.

43. Ibid.

44. Letters from Lewis Mumford, Catherine Bauer, William Whyte, Jason Epstein, Martin Meyerson, and G. Holmes Perkins to Chadbourne Gilpatric, Aug. 1958 (RF RG 1.2, series 200R, 390:3380, RAC).

45. Christopher Tunnard, letter to Chadbourne Gilpatric, Aug. 1958 (RF RG 1.2, series 200R, 390:3380, RAC). Tunnard's work was supported by the third major grant in the foundation's urban design research initiative to Yale's Graduate Program in City Planning, in 1957, for a multiyear research project on city planning and the built environment. With a title that referred to his Townscape contribution of 1950 (some called it "Outrage, U.S. Version"), the result of his foundation-supported research was *Man-Made America: Chaos or Control? An*

Inquiry into Selected Problems of Design in the Urbanized Landscape (1963), coauthored with Boris Pushkarev.

46. RF GA HUM 5862, grant-in-aid to New School for Social Research and Jane Jacobs through Oct. 1959, Sept. 8, 1958 (RF RG 1.2, series 200R, 390:3380, RAC); Rockefeller Foundation, *1958 Annual Report*, 291.

47. Gilpatric, interview with Jacobs, Jun. 4, 1958.

48. Those considered for participation in the "Urban Design Criticism" conference by Jacobs, Wheaton, and Gilpatric included Victor Gruen, William Whyte, Joseph Hudnut, Aline Saarinen, Joseph Guess, Harrison Salisbury, Fritz Gutheim, J. M. Richards, Nikolaus Pevsner, and James M. Fitch. Chadbourne Gilpatric, interview with William Wheaton et al., May 7, 1958 (UPenn—Community Planning, 456:3900, RAC); conference schedule (UPenn—Community Planning, 457:3905, RAC).

49. Memorandum, n.d. (Jacobs Papers, 19:3).

50. Chadbourne Gilpatric, interview with Jane Jacobs, Oct. 17, 1958 (RF RG 1.2, series 200R, 390:3380, RAC). The participants of a May 1960 conversation included Ada Louise Huxtable, Epstein, William Kirk, the architect William Conklin, Salisbury, Tankel, and Whyte. "Luncheon on Civic Design" (RG 1.2, series 200, 390:3391, RAC).

51. It is worth noting that Jacobs did not single William Slayton out for criticism in *D&L* just because he was closely involved with urban renewal. As commissioner for the Urban Renewal Administration, Slayton was popular, a champion of cities, an advocate of design, and an activist against racial discrimination in housing, all qualities that would have appealed to her. Cf. Eric Pace, "William Slayton, 82, Official Who Aided Urban Renewal," *NYT* (Aug. 11, 1999), C23.

52. Daniel Wolf, "Villagers Win Major Victory; Road Thru Square Shrinking," *VV* (Sept. 24, 1958), 1–3; Jane Jacobs, "Downtown Planning, Solving Traffic Problems," *Vital Speeches of the Day* 25 (Jan. 1, 1959), 190–92.

53. "A Human Victory," *AF* (Dec. 1958), 79.

54. The September 9, 1958, conference was sponsored by the *Cincinnati Enquirer*. Murray Seeger, "Experts Advise Linking Cities with Suburbs," *Cleveland Plain Dealer* (Sept. 10, 1959), 17. Also see Grady Clay, letter to Jane Jacobs, Christmas 1958, courtesy of Grady Clay. While in Boston, Jacobs had wanted to meet with Lynch and Kepes at MIT, but she ran out of time. However, she met with Martin Meyerson at the Joint Center for Urban Studies, and he suggested that she pursue a less ambitious project than a book on urban renewal and American cities. In April and May 1999, when I met with Jacobs and had a number of phone conversations with her, she said she had felt like Meyerson was trying to talk her out of writing the book.

55. Chadbourne Gilpatric, interview with Jane Jacobs, Dec. 2, 1958 (RF RG 1.2, series 200R, 390:3380, RAC). Also influential for Jacobs was the sociologist Herbert Gans's article on Boston's West End and North End, "The Human Implications of Current Redevelopment and Relocation Planning," *Journal of the American Institute of Planners* 25 (Feb. 1959), 15–25, which she cited in *D&L*. The article was an early version of ch. 14 of Gans's *The Urban Villagers: Group and Class in the Life of Italian-Americans* (New York: Free Press, 1962). Before Gans and Jacobs, the North End and Italian-American communities residing in Boston were of interest to the sociologist William Foote Whyte. Whyte's book *Street Corner Society* was the result of living in the North End, aka "Cornerville," first with a local family and then with

this wife, in the late 1940s. See *Street Corner Society: The Social Structure of an Italian Slum* (1943; Chicago: University of Chicago Press, 1993).

56. Jane Jacobs, letter to Catherine Bauer, Jan. 2, 1959 (Bauer Papers, Correspondence).

57. Ibid.

58. United Neighborhood Houses of NY, Meeting of the UNH Housing Committee, Dec. 4, 1958 (United Neighborhood Houses of New York Records, Elmer L. Andersen Library, University of Minnesota, Minneapolis).

59. "Description of and Problems Raised by the DeWitt Clinton Housing Project," n.d. (USAR, 35:7).

60. Ellen Lurie, "Tenant Leaders Meeting re New Design for Clinton Houses," Feb. 12, 1959 (USAR, 35:8); "DeWitt Clinton Housing Study," Jan. 8, 1959 (USAR, 35:8).

61. Final draft of report to Housing Authority on DeWitt Clinton, Feb. 3, 1959 (USAR, 35:8).

62. "Initial Draft of Some of the Material in Jane Jacobs' Presentation to the Housing Authority on DeWitt Clinton," Jan. 1959 (USAR, 35:8).

63. Final draft of report to Housing Authority on DeWitt Clinton.

64. Draft press release, Feb. 15, 1959 (USAR, 35:8). Copy given to Ellen Lurie by Jane Jacobs.

65. Richard A. Miller, "Public Housing . . . for People," *AF* (Apr. 1959), 134–37. Samuel Zipp has also written about the DeWitt Clinton housing project in *Manhattan Projects*, 327–31.

66. *D&L*, 397. Jacobs remained involved in redevelopment and housing matters in East Harlem into the early 1960s, and she shared information with Gilpatric about her activities during the course of their correspondence in order to encourage foundation interest and support.

67. Jane Jacobs, letter to Grady Clay, Feb. 20, 1959. Courtesy of Grady Clay. Jacobs's "hide-out" was at 224 West 4th Street.

68. Ibid.

69. Jane Jacobs, letter to Grady Clay, Mar. 3, 1959. Courtesy of Grady Clay.

70. Ibid.

71. Chadbourne Gilpatric, memo, Jun. 10, 1959 (RF RG 1.2, series 200, 390:3381, RAC); Jane Jacobs, letter to Chadbourne Gilpatric, Jun. 15, 1959 (RF RG 1.2, series 200, 390:3381, RAC).

72. Jane Jacobs, letter to Chadbourne Gilpatric, Jul. 17, 1959 (RF RG 1.2, series 200, 390:3381, RAC). It was around this time that Jacobs hired Ellen Perry (Berkeley), listed in *D&L*'s acknowledgments, as a part-time research assistant. Perry helped Jacobs confirm various ideas about city dynamics by counting the number of people sitting on stoops and their locations; inventorying mom-and-pop stores; and similar data-gathering tasks that informed *D&L*'s first three chapters (telephone conversation with Ellen Perry Berkeley, Jul. 20, 2014). Soon thereafter, with the help of Jacobs's recommendation, Berkeley was hired as an associate editor at *Progressive Architecture* and later as a senior editor at *AF*. Berkeley also helped to found the Women's School of Planning and Architecture in 1972.

73. Ibid.

74. "Woman Says Planners Look Back, Not Ahead; Urges Traffic-less Downtowns," *Flint Michigan Journal*, May 4, 1959, n.p.; "Woman Fights to Save Downtowns," *Times-Picayune* (New Orleans), May 10, 1959, 13. The latter syndicated newspaper article was

published throughout the country. See also Kent, "Jane Jacobs: An Oral History," 16–17; and Flint, *Wrestling with Moses*, 88.

75. Jacobs, letter to Gilpatric, Jul. 23, 1959.

76. Ibid.

77. Ibid.

78. William Whyte, letter to Chadbourne Gilpatric, Aug. 1, 1959 (RF RG 1.2, series 200, 390:3381, RAC).

79. William Kirk, Eric Larrabee, and W. N. Seymour, letters to Chadbourne Gilpatric, Aug. 3, 11, and 17, 1959 (RF RG 1.2, series 200, 390:3381, RAC); Charles Fahs, interview with Charles Farnsley, Jun. 15, 1959 (RF RG 1.2, series 200, 390:3380, RAC); Barclay Jones, report, Jun. 8, 1959 (RF RG 1.2, series 200, University of California, Jones & Jacobs, 433:3724, RAC).

80. Wayne Phillips, "Title I Slum Clearance Proves Spur to Cooperative Housing in City," *NYT* (Jul. 2, 1959), 13; Douglas Haskell, memo to Jane Jacobs, Jul. 2, 1959 (Haskell Papers, 79:6).

81. Jane Jacobs, letter to Chadbourne Gilpatric, Oct. 29, 1959 (RF RG 1.2, series 200, 390:3381, RAC); Jane Jacobs, letter to Saul Alinsky, Aug. 18, 1959 (Alinsky Papers, correspondence, Briscoe).

82. Jane Jacobs, letter to Chadbourne Gilpatric, May 6, 1961 (RF RG 1.2, series 200, 390:3381, RAC).

83. Chadbourne Gilpatric, letter to Jane Jacobs, May 19, 1960 (RF RG 1.2, series 200, 390:3381, RAC). The first line from White's *Here Is New York* is "On any person who desires such queer prizes, New York will bestow the gift of loneliness and the gift of privacy." Jacobs declined the suggestion.

84. Jane Jacobs, letter to Chadbourne Gilpatric, Aug. 2, 1960 (RF RG 1.2, series 200, 390:3381, RAC).

85. Jane Jacobs, letter to Chadbourne Gilpatric, May 11, 1960 (RF RG 1.2, series 200, 390:3381, RAC); *D&L*, 376 (emphasis in the original).

86. Jane Jacobs, letter to Chadbourne Gilpatric, Sept. 29, 1960 (RF RG 1.2, series 200, 390:3381, RAC); *D&L*, 376.

87. Chadbourne Gilpatric, letter to Jane Jacobs, Mar. 27, 1961 (RF RG 1.2, series 200, 390:3381, RAC).

88. Jacobs, letter to Gilpatric, May 6, 1961.

89. *D&L*, 429; Laurence, "Complexities and Contradictions," 49–60. A previous reference to Weaver's concept of organized complexity was made by the architect Richard Llewelyn-Davies in "Human Sciences, *AR* 127 (Mar. 1960), 190. Jacobs had likely read the article.

90. Jane Jacobs, letter to Chadbourne Gilpatric, Oct. 27, 1961 (RF RG 1.2, series 200R, 390:3381, RAC).

CONCLUSION

The epigraph for this chapter is from Jane Jacobs, letter to Chadbourne Gilpatric, Jul. 1, 1958, 3.

1. "Two Blighted Downtown Areas Are Chosen for Urban Renewal," *NYT* (Feb. 21, 1961), 37.

2. Ibid.; "Angry 'Villagers' to Fight Project," *NYT* (Feb. 27, 1961), 29. Jacobs discussed the fight to save the West Village in detail; see Kent, "Jane Jacobs: An Oral History," 18–47.

Glenna Lang, Alice Alexiou Sparberg, and Anthony Flint also tell the story in different ways in their books (respectively, *Genius of Common Sense*; *Jane Jacobs: Urban Visionary*; and *Wrestling with Moses*).

3. Kent, "Jane Jacobs: An Oral History," 27, 36–37. Leticia Kent, a journalist and long-time friend of Jacobs, was a member of the Committee to Save the West Village. The committee later convinced a group of "dissident" members of Mi-Cove to place a newspaper advertisement indicating their opposition to the West Village renewal proposal. See "Micove Is Attacked on Housing Stand," *NYT* (Apr. 14, 1961), 20; Edith E. Asbury, "Village Project Backed in Fight," *NYT* (Oct. 21, 1961), 24; Roger Starr, "Adventure in Mooritania," *Newsletter of the Citizens' Housing and Planning Council of NY* (reprinted in *ITM*, 53–54).

4. "Village Housing Study Fund Plea Is Put Off," *NYT* (Feb. 24, 1961), 31; "Villagers Seek to Halt Renewal," *NYT* (Mar. 4, 1961), 11; William Kirk, letter to the editor, *NYT* (Mar. 7, 1961), 34; "Dudley Asks for Delay on Renewal Study," *NYT* (Mar. 16, 1961), 39; "Dudley Predicts Wider Renewal, Says All of Manhattan May Be Studied," *NYT* (Mar. 19, 1961), 44; "Ten Big Housing Projects Approved by City Board," *NYT* (Mar. 24, 1961), 1; "Civic Groups Score Village Project," *NYT* (Mar. 28, 1961), 40. Apart from Kirk, Jacobs enlisted the support of Nathan Glazer, one of many signatories to a March 1961 statement of protest.

5. "Village Housing a Complex Issue, City's Plan Extends Only to Survey," *NYT* (Mar. 23, 1961), 35; Kent, "Jane Jacobs: An Oral History," 26–30. Lester Eisner was the father of the former Disney executive Michael Eisner.

6. "City Ready to Act in US Slum Plan, Mayor Prepares for Quick Moves on New Projects If Congress Widens Aid," *NYT* (Apr. 4, 1961), 1. See also "Davies Disputes Foes of Village Survey," *NYT* (Apr. 15, 1961), 15.

7. "Village Group Wins Court Stay," *NYT* (Apr. 28, 1961), 34.

8. "Village Housing Defended by Felt," *NYT* (May 8, 1961), 40; "Felt Sees Change in Renewal View," *NYT* (May 9, 1961), 36; "Felt Bids Council Support Renewal," *NYT* (May 10, 1961), 34; John Sibley, "New Housing Idea to Get Test Here," *NYT* (May 23, 1961), 25. Roberta Brandes Gratz discusses the 1965 Landmarks Preservation Law in *Battle for Gotham*, 38–43.

9. Charles Bennett, "City Gives Up Plan for West Village," *NYT* (Feb. 1, 1962), 30; Erik Wensberg, letter to the editor, *NYT* (May 12, 1961), 28; Kent, "Jane Jacobs: An Oral History," 2–3, 18, 21–22, passim. Erik Wensberg was a cofounder of the Save the West Village Committee. Wensberg, who was editor of *The Columbia Forum* at this time, read early drafts of *D&L* and later worked with Jacobs on the West Village Houses project and on the fight against the Lower Manhattan Expressway. See Albert Amateau, "Wensberg, Editor/Writer, Key Jacobs Ally, 79," *The Villager* 80 (Jul. 7–10, 2010), accessed online.

10. John Sibley, "Ouster of Davies and Felt Sought," *NYT* (Jun. 8, 1961), 71; "Wagner Opposes Village Change," *NYT* (Aug. 18, 1961), 23; Charles Bennett, "Mayor Abandons Village Project," *NYT* (Sept. 7, 1961), 31.

11. "Report of the City Planning Commission on the Designation of the West Village Area," Oct. 18, 1961, CP–16478, 9.

12. Jane Jacobs, "How City Planners Hurt Cities," *Saturday Evening Post* (Oct. 14, 1961), 12–14. "Report of the City Planning Commission on the Designation of the West Village," 7–9, 12–13.

13. Edith Asbury, "Plan Board Votes Village Project, Crowd in Uproar," *NYT* (Oct. 19, 1961), 1.

14. Ibid.

15. Edith Asbury, "Deceit Charged in Village Plan," *NYT* (Oct. 20, 1961), 68; Kent, "Jane Jacobs: An Oral History," 38–40, 44–45; Jane Jacobs, letter to Arnold Nicholson, Oct. 23, 1961 (Jacobs Papers, 11:6).

16. The excerpt in *Harper's Magazine*, "Violence in the City Streets," published on November 4, was acknowledged as being from the first edition of *Death and Life*, and this coincided with the book's release. Jacobs, letter to Gilpatric, Oct. 27, 1961.

17. Martin Arnold, "Felt Set to Yield in Village Fight," *NYT* (Jan. 17, 1962), 33. A few days after Wagner leaked his letters with Felt, Wagner forced the Housing and Redevelopment Board chair Clarence Davies out of office, publicly blaming him for mishandling the West Village redevelopment proposal. See Martin Arnold, "Davies Reported Ready to Quit as Head of City Housing Board," *NYT* (Jan. 19, 1962), 1; Bennett, "City Gives Up Plan for West Village," 35.

18. Reyner Banham wrote about the Washington Square and West Village battles in "Counter-Attack, NY," a reference to *The Architectural Review's* "Counter-Attack" issue (*Architects' Journal*, May 4, 1961, 629–30). See also Jane Jacobs, "The Citizen in Urban Renewal: Participation or Manipulation?" Feb. 21, 1962 (Jacobs Papers, 1:1).

19. Jacobs, "Citizen in Urban Renewal," passim.

20. William F. Buckley Jr., letter to Jane Jacobs, Dec. 27, 1961 (Jacobs Papers, 13:10); Ernest van den Haag, "Loss of Urbanity," *National Review* (Dec. 30, 1961), 455–56; Eric Larrabee, "In Print: Jane Jacobs," *Horizon* (Summer 1962); Eric Larrabee, "Book Review: Death and Life" (reprinted in *ITM*, 49–51).

21. Leticia Kent, "Jane Jacobs: Against Urban Renewal, for Urban Life," *NYT Magazine* (May 23, 1969) (reprinted in *ITM*, 20). See also Charles Abrams in "Abattoir for Sacred Cows: Reviews of *The Death and Life of Great American Cities*," *Progressive Architecture* (Apr. 1962), 196, 202; Marshall Berman, *All That Is Solid Melts into Air: The Experience of Modernity* (New York: Penguin, 1982), 314; and Fredric Jameson, "City Theory in Jacobs and Heidegger," in *Anywise* (Cambridge, MA: MIT Press, 1996), 35. For Jacobs's criticism of chain stores, which she associated socially with suburbanism and economically with monopolies, see, for example, *D&L*, 4, 147, 188, 190–92. As Jacobs discussed in *Economy of Cities*, cities grew through import replacement (i.e., local economic development and the creation of exports) and therefore would tend to shrink by replacing local production with imports (146).

22. Percival Goodman in "Abattoir for Sacred Cows," 196, 202.

23. Percival Goodman and Paul Goodman, *Communitas: Means of Livelihood and Ways of Life* (Chicago: University of Chicago Press, 1947), 16, 29, 31–32, 92, 99; Percival Goodman and Paul Goodman, *Communitas*, 2nd ed. (New York: Vintage, 1960), 52–54, 164, 174–75.

24. Percival Goodman, "What Can We Do with the City?" *Dissent* (Spring 1962), 194–98.

25. L. Mumford, "Mother Jacobs' Home Remedies," 167–68, 178.

26. Melvin Webber, "Order in Diversity: Community Without Propinquity," in *Cities and Space: The Future Use of Urban Land*, ed. L. Wingo Jr. (Baltimore, MD: Johns Hopkins University Press, 1963), 23, 25, 34, 40, 41, 54.

27. Reyner Banham, Paul Barker, Peter Hall, and Cedric Price, "Non-Plan: An Experiment in Freedom," *New Society* (Mar. 20, 1969), reproduced in *Non-Plan: Essays on Freedom, Participation, and Change in Modern Architecture and Urbanism*, ed. Jonathan Hughes and

Simon Sadler, introd. Paul Barker (Woburn, MA: Architectural Press, 2000), 16–21. In *Non-Plan*, see also Ben Franks's "New Right/New Left: An Alternative Experiment in Freedom" (32–43) and Hughes's essay "After Non-Plan, Retrenchment and Reassertion" (174–76). For another trailblazing history of the nonplanning/nondesign movement, see Anthony Fontenot, "Non-Design and the Non-Planned City" (Ph.D. diss., Princeton University, 2013). See also Robert Venturi, Denise Scott Brown, and Steven Izenour, *Learning from Las Vegas: The Forgotten Symbolism of Architectural Form* (1972; Cambridge, MA: MIT Press, 1993).

   28. *The Road to Serfdom*, written during World War II, was an antitotalitarian treatise in which Hayek attacked fascism and various forms of collectivism (e.g., communism and Marxism), as well as nationalism, racism, corporatism, conservatism, and paternalism, as steppingstones toward social control and coercion. While also attacking socialism, particularly the Nazis' National Socialism, Hayek explained in the foreword to the 1976 edition that the meaning of socialism changed after World War II, leading him to observe that "Sweden, for instance, is today very much less socialistically organized than Great Britain or Austria, though Sweden is commonly regarded as much more socialistic." In *The Constitution of Liberty*, he declared that socialism was dead in the Western world but that it had taken the form of the welfare state and its ideas about social justice. In contrast to expectations, however, in *The Road to Serfdom*, he had argued against the "dogmatic laissez faire attitude," and he wrote, "There is no reason why in a society which has reached the general level of wealth which ours has attained the first kind of security should not be guaranteed to all without endangering general freedom. . . . [T]here can be no doubt that some minimum of food, shelter, and clothing, sufficient to preserve health and capacity to work, can be assured to everybody." F. A. Hayek, *The Road to Serfdom: Text and Documents*, ed. Bruce Caldwell (Chicago: University of Chicago Press, 2007), 49, 54, 148. See also "Engineers and Planners," ch. 10 of Hayek's *The Counter-Revolution of Science: Studies on the Abuse of Reason* (Glencoe, IL: Free Press, 1952), 94–102, in which he discusses the failure of statistics to account for the particular conditions of time and place.

   29. Hayek cited Warren Weaver on the nature of scientific knowledge (not his work on complexity science) in *The Constitution of Liberty, The Definitive Edition*, ed. Ronald Hamowy (Chicago: University of Chicago Press, 2011), 77, and again in "The Theory of Complex Phenomena," in *The Critical Approach to Science and Philosophy*, ed. Mario Bunge (London: Free Press, 1964), 348–49. For Hayek's discussion of "the knowledge of the particular circumstances of time and place," which was ultimately an argument for the price mechanism, see "The Uses of Knowledge in Society," *American Economic Review* 35 (Sept. 1945), 519–30.

   30. Hayek, *Constitution of Liberty*, 466–67, 475–76, 480. The latest edition of this book cites *Death and Life* on p. 467. See also Jane Jacobs, "Performance Zoning as an Alternative to Use Zoning" (Jacobs Papers, 8:10).

   31. For Jacobs on the subject of the automobile and public transportation, see *D&L*, ch. 18, and, for a more recent discussion on the topic, her interview with Bill Steigerwald in *Reason* magazine, Jun. 2001, reason.com. The quotation concerning "atomistic competition" comes from Anthony O'Hear, "Hayek and Popper: The Road to Serfdom and the Open Society," in *The Cambridge Companion to Hayek*, ed. E. Feser (New York: Cambridge University Press, 2006), 134. O'Hear wrote, "We should surely heed Hayek's warning of the treacherousness of the apparently reasonable proposition that there is a 'middle way' between 'atomistic' competition and central direction." This slippery-slope argument for atomistic

competition is at odds with Hayek's admission of the need for social services and what is actually required to create a socially "level playing field" and with such admissions as that Sweden was socialistic, but not so socialistic as some nonsocialistic societies.

32. *D&L*, 71.

33. *D&L*, 130, 241, 248, 401; Jane Jacobs, "America and the Americans," Feb. 1945 (Jacobs Papers, 12:4), 7. In contrast, Hayek had little to say about race. While he was aware of the oppression of minorities under Nazism and totalitarian regimes, his only reference to racial segregation in America in his books on "serfdom" (slavery in de Tocqueville's context) and the virtues of American constitutionalism was to support a point about the flaws of public education. He also made abstract arguments against suffrage, observing that, "in the oldest and most successful of European democracies, Switzerland, women are still excluded from the vote" (*Constitution of Liberty*, 169). He argued that "if in the Western world universal adult suffrage seems the best arrangement, this does not prove that it is required by some basic principle" (170). Regardless of any ideas Jacobs may have shared with Hayek, she did not share these.

Hayek preferred the term "Whiggism" to "libertarianism," but he recognized it as an odd one. However, it indeed seems fitting insofar as his concerns appear rather similar to those of an old privileged class that opposed the monarchy in the seventeenth century (531). His form of libertarianism, he explained, "is concerned mainly with limiting the coercive powers of all government, whether democratic or not" (166). A reason for this is that he associated the defense of minority views and initially unpopular causes like the abolition of slavery with the "idle rich" (193).

34. See Paul Goodman, "The Anarchist Principle," originally published in *Anarchy* 62 (Apr. 1966) and reprinted in *The Paul Goodman Reader*, ed. T. Stoehr (Oakland, CA: PM Press, 2011), 29; Fred Lawrence, *Ethics in Making a Living: The Jane Jacobs Conference* (Atlanta, GA: Scholars Press and Boston College, 1989), 199.

35. *D&L*, 138, 167, 244–46, 251–56, 313–14. Discussing feedback processes, on p. 252, Jacobs quoted from Robert K. Plumb, "New Light Is Shed on Heredity Role; Neither It nor Environment, but Combination Is Vital," *NYT* (Sept. 14, 1960), 45. The term "gentrification" was coined by the British sociologist Ruth Glass in 1964, so Jacobs did not use it in *Death and Life*. However, she understood the issue in both its public (i.e., government funding for middle-class housing) and market-driven dimensions.

36. For the context of antigentrification efforts in Greenwich Village, see "Luxury Housing Gains in Village; More than 20 Structures Under Way as Boom Moves Downtown; West Village Expands," *NYT* (Mar. 12, 1961), R1. Through Jacobs's efforts, West Village Houses was supported by the New York State Mitchell-Lama housing program to allow a third of the units to be rented at a low-income rate. Jacobs and the Committee to Save the West Village sought federal subsidies to bring the remainder of the units to a similar level. See Peter Freiberg, "Village Wins 10-Year Fight for $23M Housing Project," *New York Post* (Apr. 21, 1972), 10. See also Lawrence, *Ethics in Making a Living*, 18–19. In the same conversation about those who saw her as a libertarian, Jacobs reacted to a comment that she would "do fine in Margaret Thatcher's government" by stating that "Margaret Thatcher's government *appalls*" her. (Thatcherism was sometimes associated with Hayek's economic theories and libertarianism.) See also Pierre Desrochers, "The Death of a Reluctant Urban Icon," *Journal of Libertarian Studies* 21 (Fall 2007), 115–36; and Jeff Riggenbach, "Jane Jacobs: Libertarian Outsider," Apr. 28, 2011, mises.org.

37. See Karl Popper, "Aestheticism, Perfectionism, Utopianism," in *The Open Society and Its Enemies* (Princeton, NJ: Princeton University Press, 1994), 147–57; Karl Popper, "Piecemeal vs. Utopian Engineering," in *The Poverty of Historicism* (London: Routledge, 1997), 64–70; *D&L*, 363; O'Hear, "Hayek and Popper," 141; Fontenot, "Non-Design," 341; Gerald Gaus, "Hayek on the Evolution of Society and Mind," in Feser, *Cambridge Companion to Hayek*, 238–39; *EOC*, 19–21; Jane Jacobs, "Pedaling Together," 1988 Spokespeople Conference, in *ITM*, 124.

38. Michael Harrington, "Review of *The Economy of Cities*," *VV* (Jun. 12, 1969) (reprinted in *ITM*, 102–4); *D&L*, 407. See also Saul D. Alinsky, *Reveille for Radicals* (1946; New York: Vintage, 1989) and Chester Hartman, *Between Eminence & Notoriety: Four Decades of Radical Urban Planning* (New Brunswick, NJ: Center for Urban Policy Research, 2002).

39. *D&L*, 406–8.

40. Ibid., 408–18.

41. Ibid., 425–27.

42. Ibid., 427.

43. Ibid., 408, 438–39; Jacobs, letter to Ms. Talmey, Nov. 22, 1961, in *ITM*, 4. As noted in Chapter 7, Richard Llewelyn-Davies wrote about Warren Weaver's complexity theories in March 1960, and he made the similar observation about the differences in knowledge in the 1920s and around 1960 ("Human Sciences," 190). Given her keen interest in science, Jacobs may have been referring to this article. In contrast to a strictly scientific approach, David Seamon has offered that Jacobs can be described as "a phenomenologist of urban place." See David Season, "Jane Jacobs's *Death and Life of Great American Cities* as a Phenomenology of Urban Place," *Journal of Space Syntax* 3 (Aug. 2012), 139–49.

44. Kent, "Jane Jacobs," 22.

45. C. Gerald Fraser, "Writers and Editors to Protest War by Defying Tax," *NYT* (Jan. 31, 1968), in *ITM*, 180; Lang, *Genius of Common Sense*, 109.

46. Clark Whelton, "Won't You Come Home, Jane Jacobs?" *VV* (Jul. 6, 1972), 28.

47. *SOS*, 31, 214; *EOC*, ix.

ACKNOWLEDGMENTS

This book was generously supported by a publication grant from the Graham Foundation for Advanced Studies in the Fine Arts.

Additional support during various stages of the project came from the Beverly Willis Architecture Foundation; the Rockefeller Archive Center; the Clemson University College of Architecture, Arts and Humanities; and the Clemson University School of Architecture.

Another group of institutions that must be recognized is made up of archives, along with their archivists, the heroes of history. This book would not exist without them. I must therefore thank Michelle Hiltzik, Ken Rose, Darwin Stapleton, and the Rockefeller Archive Center; Justine Sundaram, David Horn, John Attebury, and the John J. Burns Library, Boston College; Janet Parks, Julie Tozer, Nicole Richard, and the Avery Architectural and Fine Arts Library, Columbia University; Mary Daniels and the Harvard GSD Frances Loeb Library; Martin Manning, U.S. Department of State; Michelle Morgan, Susan Snyder, and the Bancroft Library, University of California, Berkeley; Carmen Hendershott and the New School for Social Research; Nancy Shawcross and the Special Collections department at the library of the University of Pennsylvania; William Whitaker, Nancy Thorne, and the University of Pennsylvania Architectural Archives; Syracuse University Special Collections; Cornell University Special Collections; Douglas Di Carlo and the La Guardia and Wagner Archive; the National Personnel Records Center; Millie Molina and Howard Marder, NYC Housing Authority; and Jean Ashton, the library director emerita of the Columbia University Rare Book and Manuscript Library and the New-York Historical Society. Dr. Ashton, whom I'm fortunate to have as part of my extended family, also helped me by reading various versions of this manuscript.

As essential as archival material is to this book, raw material is not enough. At At the University of Pennsylvania and Harvard Graduate School of Design, I was fortunate to work with some of the most distinguished historians. I am especially grateful to David Leatherbarrow, David Brownlee, and Robert Wojtowicz. This book is unquestionably better, in every way, because of them.

This book is also much better, and indeed exists at all, thanks to Bob Lockhart and his colleagues at the University of Pennsylvania Press, including the series editor Casey Blake, the associate managing editor Erica Ginsburg, and the copy editor Christine Dahlin. I thank them all for their patience, enthusiasm, and knowledgeable assistance in bringing this book into being.

For further encouragement, advice, and support, in ways large and small, some known to them and some unknown, but all valuable to me and not forgotten, I must thank a long list of people. This large group includes George Baird, Hilary Ballon, Ellen Perry Berkeley, the late Peter Blake, Wanda Bubriski, Carol Burns, José Caban, Charlie Cannon, Ted Cavanagh, the late Grady Clay, Matthew Crane, George Dodds, Kathy Edwards, Alexander Eisenschmidt, Paul Emmons, Jason Epstein, Ufuk Ersoy, Erdem Erten, the late James Marston Fitch, Marguerite Gilpatric, Rick Goodstein, Bob Gomel, Roberta Brandes Gratz, Keith Green, Nancy Hadley, Anna Vortmann Hakes, Richard Harris, K. Michael Hays, Benjamin Hemric, Sarah Herda, Juan Manuel Heredia, Dafnne Wejebe Iberri, Akel Kahera, Andrea Kahn, Kostis Kourelis, Alex Krieger, Susan Lander, Glenna Lang, Liane Lefaivre, Kasia Leousis, Zhongjie Lin, Jim London, Richard Longstreth, Judith McCandless, Tim Mennel, Susan Morris, Eric Mumford, Taner Oc, Joan Ockman, Norman Oder, Alejandra Palomares, Max Page, Linda Pollak, Hassan Radione, Jamin Rowan, Mary Rowe, Mariel Rubio, Joseph Rykwert, Hashim Sarkis, Junichi Satoh, Iram Satti, Kate Schwennsen, David Seamon, Joan Shigekawa, Michael Southworth, Krista Sykes, Russell Terry, Alexander Tzonis, Kazys Varnelis, Robert Venturi, Alexander von Hoffman, Darren Walker, Sarah Whiting, Beverly Willis, Alina Yakubova, Artemiy Zheltov, and my colleagues at Clemson.

I hope all those mentioned will approve of, or would have approved of, this book. This wish extends to the late Jane Jacobs herself—whose

invitation to her home in 1999 encouraged me to pursue this long project—
and to her family.

The last thank you, and a big one, goes to my inspiring partner,
Susanna Ashton, a prolific scholar and a master of family organization, who
wrote three or four books while I wrote this one.